THE LIFE WRITINGS

of

MARY BAKER MCQUESTEN

Victorian Matriarch

Life Writing Series

In the **Life Writing Series**, Wilfrid Laurier University Press publishes life writing and new life-writing criticism in order to promote autobiographical accounts, diaries, letters, and testimonials written and/or told by women and men whose political, literary, or philosophical purposes are central to their lives. **Life Writing** features the accounts of ordinary people, written in English, or translated into English from French or the languages of the First Nations or from any of the languages of immigration to Canada. **Life Writing** will also publish original theoretical investigations about life writing, as long as they are not limited to one author or text.

Priority is given to manuscripts that provide access to those voices that have not traditionally had access to the publication process.

Manuscripts of social, cultural, and historical interest that are considered for the series, but are not published, are maintained in the **Life Writing Archive** of Wilfrid Laurier University Library.

Series Editor
Marlene Kadar
Humanities Division, York University

Manuscripts to be sent to
Brian Henderson, Director
Wilfrid Laurier University Press
75 University Avenue West
Waterloo, Ontario, Canada N2L 3C5

THE LIFE WRITINGS
of
MARY BAKER MCQUESTEN
Victorian Matriarch

ॐ

edited by
Mary J. Anderson

Wilfrid Laurier University Press
[WLU]

This book has been published with the help of a grant from the Canadian Federation for the Humanities and Social Sciences, through the Aid to Scholarly Publications Programme, using funds provided by the Social Sciences and Humanities Research Council of Canada. We acknowledge the financial support of the Government of Canada through the Book Publishing Industry Development Program for our publishing activities. We acknowledge the Government of Ontario through the Ontario Media Development Corporation's Ontario Book Initiative.

National Library of Canada Cataloguing in Publication Data

McQuesten, Mary Baker, 1849–1934
    The life writings of Mary Baker McQuesten : Victorian matriarch / Mary J. Anderson, editor.

(Life writing series)
Includes bibliographical references and index.
ISBN 0-88920-437-3

    1. McQuesten, Mary Baker, 1849-1934—Correspondence. 2. Single mothers—Ontario—Hamilton—Correspondence. 3. Hamilton (Ont.)—History. 4. Hamilton (Ont.)—Biography. I. Anderson, Mary J. (Mary Johanna), 1931– II. Title. III. Series.

FC3098.26.M36A73 2004   971.3'.5203'092   C2004-901531-1

© 2004 Wilfrid Laurier University Press
Waterloo, Ontario, Canada N2L 3C5
www.wlupress.wlu.ca

Cover and text design by PJ Woodland.
All photographs courtesy of Whitehern Archives.

Every reasonable effort has been made to acquire permission for copyright material used in this text, and to acknowledge all such indebtedness accurately. Any errors and omissions called to the publisher's attention will be corrected in future printings.

Printed in Canada

For further information, contact the Whitehern Museum Web site at:
www.whitehern.ca

FOR MY CHILDREN
Mark James Anderson
Janelle Mary Baldwin
and

GRANDCHILDREN
Jessica Turner Anderson
Sarah Janelle Baldwin
Rebecca Jane Baldwin

and for

MY HUSBAND, THEIR FATHER,
and GRANDFATHER
James John Anderson

❧

Mr. [Thomas] McQuesten himself has told me of the large part his mother played in molding his tastes, his standards and his plan of life. Not the least of her contributions to him was to give him a love for beauty that was large enough to spread out and influence the appearance of a great city... Large areas of Hamilton are, in the last analysis, a reflection of her love of beauty.

(*Hamilton Herald* obituary for Mary Baker McQuesten, 7 December 1934)

&

Contents

❧

List of Illustrations

❧

Preface

❧

One morning in the Spring of 1971 I was taken down to the offices of the Parks Board in Gage Park. There I was shown three large carton boxes full of family papers found at "Whitehern."... I worked for nearly two years, deciphering the old-fashioned handwriting of the 19th [and 20th] centuries and collating and arranging over 8000 handwritten pages.

Mary Harrington Farmer, *Wentworth Bygones*, 15 October 1976

This book has a similar story to tell about its inception: One afternoon in 1988 I visited Whitehern Museum, located at 41 Jackson Street West, Hamilton, Ontario, Canada. As I was graciously received at the front door by an attendant in period dress, I was immediately captivated by the floor-to-ceiling book-lined walls of the library, just to the right of the front hall. I knew then that the McQuestens had been an educated and literate family. I enquired if any of the family had been writers, perhaps, of diaries, poetry, or short stories, but was told that most of the writings in the house were in the form of personal letters—at least 10,000 pages of same—dated between 1819 and 1968, some of which had been untouched since the death of the last family member in 1968.

I then continued with the tour and was struck by the fascinating McQuesten family story that had all the earmarks of a family saga. I asked permission to view the letters and found that the literary and narrative quality in the collection was unmistakable. I then determined to do my PhD thesis for the English Department at McMaster University on the recovery of Mary Baker McQuesten's letters, the matriarch of the last generation of six children at Whitehern. After completing the thesis in 2000 I found that the strong narrative qualities of the story continued to be both compelling and insistent. Thus this book was born, with the generous assistance of SSHRC and WLUP. At the same time, with the help of my daughter, Janelle Baldwin, we determined to digitize a larger number of the family writings to bring them to the public's attention—and received generous funding from Canada's Digital Collections (Industry Canada) to do so.

And so it grows! From the humble beginning of the "three large carton boxes" excavated by Mary Farmer, we have now produced this book which is a concise narrative, and have also complemented it with a Web site: **www.whitehern.ca**, the "Whitehern Museum Archives," which is a much larger body of McQuesten writings. The Web site now contains phases one, two, and three of the completed digitization projects. When finally completed it will contain more than 3,000 letters, writings, and photographs, dating from 1819 to 1968, written by the extended McQuesten family in New England and at Whitehern. We have also presented various lectures based on the wide variety of subject material in the archive.

Two biographies have been written on Thomas Baker McQuesten, the successful lawyer/politician of Whitehern: Roland Barnsley's *Thomas B. McQuesten* (1987) and John Best's *Thomas Baker McQuesten: Public Works, Politics and Imagination* (1991). John Best has also produced a video based on his research which is available at Whitehern. Also, the *Dictionary of Hamilton Biography*, Volumes I-IV, edited by Rev. Dr. Thomas Melville Bailey, provides invaluable material on the McQuesten family. I am indebted to these writers and have found their work very helpful in my research.

The letters at Whitehern are dated from 1819 to1968 and cover three generations of the extended McQuesten and Baker families. Mary Baker McQuesten's life writings consist of approximately 1,000 letters and other writings. The largest portion of these are Mary's letters to her children when they were away from home. Mary also wrote and delivered many public addresses for the women's missionary societies at her church, MacNab Street Presbyterian Church, and during her travels to other churches and missions throughout Ontario and Western Canada. A selection of these addresses is included here.

The complete archive of life writings at Whitehern consists of personal letters, school essays, wills, eulogies, sermons, church correspondence, missionary addresses, legal and business correspondence, diary and journal writings, many photographs, and two unpublished book manuscripts written by Rev. Calvin McQuesten. There is also a large library at Whitehern, consisting of 3,500 books as well as paintings and engravings, all of which have been catalogued. The library, the family's writings, and the art work reflect the family's broad cultural and professional interests in law, politics, medicine, education, journalism, art, literature, architecture, industrial and parks development, religion, missionary work, and social reform.

Time and space have forced me to be selective in my use of the letters, and so I have used only a relatively small portion of the material at Whitehern. Of the approximately 1,000 letters extant in Mary Baker McQuesten's hand, I have selected 150 letters and life writings in order to highlight key moments in her adult life, including her marriage in 1873 at the age of twenty-three, through the birth of her seven children (one of whom died in infancy), and then her widowhood and impoverishment at the age of thirty-eight. The story then proceeds through her efforts to raise and educate her six children while continuing her executive Missionary Society role in the community. After twenty years of worry and struggle she was successful in partially restoring the family, which then proceeded to implement its Social Gospel and City Beautiful plans for the community and the province. Mary's matriarchal influence on her family and community continues to her death at the age of eighty-five in 1934 and beyond. This book thus offers not only an autobiographical view of Mary in an epistolary and narrative form, it also provides a cultural study of Hamilton, Ontario, and Canada, during the years of Mary's adult life, and especially for the Victorian and Edwardian periods.

Editing Decisions

After some consideration, I decided to use complete letters rather than selected fragments, because the complete letter provides a truer picture of family dynamics, the social scene, and the day-to-day lives of a Victorian community. I have included extensive annotations to the letters which sometimes contain fragments of other letters in order to provide narrative or thematic continuity. The annotations also give the reader some idea of contiguous events of a personal or historical nature that might contextualize the circumstances described in the letters, and they contain some biographical details about the McQuestens' friends and neighbours, and about prominent or interesting people. I have also provided photographs and a genealogical "tree" to assist the reader in identifying the characters from three generations of the extended McQuesten family.

The letters and documents in the Whitehern archive exist in their original handwritten form and on microfilm. Many have been transcribed, when time and funds have been available, under the diligent supervision of the curatorial staff at Whitehern. In checking for accuracy, I find that the transcriptions are, for the most part, true to the originals, but I have made corrections or filled in the blanks where necessary. I have also transcribed many of the letters myself and know what a monumental task it presents, especially when inkblots or folds in the fragile paper render some parts illegible, or when microfilm is blurred. In those cases in which parts of originals are illegible, missing, undated, or dated incorrectly, we have added blanks or dates (if known) in square brackets.

As in all personal correspondence, some letters are quite formal and carefully composed, while others are informal and hurried, in which case punctuation and/or spelling have been sacrificed. The letters have been transcribed to retain their original spelling and punctuation; however, where significant corrections or interpolations have been made to make sense of the letter, they also appear in square brackets. (If minor they have been made silently.) Mary's letters are very densely written to economize on paper, so she used dashes to indicate paragraph breaks. I have used these dashes as indications for divisions into actual paragraphs with indentations. The marginalia which appear on many letters and even on the envelopes are impossible to reproduce here, but have been noted when significant. For purposes of consistency, I have standardized the initial presentation of each letter so that numbering, dating, letter headings, and salutations are more easily accessible for reference purposes. In making these editorial decisions or alterations, I have followed the lead of Robert Halsband, who advises: "We as editors should at least clean, frame, and light them [the letters] for all to see and enjoy" ("Editing" 139).

The letters have been placed chronologically; however the numbering of the letters bears some explanation. I have provided the Whitehern catalogue number of each letter or document in the upper left hand corner of the presentation, but since I collected the letters from various parts of the archive, the numbers are not always consecutive. To overcome this problem I have given each letter an "A" number, which is consecutive from A1 to A150, and which precedes the Whitehern Calendar number, as in the example of A17-(4436). The "A" is necessary so as to avoid a future conflict with any letters already bearing the numbers 1 to 150 elsewhere in the Whitehern collection. The consecutive "A" number provides a finding aid for the letters that are cross-referenced in the annotations or noted elsewhere in this book. If a number appears in an annotation bearing only the Whitehern archive number, then that letter will not be found in this book; however, it can likely be located by a search on the Web site: www.whitehern.ca.

The obvious gaps in dates between some of the letters are unavoidable and result either from the loss of letters, the fact that some letters had not yet been transcribed, or the fact that no letters were written in that period.

In making this selection, I am aware that I have imposed, to some extent, my own interpretation on the text of these writings; however, I do so in full recognition that mine is only one interpretation and that there may be others. Although my sense of encroachment and voyeurism is strong, I have attempted to present the material as objectively as possible. I rationalize my uneasiness with the consideration that the family carefully preserved these writings and appreciated their literary, historical, and cultural value and, in making their bequest to the city, they anticipated that some day their collection would be publicly recognized. The personal letters and writings from Whitehern provide an intimate appreciation of Mary Baker McQuesten and her family, of the events and experiences they felt compelled to record, and of the form in which they are recorded.

Whitehern Historic House and Garden

The archives of the "Whitehern Historic House and Garden," are preserved on site at 41 Jackson Street West, Department of Culture and Recreation, Hamilton, Ontario, L8P 1L3, (905) 546-2018. Whitehern (originally named Willowbank) was the McQuesten family home for 116 years, from 1852 until the death in 1968 of the final remaining family member, Rev. Calvin McQuesten. Mary Baker McQuesten's father-in-law, Dr. Calvin McQuesten, purchased the stately home in 1852, and three generations of McQuestens lived and died at Whitehern. Since Mary's six children never married there were no heirs or successors and, in 1959, the three remaining children, Mary, Hilda, and Rev. Calvin, prepared a bequest agreement leaving their stately home to the Board of Parks Management of the City of Hamilton, that was implemented with Calvin's death. One of the terms of the bequest is that Whitehern be preserved intact as a period piece.

Consequently, Whitehern as a museum is unique because nothing was dispersed; it is complete with all family furnishings and possessions, including the family's life writings. Furthermore, because the family became impoverished in 1888, very little was changed at Whitehern from that time, except for some redecorating and upgrades such as the addition of electricity and indoor plumbing. Even the garden has been maintained as nearly as possible in its 1930s state, at which time Mary's son Thomas had altered it for his mother with the help of his associates, the husband and wife landscape design team of H. B. Dunington-Grubb. As the Whitehern brochure describes the estate, "The collection is unique, demonstrating the fine taste of a cultivated family in Canada for a period of over 100 years" (Farmer, *CMQPW* 3). Whitehern is a virtual time capsule.

Abbreviations

਍

CMQPW	*Calendar of McQuesten Papers at Whitehern: January 1973*
BDKC	*Biographical Dictionary of Knox College: 1845-1945*
CBD	*Chambers Biographical Dictionary*
CE	*The Canadian Encyclopedia*
CBE	*Cambridge Biographical Encyclopedia*
DHB	*Dictionary of Hamilton Biography, 4 volumes*
EHB	*Encyclopedia of Human Behavior*
FMC	Foreign Missions Committee
HPL	Hamilton Public Library, Special Collections
MCML	McMaster Library, Mills Reference and Special Collections
MCP	McQuesten Papers (on microfilm)
MDCB	*Macmillan Dictionary of Canadian Biography*
OCCL	*Oxford Companion to Canadian Literature*
OCEL	*Oxford Companion to English Literature*
OED	*Oxford English Dictionary*
POH	*Presbytery of Hamilton: 1836-1967*
VDCH	*Vernon's Directory of the City of Hamilton*
WFMS	Women's Foreign Missionary Society
WHMS	Women's Home Missionary Society
WMS	Women's Missionary Society
WNCD	*Webster's New Collegiate Dictionary*

Acknowledgments

ॐ

I am grateful to Wilfrid Laurier University Press and SSHRC for the confidence they have shown in this book and for their assistance, both financial and technical, in bringing it to publication. I wish to thank my professors at McMaster University, Drs. Carl Ballstadt, Lorraine York, John Ferns, and Richard Morton, for their guidance in bringing this work to its former incarnation, the PhD thesis stage. I am grateful to my family for their love and encouragement throughout the extended period of this writing: my husband, John Anderson (now deceased), for his inspiration, encouragement, and support; my son Mark James Anderson, for his technical mind and hands and perceptive ear; and my daughter Janelle Mary Baldwin, for her scholarly mind and keen eye. I am also grateful for three beautiful and intelligent grandchildren who have shown an enthusiastic interest in my writing and research. My good friend Beverley Everest has provided her usual ready ear and incisive mind to support and challenge me in my life and work. The former curator at Whitehern Museum, Ania Latoszek, and the present curator, Ken Heaman, as well as their busy staff, have been very cooperative in opening the archive to this project, and I give a further thanks to Georgina Minnes at Whitehern who "gave me the facts." I am also grateful to Mrs. Falladown and the staff at the MacNab Street Presbyterian Church for the use of their archives. I should also like to acknowledge my Salon group for their creative influence: Janelle Baldwin, Pamela Doidge, Tara Gammon, Eleanore Kosydar, and Sheila Russell, with a special thanks to Sheila for her professional and discerning eye and assistance with the editing. Finally, to Pat Kirkley, my computer wizard, who kept my "windows" and "desktop" in order.

McQuesten-Baker Family Tree (1675-1968)

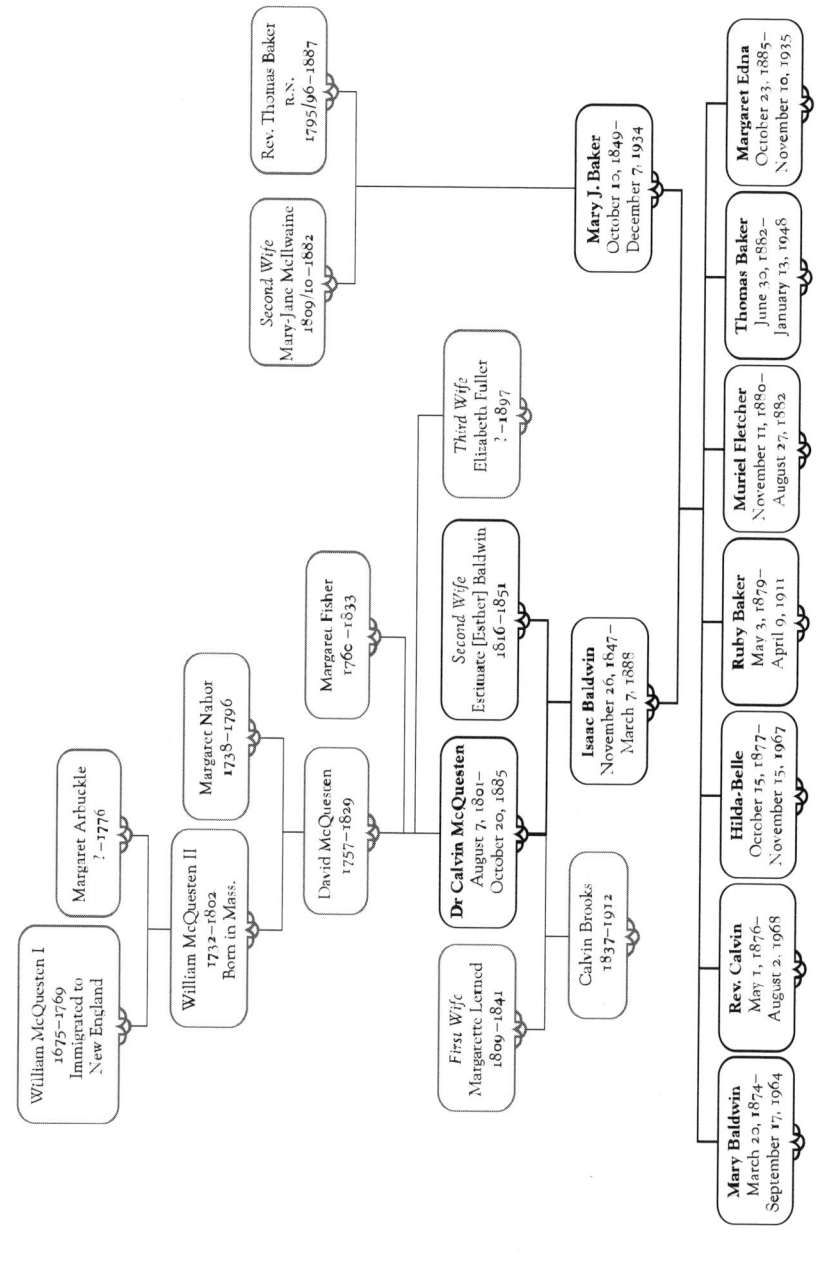

Rev. Thomas Baker, Mary Jane Baker, Mary-Jane (McIlwaine) Baker

Mrs. Dr. Burns' Ladies Collegiate Institute (circa 1868)
Gerrard St. W., Toronto, Canada West—Mary J. Baker, centre back

Mary J. Baker and Isaac B. McQuesten on their wedding day, 18 June 1873

(3885) MARY BAKER'S WEDDING TROUSSEAU[1]
TO MRS. BAKER FROM SARAH ALEXANDER (Seamstress)

JUNE 12 [1873]
To making (travelling) overskirt with
   deep flounce, scalloped pieces and reversed
   pleating all bound with Silk, Polonaise,[2]
Cape trimmed with pleating . . . . $ 7.25
Body lining .53, Sleeve lining .20, Crinoline .30 . . . .   1.03

1 See wedding photography, unfortunately blurred, which indicates the voluminous material in
   Mary's gown.
2 Polonaise" waist and drapery in one piece worn over a separate skirt (*WNCD*).

---

53 yds. Silk, 1" 25 yd. Gimp, Buttons 25 Braid 18	7.62½
Ribbon for cape .75, Dress shields .13	.88
Whalebone, Sewing Silk	.50

JUNE 13

To making Black Skirt with deep flounces and	
ruffles and leaves, Basque[3] Apron front, Sash	
trimmed with leaves all bound with Satin.	9.25
Back Body lining .53, Crinolin .45, Braid .18	1.16
Sleeve lining .25, 3 ⅛ yds. Satin 2.87	9.25
Sleeve facing .45, Ribbon .35, Buttons .35	1.15
Whalebone, Sewing Silk .65 Dress shields .13	.78

JUNE 14

To making one Mauve Silk Skirt with fine finished out	
ruffles, puffings & rucks in front.Overskirt & Basque	
trimmed with pleatings piped and turned back	6.75
Body lining .53, Skirt lining .75	1.28
Sleeve lining .20, Crinoline .30, Braid .15	.65
4 yds. Silk 1.25. piped Tarleton .75	6.08
Buttons .40, Dress Shields .13	.53
Whalebone, Sewing Silk etc..	.65

JUNE 16

To making dove Colour Silk Shirt with front and sides	
trimmed with ruffles & double box pleats.	
Basque trimmed with folds & turn back tucks.	7.75

Total . . . . $ 62.55 [sic]	
Brought forward $62.55	

JUNE 16

Body lining .65, Skirt lining 1.20	1.85
Sleeve lining .65, Sleeve facing 1.20	1.45
1 ¼ yds corded silk 2.25. Tassels .75	3.56
Ribbon .50, Buttons .28, Braid .18.	.96
Crinoline .45, Net for rucks .17.	.62
Dress Shields .13, Whalebone, Sewing silk .65	.78

JUNE 17

To making one Print Skirt with four ruffles and two bands above.	
Polonaise & underbody	3.75
Body lining .25, buttons .55, Braid .15	.95
Silk, Whalebone, Thread etc.	.45

JULY 2

To making one Muslin Skirt with nine ruffles in front, deep flounce,	
and ruffles in back, Basque and Pannier[4] trimmed with ruffles	4.50
Extra muslin .62 ½, Ribbon for bows .45	1.07 ½
Ribbon for binding .20, Thread etc. .35	.55

3 "Basque" a fitted jacket-like waist (*WNCD*).
4 "Pannier" an expanded framework for overskirt, puffed full at the sides (*WNCD*).

JULY 4

To making one blue Silk Skirt with 3 ruffles
bound & five bands above stiched Empress
train, trimmed with band, turn back pieces,
Collar and Cuffs 8.00
Body lining .53, Skirt lining .75 . . . . 1.28
Sleeve lining .20, Crinoline .45, Braid .25
Muslin 1.00. Sleeve facing .45 90
4 yds Blue Silk 2.00. Buttons .80 . . . . 8.80
Ribbon .30, Dress shields .13 43
Whalebone, Sewing Silk etc. 75

JULY 7

To making white Muslin Skirt, overskirt
& Basque trimmed with pleating. 4.25
Extra Muslim for Skirt and hem 69
Buttons .30, Braid, Thread .40. 70

Total . . . . $ 115.29 [*sic*]

Received Payment in full, Toronto, July 11, 1873
[signed] Sarah Alexander

Mary B. McQuesten   Isaac B. McQuesten
(1849-1934)   (1847-1888)
(circa 1880)

Part One

Mary Baker McQuesten's
Biography

Mary Jane Baker's Childhood

❧

Seek after self-improvement [for] all that you have yet acquired only places
you on the threshold of the temple of reason. (3004)
—Rev. Thomas Baker to daughter Mary, 18 June 1867

Mary Jane Baker was born on 10 October 1849, in Brantford, Ontario,
the only child of the second marriage of Commander the Reverend
Thomas Baker (1796-1887) and his second wife Mary-Jane McIlwaine (1809-82). She later shortened her name to Mary Baker and, after marriage, always signed her letters "M. B. McQuesten."

Mary's father applied for commission in the Royal Navy in 1805 at the age
of nine. He then went to sea at the age of eleven as a midshipman aboard the
Antelope during the Napoleonic Wars, and continued his education while on
board. During the war of 1812 he was a lieutenant on the HMS St. Lawrence
on the Great Lakes, which was the largest freshwater sailing vessel at the time.
He was granted a lieutenant's commission and pension and, after retiring from
the navy in 1817, at the age of twenty-one, he attended the Theological College in Portsea. He then emigrated from England to Upper Canada in approximately 1835, where he pursued further theological studies and took up a position
as the first minister of the first Congregational Church in Upper Canada at
Kingston, Ontario in 1835. He continued his ministry at other locations in
Ontario. In 1870 he was granted the rank of "Commander in H.M. Fleet" and
was awarded a retirement commission of eight shillings and sixpence a day in
recognition of his military service (Minnes 1; *DHB* 3:4; 3038).

Thomas Baker and his first wife, Sarah Hampson, had eight children. By
the time of her death in 1846, the eight children from this first marriage were
grown. He married for the second time in 1847 when he was fifty-one years old
and his second wife, Mary-Jane McIlwaine, was thirty-eight. Mary Jane Baker
was born two years later and became the precious and only child of this late marriage. Mary's secure childhood likely provided the stability that sustained her
later in life. Thomas Baker's correspondence at Whitehern provides details of
Mary's upper-middle-class childhood and education, and gives insights into his

Notes for Part One start on page 239

influence in determining her strong sense of duty, moral fortitude, strict Calvinist views, and critical spirit.[1]

The McIlwaines originally came from Ireland and were also a naval family. Mary's uncle, William McIlwaine, served like her father in the Napoleonic wars. The McQuestens have stated that, in the historical painting by Sir William Quiller Orchardson, "Napoleon on Board the Bellerophon," he is the young midshipman leaning over the rail in the background (Farmer, *CMQPW* 10). Little is known of Mary's mother except that she was a minister's wife, and a leader in organizing the women of the church in collecting for the Bible Society from 1853 to 1857. They were charged with calling on the "poor and unchurched ... [and] ascertaining whether any families are destitute of the Holy Scriptures" (4194). Women in the Bible Societies were forerunners of the women's missionary movement and they brought years of experience to it (Brouwer 64). Mrs. Baker likely provided a model for Mary's later participation in the women's missionary movement in the Presbyterian Church.

On both sides of Mary's family, the strongest influences in her early life were both military and religious. They provided a strong code of discipline, morality, and social responsibility. Mary, in turn, inculcated in her children the same strict discipline and moral and religious code. She also imposed her convictions on her community with dedication and vigour. Although she was physically a small woman, she was a formidable presence.

Mary's father was a model of Calvinist rectitude in his pastoral dealings and he demanded a very high moral standard from his congregation. His letters demonstrate his patriarchal expectations regarding his congregation. For instance, in his letter of August 1841 to his congregation in Paris, Ontario, Thomas Baker tendered his resignation because they had not fulfilled their promise to erect "a comfortable and commodious Place of Worship":

That in this aspect you are behind every other Congregation of this denomination in this Province, you are the only people who have allowed a year to pass away without the effort required of you and which I was encouraged to expect when invited to become your Pastor. It was well known that I had pledged myself to leave if the measure was not carried out in the time proposed.... It must be obvious to you that the necessity of dissolving my connection has been forced upon me. (4126)

The chastising and judgmental tone of the letter justifies his stance with a legalistic thoroughness. It bears noting that the flawless form and flourish of his penmanship was also a reflection of his fastidious nature.

Thomas Baker's writings also contain a lengthy account of dissension within the church, which is significant for two reasons. First, it discloses that his subsequent ministry in Brantford was also riddled with discipline problems that he proceeded to rectify with the same stern measures. The lengthy account for the years 1841 to 1848 concludes that the Brantford members were "most pertinaciously adhering to their opinions," and the matter was finally resolved in 1849 with "resolutions ... and names of church members expelled and suspended" (4129, 4142). It is evident from the form and content of these accounts that Thomas Baker was a highly principled and inflexible pastor, and meted out disciplinary measures with an Old Testament justice and a military rigour.

Second, and equally significant to Mary's development, is Thomas Baker's defence of women's rights. Although he was rigidly patriarchal in dealing with his flock, he openly defended the right of women to participate in church meetings and politics. His account relates that a member of the congregation "objected to females speaking in the church." At the next meeting, one month later, he "spoke at some length to the right of females to take part in transacting church business, showing that their being forbidden to speak related to Worshiping Assemblies and not to meetings for the transacting of church affairs." In his lengthy sermonical reply he quoted extensively from the New Testament, and then abruptly concluded that he hoped he had now "set the matter to rest" (4129e).

It is evident that, as a woman, Mary gained the courage to voice her opinions and criticisms at church meetings and in missionary circles from her father's example and teaching. Mary particularly deplored the fact that women were not allowed to vote in church politics (A127-24 April 1923; *DHB* 3:6). However, if her work or opinions were not always appreciated, this did not dissuade her. She had the utmost confidence in her own interpretations, assessments and judgements of people. She never hesitated to be critical of church politics or of ministers, either for the style and content of their sermons and their oratorical skill, or for their dress or appearance (A35-4803). In March 1905, when Rev. Dr. Donald Hugh Fletcher was retiring, she traveled to Markham to hear a possible new minister for the church but rejected him because "he has no attractive force about him" (MCP 1-3a.16). She rejected another minister because "he is not Scotch, which will be [held] against him" (MCP 1-3a.30). She then recommended Beverley Ketchen because "he was very good looking and manly; more of a born gentleman than any of the other young men" (MCP 1-3a.11). In fact, Mary placed the gown on Ketchen's shoulders at his induction and also, reportedly, gave a "remarkable address" (A144-Eulogy). Mary was equally outspoken on political, civic, and social issues. She was a staunch Liberal and a temperance worker; she supported labour unions and defended their right to strike (MCP 2-4.34).

Although Mary Baker did not receive a university education (very few women did at that time) she did receive a classical education and achieved "Most Satisfactory" or "Excellent" grades. Her report card from Newmarket County Grammar School in June 1865 lists her curriculum and grades (4221). In "The McQuestens and Their Letters," Mary Farmer states that "[i]t was probably at this school that she was so well grounded in public speaking that she could be critical of preachers and preaching" (33). Mary also attended

Mrs. Burns' Ladies' Collegiate Institute in Toronto for four terms and distinguished herself there. The report card for the French Department reads: "1st class, This is to certify that Miss Baker is the only Young Lady who obtained 1st Class at the Monthly Examination. Signed, Emile Pernet Mrs. Dr. Burns' School: Toronto, March 16th 1868" (Box 4.2).

Newmarket County Grammar School*
QUARTERLY REPORT FOR MISS M. J. [MARY JANE] BAKER
For the Quarter Ending June 30, 1865

Subject	No. in class	Relative rank	Progress
Greek Grammar	4	1	Most Satisfactory
Latin Grammar	6	1	Most Satisfactory
Greek		1	Most Satisfactory
Greek Prose Comp.	1	1	Most Satisfactory
Latin Prose Comp.		1	Most Satisfactory
Latin	1	1	Most Satisfactory
English Grammar	X		
English History	14	1	Most Satisfactory
Ancient History	1	1	English History
Canadian History			
European History			
Geography	15	1	Most Satisfactory
Reading			
Dictation			
Spelling			
Arithmetic	11	2	Most Satisfactory
Euclid	1	1	Most Satisfactory
Algebra			
Trigonometry			
Mensuration			
Natural Philosophy	9	1	Excellent
French	2	1	Excellent
Elocution			
English Composition			Excellent

Conduct: Very Satisfactory
Principal: W. H. Vander Smissen B.A.

---

* Mary also took German lessons at a cost of $5.25 per quarter (4222, 30 June 1865)

Thomas Baker's pride in Mary and his expectations are evident in his letter to her of 18 June 1867: "Seek after self-improvement [for] all that you have yet acquired only places you on the threshold of the temple of reason" (3004).

These injunctions are later echoed in Mary's instructions to her children, as in her advice to Calvin to attain "a well furnished mind" (A31-4686).

Thomas Baker also guided his daughter's education and reading, and some of the books in the Whitehern library contain his inscriptions to Mary on the occasion of a birthday or Christmas. For instance, her father presented her with a Latin dictionary, inscribed: "To Mary Jane Baker, This copy of Walt-shmidt's Dictionary is presented on her eleventh birthday, as a reward for diligent attention to her Classical Studies, October 10, 1860." Several of these gifts were texts of Bible exegesis, such as the nine volumes by Albert Barnes on interpretations of the Old and New Testaments (1847-63). Mary, in turn, presented some of these books to her children, sometimes re-inscribed from her.

Significant to the issue of women's education in Ontario, Thomas Baker's collection also contains supportive letters about the opening of women's classes at McGill University and the Congregational College in 1884, following their affiliation one year earlier (3813; 3831). Mary Baker was also fortunate in that she married into a family that encouraged an enlightened attitude toward women's education. Her father-in-law, Dr. Calvin McQuesten, had been involved in the establishment of the Wesleyan Ladies' College in Hamilton in 1861, which, in spite of its name, granted a non-sectarian degree. He was vice-president of the college until 1872 and president until his death in 1885.

Mary's family consisted of educated members who had graduated in the major professions: the military, the clergy, medicine, law, and teaching. She became keenly interested in these professions through her family and through the education and direction of her children's lives.

Mary Baker's Marriage to Isaac B. McQuesten

૨ે

My sweetest, I have been very impertinent so far, and I know and confess it. Darling what a happy, happy time it will be when you are not to be taken away from me nearly all the time, and I can be at liberty to pet you just as much and just as often as I wish. (2352)
—Isaac McQuesten to Mary Baker, 20 March 1873

Mary Baker and Isaac Baldwin McQuesten met formally in 1869 and they were married four years later, on 18 June 1873.[2] Mary had broken off their engagement at least once (the reason likely was Isaac's habitual use of alcohol) and he wrote in contrition: "My darling, it will be a lifelong wonder to me that you could have ventured to renew an engagement so justly broken off with one ... who gave you such sufficient cause to fell him, and that forever. However, sweet, it did me good" (2340). For the most part, Isaac's letters are playful and teasing and express his longing for their marriage, and theirs was a loving marriage.

Mary was a strikingly beautiful young woman and, at the time of their marriage, Isaac was a handsome young lawyer with excellent prospects, the son of a prominent and wealthy Hamilton industrialist, Dr. Calvin McQuesten (1801-85). McQuesten had come to Canada from New England during the 1830s and established the first foundry in Hamilton. This was the beginning of the steel industry in Hamilton which eventually grew to become known as "the Birmingham of Canada." Calvin McQuesten was very successful in his enterprises and, in 1857, at the age of fifty-six, he retired with a family fortune of $500,000 as well as real estate and other investments. He then indulged himself in his favourite avocation, evangelical Protestantism, and participated in the design and development of Presbyterian churches in Ontario and in other parts of North America (*DHB* 1:146-47). Becoming increasingly senile with age, he died in 1885 at eighty-four.

Isaac graduated in law in 1873 and took control of the family finances until his father's death in 1885, at which time he inherited Whitehern (then Willowbank) and moved in with his family. Mary promptly changed the home's name to Whitehern. Unfortunately, Isaac had lost the family fortune by 1888 through bad management and poor health.

Several factors contributed to Isaac's decline, including a long-standing poor relationship with his stepmother, his father's third wife, Elizabeth Fuller McQuesten. Isaac's mother, Estimate Baldwin McQuesten (his father's second wife), died when he was four years old, and Elizabeth Fuller became his stepmother two years later. It was a poor relationship from the start, and she sent the children, Isaac and his half-brother Calvin (his father's son from his first marriage) away from home to be educated. She was cold and distant and instructed the children to call her Mrs. McQuesten, and spent much of her time on long shopping trips to the United States and to Europe. Many of the fine furnishings at Whitehern are the result of her excursions.

Elizabeth Fuller McQuesten and Isaac engaged in a long struggle over the family finances (2321). She sought to turn his father against him by charging him with irresponsible behaviour and with drinking and carousing at school, some of which was true. For instance, an 1869 letter from his friend Robert Hope confirms his reputation as a "mighty mingler" and "drinker of strong drink" (2275). Unfortunately, Isaac did suffer from alcoholism and possibly other addictions. He also suffered with insomnia and depression, which deepened into mental illness, requiring treatment. Isaac also made a series of poor investments involving patents for a railroad car coupler and a textile mill in Hespeler, Ontario, which failed.

Isaac's half-brother, Dr. Calvin Brooks McQuesten, was practising medicine in New York, and the letters between the brothers during this period reveal that, although they were united in their struggle against their stepmother, they also became divided themselves over Isaac's handling of the finances. Mary's letters to Dr. Calvin Brooks McQuesten in May and July 1885 relate her increasing distress and anxiety about the urgent family problems: Isaac's father's health, Isaac's "nervous disease," and the continuing bitter struggle with their stepmother (A5-4323; A6-4327). In 1886 Calvin Brooks McQuesten wrote to Dr. Mullins, the family physician, and inquired about Isaac and his addiction. Dr. Mullins confirmed his suspicions when he replied: "an unfortunate habit had been established and I believe that a sincere effort has been made to resist it" (1592).

Isaac's letter to Calvin of 1 October 1887 (2511; A6-4327n) reveals the extent of his unstable condition. The letter was written on his return from Homewood sanatorium in Guelph, which he entered for treatment of his addictions and mental illness, during the failure of the Hespeler Mill. Isaac's letter describes his symptoms as "an unhealthy excitement ... [and] wakefulness," followed by "sluggishness" and "despair."[3] The letter contains a frank admission of his addiction: "[I was] systematically using stimulants.... It is these sudden impulses that I must look out for. It is one long continuous want or craving." The letter also bears a cryptic and portentous statement about a plan or course of action, possibly violent, that Isaac was contemplating, and that "must be done," and he warns his brother to "be prepared, when such occasion may occur, to quickly and calmly use your best judgement." It is impossible to know the precise meaning of the letter, but five months after it was written, Isaac died very suddenly on 7 March 1888, at the age of forty, reportedly as the result of a combination of a sleeping draught and alcohol.

Isaac's death was publicly rumoured to be a suicide, but this is not conclusive and he was given an elaborate and honourable funeral with many prominent dignitaries and politicians as pallbearers. There were various conflicting reports about the cause of death, including suggestions of heart disease or lung congestion, but I have found no letters that give any precise details about Isaac's death (A8-2520). However, there are many letters of condolence in a commemorative journal at Whitehern.

The suicide rumours gained further credence when Isaac's death revealed the extent of his bankruptcy, with liabilities totaling $900,000 (Minnes 2). To make matters worse, Isaac also lost much of Mary's inheritance from her father, as well as most of his half-brother's share of the estate.

Isaac's death ended fourteen years of their marriage, and although it was a loving relationship, they were tumultuous years for the family. During the first twelve years Mary gave birth to seven children. The year 1882 was particularly traumatic for the family: Thomas, the sixth child, was born in June, Mary's mother died in August (of diabetes), and, two weeks later, Muriel, the fifth child, died at twenty-two months of age. Then, in 1885, Mary's father-in-law died, and on the day of his funeral, 23 October, Edna, the seventh child, was born. Mary's father then died in 1887. If we also consider the financial difficulties and struggles with Isaac's stepmother, and Isaac's addiction and recurring mental breakdowns, it is little wonder that Mary occasionally suffered during this period from exhaustion and emotional collapse and had to seek treatment herself. It is difficult to comprehend that, during the same period, she was also a very active executive in the women's missionary auxiliaries. Indeed, on the very day of Isaac's death Mary had attended a missionary meeting at her church.

Mary Baker McQuesten's Widowhood and Matriarchy: Six Children and Lives of Genteel Poverty

ॐ

Surely a man was never blessed with a better mother in every way.... You seem to demand the best of a man ... we know distinctly the difference between right and wrong, and I don't know that any mother can achieve a much higher result.... You were always thoroughly consistent.... I have seen you actually stinting yourself so that we could have more.... I do know my dear mother that if I am going to achieve anything and come to you for commendation, I must come with clean hands. (5440)
—Thomas McQuesten to his mother, Mary Baker McQuesten, on the fourteenth anniversary of his father's death, 6 March 1906

With Isaac's death, Mary's story changes abruptly from one of privilege to relative impoverishment, as she became the single parent of six children between the ages of fourteen and three: Mary (fourteen), Calvin (twelve), Hilda (eleven), Ruby (nine), Thomas (six), Edna (three). Isaac had had the forethought to arrange with a law partner to place the house in trust for Mary and his family, and so Whitehern was preserved. However, the widowed Mary was forced to raise and educate her children, and struggle to maintain the large family home, on a greatly reduced income of approximately $1,700 per year at a time when taxes and water rates alone on Whitehern were approximately $300 per year. Mary received legal assistance from Isaac's law partner, James Chisholm, and managed to retain ownership of Whitehern, some investments in her name, and the two attached houses on Bold Street that she and Isaac had shared with her parents. These houses were badly in need of repair, and when she was finally able to make repairs in 1903, she rented them for $40 a month as boarding houses (later raising the rent to $75) (A43-5012n). For a very short time, according to the 1891 census, Mary managed to keep two servants but for many years thereafter she was unable to hire help except occasionally for heavy work (A9-4343n).

A very strong influence on Mary at this pivotal point in her life would likely have been the memory of the negative moral example set by a widowed female member of her father's first family. Thomas Baker's son James Alfred (1825-76) had suffered bankruptcy and died, leaving his second wife, Maria Mudge, impoverished, with *his* seven children to raise (2953). A neighbour reported the rumours to Thomas Baker that Maria was entertaining men in the house who "stay undue periods" (3156). Mary Farmer notes that "the unfortunate woman knew of only one way to augment her income" and Rev. Thomas Baker then had the difficult task of placing his grandchildren elsewhere and providing for their education and upkeep (Farmer, CMQPW 12). However, there is further evidence in the letters that Maria may have been unjustly maligned by the gossip "in the mouths of old women" (3156)

Thomas Baker's patriarchal attitude likely provided a model for Mary's matriarchal development when she was forced to take charge of her family. Her strong character developed as she had to make decisions alone, and she gradually took charge of every aspect of her children's lives.

It is impossible to imagine the devastation that Mary must have felt. It is facile now to look back and say that she had a plan, and that things worked out according to that plan, and that she was in control and, even, controlling. But that is not the case; they lived a day-to-day existence for more than twenty years. Most of the time Mary was terribly worried and even physically and emotionally ill with the responsibility and with not knowing what the future would hold for all of them. In the darkest years it was impossible to look forward to any relief. At one point, when finally the finances began to ease just a little, she remarked to Calvin: "We can look back now to the time when we could not look forward at all" (5347, 6 July 1905). However, even after that glimmer of hope, more tribulation was to follow before things got better.

We can try to see this predicament through Mary's eyes and feel her desperation during the worst times. What was Mary to do with this large house and six young children? If she sold it, she would still need space for seven people. How was she to manage their day-to-day lives, physical needs, education, and moral upbringing? How was she to restore her family's social standing? The miracle is that she did succeed. In retrospect, we can see how she did it, but it was a very gradual and painful process.

In true matriarchal fashion, Mary assessed each of the children for their potential to restore the family to its former status, and she guided them accordingly. Four of the children were girls and, during the Victorian age, they would never be able to earn enough to support a family. Consequently, since Mary could no longer afford to have servants, the two eldest daughters, Mary and Hilda, were assigned to look after the home and to take care of the younger children. They were not especially scholarly and spent their years at home; thus, there are fewer letters from, or to, them. They both lived to the age of ninety and continued their mother's work in the church.

Mary's eldest son, Calvin, was twelve years old when his father died. He had been born with a deformed left hand and some paralysis on his left side, and as he grew older he began to exhibit signs of the family's inherited nervous disease. This condition was characterized by phases of great energy and creativity, followed by phases of depression and lassitude.[4] Calvin was never able to earn an income for the family, but, in spite of his limitations, he achieved some success as a journalist in Toronto and Montreal from 1901 to 1903. For the Toronto *News* he wrote, among other articles, "A Corner for Women Readers" under the pseudonym "Nina Vivian." At the Montreal *Herald*, he wrote a "Tatler" column after the fashion of the Addison and Steele "Tatler" of 1709-11 (*OCEL* 804), with rich commentary on politics, literature, art, history, religion, and world events. In these articles Calvin demonstrates literary skill, wit, and a broad and eclectic knowledge.[5]

The pay as a journalist was very small so it was very seldom that Calvin could send money home to his needy family. In fact he often required assistance from his mother, his sister Ruby, or, later, his brother Tom. On a rare instance in 1903 when he was able to send ten dollars home, his mother was very pleased and listed all of her expenses in order to show "how much help your ten dollars is" (A43-5012). This provides a valuable record of some of the family's household expenses in Hamilton in 1903.

Calvin had undergone a religious conversion in 1896 at the John Dowie "Zion" "Divine Healing Mission" in Chicago and, although his mother did not approve of his remaining there because of the cost, the effects of this religious experience remained with him as a "rebirth" experience all his life (A12-MCP 1-3B.16; A13-MCP 1-3B.9; Diary, Box 14-082). After he found journalism too stressful, Calvin, with his mother's encouragement, decided on an education for the ministry, although she frankly stated that she would be unable to help him financially. He then worked as an itinerant missionary preacher in the summers to pay for his university education during the fall and winter. Calvin's education took many years, but he finally graduated with a B.A. in 1908 and was ordained in 1909 at thirty-three years of age. He spent another year at university to attempt a master's degree, and passed some exams, but did not receive the degree. Nevertheless, his mother declared that he was "finally launched" and should never again attempt examinations, since they were too stressful for him (A102-6676n).

Calvin tried preaching and was considered an excellent orator. He also tried homesteading in Saskatchewan in 1907-10 but with very little success (7667). He had several breakdowns and came home to stay in 1916. From 1920 to 1950 he held a semi-volunteer position as chaplain at the Hamilton Mountain Sanatorium for the treatment of tuberculosis, where he was much loved by the patients. He also wrote two book manuscripts but they were never published.[6]

Because Calvin was away from home so much between 1895 and 1916, many of Mary's letters are to him. Their relationship was somewhat ambivalent; she sometimes confided in him and asked his advice, but at other times she grew impatient and treated him like a child: "we have all suffered enough in the past, for your persistent taking of your own way" (A81-5984). Mary was ever vigilant for signs of an impending breakdown and constantly warned him about this possibility. Her letters acted like a kind of umbilical cord between them. Both Calvin and Tom preferred to live away from home, but both also ended up back at Whitehern. Calvin was the last surviving family member and he died at the age of ninety-two at Whitehern. It was Calvin who, after some discussion and urging, arranged with his sisters to bequeath Whitehern to the City of Hamilton (Box 4-113).

Ruby was nine years old when her father died in 1888. She was very beautiful, artistic, and scholarly. With her mother's guidance, she became a teacher, took a position with the Presbyterian Ladies' College in Ottawa in 1899, and sent most of her income home for Tom's education and for the maintenance of the home (A22-4535; A23-4544; A43-5012). She also helped Calvin with his school expenses. Her salary was the only means of gaining enough money to see Tom through school, so that ultimately his income would provide some solvency and status for the family.

Ruby was often homesick, though she never complained (A20-4521). She was repeatedly ill at the drafty old school (A24-4549), but in spite of her illnesses Ruby managed to work just long enough to earn Tom's tuition until his graduation in 1907. After several false diagnoses (A87-6135, A88-6173), she was eventually diagnosed with tuberculosis and sent to a sanatorium in Calgary in 1908 and then to another in Muskoka in 1909. Ruby's medical expenses were a great burden. She was brought home in the fall of 1910 and lived in a cottage on the Hamilton mountain, where the family cared for her, but she succumbed to the tuberculosis and died in April 1911, at the age of thirty-two. Ruby was a tragic heroine in the family; her intellect, beauty, charm, and talent were sacrificed for Tom's education and for the family. However, her letters are always charming and witty, even when written from the sanatorium.

Edna, the youngest child, initially showed great promise as a scholar and a musician. She won a scholarship in classics to Queen's University in 1904, at the age of eighteen, but was never well enough to attend (MCP 1-1.25). Edna suffered from a severe form of the family mental disease and had several breakdowns, each progressively more debilitating. Her medical expenses were also a great burden to Mary. Edna was hospitalized on several occasions and institutionalized in 1920 at the Homewood Sanatorium in Guelph, where she received several shock treatments and, eventually, a hysterectomy and a partial lobotomy. She died in 1935 at the age of fifty, one year after her mother died.

Thomas, the second-youngest child, was robust, scholarly and athletic, and Mary soon perceived that he embodied the best hope for the family's return to solvency, so Mary concentrated the family's resources on his education. Thomas was clearly her favourite and her letters to him often express an extra warm greeting: "You are much in my thoughts and always in my prayers my dearly beloved son. May God bless and help you! Your loving mother" (MCP 1-3a.25). More than that, she told him explicitly of her reliance on him:

My own darling boy: You do not know just what a help and strength you have been to your mother. I am so very nervous and anxious minded that if you had been anything else but what you are I would certainly have broken down ... it seems to me I would have died, for people do die of broken hearts. To one of my disposition and views it would seem to me life would have been impossible. As it is you were strong and vigorous and unlike son Cal, physically fit ... and thus have been an unspeakable strength to me. (A75-MCP 2-4.37a)

Thomas came very close to winning the Rhodes Scholarship in 1904, the first year that it was offered, but was passed over for another candidate. Mary expressed her severe disappointment at the loss of the opportunity, the income of $1,500 per year, and the honour: "It seems as if I cannot forget it.... I would just have been too proud" (A50-5199).

Tom graduated in law in 1907 at the age of twenty-five and then articled in Toronto and worked in Elk Lake in 1908, during the Cobalt boom. His mother encouraged him to come back to Hamilton, stating to Calvin: "[i]t is difficult to decide as to Tom's final start, but he thinks, and I think, perhaps it is as good a place as anywhere here in Hamilton ... here I may get him interested in some good works besides his business" (as, indeed, she did) (A90-6318). In 1909, Tom secured a permanent position in Hamilton with John Chisholm, his father's former law partner, and began to earn an income of $1,000 a year.

The Restoration of the Family

છે.

It is certainly wonderful to look back over the years and realize that they are past and that we are in such easy circumstances. Sometimes one is tempted to think that the sorest trials might have been averted if there had not been such a scarcity of money, but then we feel that is not for us to say. God was managing our affairs for us, and He surely knew the best way. (Box 12-720)
—Mary Baker McQuesten, 7 March 1912

With Thomas's income, the family finances finally began to improve a little, but the heavy bills for Edna and Ruby and for the maintenance of Whitehern continued. However, the McQuesten family was finally restored to political and social prominence by Thomas McQuesten, who eventually fulfilled his mother's expectations and his own potential. Tom was remarkably successful in politics and public works in Hamilton and throughout Ontario. On the Hamilton

Parks Board, as part of the "City Beautiful" movement, he commissioned many parks and building projects, including Gage Park, Cootes Paradise, King's Forest Park, Chedoke Civic Golf Course, The Royal Botanical Gardens (The Rock Gardens), the High Level Bridge (later, the McQuesten High Level Bridge), and many more. Tom was also instrumental in bringing McMaster University to Hamilton from Toronto, which was finally accomplished in 1931. Tom considered this success to be one of his finest achievements (A134-7085n), and the chancellor of the university, Dr. H. P. Whidden, clearly stated his indebtedness to Tom by acknowledging that Tom was "one of the great big factors which has made the whole thing possible"(A136-7111n).

Tom, in turn, stated his indebtedness to his mother. In Mary's obituary Tom openly acknowledged his gratitude to his mother for her inspiration, encouragement, and imagination. Tom fulfilled his familial and his public duties admirably. After his mother's death in 1934 he continued their beautification vision at his dual portfolio in the provincial cabinet and then, with his collaborators, built the Queen Elizabeth Highway, the Rainbow Bridge, the Niagara Parkway and Parks system and its School for Apprentice Gardeners, the Floral Clock, the Carillon Tower, the Clifton Arch, and the Oakes Garden Theatre. He also rebuilt several forts and was involved in many other public works, parks, bridges, and roads in the Niagara peninsula and in other parts of Ontario (Best 192).[7]

Mary's obituary in the *Hamilton Herald* (7 December 1934) credits her with being the primary influence in Tom's life and work:

Mr. McQuesten himself has told of the large part his mother played in molding his tastes, his standards and his plan of life. Not the least of her contributions to him was to give him a love for beauty that was large enough to spread out and influence the appearance of a great city.... large areas of Hamilton are, in the last analysis a reflection of her love of beauty. (Box 8-140a)

Many of Mary's letters in the late 1920s and '30s describe her frequent trips with Tom to survey his projects (A134-7085).

Tom died in January 1948 at the age of sixty-five, reportedly of throat cancer (Minnes 5). In a letter to Tom, Beverley Ketchen acknowledged a public debt to him: "Very few men can point to so many public benefits of enduring value. Like Christopher Wren's, *Your* monuments are beauty spots" (Box 8-202, 12 July 1947). Mayor Walters paid a similar tribute to Tom in an obituary statement (A123-6975n).

Thomas did fulfill Mary's ambitions for him and he did finally restore the family to honour and prestige, if not to wealth. However, for more than twenty years Mary had struggled day-to-day with the terrible fear and anxiety of not knowing if they would succeed. There were times when Mary expressed despair because the burden seemed impossible, and several times she collapsed under the strain, but she never gave up.

Twenty years after her husband's sudden death, Mary assessed the struggle so far and was grateful for the relative "comfort and luxury" they had achieved:

Isn't it just wonderful to look back over the twenty years since your father was so suddenly taken from us and think of the serious illnesses of different members of the family and how we were brought through them all and now look at the comfort and luxury in which we are living! (A85-6063)

However, in the same letter Mary notes she is still unable to send Calvin the money for his trip home from Toronto, and debts remained heavy for several years after this.

During the hard times Mary considered selling Whitehern, but the price was never high enough to make a move worthwhile. In 1895 the encroaching TH&B railroad line was built at the rear of Whitehern which had devalued the property, and the house was falling into disrepair. After careful calculation, she concluded that she would still require a large home for her family of seven, and she reasoned that their "beautiful things" would be dispersed with little monetary gain (A73-5788). Also, their stately home was invested with a great deal of social prestige that Mary was no doubt loath to give up.

In 1907 Mary accepted an offer from the Hamilton Club, an exclusive men's club, to rent Whitehern for eight months for $900. The income helped to sustain the family during a particularly dark period in financial and health concerns (A76-5800). Mary was appalled by the condition of the home when the rental period was ended, particularly when they finally located the source of the stench of "5 kegs of rotten oysters in the coal room" (A83-6012). However, she had finally earned some money for repairs and redecorating, although she was still deeply in debt (A87-6135).

During the rental period Mary took a cottage in Oakville for herself and her daughters while her sons were away from home. The rental of the cottage was $200 for the period of May to 15 October, and $15 per month if needed longer. The down payment from the club covered the rent. Her daughters, Ruby and Edna, were both ill at the time; Ruby was generally run down and suffering from bronchitis, later diagnosed as tuberculosis, and Edna was recovering from a mental breakdown (A71-5744; A87-6135). In time, as the two girls required treatment and hospitalization, their medical expenses increased.

In 1911 Tom was able to reassure Calvin, stating: "Don't worry about the money there's plenty of it" (8237), and again, "I am fairly flush just now. Got a small raise in salary" (8239). The financial burden finally eased considerably in 1912, when Uncle Calvin Brooks McQuesten, Mary's unmarried brother-in-law, died and left her $36,000. The financial relief is dramatically evident in the abrupt transition from Mary's frugal 1911 vacation at $5 a week for room and board (A107-6752), to her comparatively lavish vacation of 1912, when she expressed no distress at the expense of $600 to travel to Vancouver and the Rockies (A111-6780).

However, through those long hard years Mary did preserve the family home, took charge of all aspects of her children's lives, and finally managed to restore the family to social and political prominence. It is not surprising, therefore, that on several occasions she required rest and treatment when she suffered "nervous prostration," a term she used to describe an emotional collapse caused by stress, anxiety, and overwork (A22-4535; A81-5984; 8756).

John Best, in his biography of Thomas Baker McQuesten, speculates on the rumours that it was because of the inherited mental illness in her family that Mary actively broke up any prospective marital union for her children (Best 20, 203, n10; *DHB* 3:8). Although this is a compelling assumption, it remains unconfirmed. However, it may be significant that Isaac's half-brother, Dr. Calvin Brooks McQuesten, also remained unmarried. He was often consulted by the family on matters of science and medicine. He may have warned the family of the possibility of perpetuating any hereditary illnesses and, as a result, they may have agreed on a form of eugenics (Dr. Calvin Brooks McQuesten's diary entry, n.d.). It is evident that the family was aware of the system of eugenics in Plato's *Republic* since it was noted briefly in Isaac's letter to his brother Calvin of 1 October 1887: "A more deplorable union than Mamie's with young Brown I cannot well conceive. If ever the principles of Plato's Republic as to marriage ought to be invoked, they should in this case" (2511). Also, there were strong influences in Canadian Victorian society at that time that favoured eugenics as a means of preventing the breeding of the "feeble minded" and "unfit" (*Electric Library Canada*, 22 October 1999). Dr. C. K. Clarke (1857-1924) also advocated eugenics, and practiced sterilization of the "feeble-minded" in Toronto during his career. That broad category, "feeble-minded," included immigrants, women, mental patients, the unemployed, and criminals, (*Ideas*, CBC Radio, August 2000). This practice of eugenics persisted for many years: in the United States, the Lynchburg Colony in Virginia performed routine sterilization on the young "feeble-minded" inmates from 1904 to 1972 (*The Lynchburg Story*, PBS Documentary, 16 November 1999).

Mary actively intervened in the marital prospects for three of her children—Hilda, Ruby, and Tom. In each situation, she exerted her matriarchal power, the engagements were terminated, and they remained single. In fact, none of the children ever married. It is possible to glean several reasons for Mary's interference but it is impossible to extract a single motive for all three cases. However, it is likely that in all three cases the social station of the prospective partner was not acceptable to Mary's aspirations for her family. She expresses regret, on several occasions, that her daughters did not receive sufficient invitations to a "really nice home" or have "a chance to meet any one" (A24-4549). She also shows some anxiety that her standards had "been too puritanical" and had "shut out the girls from any opportunities" (A75-MCP 2-4.37). There is also some evidence that

Mary may have regretted her role in the break-up of some of the relationships and she speculates that her motives may have been "self-seeking" (A67-5654).

At times, Mary encouraged her son Calvin to marry but also warned him about the dangers of being "caught" (A22-4535). The family's financial circumstances, the rumours and stigma of their father's possible suicide, and the family's mental disease were all factors which hindered any early union for Mary's children, even though they were intelligent and attractive. By the time that the family was solvent again, the children were all mature and their lives and energies had been directed by Mary into good works for the community. They were imbued with a strong sense of duty and social conscience and fulfilled themselves in that way, according to their capabilities.

Mary tried to keep abreast of even the smallest details in her children's lives and instructed and even manipulated them when she felt it necessary. When the children were away from home, the constant communication by letter was the conduit of her control: "so be wise and obey your mother" (A81-5984). She often used the behaviour of their friends as negative examples. Mary criticizes Annie Fletcher, the minister's daughter, stating "[i]t is really terrible the way that girl has been allowed to run loose & the extravagance.... It just shows what trying to keep in with the world does for people, one step surely leads to another" (4562). Of Percy Robertson (a friend), she says: "[he] would play the mandolin all day, has no particular fancy for any calling. I feel very sorry for his mother. She had to give up keeping a servant ... and I do not think he appreciates it one bit" (A74-5794).

Mary required of her children the highest moral standard based on Christian principles and she demanded no less of herself. Guilt and duty were powerful incentives, and her leadership in self-sacrifice was the model of moral behaviour. Her directions were always lovingly intended and she sought the guiding hand of God in prayer for all her decisions. This is not to suggest that Mary's judgements were always sound. It is possible that, as a single parent of six children, forced to make decisions alone, Mary found it convenient to impose an excessively strict morality on her growing children as a means of control. She also confessed that, because there was no money for any frivolous extras, it made it easier to deny them these many temptations. As early as 1902, she stated to Cal: "Many an hour I have laid awake, thinking if I had stood in my children's way by not joining in the pleasures of the world, but I believe any other course would have been wrong & I leave their future in God's hands. Of course the lack of money made it easier" (4562). Again in 1904 she admits that "this shortness of money has really developed the family. I just think I have the finest family in all the world but I must not be too proud" (5297).

It may be possible to fault Mary for her excessive control of her children's lives, but it is not possible to fault her for neglect or lack of caring. Whatever Mary's role was in the unmarried status of her children, there is little doubt that she did what she thought was best for her family at that time, from a financial and moral standpoint. In retrospect, it would be facile to judge Mary as merely self-centred, demanding, interfering, and tyrannical. She was not a one-dimensional character but complex and many-faceted. The debate in judging her character is between matriarchy and tyranny—that is, between maternal control and oppression. When reading Mary's life through her letters, one is constantly being swayed between the two poles, and I leave it to the reader to make that judgment.

There is evidence that the family suffered gossip and social stigma because of the rumours surrounding their father's alcoholism, possible suicide, and bankruptcy, as well as the family's mental instability, tuberculosis, and the six unmarried siblings. Therefore, the best social prospects were likely not available to Mary's children. At that time being an "old maid" was a disgrace and, in fact, some friends openly expressed that they were "terribly concerned that none of the girls were married" (5691). The effort to conceal some of the family's circumstances required secrecy and insularity in the family: "In Tom's letter I warned him that if people become too inquisitive about Edna.... We do not mention her name unless people ask after her particularly" (5430).

The rumours created an aura of mystery that surrounded Whitehern during the family's occupancy, and this aura persists to the present day. In tours and lectures at Whitehern Museum visitors often express the sense that the house continues to guard its secrets and they probe the McQuesten mysteries with questions and conjecture. The McQuesten letters provide some verification for all of the rumours. There are no real conclusions to be made, but from a literary and cultural point of view, the aura of mystery is the stuff of lore and legend that lends a Victorian Gothic cast to the mythology of Whitehern.

However we might assess Mary's matriarchy, it cannot be denied that her single-minded determination and devotion to her family kept them all working together and eventually restored their status in the community. Her children reflected this model of duty and fortitude in their relations with one another, and with her. The role of family head was thrust upon her and, in the best sense of matriarchy, she was a dynamic and resourceful woman who took charge of her family, assessed each member's potential, and demanded the best of them, and of herself, for the sake of the family, the church, and the community.

Merely surviving was not enough for Mary; in the best biblical tradition, she demanded blameless moral behaviour, self-sacrifice, and good works as well. From an Old Testament point of view, it is possible to see her as a female Moses who led her children out of the wilderness with a strong moral code and guiding hand, and made of them a great family. Like Moses, her moral code was just as inflexibly "written in stone" and, like the New Testament epistles of Paul, her letters to her family are also her legacy to us.

Part Two

Mary Baker McQuesten's Work with
the Presbyterian Missionary Societies

Mary Baker McQuesten's Work with the Presbyterian Missionary Societies

ॐ

MISSION CAUSE LOSES FRIEND
Mrs. M. McQuesten Wielded Powerful
Influence in Presbyterian Councils

In the passing of Mrs. McQuesten, the Presbyterian church has lost a devout and faithful daughter, and the mission field one who was ever on the alert to help the cause. Mrs. McQuesten's advice, always considered and wise, was much sought on many matters, and in the organizations in which she was such a power her loss will be keenly felt. No woman in Canada, probably has filled high offices with such dignity, ability and tact; and her gentle personality and wide sympathies make her beloved, far beyond the confines of her own city.

A pattern of Victorian womanhood, her home and family and her church constituted her world, and in all that pertained to them she upheld, by her life and works, her own high and impregnable sense of duty. Many friends will mourn her. (Box 08-183)

— Newspaper obituary, source unknown, Hamilton, 7 December 1934

When one considers the financial and health difficulties that Mary Baker McQuesten encountered in raising her six children, it is difficult to imagine how she also managed to devote a great deal of time and energy to the Presbyterian Church and the Women's Missionary Societies. Her daughter Mary said of her: "Saw Mamma off for Winnipeg ... I tell you what, there isn't a woman can touch her" (5447, 29 May 1906).

Mary viewed her commitment to the missionary society as part of her responsibility for social reform, and she worked tirelessly—accepting executive office, conducting meetings, and writing and delivering addresses. Her zeal and persuasive powers are evident in her missionary society addresses, urging and exhorting members to greater efforts for their "heathen" sisters abroad.[1] Mary also travelled throughout Ontario and to the West to establish auxiliaries or to inspect missions.

Mary's work for the missionary societies demonstrates her matriarchal leadership and organizational abilities and the high standards that she

---

Notes for Part Two start on page 239

demanded of herself and of others. She was a zealous leader, liberal in voicing her opinions on all subjects and inflexible in her moral judgments. This did not always endear her to the established patriarchal authorities.

Soon after Mary's marriage in 1873 she was elected to the executive of the Women's Missionary Society in the MacNab Street Presbyterian Church in Hamilton. Mary was also a member of a group of fifty women who met in 1876 at Knox Presbyterian Church in Toronto to establish the Woman's Foreign Missionary Society (WFMS). By 1878, she was also a member of a joint missionary society between three local churches. In January 1887 Mary was instrumental in establishing a separate auxiliary group of the WFMS at her home church. At the outset she was its secretary and, in 1893, became president. The minutes of the meetings, in her own hand, demonstrate her facility with language and organization and provide insights into her missionary zeal. For instance, at the first meeting she noted that the only hindrance to action was the lack of funds, and the meeting closed "with an earnest appeal to us all, to see to it that we hinder not the spread of the work by any want of liberality on our part" (11 January 1887). At each meeting, Mary's minutes recorded a similar moral directive. Mary McQuesten was president of the WFMS for twenty-five years and was an active member for more than fifty years.[2]

As her executive skill flourished and was recognized, she was elected to a Board of Management in 1882 and was charged with forming new missionary groups. She travelled to Manitoba and Quebec by rail, and by horse and buggy, giving addresses as she organized these groups, inspected residential schools for Aboriginal children, or attended conferences (A60-5464; A62-5487). Her enthusiasm and industry prompted her daughter Hilda to exclaim: "Mother has been stirring up things considerably these days, hope she won't be a wreck after the meetings" (6840).

Shortly after the turn of the century, Mary accepted an executive position with the newly formed provincial Women's Home Missionary Society (WHMS), but she was reluctant to be president, and she and other women executive members felt they had been coerced into joining the home mission group (Brouwer 51; A72-5765). The WHMS was formed, initially, to minister to the men flocking to the Yukon and Alaska Gold Fields and to provide medical and spiritual aid and education to Aboriginal women and children in the Canadian North and West (*Wee Kirks* 194; *DHB* 3:6). However, Mary's loyalties remained with the foreign missions abroad whose work was exclusively for women. She felt that the foreign women's needs were greater because they were often sequestered as in the zenanas in India, and could not be reached except by other women. In this regard it is possible to see that Mary's attitude to missionary work was also matriarchal in that she favoured a society of, and for, women.

For all of their colonial and Christian zeal, the missionary societies were not without internal strife, and Mary's letters record some of the gender conflicts that occurred at home and abroad. At home the conflict was between the all-male Foreign Missions Committee (FMC) and the women's executive body in Canada, and abroad the conflict was between the FMC and the actual women missionaries (A30-4651; A49-5172; A72-5765; A120-6853). In both cases the dispute involved the control of funds that the women's societies had raised for women's missions and were reluctant to give up to the men for other uses. The WFMS proved to be extremely successful at fundraising, while the FMC had "perennial budgeting problems." Initially "the power of the purse" prevailed and the women insisted on "financing only women's missionaries' activities" (Brouwer 32, 34, 38). The dispute continued for many years while the FMC used pressure tactics and placed restrictions on the WFMS and, in 1910, the provincial WFMS and the WHMS agreed to negotiations to try to work out a basis for union. In the same year Mary became vice-president of the Ontario Provincial Society and spoke out strongly against this union. However, in 1914 the WFMS and the WHMS were forced to unite and became the WMS. The women were defeated and, although they provided a "show of unanimity and brave talk," they could not "mask the fact that their leaders had been coerced into union."[3]

Ruth Compton Brouwer's analysis of this period is very thorough, and she notes that the women dutifully agreed and that "their tone and tactics were moderate"—in keeping with the Presbyterian tradition "through Calvin and Knox" of women's "subservience [after] various church assemblies had reaffirmed the Pauline injunctions against women's speaking or preaching in mixed assemblies." Presbyterian women, in this regard, were unlike the Methodists and Quakers, who had already established a tradition of female leadership in religious roles. Nevertheless, the Presbyterian WFMS could look back with pride on their "total income of more than one and a half million dollars over the life of their organization" and on the many schools, hospitals, and other facilities they had sponsored.[4] Brouwer notes the added benefit that, "in seeking to liberate their 'heathen sisters,' they had made considerable progress in enlarging their own sphere" (27, 52).

After the amalgamation creating the WMS, Mary's letters became gradually less concerned with the missionary societies, and she transferred her missionary zeal to the Social Gospel reform movement that was sweeping the country. The Presbyterian Church in general became concerned with a social reform movement to counteract the urban moral decay caused by industrialization and immigration in the aftermath of the war (A57-5359n). This was a strong international and interdenominational movement that saw a moral parallel between beautiful surroundings and moral behaviour. Mary then began to focus her efforts increasingly on the work being accomplished by her son Tom and his collaborators in the "City Beautiful" movement.

Presbyterians paid special attention to the needs of young women travelling unaccompanied and the missions were urged to attend closely to their welfare after they arrived in Canada (Moir, *Enduring* 168). The threat of immigrant women being led into prostitution in the Northwest gold fields was an even more immediate danger, and a "vivid warning" was issued to Presbyterian women to extend their efforts to this new challenge "if the motherhood of the nation was not to be permanently debased" and if their own sons were not to be corrupted (Brouwer 46). Mary actively supported this missionary work in the West and, for the same reasons, she also helped to establish the YWCA at home:

In March 1889 Mary proposed that Hamilton establish its own chapter of the YWCA. The fledgling organization's objective was to care for the educational and moral well-being of the many young women who ... were heading to the cities in search of work ... in part, to ensure the continuance of the existing social order ... and to counteract sexual exploitation. (*DHB* 3:6)

However, in Mary's YWCA work she made it clear that she favoured the Christian part of the organization over the teaching of domestic science, which was being promoted by Adelaide Hoodless (*DHB* 2:72). Mary notes the controversy in her letter of February 1903:

I have been spending all of my spare time for several days on Y.W.C.A. but have about come to the conclusion it is hopeless to try to keep it up, so many different things to be kept up and where it is religious work, so few interested or capable of doing anything and when it cost $100 a month to keep the building heated & pay the salaries, without employing a secretary for religious work, it is useless to go on with it. Mrs. Hoodless has two top stories for her school and declares she cannot pay any rent. (4795, 5183, 10 May 1904)

Mary's daughter Edna also describes, somewhat humorously, the futility of her experience at the school: "I have had enough of domestic science down at the school for a while. We spent an hr. and a half boiling a few parsnips" (4922, 29 April 1903). Nevertheless, Mrs. Hoodless's school prospered; she campaigned for domestic science in the schools, she founded the first Women's Institute in Canada, and she helped to found the National Council of Women, the Victorian Order of Nurses, and the national YWCA, but she, like Mary, never, supported the women's suffrage cause (*CE* 1006).

Although there is no record that Mary ever joined a suffrage group, her feminist inclinations are evident in her membership in the National Council of Women (*DHB* 3:6). However, it was likely that the lack of a clear Christian thrust in the NCW made Mary favour the women's Presbyterian missions. In 1894 it was proposed that the WFMS unite with the NCW, but "the council's decision not to open its meetings with public prayer provided further reason to remain aloof" (Brouwer 43).

Mary's feminist leanings took the form of demands for more opportunities for women in the church and mission societies, and she developed the courage to voice her impatience with the male establishment, particularly in matters of leadership, intelligence, and ethics. In 1903 she deeply regretted her silence in one of the "gentlemen's meetings," especially since the other women had looked to her for leadership (4745). In August 1905 she complained to Calvin about the quality of preaching by a minister at Central Church:

We had Logie Macdonnell, on Sabbath evening, he managed to give a sort of an address on a Psalm without mentioning the name of Jesus Christ. In fact not one word of the gospel in it. It is almost impossible to conceive of a preacher being really a converted man, who has so little conception of his duty and opportunity in the pulpit. They can never have grasped the thought of a lost soul, or they could not stand up in a pulpit and talk such twaddle. It is really terrible to think of the church in the hands of such men. Certainly Dr. Lyle has been most unfortunate in his assistants. (A58-5382)

In 1906 Mary delivered an address to a group of men at Knox Church in Hamilton, and later denounced them for their lack of interest and poor attendance: "doubtless they would not think me worth listening to, at the same time I have a feeling there are very few men there, who are of much value" (A69-5709; A123-6975).

It might be expected that the WFMS's growing power base would eventually lead it into the suffrage movement; however, this did not happen because the foreign missionary cause was given priority. Brouwer explains that the Presbyterian women's "strong convictions about Eastern [Asian] women's disabilities and about their own incomparably more emancipated status undoubtedly served as an effective damper on any tendencies toward militancy." They could not forsake the "'heathen women's pathetic cries for help" without "concluding that they had little reason to protest women's lot in Canada" (Brower 190-91). Mary makes this priority clear in one of her addresses to the WMS, in which she quotes Dr. Elizabeth Beatty, the first Canadian female missionary physician: "if the women of Canada knew what the women and children of India suffer they would spend their last dollar to help them." Mary continues: "Then it was that the members of our WMS realized the wonderful difference in their condition ... [and must] pour out their hearts in thankfulness to God for His unspeakable goodness to them" (MCP 2-4.23).

In some of Mary's addresses there appears a definite note of resistance to the suffrage movement:

The very freedom we enjoy of going in and out when we please treated with all consideration and courtesy by men, especially those near and dear to us, of saying and doing as we like.... This very freedom, I repeat, if we think at all, must be a constant reminder of those millions of women who are valued as a man values his cattle, who lead lives of drudgery and degradation who have no one to come to their help and unless we do, they have no one else to take up their cause. (MCP 2-4.23)

Nellie McClung had made the case for suffrage by linking it with the Methodist missionary cause with some success; however, the Presbyterians had no feminist of her "stature and inventiveness." McClung and other radical feminists "might deplore the false consciousness that the church-generated propaganda promoted, but their attempts to counteract it met with little success." Even the Methodist WMS "declined to associate themselves with the suffrage cause," in spite of McClung's efforts. Many Presbyterian women and men did advocate suffrage but they did it "while wearing a different hat." In fact, "Presbyterian men were strongly represented in the ranks of acknowledged suffrage advocates" (Brouwer 190-91).

There is also no evidence that Mary ever joined the Woman's Christian Temperance Union, and the WFMS declined to support them as well. Again, the likely reason was their single-minded devotion to the missionary cause, which had its own temperance agenda (Brouwer 43). During the Ontario Temperance Referendum of 1902, Mary worked feverishly to convince the women to influence their men to vote for temperance, but it was narrowly defeated (A96-6419). In Mary's missionary speeches she often targets alcohol as a primary social problem and as one of the main deterrents to Christian and social reform.

Two contentious issues that engaged Mary and divided the Presbyterian Church in the first quarter of the century were higher criticism and church union. Mary objected to both. She rejected any modernization in biblical exegesis that was being debated by some of the "professors and preachers" and was creating a "storm centre" in the church. Mary's frequent criticisms of preachers were often based on her objection to modifications of doctrine that challenged her fundamentalist interpretation of the Bible (A52-5283n; A17-4436; A79-5868).

Those who favoured higher criticism also tended to favour church union—the organic union of the Methodist, Congregationalist, and Presbyterian churches. Mary was fiercely opposed to union as well and, in 1923, although she was seventy-five years of age, she spoke out forcefully and publicly against it (A127, 24 April 1923; A52-5283; A97-6446). In a speech in 1923 she asserted angrily that "it was time to stop the nonsense of government of the church by men.... If we women can't get into the general assembly and have a vote, we are going to show them that we can do something to block this church union" (Hamilton Spectator, 24 April 1923). Finally, union did occur in 1925 with the formation of the United Church, and the Presbyterian Church in Canada was left fractured and weakened, with only a quarter of its former members. In fact the vote was defeated in one third of the Presbyterian churches in Canada, which voted to perpetuate "a distinctive Presbyterian denomination in Canada" (A127, 24 April 1923). The MacNab Church voted to remain Presbyterian, and the Hamilton Presbytery lost only four churches to union (Wee Kirks 213; John McNeill 245, 260).

Mary was an effective leader and her executive positions in the women's missionary societies provided a good deal of status for the family. It is likely that the McQuestens worked even more diligently in the church in an attempt to regain the social prestige that was lost with Isaac's bankruptcy and death. The church provided a continuity of social life for the family, and Mary's letters give a rich and colourful account of the Victorian cultural scene in Hamilton during the McQuesten era. However, the endless teas and visitings were not merely frivolous society affairs; they were a mandatory part of church and social life. Indeed, Tyrell's *Society Blue Book* (1900) lists a day and time for "receiving" for each family registered. The church members were required to make regular visits to one another and to new members, which were then reported at the auxiliary meetings. The visiting, and the gossip, were also part of the Presbyterian emphasis on "neighbours' watchfulness," which was viewed as an incentive to moral behaviour (MacGillivray 52).

Mary sometimes grew weary of the constant visiting and of "having to make conversation for a whole afternoon," and she complained that she was "simply tired to death of transients" (5392). Whitehern was just a block from the church and the McQuestens often received these transient visitors. On the other hand, there were also times when Mary deplored the lack of social life for her children: "we do not like to live always to ourselves" (A69-5709).

From time to time, Mary suffered extreme exhaustion, depression, and "nervous prostration" because of the stress of her missionary work. In her letter of 15 January 1907 she complained that she was finding it difficult to concentrate and could not "stand too much in the way of being responsible" (A72-5765). By 6 February, she had rallied sufficiently to deliver another paper to her auxiliary (5784), but she remained exhausted throughout that year.

Mary's work with the missionary societies demonstrates that she had the Victorian attributes of a clear social and political sense of responsibility, a deep sense of mission, a firmness of will, and an unwearying industry. She also had the matriarchal attributes that favoured women's organizations to the exclusion of men. She was remarkably practical and determined to create change in her world, which was circumscribed by the Scottish Enlightenment ideas of progress, complete confidence in the British imperialist vision, and a firm Calvinist Presbyterian morality. She was a dedicated leader for social change for women and children, for immigrants, and for families in general, wherever she could effect it, and her every act for herself, her children, her church, and her community, was calculated toward that end.

Postcolonial Considerations

ॐ

> You will notice that just accordingly as a church is interested in missions or
> not it is an alive or dead church. (A145-7193)
> —Mary McQuesten, address to WHMS, Grafton, Ontario, 6 July 1892

There are obvious political aspects to the recovery of writings and they are
essential for revisionist analysis and postcolonial considerations. Just as there
are political aspects in the initial writing, the collected works will offer an even
greater potential for political and historical comparison. Mary McQuesten's
writings are not static but dynamic entities, and her letters and missionary
society addresses provide the primary material by which to analyze and assess
the political and personal motivations behind the colonial enterprise in Canada.

The women's political sphere was widened expressly by their participation
in missionary work. It had some liberating aspects for women and facilitated
their education and entry into the professions, especially medicine. Some of
the first women doctors were educated in medicine in order to treat and to
teach the women who were sequestered in foreign lands. The following is a
farewell sermon preached to a women's missionary group and to missionary
wives who were leaving for the field:

> It will be your business, my dear children, to teach these women, to whom your husbands
> can have but little, or no access. Go, then, and do all in your power, to enlighten their
> minds, and bring them to the knowledge of the truth. Go, and if possible, raise their char-
> acter to the dignity of rational beings, and to the rank of Christians in a Christian land.
> (Brouwer 16)

The sermon is deliberately biased and patriarchal, and demonstrates the
colonial view of the recipients as lesser humans, without rationality or dignity.

Mary's trip to Winnipeg in 1906 to inspect the File Hills School and other
missionary schools and enterprises (since discredited as inhumane), demonstrates
her deep moral conviction and her optimism for their success. It is only in the
mid- and later twentieth century that we have come to assess the damage that
was done to some of the Aboriginal children at these residential schools.

This political and colonial aspect is especially apparent in Mary
McQuesten's missionary writings and speeches, in which she exerts her
matriarchal influence in person and seeks to inspire large groups. In the
recovery of these writings it is possible to perceive the political dynamic at
work and the motives implicit in the colonial enterprise.

A thorough revisionist analysis must include the first-hand accounts and
the original motivation of the missionary effort. For example, note Mary's
impassioned speech in "The Necessity of Foreign Missions":

[The missionary is] the noble champion of poor degraded womanhood, who has shown how much can be done to lift-up by a kind, encouraging word and a loving helping hand ... on the behalf of those poor down-trodden sisters in heathen lands ... with no hope either for this world or the next. (A144-8432)

The missionaries' first motivation was Christian evangelism. In their efforts with the immigrant groups in Hamilton, the object was not only to teach the English language, but also to convert immigrants to Christianity, and it was considered a failure if the immigrant stayed just long enough to learn the language and not the religion.

The McQuesten writings in the Whitehern archive are valuable as postcolonial research material. They have broad interdisciplinary appeal, they are valuable in the recovery of women's writings, and they are a rich repository for enriching our understanding of family life and society in Ontario and in Canada—and of the Victorian ideas and ideals that shaped them. As such, these life writings reflect the ideology of a particular world view that had been determined by the philosophical forces of the Scottish Enlightenment and the ideals of liberty and progress. However, during this era that world view was already in a state of flux as a result of the economic forces of migration and industrialization.

The writings were produced by educated and enlightened individuals who expressed a sense of optimism, autonomy, purpose, and participation in a period of world change. At the time, even their Presbyterian fundamentalism was being challenged by various controversies surrounding doctrine and church politics, such as higher criticism in studies of the Bible, gender conflict in the missionary groups, (both at home and abroad), and Church Union, the political movement toward union of the Presbyterian, Methodist, and Congregational churches.

The McQuesten writings also reveal the political situation for women and the changes that were taking place in their lives. That Victorian period ushered in great changes that formed the basis of modernism and led to accelerated change later in the twentieth century. For these reasons the letters are invaluable in order to gain a more comprehensive view of the ideologies that governed that period in history. A broader understanding of all of the dynamics of the era, including the woman's role, is vital to an understanding of the ethics of the present, and to the politics and policies of the future.

The McQuestens were greatly influenced by Victorian writers such as Matthew Arnold (1822-88). Arnold's work represents the high culture of the Victorian age with its moral ideal of a love of perfection and a social and moral passion for doing good. He also posits the "social idea [that] men of culture are the true apostles of equality" (Arnold 21, 32). In postmodern criticism, Arnold's theory has come to be negated because it is high culture and utopian; however, in his age, "high culture" was considered the highest praise. In fact, in her death notice in 1934, Mary Baker McQuesten is described as a woman of "high culture," among other tributes (news clipping, Whitehern, M49). It is precisely the moral ideal of the Victorians that is demonstrated by the McQuestens' colonial ideals; and their absolute and unquestioning confidence in their "moral passion for doing good" is implicit in their writings.

A postcolonial view of the McQuesten writings reveals their Victorian colonial attitudes in their Presbyterian missionary zeal to impose their ideal of British cultural superiority on the "heathen" of distant lands, on immigrants, or on Aboriginal Canadians. Brouwer notes:

A sense of shared responsibility with Britain for the uplift of lesser breeds was the key element in their imperialist vision, and participation in foreign missions was seen to be one of the most vital and concrete ways of giving that vision expression.... Missionary literature broadened the horizons of ordinary Canadians, providing them with the materials for a world view whose optimism and idealism would for a long time mask its less attractive aspects. (4)

This was true also of the various ethnic groups and "lesser breeds" in Canada, and it is a cultural and postcolonial irony that Aboriginal Canadians were originally considered "foreign" by the Victorian missionary societies (*DHB* 3: 5, 6).

In the early part of the twentieth century, immigration to Canada rose steadily each year until it reached its peak of 400,000 new arrival in 1913; these immigrants came from fifty-nine countries (Moir, *Enduring* 165). In Hamilton, the immigrants drawn to industry were targeted for conversion, and Mary often refers to teaching the "Jews," "Japs," or "Chinamen." Mary was dedicated to the immigrant cause and reports that she spent all one morning "trolling from one end of the city to the other looking for work for a Jew" (A33-4717; 4847; A50-5199; 5245). The Presbyterian Church set up missions for "foreigners" within Canadian cities, and Mary was vice-president of the Jewish Mission in Hamilton where they conducted classes for all immigrants in order to "Canadianize and Christianize, on terms dictated by the older Canadians, an approach that too often engendered a type of defensive nativism" (Moir, *Enduring* 165).

The Presbyterian attitude to immigrants at that time was deliberately and unapologetically colonial. The Victorian goal was to assimilate them "to the Canadian way-of-life, which meant assimilation to an idealized model of Anglo-Saxon society" (Moir, *Enduring* 165). A headline from the *Hamilton Spectator* of 23 March 1915 gives an indication of the prevailing attitude: "Judge Advises Foreigners to Change Names ... to plain English."

The work ethic was, of course, an important part of Presbyterian teaching. Moir provides an example of the prevalence of a perception of a lack of an appropriate work ethic among foreigners. He notes that the attitude was reflected in books such as R. G. MacBeth's *Our Task in Canada* (1912).

Generally speaking ... the foreigners that come to this country menace ... the welfare of our labouring class. A great many foreign immigrants do not consider pauperism discreditable, and this is something new on Canadian soil ... foreigners of certain classes furnish the criminal list beyond all proportion to their numbers ... their presence is menace of a very deadly kind to the body politic.

The sense of urgency is clear in the above statement, and it was also considered that the immigrants in their "insufficient literacy, virtue and intelligence posed a threat" to democracy itself (Moir, *Enduring* 165-66, 168).

The Presbyterian General Assembly of 1912 set up a "Department of the Stranger" with chaplains to meet immigrants at the borders, and the women's Missionary Societies created "Stranger's Committees" to maintain the contacts. Some of these missions were "less successful" than others. For instance, many of the Jews did not welcome the missionary efforts to "bring a ray of true light to illuminate Israel's gross darkness," and many of the Chinese took advantage of these missions only long enough to learn "enough English to assure them of good jobs" (Moir, *Enduring* 167-69).

Those readers interested in postcolonial considerations will find that the McQuesten writings will provide valuable material for the study of the Victorian colonial attitudes that formed Canadian culture, both its positive and its negative aspects. The letters clearly demonstrate that, at the time, this colonial attitude was a shared ideal, supported by the churches as well as by the government and the courts. As we come to know the Victorian writers through their own words, we receive an ever-expanding portrayal of life in Canada during the Victorian era. The increasing accumulation and analysis of diaries, letters, and extant writings will provide us with a larger, but never complete, picture of the culture of the era. Indeed, as time progresses, it will always be subject to yet another "post" analysis.

Selections from Mary B. McQuesten's Missionary Society Addresses

And now let me try to enlist your sympathy, on the behalf of the women & children, in those heathen lands. I want each one of you to-day to picture herself as born in a heathen country, and not in our own Christian Canada. Remember, it was only the kind Providence of God, that made us Canadian women & not heathen (A146-8432). Either we must go ourselves to the nations that are in darkness, or if it is impossible we must do our very utmost at home to send others. If we cannot go down the mine—remember, we must hold the ropes. (A145-7193)

A145-(7193) ADDRESS TO WFMS
(GRAFTON, ONTARIO, 6 JULY 1892)

As one reads these accounts of the first attempts at Foreign Mission work, what strikes one as the most remarkable fact is the extraordinary opposition of Xtian[5] people to the movement, that the Christian Church could ever have sunk to such condition of selfishness & narrowness as to forget that its peculiar mission was to spread the good tidings of a Saviour to the World. It is really inexplicable, how those professedly Christian men, the ministers of the church could read their bibles without accepting the commandments of the Saviour as there laid down, moreover it is very difficult to comprehend how they could be Christians at all, just the same as it is very difficult to understand now, how any one can possibly be a follower of the Lord Jesus Christ and not obey his commandments. For if we will not shut our eyes to the real duty that is laid down for us in the Word of God, there are just two courses indicated for the true disciple of Christ,— Either we must go ourselves to the nations that are in darkness, or if it is impossible we must do our very utmost at home to send others. If we cannot go down the mine—remember, we must hold the ropes.

Therefore it comes to this, either those who call themselves Christians do not read their Bibles or they deliberately disobey the Saviour's commandments. Is this a safe thing to do? Then the question arises Can any one be a Christian without reading the Bible. It is the word of God, it is the Revelation of God's will to man, of what we must do to be saved, and having read this revelation of the Father's Will, how can we dare disobey? No matter whether we succeed or not; no matter if the heathen are to be saved without us, we cannot set aside our Lord's bidding to us to "Go unto all the world[6] &c. &c."[7] & the responsibility thereby. Did it ever occur to you Christian women that the reason there is so much indifference & lethargy & deadness, utter stagnation, in our churches, and that worldliness has come in upon us like a flood, drowning out all vitality and life is because the Church has failed to obey Christ's commandments and has thus lost God's blessing, for you will notice that just accordingly as a church is interested in missions or not it is an alive or dead church. As MacKay of Uganda writes home in all of his letters "Of one thing I feel sure nothing could be better for rousing the spiritual life of a congregation & leading it on to a higher life, than the cultivation of the spirit of missions. The progress of the Kingdom of God in the world is a study well calculated to enlarge the mind & soul & rescue torpid congregations from their self satisfied ease. What a power for good would be our home millions of Christians if really alive to their privilege & duty in helping forward the work [illegible, torn page]."

The Missionary Spirit strikes a death blow at selfish piety. Now then how are we to awaken this missionary spirit (first of all in ourselves); by the conscientious study of our Bible, for it seems to me either we have forgotten to read it or have been dozing & dreaming whilst we read. How can we find out the exact command of God, how can we know what He expects of us, if we do not study his rules laid down? They grow faint in our memories. We have to keep continually repeating to ourselves "If ye love me &c ye are not your own &c." I often think if we would go back to our Catechism which we all have learned from our childhood, there would be a more perfect obedience. And [?] you do not give up teaching it. Now let us try it; what is the first portion "Man's chief end is to be?" Then follows most naturally "What rule hath God given &c." Thus we see we must go to the Bible to find out the duty expected of us. "Hereby we know, that we know him, if we keep his commandments." Now we are also told in God's word that we are justified by faith but that we are also told that "Faith without works is dead." Now dear friends it is just up to this point— we want to lead Christian Work. Religion is a practical thing not a theory it is a conduct a practice, it is the act of obeying Christ. Christianity is not a treasure to be stored, it is a message to be delivered. God never bestows spiritual power for private & exclusive use. It has been truly said "We are not reservoirs of spiritual blessing, but channels; as soon as we begin to dam up the blessing, it evaporates like the dew or stagnates into an unhealthy pool, generating disease & death." How? Why, if our influence does not bring strength & power, life & energy to the work of the church it diminishes & weakens. Since there is nothing more deadening to the vitality of any church than phlegmatic indifference that wretched lack of interest, which chills and cools the ardour of the most enthusiastic worker. As Mr. Macdonald said "Do not let us be mere hangers on to the camp." Then having learned from our Bibles the duty laid upon us of working for Christ; the next means I would suggest for awakening interest in the work of the churches, is to make ourselves thoroughly acquainted [with] the various schemes of the church their aims, their objects & their needs. To do this read the religious newspapers and specially do I commend the effort of the F.M. Committee to your attentive perusal. It is a great mistake that reports are necessarily dry. The report of the F.M.S. is exceedingly interesting & full of information, as a young lady of our M.B. said. So too is the report of our own W.F.M.S.

How can you possibly have any interest in our missionaries & their works if you know nothing about them. A great deal, if not all the indifference, which prevails is due to evilful ignorance, for I cannot believe our Christian people could be so heartless, so wickedly selfish, so deaf to the imploring cries, that come to them from every quarter of the heathen world, if they really knew the facts. If they only knew the work of those brave servants of God amidst many dangers & discouragements, principally because there are so few labourers amongst such a multitude, if they read their appeals for help, their noble self-sacrifice and joy in it. It seems to me the hardest heart would be melted, the tightest purse string would be untied.

Then if we are to be of service, we must show our interest, let us manifest our interest by a regular attendance at all the meetings of the Society. This is the Lord's work not ours to do or to leave undone just as we please. Our W.F.M.S. is one of the recognized schemes of the church and should have the interest and support of every Presbyterian Woman, and should not be treated as if it were the mere whim & fancy of a few enthusiasts.

Now just let us consider what we can do to help in this matter. It is exceedingly discouraging to the President & those actively engaged in the work, that so few seem to have any real interest in the work, sometimes they come sometimes they don't; they forget the day altogether or give the most trivial excuses. Now, I think the rule for us should be as binding as that of the Christian Endeavour, its members are bound to attend their meetings except when burdened for a reason sufficient to offer to Jesus Christ Himself. All the women young and old, not the two or three, should feel it is our meeting. You know there is nothing more discouraging than empty seats. There is a great stimulus in members, & if you can do nothing more than fill a chair and look interested, I entreat of you to come, it will be a great help & bye and bye you will be able to do more than look interested. How? Well, always be on the outlook for missionary intelligence & when you come across an item of interest or a thrilling account mark it; lay it by and take it to a meeting. Read it, read it as if you felt it, naturally, not in a dull monotonous voice. Let each one feel, I must do something to make it more interesting, & this is only right, it is not to be the President's Society (it is not fair). We should not leave the whole burden on her, and in doing so, you will be astonished how your own heart will be stirred & aroused. On the other hand I would like to say, that no one should come to the meeting with the idea that necessarily something interesting must be provided for them, it is not a meeting for entertainment it is a meeting for work in which we have to come together to receive intelligence of our missionaries as to their work & success to consult as to the best means of helping them & keeping up the interest in our hearts & the hearts of others & in spreading that interest to all around. It is a meeting for devising means of how to gain contributions for spreading the gospel and encouraging each other in acts of self-denial so that we may be able to give more and more. Above all things it is the place of prayer, where we must lift up our hearts & voices in most earnest supplication for the help & blessing of God in our efforts.

O dear Christian Sisters, we do not pray enough. If our society is to be of any service our auxiliary meetings must be <u>prayer-meetings</u>. And this brings us to another point & you will excuse me if I speak very plainly on this matter, but I want to bring home to your hearts the duty which is laid on each one of us of always doing what we can to help & therefore to be ready & willing to lead our sisters in prayer when it is required of us. We are <u>exceedingly in earnest</u> about this, because we are convinced, that societies are not formed & societies die out & societies are cold & dwindling simply because there are sometimes not even two or three Christians who will take this part, who, in plain words, love their Saviour enough to cause them to forget themselves and render this service for Christ's sake in order to help on the cause of sending the news of a Saviour to a perishing world. You must see that the work of our society will be a failure without prayer & that first & foremost our meetings must be prayer meetings & how can this be if every one refused to take part. If this duty is left to one or two, it becomes so monotonous & wearisome that it is almost useless & therefore I entreat of you to put it before your own minds as a duty, as a service to God Himself & then you will feel very differently about it. You would not surely let a selfish feeling on your part be an obstacle to the work, because really it is selfishness we are so afraid of hearing & of the remarks that may be made upon us. Now, think of it, cannot we be brave enough to risk that much for the sake of Him who gave his life for us? What is this little sacrifice in comparison with the sacrifices of our Missionaries? As to criticism I never heard Christian women unkindly criticize one another, we all know how simply weak & nervous we are, and as to breaking down, if we prepare our thoughts as well as we can before hand & rely upon God's help we can never break down for God never fails those who strive with his help to do their duty. Do not say I have no gift or I am nervous, we know all about it but put yourself, in God's hands. We must "expect Great things &c." A great help to this duty is a suggestion I read in a leaflet, that is to make a habit when we are offering our own private devotions, of putting our thoughts into audible words. Many pray in their minds but learn to do it in words. I thought this a very helpful suggestion.

Some one says I cannot express myself and the words seem to leave. Why it seems to me if you keep your minds full of the terrible need of those poor heathen souls, of the terrible sufferings of those poor women and children, you cannot keep silent, involuntarily the longing of your souls will spring to your lips. The need of help is so great, &c. & Miss Harris & Dr. Beatty's appeal. [balance of page blank] Grafton [Ontario] July 6, 1892

A146-(8432) ON THE NECESSITY OF FOREIGN MISSIONS (WELLAND, WOODSTOCK, GUELPH, PORT HOPE, APPROXIMATELY 30 JANUARY 1913)[8]

Last week we in Hamilton had the great pleasure and privilege of listening to an address by Miss Frances Willard, the noble champion of poor degraded womanhood, who has shown how much can be done to lift-up the fallen by a kind, encouraging word and a loving helping hand. In the course of her remarks she referred to that old adage "Speech is silver but silence is golden," saying "it seemed to her, that for a Christian women, speech is golden and silence criminal."

And it is this thought that has impelled me to attempt to say a few words to you to-day. Why, indeed, should we be silent, when we owe all we have and we are, as women in a Christian land, to that blessed Redeemer, whose Gospel has given all the liberties and privileges which we possess! Why, indeed, should we keep our lips tightly sealed, and not lift our voices in earnest protest and pleading, on the behalf of those poor down-trodden sisters in heathen lands, who are living lives of most indescribable misery, with no hope either for this world or the next? As the Rev. John McNeill, the noted preacher and pastor of Regent Square Presbyterian Church London, said the other day "When I see how dumb people are when it comes to speaking about Jesus, I am wild with suspicion, that after all they have never found Him" Therefore I trust you will forgive me, if I speak somewhat plainly on this subject, but it is a very serious vital question, and I want particularly to speak to those who have not yet taken an interest in the mission work of our Church. Why is it? I want to ask this question still more particularly of those whose names are on the church roll. For as I view it, when we join the church, we should join the missionary society the one natural consequence upon the other: and the thought has come to me with fresh force since the past Sabbath was our season of communion, and when I looked around upon that large gathering of professedly Christian Women, and compared it with the tiny gathering of the faithful few at the missionary auxiliary meeting, I could not but say to myself, what does this profession mean? What is it all worth?

Let us deal plainly with ourselves. When we came forward and signified our desire to become members of the church, what did we mean by it? Was it simply that we might have the right to partake of the bread and wine and sit with the communicants on communion Sabbath? Surely it was not this, surely we had some higher conception of its meaning. But how are we to be judged? The Saviour said "By their fruits ye shall know them." "Faith without works is dead." If it does not, it ought to mean to every one of us, our entire consecration of ourselves to God, our means, our time, our talents, every thing that we possess. "For we are not our own, we were bought with a price." Does it not mean, that we have taken the oath of allegiance to the King of Heaven, and having entered His service, we are bound to obey His orders implicitly instantly, conscientiously? Does a soldier when the word of command is given, ever think of saying "I feel rather tired" or "I am not very well" or " It is not quite convenient for me to go just now"? Does it ever enter his head to say anything of the sort? Well, what are we doing, when we are found absent from our posts of duty? What do we mean, by making all sorts of excuses for not obliging the commands of our divine Sovereign in labouring to extend his Kingdom over the whole earth? Dear Christian friends, is there not too little realization of what God expects of us, too much indifference, too much of this putting our work before the Lord's work?

Now, think of it, Christian women, who know the truth of the Gospel, who believe in Jesus Christ, and the awful fate awaiting those who do not; think of us, giving our time & thought entirely to what concerns ourselves. Do not think I wish to make little of home duties, for a true Christian never neglects her home or her family, (this is most important part of our mission), but I do say that we may make too much of it, we may make a continuous idol of our house or our housekeeping. As an illustration of exactly what I mean, suppose the Missionary Meetings comes on Tuesday and the ironing day also, let the ironing be put off till Wednesday, it is not of vital importance, nobody will die if it is left for a few hours, so with many other every day duties, altogether necessary & right in themselves, but not so binding, that we can never postpone them for a little, while we attend to God's work. There is a great deal in planning [and] "where there's a will there's a way," and you will certainly find, (I speak from personal experience) that time spent at a missionary meeting is not wasted. You will come back to that monotonous routine of everyday tasks with fresher minds, better tempers, brighter faces, with something to talk of to your children, & something to live for besides yourselves. And here comes in the question of parental example, "Example is better than precept" saith the proverb. There is not time for me to enlarge upon this proverb namely the mighty force which we mothers, Christians, have in our possession, for influencing our children by a consistent beautiful Christian life, but let me ask, how can we expect our sons and daughters to be interested in the work of the church, if we are not. If we give only the leavings, the mere scraps of our time and money to the cause of God, what importance can they attach to our Christian teachings? We must practice what we preach.

Now my dear friends, let me entreat of you, to think of this matter very earnestly for a little while. Let us bring that scene before our minds, when Christ Jesus, the Son of God, looked out upon the world lying under the terrible curse of His Almighty Father, must He not have foreseen, that an awful future awaited the human race, if He did not do something to save us? It is neither the time nor the place, to enter into the discussion of the doctrine of future punishment, but Oh! it seems to me that the Son of God would not have left His beautiful home in glory, that seat beside his father for nothing; surely there must have been some awful woe in store for us, to induce Him to make such a sacrifice; and would God the Father have given up his only son, "the brightness of his glory, the express image of His person," to such a death, if his heart had not been stirred to its very depths in pity for us.

O dear Christian friends, sometimes it seems as if we must have forgotten the truths in our Bible, that we have too many papers, too many magazines, and we read too much the sayings of man, that we have forgotten the sayings of God, or have become too familiar with the plain teaching of the scripture that we fail to take it in, and live it out in our daily lives. Then too if the Saviour had only to die to save us, why did he endure thirty years of privation and suffering on our Earth? Was it not because He also foresaw that He must live upon earth long enough to show us what a Christian life ought to be; to teach us that in order to be acceptable in God's sight, we must take up a course of life such as the Saviour did. What kind of a life was His? Was it not one of entire self-renunciation, self-sacrifice for others? The great Teacher was not self-absorbed, He could spare time to be kind and gentle even to little children, He went about continually doing good, preaching the gospel, healing the sick, sought not to be ministered unto, but to minister, "Even Christ pleased not himself." His death was but the last & steepest step of the altar of self sacrifice, He had been so long ascending. On this pivot of self-denial hangs the whole secret of a life pleasing in the sight of God. (Now then possessing the knowledge of what God demands of us if we will have everlasting life, and the only way of salvation). Nor can we rest in peace for one moment, so long as there is a single soul on the face of the Globe who knows not the way of life. And what are the facts of the case? Dr. Pierson tells us, that of the 1500 millions who people the world, not more than 30 millions could be considered as evangelized. What has the church been doing all these years; that Church in whose keeping the Saviour left the knowledge of his Salvation with the command "Go tell all nations." As Canon Farrar has said "Had Christ and His apostles acted with the excuse of modern selfishness, Christianity would have died away as the religion of some obscure sect on the Dead Sea shore. Were there no unbelievers in Judea, when Christ told His disciples to go tell all nations? Were there none in Nazareth, when He went to Capernaum? We must still leave the dead to bury their dead." Do not misunderstand me, I do not wish to detract from the importance of Home Mission work, but that of the Foreign is equally binding upon us.

And now let me try to enlist your sympathy, on the behalf of the women & children, in those heathen lands. I want each one of you to-day to picture herself as born in a heathen country, and not in our own Christian Canada. Remember, it was only the kind Providence of God, that made us Canadian women & not heathen. First of all let the aged think and contrast their lot with that of the old in those dark lands. When Mrs. Annand, the wife of one of our missionaries to the New Hebrides returned a few years ago from the Island of Aneutyum [sp?], she gave us an account of life amongst the natives, and amongst other things told us how the old women were treated when they had become helpless & infirm; instead of being loved & tenderly cherished, as we love our dear mothers and grandmothers, a hole was dug, and into this was put the poor old creature alive, and never shall I forget how Mrs. Annand described those piteous cries growing fainter and fainter, as the earth closed in upon them. Then as to the young girls, when they were married, it was not with a ring put on tenderly & lovingly, but with a rope put round the poor girl's neck, which she was henceforth to wear, so that at any time, if she chanced to displease her husband he might use this, to strangle her. And do you (as many here) know those brave missionaries Mr. & Mrs. Annand worked on till, by the blessing of God, these frightful practices were abolished and that island became a Christian Island, and sends in contributions to our Mission fund.

Now, they have begun work in another island. Espiritu Santo. Would I be detaining you too long, if I read you an extract from (one of) Mrs Annand's (last) letters (at that time) just to show you what the refined delicate lady we all, or some of us may remember her, is enduring for the sake of saving immortal souls. After describing some of their customs, and the style of their huts, she says: "They sleep cook and eat in this hut, lie there when sick, & when they die are buried within them. This is one of their most abominable customs, namely burying their dead in their dwelling houses, sometimes not covered more than one foot in depth. For fifty or more days, the husband at least must remain indoors the greater part of the time in the house where his wife is buried. A fire is kept burning most of the time over the grave to consume the gas rising from it.... They seldom or never wash during the mourning, so you can imagine what they are like." What self sacrifice do we make in comparison with these devoted missionaries, spending their lives with these disgusting savages? Then you all know the lives of the women in India, and far worse than that the lives of the children, many of them wives or widows. Does it not make our blood run cold, when we think of giving our little girls over to married life at eight and nine years of age? No child life in India. (Fancy). Just try and realize what bondage they are under, from a notice in the newspaper, a short time ago, that the barbers of Bombay had revolted against the cruel practice of shaving the heads of the widows once a week, as had been the custom in that city. Now dear friends, forgive me if I have wearied you, and detained you too long, but life is very short and very uncertain, and I have been very anxious to awaken your attention to your own duty & responsibility, and the needs of your dying fellow creatures, remembering the solemn injunction, "to him that knoweth to do good and doeth it not, to him it is a sin. Whatsoever thy hand findeth to do, do it with thy might, for there is no work, nor device, nor knowledge, nor wisdom in the grave, whither thou goest." [Written at bottom of page] Given at Welland, Woodstock, Guelph and Port Hope.

A147-(7172) REVIVALS; CHINA AND SIERRA LEONE
[EXCERPTS, ESTIMATED DATE 1905][9]

Great progress reported in mission fields.... A revival in Madagascar in the Betulin country which was first evangelized by Welsh missionaries 80 yrs ago has many Welsh men still at work. These missionaries hearing of the Welsh movement told the native Xtians about it & formed a solemn league & covenant among them to prepare & pray for a similar revival. Quarrels were made up (injuries forgiven) & as far as possible every hindrance removed. A few weeks were spent thus in preparation & prayer & then the answer came in a profound sense of God's presence & power at a prayer meeting. This led to the decision of 83 nations on the following Sabbath and a wave of blessing followed.

Revivals Prayer

In India a great revival had come and in connection with this we wish specially to notice, that a week of prayer for India had been arranged in England and on the first day of that week when the first great wave of prayer reached India the spirit of God broke out in melting power and marvellous have been the results. I am sure all our hearts must have been thrilled & melted as we read of these revivals and so has come to us a reflux of the blessing. This the "flux & reflux" which Madam Griegore [sp?] speaks about of the life of God flowing from Him into—I thought all who are in communion with Him. O how little we realize the possibilities & power of prayer & the surging life which is ever more flowing from the heart of God into the world, ready to break forth in quickening power whenever hearts are prepared by seeking Him. What a view of themselves men & women received under the great search light of the Spirit of God, how clearly they saw dishonesty & hatred & spite & how the missionaries were convicted of lack of faith, lack of prayer & consequently little fruit bearing. And we noticed too how as on the day of our Lord the devil fought against God, as it were openly. O how busy he always is, though he hides his work so cleverly, suggesting all sorts of reasons why we should not engage in various kinds of work for God, putting all kinds of excuses into our minds even when we are on our knees distracting our thoughts, paralysing our memories, so that we lose our connection with God, and the channels of blessing are broken.

China

Four Viceroys, rulers of 8 provinces with a population over 179,000,000 appealed to their own government to seek the aid of Great Britain in saving their country from ruin through opium, because they say China can never be strong and stand shoulder to shoulder with the powers of the world when 1/4 of her subjects have been reduced to skeletons and look half dead. They call upon them to use the Japanese methods in Formosa and by doing so China can be saved in 30 years.

Sierra Leone

Zackary Macaulay, father of the great historian had been for 10 years overseer of a West Indian Estate, he was of high character & great mental power & laboured hard to promote the Slaves' interests. In 1792 compelled to return to England on account of ill health, he became acquainted with friends of Africa, who induced him to go out to Sierra Leone. He became Governor.

In 1799 the Sierra Leone Co made him their English Secretary & he resided at Clapham in close communication with the founders of the Church Missionary Society for Africa & the East. Among these founders were Charles Simeon of saintly memory, Wm. Wilberforce, the Champion of the Slaves in Jamaica & the venerable John Newton. Lying off the Southern promontory of Sierra Leone are the Banana Islands, now the seat of a flourishing Xtian Church. Upon one of these islands there landed in 1746 a wretched youth, clothed in rags who entered the service of a white slave trader living nearby. Many bitter hardships did he suffer from the severity of the climate & the cruelty of his master's negro mistress. He had lost all faith in God or man, but was brought out of his troubles by a series of remarkable deliverances. His future career is briefly sketched in his epitaph written by himself & now to be seen on the walls of St. Mary Woolnoth Church, of which he was for many years Rector: "John Newton once an infidel & libertine. A servant of slaves in Africa, was, by the Rich mercy of our Lord & Saviour Jesus Christ [?] restored, pardoned & appointed to preach the faith he had long laboured to destroy."

Egypt

At Cairo the mission is experiencing many encouraging opportunities for speaking & preaching to moslems & even to students of Al Azhar. Rev. D. M. Thornton has recently addressed men from Sierra Leone, Timbuctoo, Shangit, Yemen, Fez & Turkey. The Bible bought at the mission depot is possessed by a number of Moslem students & is even read openly within the walls of the great Moslem University Al Azhar itself. Mr. Thornton writes: "Praise for blessing coming, for hearts-softening, for doors opening, for converts openly preaching & teaching Christ up & down the land. Let the brethren know that the time is ripe & the harvest coming soon so keep on believing." I find that Toney is right "Preach for results & you get them," though Lord Cromer would not have Xtian Missions work in Sudan. Xtians belonging to U.P. churches in [?] are moving into Sudan for business purposes, are taking Xtianity with them & are now arranging to have pastors & preachers, so the gospel will be preached in Sudan.

The British and Foreign Bible Society reports that the demand for copies of the Scriptures is three times what it was a year ago & one bookseller writes "No trouble now to sell Bibles, the trouble is to get them."

A148-(7181) ON NESTORIANS [EXCERPTS, ESTIMATED DATE 1906]

During the past months we have been studying (eating-up) China (consecutively) as to its geography, its dynasties, its religions, its people; and to-day we are to have the entrance of Xtianity from its first dawn. We find that the first news of a divine saviour was carried by Nestorian

Xtians & as we often hear the Nestorian Church referred to in Church history let us first refresh our memories as to its origin. The Nestorian Sect was called after its founder Nestoramus a native of northern Syria near Antioch, where he received priests orders & became so eminent for his eloquence as a preacher and his exemplary life that in 425 A.D. he was summoned by the Emperor of Rome, Theodosius, to be made Bishop of Constantinople. He was by no means a loveable character, a monk of austere & ascetic life. Gibbon tells us that in his first sermon before the Emperor he cried "Give me O Caesar give me the Earth purged of heretics & I will give you in exchange the Kingdom of Heaven. Exterminate with me the heretics & with you I will exterminate the Persians." He fiercely persecuted the Arians, these were the disciples of Arius, who did not believe in the [?] denying the divinity of Christ. In the Syrian school Nestorius had been taught to discriminate between the humanity of his master Christ & the divinity of the Lord Jesus: he revered the virgin as the mother of Christ but resented the title mother of God which had been adopted by the Arian controversy out of the love & reverence for everything connected with the redeemer [very faint script] had grown up in the church at that point worshipped the virgin mother. And when Nestorius & his fellow presbyter Anastasius preached sermon after sermon of great power & eloquence against this favourite doctrine, there was a storm of wild indignation: the presbyters & priests went against the bishop. Nestorius does not seem to have borne this quietly, he had the offenders tried & cruelly scourged. This holy war spread from Constantinople to the far East. Cyrilpatian[?] of Alexandria full of an inherited jealousy & animosity to the Bishop of Constantinople & who under the cover of being a Xtian was a persecutor of the cruellest & bitter type stirred up a violent opposition.

Some of you may have read Hypatia by Kingsley. It was at his instigation she was so cruelly murdered. She was a beautiful woman, a Greek; she had inherited from her father great gifts as a mathematician. Cyril's jealousy was aroused because the [?] of her academy of philosophy was crowded by the gorgeous train of horses & slaves of the illustrious persons who attended her teaching. Accordingly a false rumour was circulated amongst the Xtians against her, she was dragged from her chariot & torn limb from limb with the most frightful deed of atrocity. Such was the religion of those so-called Xtians of the day.

The Knowledge of this has come to us in a very remarkable way through the discovery of a tablet which was presumably buried in China for 7 or 800 years.... Near the great city of Ch'ang-an ... North Western China, some workmen digging a trench in the year 1625 came upon a stone tablet 7ft long & 3ft wide covered with characters mostly Chinese, but a few of them Syrian. Fortunately the Chinese love for ancient monuments preserved this one and a native Xtian sent a copy of it to some Jesuit missionaries. Competent Scholars have decided that this was a genuine monument inscribed by Nestorian missionaries A.D. 781 and proved to be of surpassing interest. The first part is a statement concerning the being of God, the sin of man, the coming & teachings of Christ & the beneficent work of Xtian Missionaries. The second part is a sketch of Nestorian missions in China from A.D. 655 to 781. The third part is a poem in praise of the "Illustrious Religion" as Xtianity is always named on this monu-ment & Eulogistic of the Chinese Emperors who favoured this religion. Several notes are added giving the names of [?] and that of the writer Yezd-buzril. The whole inscription as translated by Prof Legge of Oxford has some 3500 English words. Here is a brief extract from the historical portion of the record, page 109 (2000 yrs. before Carey).[10] [Extract not written in address.]

A149-(8447) ON THE SENEGAMBIANS [ESTIMATED DATE 1904]

In the region bounded by the East Sahara; the great River Niger and the Atlantic, dwell many distinct tribes. Here in Senegambia, which lies between the Senegal and Gambia, are the tall Wolofs and Mandingoes, the finest types of the Negro race who seem to have been a very poetic people of whom Mungo Park the great early traveller tells so many tales. Among them roam the Foulahs, meek & peaceable. Along the Niger dwell the [?] & the Yorubas, powerful warlike tribes. The Yoruban capital Eyer being described as 15 miles round and width of 7 miles. Its monarch boasted that his wives linked hand in hand would stretch across his kingdom. But most renowned of all the West African people are the Ashantis, not only in war & commerce but also in agriculture & arts. With them the British ever [?] waged war. In 1873 they surrendered to Sir Garnet Wolseley. The Capital Kumasi has become a word for cruelty.

There is also Dahomey with its army of 8000 Amazons 600 of which were counted as wives of the King. Fearful tales are told of these cannibals. In a palace guarded by Amazons, the walls of the King's bed chamber were ornamented with human jawbones & the path approaching was paved with skulls. Fortunately the French put an end to the Kingdom in 1893.

Nearby the bloodthirsty Benins, treacherous & cruel beyond description, all dealt with the most frightful practices, offering human sacrifices until the British put a stop to it. All along the coast the

British Government & the missionaries have waged incessant war against these fearful people.

Lagos, the Liverpool of Africa. Bishop Tugwell once asked a Lagos chief "What makes the hearts of your people so hard, and their houses so shabby." Pulling aside some bushes, the chief asked him to look beneath, there lay thousands of empty gin bottles.

A150-(7191) CLOSING WORDS OF AN ADDRESS [BALANCE OF ADDRESS ILLEGIBLE][11]

Did it ever occur to you Christian women that the reason there is so much indifference & lethargy & deadness, utter stagnation, in our churches, and that worldliness has come in upon us like a flood, drowning out all vitality and life is because the Church has failed to obey Christ's commandments and has thus lost God's blessing, Mission work is not a department of Church work, but the heart and soul of Church work.

Part Three

The Victorian Narrative

Mary Baker McQuesten's Letters as Literature:
A Victorian Narrative

ख़

And I understand that all these materials for a work of literature were simply
my past life.   —Marcel Proust, *Time Regained*

Proust's reference to "materials for a work of literature" suggests the broad
and inviting possibility of constructing narrative out of a broad range of
documents such as personal letters, diaries, journals, photographs, oral histories, and, more recently, digital collections. All these forms are records of
"past life" and, as such, constitute literary "materials."

Mrs. Mary Baker McQuesten's letters and other writings in this collection that record her past life are just such "materials for a work of literature."
On the basis of narrative content alone the letters could be read effectively as
a novel set in the Victorian age[1] in Hamilton. With that view in mind, the letters have been selected to foreground the natural narrative and the dramatic
content. As a collection, they have an inherent plot structure with various
themes, mystery, romance, tragedy, dramatic effects, characterization, character development, rising and falling action, and a dénouement.

The story, as it emerges, reveals the ideal young couple—a beautiful and
privileged young woman, Mary Baker, and a handsome and wealthy young
lawyer, Isaac McQuesten—and their loving marriage in 1873. It follows the
birth of their seven children in twelve years, and then describes the abrupt
collapse of the family's fortunes with Isaac's mental illness, alcoholism, bankruptcy, and possible suicide in 1888. The story then continues with the tale of
the widowed and impoverished Mary and her six living children and their
struggle to maintain their genteel social status as they perform remarkable
social and political activities in the community and throughout Ontario.

The story also describes Mary's matriarchal development as she takes control of her six children's lives, and also presides over the Women's Missionary
Society, first at the MacNab Street Presbyterian Church and, later, provin-
cially. The story then gradually reveals some of the details about Mary's role in
the romantic disappointments in the lives of three of her children. She does
not clearly expose her motives and, as in any good novel, the mystery of why

Notes for Part Three start on page 240

none of the children ever married must be left to the reader's judgment. The dramatic dénouement in the extended narrative occurs in the family's gradual demise until the death of the final member in 1968 and the dedication of Whitehern and its contents to the City of Hamilton to become a museum— and a valuable archival legacy. There are thus elements of both tragedy and success in the story.

The Victorian Gothic elements in the tale are quite apparent, even in the sketchy outline above. We can add a wicked stepmother, a madwoman in the attic, a tragic heroine, inherited mental disorders, institutionalization, social stigma, and secrecy. The narrative presents the paradox of an intelligent, loving, and devoted mother who also demanded an inflexible Calvinistic morality and exerted a dominant will to control all family events and values. We are reminded here of Alice Munro's term, "Southern Ontario Gothic," by which she describes a similar stern Scottish, "life-denying" Presbyterianism (Redekop 21-26).

The McQuesten story has many of the qualities of a saga, which unfolds in the chronicle of the extraordinary family at Whitehern and their near-legendary status in Hamilton lore. When reading the story of Mary's life through her letters, one is amazed that she could have accomplished so much and remained so determined, in spite of so many personal trials and hardships, including her own health problems. That she was able to restore her family to social and political prominence is remarkable; that she was also able to accomplish so much in the community, and in missionary work, is astonishing. Her life and death are commemorated in the eulogy by the Rev. Beverley Ketchen, the family minister for thirty years. Ketchen knew her well, and he pays tribute to her formidable strength of character and indomitable will as he celebrates her life and contributions. The eulogy provides a fitting closure to Mary's letters (A144-Eulogy).

Mary's letters reveal the social, financial, and cultural forces of the era that both governed and limited a woman's aspirations for herself and her children. As a widowed mother of six children, the most vital recurring themes in her writings are those of family finances, health, education, the Presbyterian missionary societies, and Victorian society and culture. These themes provide a framework which reveals the day-to-day lives and concerns of a cultured but impoverished upper-class family in Ontario. They also reveal the gradual development of the character of Mary Baker McQuesten from a privileged young matron into a powerful matriarch and a forceful social activist.

The McQuestens' personal experiences with illness, death, and impoverishment are tragic; however, they also add a broader cultural perspective to their writings that would not have been revealed if their financial circumstances and elite social status had remained unchanged. The letters frankly confide the family's anxieties about financial problems and health concerns, both mental and physical.

Mary was the acknowledged inspiration behind her children's achieve-ments in education, journalism, the ministry, law, politics, and city planning. Most of her writings take the form of family letters in which she guided all aspects of her children's lives according to an inflexible Calvinist, Presbyter-ian morality. As Mary Harrington Farmer writes, "Her advice, opinions, and reactions are as firm and un-negotiable as were the laws of the Medes and Per-sians" (Farmer, *CMQPW* 14). Mary's letters demonstrate her ability to influ-ence and control her children even from a distance. At the same time she urged them into social activism. She demanded of them the same strong social and moral conscience and sense of duty that she had learned from her father.

Mary's letters very often contain instructions about finances, diet, appear-ance, and behaviour, or warnings to guard against an emotional collapse, and most often she gave counsel on a moral or religious theme. As Thomas writes to his mother, "You seem to demand the best of a man ... we know distinctly the difference between right and wrong" (6 March 1906, 5440). Mary herself writes to her son Calvin that "I must lay the truth of the circumstances before you, no one but myself could do it" (17 March 1914, A115-8757).

Mary's children never married and her matriarchal power is evident in that she actively broke up the prospective engagements for her three children, Hilda, Ruby, and Tom. It would be difficult to single out any one reason for her objection to these unions. Were the prospective partners not suitable by edu-cation, profession, wealth, or social standing? Or was Mary intent on a eugenic solution to the inherited mental affliction that several family members suf-fered, including, to some extent, herself? Her reasons are not always clearly divulged in her letters, and I leave it to the reader's speculation and interpre-tation to judge her motives. It is evident that she experienced some regret:

Many times, I have had grave anxiety as to whether my standard of right has been too puritanical and has shut out the girls from any opportunities, but yet I could not forget that "we are not to do evil that good may come," and I believed that it is only when obey-ing God, that we receive His help, and I always felt far too weak to go into anything without His approval. And as I look back and read my Bible, it still seems to me the only Safe Course." (MCP 2-4.37a, 7 March 1907)

Mary is somewhat conflicted in this statement; she reflects that she may have made a mistake, but then justifies it by a virtuous motive based on her belief in the personal and guiding hand of God.

Mary saw it as her duty to write twice a week to her children when they were away from home at school or at work, and they were to write home at least once a week. Since Calvin (the eldest son) was away from home most often, many of the letters are to, or from, him. Although Ruby was away also, very few of the letters to her are extant. Perhaps Mary felt that Ruby did not require her guidance as much as Calvin did. Nevertheless, letter writing was a family obligation which the members discharged with loving attention to one another, and Mary insisted on this program of communication, although writing was not permitted on the Sabbath. She was the centre of the family and her epistles were circulated among family members, as was the custom of the age (19 January 1909, 6331). In one letter Ruby aptly describes her mother's role: "You're the indispensable hub of the whole family wheel and your family would be utterly wretched and lost without you" (13 February 1910, 6446). Many of the letters, especially those to Calvin, were carefully returned to Whitehern and preserved for posterity.

The family members rarely show a note of anger or impatience with one another in their letters and, in spite of their financial constraints, they are always generous, loving, encouraging, informative, and often witty and teasing. They paid special attention to birthdays and health concerns, and often exchanged rich commentary on literature, social and world events, and politics. The children rarely challenged their mother, and sought always to spare her feelings or to avoid her wrath. However, there is some suggestion that some correspondence was carried on in secret or written on a separate page with injunctions to burn or destroy (6281; 6310; 8164). For obvious reasons only a few of these are extant.

The value of the McQuesten writings is also apparent in the quality and the art of the writing. They were written by educated upper-class people who demonstrate an awareness of epistolary form and an elegance of language that are beyond the requirements of the mere transmission of information. The McQuestens received a classical education and were aware of their roles as writers, as they recorded and transmitted life events in a formal, creative, and often imaginative way. Although letter writing was a family duty, a particularly good letter was always applauded by family and friends. They considered letter writing an art form, and often consciously projected their aesthetic sensibilities in the use of colourful and descriptive language and humour.

The complete McQuesten archive at Whitehern Museum contains the private letters of individuals who reflect the ideologies and influences of the post-Enlightenment period, and especially of the Scottish Enlightenment, and the experiences in the letters can be mined, or "re-collected," for their historical, cultural, and literary relevance.

The ideas of the "Scottish Enlightenment" are embodied in the eighteenth-century philosophies of "David Hume, Adam Smith, Adam Ferguson, and others, who were deeply indebted to the Frenchman Montesquieu" (*Enlightenment* 15-16). Montesquieu advocated a "philosophy of individual liberty, holding up the English state as a model," which later supplied the emphasis on freedom in "the drafting of the American Constitution" (*OED* 936). The movement is characterized by an intellectual rigor in criticism of superstitions, political systems, laws, and any institutions that hindered the intellectual and moral development of human nature. It was an optimistic "Age of Criticism," that believed that human nature, through advancement in knowledge, "would change the world—for the better" (*Enlightenment* 17-19). The Presbyterians embraced and implemented these ideals in their emphasis on education, the work ethic, morality, individual commitment, and moral responsibility. This gradually developed into the "higher criticism" of scripture in the colleges, and into the "social gospel" and "city beautiful" movements, which believed that education and a healthy and beautiful environment would promote moral-ity. The McQuesten letters and their library reflect their passionate commit-ment to these Enlightenment beliefs.

The McQuesten writers were clearly aware of the historical importance of their writings and in the circulation possibilities in their collection. They consciously accumulated and preserved the letters of three generations of the family. This suggests an awareness of their value into posterity far beyond the immediate addressee of each letter. Indeed, they initiated the heritage process in their bequest agreement which stipulated that their home and all contents were to be made available to a wide public audience as a "period piece." In some cases, family members carefully collected and returned the letters, and the careful retrieval of letters to provide both sides of the correspondence is a striking example of conscious literary and historical archive building. It is sig-nificant to note that the McQuesten letters were gradually passed on from one relative to another, as was often the custom among families in the past. The person-to-person distribution, or the reading out loud of letters to friends or family, also suggests circulation, and the dramatic value is apparent in the text's ability to evoke pain or pleasure even long after the news is no longer current.

Mary's letters are very forthright and personal and, as a collection, have an obvious affinity with autobiography. Evelyn J. Hinz confirms the genre's current popularity and its relationship with art and drama. She argues that it has three basic features in common with drama: "An element of conflict and dialogue, a sense of performance and/or spectatorship, and a mimetic or refer-ential quality." She states further that "drama shares with auto/biography an interdisciplinary dimension" and that auto/biography has dramatic affinities, a narrative quality, and it has plot, characterization, setting, and evokes the Aris-totelian "pity and fear" in its emotional, and often tragic, content ("Mimesis" 195-98). All of the above elements of autobiography, drama, and narrative are also present in the McQuesten letters. In themselves the letters are autobio-graphical, but when selected and published later as a collection by a second writer they become biographical.

There has been an explosion of interest in the epistolary tradition and in biography and autobiography since the late twentieth century. Biographical forms invariably make use of extant personal letters to provide authenticity in historical and cultural details, and for narrative and dramatic effect. There is an intense curiosity about what constitutes a private self and a public self, and the life writings of earlier generations who were also living on the cusp of change, or were caught up in the prevailing ideas of "progress" and "freedom," are very useful as cultural documents.

As a means of providing a local literary context for Mary's letters, we can examine three surviving diaries of women from the Hamilton area, two of which have been published and have enjoyed growing interest. For years the diary of Sophia MacNab languished in the halls of Dundurn Castle, the Mac-Nab mansion in Hamilton, until it was published in 1968. It was written by thirteen-year-old Sophia during the period of January to July 1846, and describes life at Dundurn Castle, including details about her father, Sir Allan Napier MacNab (1798-1862)—a lawyer, railway entrepreneur, and politician who became premier of the Canadas (1854-56) (CE 1279-80,13). Sophia's diary has become popular and is often presented on special occasions in Hamilton; in dramatizations at Dundurn Castle, Sophia speaks her own words, tells her own story, and lives for us once again.

Curiously, the McQuesten writings at the Whitehern archive rarely mention the MacNab family, and the omission serves to illustrate how insular the various groups in Victorian society could become. There are several reasons for this, relating to political, religious, and business issues. The McQuestens were staunch Liberals, while the MacNabs were "extreme Tories" (CE 1279-80). Also MacNab and his first wife and daughter were Anglican, and MacNab's second wife was a Catholic, as were their two daughters. On the other hand the McQuestens were Presbyterian, and they were critical of the Anglicans and Catholics, partly because of an old controversy over clergy reserve lands. Mary found "no spirit of Christ in them only the spirit of the devil" (A52-5283 & note, 5289). The business problem involved the fact that the McQuestens were viewed as American upstarts, having emigrated from New England, unlike the MacNabs, who came from old, established, well-connected Canadian stock. As president of the Gore bank, MacNab turned down Calvin McQuesten for a loan because he was American (280, 6 May 1837). This serves to illustrate that, when making a comparison of writings from any given era or area, much historical and cultural detail can be gleaned from information that appears, initially, to be absent.

The diary of Catherine Bell Van Norman was written in 1850 in Nelson Township, near Hamilton, and it remained largely unknown until its publication in1981, when it became valued as a historical and cultural document. It is a religious diary (Methodist) and it reflects a deep religious spirit similar to that found in Mary Baker McQuesten's letters. Catherine and Mary were both strong women and both criticized their preachers; however, it is not known if Catherine did so publicly, because a diary is much more private than a letter and a letter engages at least one other person and often several. It is evident that Mary felt the freedom, or the need, to speak openly in criticism of a preacher, or of men in general. Catherine's diary, written by a farm housewife about her "wholly domestic" life for a brief period of less than six months, while her health was failing, was yet considered of such great value that it was hand-transcribed and then finally published. These works are not merely isolated historical novelties, giving us some brief details about life in Ontario in a bygone age, they also have dramatic stories to tell. They are real people, with real life and death experiences. Catherine Bell Van Norman's tombstone is inscribed: "She being dead yet speaketh," which is also the epigraph used in the publication of her diary. It also aptly describes the current impulse to recover women's voices.

A third work extant from the Hamilton area is the diary of Queenie Crerar, the daughter of a prominent Hamilton lawyer, John Crerar, and his wife, Jessie Anne Hope (Tyrell 135), which she wrote from May to September 1887 and from June 1891 to February 1892, between the ages of fourteen to eighteen. It has not been published but is available in Special Collections at the Hamilton Public Library. It provides a social comparison particularly with the children in the McQuesten writings, since Queenie is approximately the same age as was Mary McQuesten's eldest child (also named Mary) when Isaac died so suddenly in 1888, leaving them impoverished. Consequently, Mary and her siblings were strictly limited in their opportunities for amusement or entertainment, and Mary and Hilda were immediately assigned to look after the house and the younger children. In contrast, at the same time and in the same city, Queenie lived a privileged and carefree life with many outings, the theatre, concerts, music, art lessons, regular sporting events, school in England, and the Grand Tour in Europe in 1891 at the age of eighteen.

There is no mention made of the McQuestens in Queenie's diary, in spite of the fact that the Crerars lived on MacNab Street just a few blocks from the McQuestens. However, there are a few mutual friends in both writings—the Glasscos, the Hopes, the McPhies, and George Brown—and both mention going to Crawfords for ice cream and cake (Crerar diary, 7 September 1887 and letter 4367). There may have been the same social division that occurred between the MacNabs and the McQuestens, in that while Queenie had relatives who were Presbyterian, she also had others who were Anglican (*DHB* 2:35, 70, 1.55,105, 4.63), while the McQuestens were strictly and sternly Presbyterian and intolerant of Anglicans. For her part, however, Queenie showed no hostility in either direction. In the diary she notes a renewed awareness of pride in her "Scotch" connection through her father and both grandmothers, and she enjoys an Evangelical Presbyterian service in London, England (15 August 1887, 19 November 1891). Queenie's family practised a much more liberal Christianity, so that on Sundays Queenie was allowed to write letters and diary entries, go to the beach, and often miss church, while the McQuestens' Calvinistic Presbyterianism allowed for no such frivolities on the Sabbath. Also the Crerars were involved in the Garrick Club, a drama and theatre club in Hamilton, and Mr. Crerar's brother Peter Duncan was president of the Hamilton Distillery, both of which would have offended the McQuestens' puritanical and temperance sensibilities (*DHB* 1:55; *DHB* 2:34, 35).

However, the contrasts found between Mary's letters and Queenie's diary must also take into account the difference in finances of the two families. Mary was likely more strict with her children because of a lack of money, a circumstance to which she herself admits. This suggests that other Presbyterian children, if they were also privileged, were not denied some of these pleasures, and indeed Mary criticizes some of them on that very account. Queenie's diary thus provides yet another view of Hamilton's cultural scene, and reinforces the fact that it is necessary to recover as many writings as possible for any given era or place so as to avoid the conclusion that any one experience is typical.

The aforementioned texts represent a variety of ages and walks of life, but they are all women's voices of the Victorian era. They represent media often favoured in the Victorian age through which women were allowed to imagine, envision, emulate, and project different versions of the self. The woman's voice in the diary will be more private than that of the letter, but also, perhaps, more honest, unless she is writing consciously for posterity, in which case it will have political undertones intended to influence or persuade the reader. In fact it could be argued that the very concrete fact of writing in any form—whether letter, diary, or memoir—will have a social or political purpose which seeks to influence the reader. The letter, however, is a more consciously public and political medium in the sense that it has the explicit intention to instruct, persuade, and influence another person—or a whole family, as in the case of Mary McQuesten's writings.

The letter form itself represents a fundamental human desire—the attempt *and* the intention to communicate with another human being, in spite of the distressing limitations of space and time. It is solely because the two parties are separated that the letter is being written, and it represents the speaking voice and body converted into text. In this sense, the body is always central to the letter, and the letter compensates for its absence.

The physical nature of the written word is embodied in the language we use to describe the letter form: it has a "salutation" and a "body" and, therefore, is a substitute for greeting and meeting. An example of this is found in an account from the *Hamilton Spectator* in June 2000 of a man whose knowledge of his father was limited to a few photographs and his mother's stories. On finding one of his dead father's letters, the article states, "[a]t that moment, the face in the frame became a person. After 56 years Bob met his father . . . and couldn't stop crying" (Hanley, 6 June 2000). Mike Hanley's lengthy and very moving article makes much of this experience of the living nature of the written word. In the dead soldier's single letter he was immediately transformed into a real person. In the father's salutation to his son as "Dear Bobby," and in his closing of "Your Daddy," he took on a reality of character and meaning for his son. This report is a graphic example of the vital nature of written fragments from the past, and also attests to their need for classification and preservation so that they can be alive for the present.

In the early part of the Victorian age the letter was the only means of communication across distance. Personal letters often expressed, emotionally, the regret and pain of separation, but then proceeded into communication, with the expectation of return dialogue. Letters were a substitute for a personal visit and, as such, they conveyed the personality or subjectivity of the writer, however faintly and imperfectly. Signatures and dates argue for a sense of time, place, and agency in history, and for attempts to create and to project the self. Note this letter from Eliza McQuesten to her brother, Calvin McQuesten.

Often have I wished that I could know how you are passing your time … the family have retired and I am seated alone by a warm fire in our kitchen. Imagine to yourself what a pleasant chat we should have could you make yourself a guest of my happy department; but as this is impracticable, I will suffer my thoughts to roam till they have wandered over that little streak of country which separates us, and enter your study and hold "silent converse" with you. (11, 23 March 1830)

The letter becomes the graphic example of the "word made flesh," in which Eliza expresses poignantly and poetically the pangs of separation. Many of Mary's letters also express her concern at the separation from her children and her eager anticipation of their homecomings.

There is a long history that has already established the literary quality of personal letters. In the eighteenth and nineteenth centuries, personal letters were a preferred form of literature that developed into the epistolary novel, in such forms as Samuel Richardson's *Pamela; or, Virtue Rewarded* (1740) and *Clarissa, or History of a Young Lady* (1747-48). These have achieved canonical status as the first English novels dealing with character portrayal and consciousness (Cook 19, Harmon 351-52).

During the eighteenth century, as printing and publishing developed into an industry, the demands of a rapidly expanding literate public that encouraged letter writing contributed to a hunger for any literature that explored the boundaries between the public and private. The public's intense curiosity about the private habits of others encouraged a kind of cultural voyeurism which was exploited by the publication of personal letters, whether they were discovered by chance, stolen from private homes, or deliberately written and misrepresented as "real" letters. Letters of all types were marketed and published in "collections of letters with no common theme, save their form." At that time the very letter form attested to their legitimacy:

Billed as letters between friends, between lovers, collected from long journeys, and so on, these collections were often explained as turning up in deserted houses, in anonymous deliveries, or as being deliberately published by their owner to publicly heal a reputation, correct misinformation, or to give a wayward, heedless public the benefit of another person's experience. (Perry 66, 72)

Indeed, the "attempt to construct the body" was so "central" that it became sexual, and if a woman consented to write a letter to a man, it actually signaled her erotic willingness, and was a prelude to her sexual capitulation. In drama, the "writing cabinet" became the symbol for either guarding the chastity (body), or creating the self (mind), and letters gradually became the expressions of individuality and consciousness (132-35). This is apparent in Richardson's *Clarissa*, where he makes much of the fact that Clarissa grants Lovelace a private correspondence. So even in the private or "real" letter, the literary skills of art and imagination are necessary to bridge the distance between writer and reader and both must be evoked in the act of writing itself.

The epistolary novel enjoyed a long and successful tradition, but gradually became eclipsed in the twentieth century in favour of the fictional novel, as so-called *pure* fiction. The fictional novel then achieved canonical status in literature as being more authentically artistic—in having been created out of the artist's imagination. However, the personal letter and other forms of life writing based on lived experiences are once again being recognized within the scope of literature, not merely for their historical, cultural, and biographical value, but also for their literary, imaginative, and narrative qualities.

Throughout written history, an established author's personal letters and other writings have been readily accepted as literature because they are often complementary to publications that have achieved canonical status. However, the fact that Mary McQuesten's writings were produced by an "ordinary" person, rather than by a celebrated author, does not diminish their intrinsic value as writings from life and experience. Indeed, it is now recognized in our postcolonial age that the personal letters of writers in the Victorian era, at the height of the colonial age in Canada, play a vital role in our literature and in our history, and can contribute to a fuller understanding of our cultural heritage.

Personal Letters as Life Writing

ह

Marlene Kadar, in her collection *Essays in Life Writing* (1992), argues for the inclusion of letter writing within the genre of life writing. She notes that life writing as a term was popular "for a part of the eighteenth century, before the Greek and Latin rooted words 'biography' and 'autobiography' fell into current usage" (4) and goes on to state that

[i]t is a kind of writing about the "self" or the "individual" that favours auto-biography, but includes letters, diaries, journals, and (even) biography. This kind of life writing may be written by literary men and women, or it may be written by "ordinary" men and women.(5)

In the genre of life writing Kadar includes "archival materials by women or men who never became celebrities, or diaries and letters to loved ones and friends, some notable examples of which have been uncovered in recent years" (6). Clearly, the McQuesten letters match these criteria and will add to the publications already existing in the genre of life writing by providing some further "notable examples."

An important companion to Mary Baker McQuesten's letters, is Marilyn F. Whiteley's *The Life and Letters of Annie Leake Tuttle: Working for the Best* (1999). It contains the letters and memoirs of Annie Tuttle (1839-1934), who was the matron of the Women's Missionary Society of the Methodist Church in Victoria, British Columbia, in 1887. Mary Baker McQuesten's life and writings cover approximately the same dates, and also have a strong women's missionary society content. Together, they provide a cultural comparison of women's voices and contributions from both Western and Central Canada. They also provide insights into the political or ideological variations within the Protestant churches and their missionary enterprises.

Another book that provides important material for Canadian women's writings is Frances Hoffman and Ryan Taylor's *Much to Be Done: Private Life in Ontario from Victorian Diaries* (1996). It is a collection of nineteenth-century women's diary and journal writings that provides "selections" and "whispers" from a large number of women, as they portray all aspects of women's domestic life in Ontario from childbirth to funerals. Some of the characters and events can be compared with the McQuesten letters. For instance, Van der Smissen is mentioned as a professor at University of Toronto (143-44); he had been Mary Baker's teacher at grammar school and Tom's professor at the university, where he had assisted Tom in his bid for the Rhodes Scholarship (A51-5233). Notes in the Hoffman and Taylor volume about the temperance movement, itinerant seamstresses, tea parties, and fashion also play a part in Mary's letters, as well as items about Hamilton and Burlington. Although Mary's letters represent one long, sustained dialogue with a constant cast of characters and a narrative continuity, both styles of recovery have cultural value and are complementary to one another for historical and literary purposes.

Margaret Conrad's *No Place Like Home: Diaries and Letters of Nova Scotia Women 1771-1938* is a recovery of women's voices from a feminist perspective. It contains the writings of ordinary, unpublished women and establishes their writings as stories and chronicles. It also seeks to blur the boundaries between disciplines in its collaboration of editors from the disciplines of history, English, and education.

A useful comparison with Mary McQuesten's missionary work is found in Shirley Jane Endicott's *China Diary: The Life of Mary Austin Endicott*, in which Endicott writes her mother's life in the form of her personal memories, blended with excerpts from her mother's memoirs, diaries, and letters. The resulting narrative is a gripping story of the experiences of the generation of missionaries who went to Asia after the United Church was formed in 1925. The Endicotts did teaching and foster care, but also took a strong political stance to became peace activists and endured several crises in China during the Chinese Revolution and its aftermath, when Jim Endicott was accused of treason.

In Canadian literature, the epistolary tradition is strongly evident. Frances Brooke's epistolary novel, *The History of Emily Montague* (1769), has claim to be the first Canadian novel. Catharine Parr Traill's epistolary form is clearly revealed in the long and descriptive title *The Backwoods of Canada: Being Letters from the Wife of an Emigrant Officer, Illustrative of the Domestic Economy of British America* (1836). Anna Brownell Jameson's *Winter Studies and Summer Rambles in Canada* (1838) presents "'fragments' of a journal addressed to a friend" (Jameson 9). Margaret and Thomas Blom's *Canada Home: Juliana Horatia Ewing's Fredericton Letters 1867-1869* (1983) is the work of an established author and her personal and informal letters are selected to concentrate "on what she has to say about Canada and about her activities as an author" (xxii).

There are also several examples of the publication of collections of the personal letters of literary persons in Canada, notably, *Susanna Moodie: Letters of a Lifetime* (1985), and *I Bless You in My Heart: Selected Correspondence of Catharine Parr Traill* (1996), both edited by Carl Ballstadt et al. There is no difficulty in declaring these letters as literature since they are written by published authors and therefore serve to complement existing publications and scholarship. For example, in Carl Ballstadt's essay "'The Embryo Blossom': Susanna Moodie's Letters to Her Husband in Relation to *Roughing It in the Bush*," he notes that Moodie's letters "serve as a gloss" on her published work, and sometimes reveal more about backwoods society than the book itself (Ballstadt, "Embryo"). Similarly, the recuperation of the letters of unpublished writers in Canada serves to expand the literary base for any particular era.

The Whitehern archive also invites specific literary and historical comparisons with the Moodie letters in *Susanna Moodie: Letters of a Lifetime* (1985) and her writings in *Roughing It in the Bush*, published in 1852. It was also in 1852 that Calvin McQuesten purchased Whitehern (then Willowbank), and together these sources provide a comparison between two different settlement cultures in Ontario, the rural and the urban. Susanna Moodie (1803-85) came from England in 1832 and her work describes the hardships of frontier and backwoods settlement near Peterborough, about one hundred and fifty miles northeast of Hamilton, Ontario. At the same time Calvin McQuesten (1801-85), an entrepreneur from New England, emigrated to the thriving urban community of Hamilton, establishing its first foundry. From this humble start, Hamilton grew to become "the Birmingham of Canada."

The life and journal writings of Lucy Maud Montgomery (1874-1942) also provide some areas of comparison and contrast with Mary McQuesten's life and letters. Both women were educated, intelligent, outspoken, and closely involved with the Presbyterian Church and missionary societies in Southern

Ontario. However, Montgomery, even though she was a minister's wife, was a reluctant participant. She avoided leadership or giving addresses, and she found church meetings "deadly dull" (Rubio and Waterston, *Selected Journals* Vol. II, 139). Montgomery had a fulfilling alternative role as a writer, while Mary's alternative role was precisely that of the zealous missionary society leader that Montgomery avoided and found "hopelessly uninteresting." Even though Montgomery was twenty-five years younger (the age of Mary's firstborn daughter), it is likely that they encountered one another at some of the meetings or conventions at which Mary gave her passionate pep-talks,[2] but they likely had little in common. It is interesting to note that none of Montgomery's books are in the Whitehern library, and I have found no reference to her in the writings. The library holds a large collection of writings by many other Canadian woman authors of the Victorian era.

An interesting variation in life writing is the use of oral accounts in literature, which is evident in Bill McNeil's *Voices of a War Remembered: An Oral History of Canadians in World War Two* (1991). McNeil's stated purpose in making the collection is the recovery "of individual stories [which] need to be saved for future generations" (1991). This is a valuable record for life writing and for cultural studies since it chronicles the experiences of Canadian servicemen and women in foreign and hostile countries under extreme conditions of danger, fatigue, and loneliness. Since many of their letters are lost, the oral histories must bear witness to the horrors that they endured. In the book, one James Anderson describes the liberation of Buchenwald, which, together with his own photographs, makes this a valuable historical, cultural, and literary text.

Mary McQuesten's letters relate some of Canada's experiences in World War One, and provide the details of her objection to the war and her adamant refusal to allow her son, Tom, to enlist. Mary states: "The war is so terrible and all these young Canadians cut off in the prime of life and their mothers left to mourn them all their days" (30 April 1915, A119-6828).

We can now add Mary Baker McQuesten's comparatively lengthy saga to the growing collection of published Canadian diaries and letters that serve to recover the voices of ordinary people and their stories. Among the increasingly numerous women's voices in this epistolary literature, there is revealed a gradual shift from the private and domestic sphere to a more public sphere, beginning with women's involvement in church organizations such as the missionary auxiliaries, and expanding later into the professions.

The McQuestens and Their Victorian World

৵

> Mrs. McQuesten had a real Puritanical sense of right and wrong. Her uncom-
> promising conscience would not countenance anything that was not utterly
> honourable. But with all that inflexible integrity were blended a very great
> kindliness and the graciousness of a true lady. She was an aristocrat by birth
> and breeding; she was an aristocrat intellectually and spiritually, too. (A144)
> —Eulogy by Rev. Beverley Ketchen, 10 December 1934

Mary Baker McQuesten was among the most enlightened women of the Victorian and Edwardian age in Canada, yet she is little known. Although Mary
never wrote for publication (few women did at that time) she was a "prolific
and uninhibited letter writer" (Farmer, *CMQPW* 13), an articulate public
speaker, and an outspoken critic of the times. Her forums were the home, the
community, the Presbyterian Church, and the Missionary Societies. The recovery and presentation of Mary's life writings will add to the growing body of literature about women's political history in the Victorian era in Hamilton, in
Ontario, and in Canada. These writings are important artifacts that provide
insights into the Victorian family and society from 1873 to 1934.

Mary McQuesten's writings reveal the political strength and matriarchal power that an exceptional woman was capable of gaining in Ontario during the strongly patriarchal Victorian age. In Mary's case her matriarchal
power was likely gained partly by nature, partly by nurture, and partly by
necessity: by nature through a naturally strong will and constitution, by nurture through her father's example and teaching, and by necessity through
the need to be both father and mother to her children. Little is known of
Mary's mother except that she was a loving mother, a minister's wife, and
involved in the women's group in the church, which likely also provided a
model for Mary when she matured.

Mary was a powerful matriarch in both the home and family and in society. In the home, she regulated every aspect of her six children's lives. She was
also a powerful matriarch within the women's community of the Presbyterian
Church as she organized and guided the women's auxiliary groups for the exclusive benefit of other needy women and children. Mary also brought a strong fem-
inine influence into church politics as she sought to influence all church
decisions, from the selection of new ministers to issues of higher criticism and
Church Union. This often brought her into direct opposition to the wishes and
demands of the male church establishment.

Mary's life saw the reign of three monarchs: Queen Victoria (1837-1901),
King Edward VII (1901-10), and King George V (1910-36). These years spanned
a time of great change in Canada and the Western world, witnessing such significant events as Canadian Confederation, the Boer War, industrialization,

immigration, World War One, the Depression, and the increasing effects of Darwinian theory, humanism, liberalism, and modernism. The turbulence of the age was accompanied by a growing optimism inspired by the progress promised by science and technology. Presbyterians were particularly influenced by the social ideas of the Scottish Enlightenment and demonstrated the missionary evangelical and colonizing spirit that presumed the cultural superiority of Britain and its "manifest divine destiny" (Moir, *Enduring* 185).

During the Victorian age a demand for the education and liberation of women was accompanied by a growing criticism of the rigid patriarchal forces of society that prevailed in religion and politics and that tended to disregard the needs of women. One of the earliest forums of the feminist movement in the Victorian age was the Women's Missionary Society, and it provided a focus for women's desire for social change. Mary's letters reveal that it possessed a matriarchal structure, being organized and led by women for the benefit of women; they raised their own funds and administered them, and resisted male dominance in their gender struggles both at home and abroad. Mary was one of an emerging body of newly organized women who were educated, outspoken, and highly motivated by a feminist impulse, although they may not have recognized that impulse as feminism at the time.

The McQuesten's family life was circumscribed by the MacNab Street Presbyterian Church, the church which Calvin McQuesten (Mary's father-in-law) had helped to finance in 1854. It is only one block from Whitehern, and the McQuesten family attended twice every Sunday for more than a hundred years. Mary's faith in a personal and loving God sustained her in the darkest times, although there is some evidence that she occasionally grew discouraged and impatient with His plan (4670). This once prompted her son Calvin to pray that "mother may get more comfort and happiness from her religion" (*Diary* 1918, 1920).

Mary's strict Calvinist moral interpretations and fundamentalist beliefs were aligned with the most restrictive injunctions of Presbyterianism. At the same time, and with apparently no concern for any rational conflict with fundamentalism, Mary demonstrated the enlightened Victorian interest in a kind of social Darwinism—a trust in progress through the natural sciences, eugenics, social reform, and the belief that humans are shaped by their environment as well as their wills (Moir, *Enduring* 174-75; Allen 383-87).

The Whitehern library contains books by and about Charles Darwin and his theories. One might expect that Mary's fundamentalist convictions would have caused her to restrict her children's reading and education, but she maintained and encouraged an educated and enlightened outlook. She insisted on a classical education for her children and promoted an interest in the broader world of literature, art, science, and travel, all in the interest of preserving a very high intellectual and scholarly standard. She also guided her children's reading, just as her father, Thomas Baker, had guided hers.

The library at Whitehern consists of more than 3,500 books, the oldest of which is a four-volume set dated 1569 and entitled *Corpus Litis Civilis. Digesta. Digestum Vetus* (A Compendium of Civil Law based on the compendiary of Florence, formerly called Pisan, Lugdunum, Lyons, 1569). The library reflects the professional interests of three generations of the family in the classics, law, medicine, religion, politics, philosophy, architecture, town planning, the natural sciences, and Biblical exegesis. The library also contains an excellent collection of fiction, poetry, drama, Canadian literature, and women writers. There are several books that demonstrate an appreciation for the epistolary tradition in literature. For instance, Mary comments on reading the three volumes of *The Letters of Queen Victoria* (1908):

I have been reading the Queen's letters, she certainly, as a girl of seventeen, had a great deal of ability and of the fear of God.... It is really a good thing to read for it refreshes one's mind on so much of her early reign and interests me particularly as I used to hear your grandpapa speak of so many of the mentioned. (A93-6347)

Another epistolary text in the library is the *Historical and Literary Curiosities: Consisting of Facsimiles of Original Documents* (1875), which contains copies of the handwritten letters of James Granger from 1769 and Tobias Smollett's from 1756, along with many others. The latter was presented to Thomas Baker by Mary and Isaac for Christmas 1879. Books were often the gifts of choice and were discussed frequently as Mary guided her family's reading and education, or as the children commented on their reading. The books were often loaned out but also diligently sought after for their return.

The many books in the McQuesten library on history and social reform reflect the family's interest in social planning. They include Thomas Malthus's *An Essay on the Principle of Population* (1872), which advocates "checks" on population growth (*OCEL* 509). Among the twenty-nine volumes by Ruskin in their library is *The Political Economy of Art* (1870), and the McQuestens were likely influenced by his social and moral philosophy in urban planning, architectural design, "organic nature," "national education," and "organization of labour." Ruskin was considered to be a "moral guide or prophet" (*CBD* 1275-76; *OCEL* 716). Ruby's letter of February 1903 describes a lecture given by a very young and "unabashed" William Lyon Mackenzie King on "Social Settlements," including Hull House in Chicago and Toynbee Hall in London (4785). Ruby also writes at great length of having attended a lecture by Booker T. Washington on slavery and judged him "a Great Man" (February 1906, MCP 1-3a.21).

The McQuestens' missionary zeal was inspired by the Victorian social conscience which linked aesthetics to social reform and was known as the Social Gospel movement. It was a belief that morality was directly related to beautiful surroundings and to the quality of public spaces. The McQuesten's philosophy of social reform included a sense of the importance of the organic world; therefore, nature, gardens, beauty, health, and morality were closely connected in her world view. She was the active and acknowledged influence behind her son Thomas (a lawyer, politician, and member of Parliament) and his commitment to the "City Beautiful" movement. Thomas's planning of parks and bridges was based on a renaissance ideal and he "was possessed with an almost obsessive impulse to restore and beautify his surroundings" (Best 192). This was a reflection of optimism in the Victorians, who sought to control both nature and human nature in their response to the wilderness of Canada, the disorder of the settlement era, and the new waves of immigration for industry.

Whitehern's large library, its works of art, and its three generations of life writings were all accessible to the McQuesten children, and provided a deep sense of pride in their heritage. Mary had an aristocratic sense of self-worth and a frankly elitist attitude that she instilled in her children and that gave them all the courage to be critical of others, especially figures of authority such as ministers and politicians. In spite of their impoverishment or, perhaps, because of it, Whitehern itself became an emblem of the family's status, and its possession and preservation was vital to their self-image.

We must credit Mary with consciously preserving the Whitehern archive even when she might have sold the home and sought more economical accommodation, as she considered doing several times. Even when she rented Whitehern to the Hamilton Club in 1907, she carefully packed all of the family possessions and placed them in storage. It was likely a culmination of Mary's influence and sense of posterity when, in 1959, twenty-five years after her death, her three remaining children collaborated to deed Whitehern and all their possessions to the City of Hamilton so that everyone "may enjoy ... the beautiful rooms of Whitehern and eat their lunches in its pleasant garden" (Box 08-140, address by Calvin McQuesten, 3 November 1959).

Mary Baker McQuesten and her six children (circa 1889)
(From left to right, back row) Hilda, Thomas, Mary, Ruby, Calvin
(front row) Mary B. and Margaret Edna

Hilda and Ruby McQuesten and dolls (Christmas 1882)
These dolls are displayed at Whitehern (4309).

Mary Baldwin McQuesten (1874-1964)   Rev. Calvin McQuesten (1876-1968)

Hilda Belle McQuesten (1877-1967)   Ruby Baker McQuesten (1879-1911)

Thomas Baker McQuesten (1882-1948)   Margaret Edna McQuesten (1885-1935)

The six McQuesten children at Whitehern

Aged Mary B. McQuesten and son Thomas (circa 1934)

An excerpt from a letter in Mary B. McQuesten's hand (8737, 1913)

Part Four

❧

Mary Baker McQuesten's Letters

1873-1903

۶🐚

✦ A1-(1380) To Dr. Calvin Brooks McQuesten[1]

213 East 53rd St. New York　　　　　34 Gloucester Street
　　　　　　　　　　　　　　　　　Toronto, June 8, 1873

My dear Calvin

You will, I trust, question this rather familiar manner of addressing you, but I didn't like the idea of treating as a stranger one who is soon to be my "big brother" too, and with whom I hope, to be ever on terms of warmest friendship.

But I have not time to write a lengthy epistle and therefore I must come at once to the point, which is to invite you to my wedding. We shall all be very glad to see you and in fact will be very disappointed if Isaac's only brother is absent. It is to be a quiet affair, and therefore not very much inducement to come so far, and I know, it must be difficult for you to get away from your engagements, but still, if you <u>can</u> come I shall take it as quite a favour to <u>myself</u>, and Isaac is <u>very</u> anxious to have you.[2]

　　　　　　　　　　　　Believe me,
　　　　　　　　　　　　yours very sincerely
　　　　　　　　　　　　Mary Baker

✦ A2-(4283) To Dr. Calvin Brooks McQuesten

New York　　　　　　　　　　　Hamilton
　　　　　　　　　　　　　　　December 28, 1875

My dear Brother,

When I came home from posting your handkerchiefs, I found your magnificent presents awaiting me, and if I could have recalled my order, I certainly should, for your [illegible] quite made me ashamed of it. Many many thanks dear brother Calvin for your kindness, but it was altogether too much, one half would have been a large gift. Such a grand book and the little I could glance into the reading matter very interesting. The [illegible], I

---

assure you, was greatly admired. I never saw any so pretty before and such a fine quality. I told Isaac you ought to charge the latter to him because it was altogether too much. And I am sure you have just robbed yourself.

I intended to write you immediately but I had hardly time to look at the presents when I began getting blind with a sick headache. I suffer so fearfully from heartburn and indigestion that I can hardly walk down town and back without being knocked up. But I fancy I can do nothing but endure it for a while any way. When I can't stand it, I take something that relieves me for the time but it will be on again in half an hour, the worse of it is you know that I am always hungry and it is such hard work to keep from eating. I wish you could see Tiny.[3] She is just the picture of health but I am afraid she would lead you a sad life of it, for Isaac never has a minute's peace, the moment he comes in she goes for him. Isaac thought it was so troublesome getting anything through the custom house, we would just post the handkerchiefs. Hope they reach you. With many thanks.

Believe me,
your loving sister
M. B. McQuesten

✦ A3-(4297) To Calvin McQuesten

c/o Dr. Calvin Brooks McQuesten   Hamilton,
New York   September 9, 1882

My own dear Cally,

Every day I have been trying to find time to write you a letter, but I have been so busy. We all miss you very much, and so many ask me "where is Cally," and when I tell them "Cally is in New York," they seem quite surprised to hear he is such a traveller. Yesterday morning your papa took Tiny [Mary] and Hilda up to see the exhibition at the Crystal Palace,[4] and they were all sorry you were not here to go with them. They came home with a balloon each. Tiny is going to school to Mrs. MacKay on Monday and when you come home you are to go too.[5]

I hope you are not feeling homesick, I often feel very lonely without you my dear little boy and will be so glad when the time comes for you to come home. Katie came back to-night and they all had a great frolic in the kitchen.[6] Papa went up to Hespeler yesterday and is not coming home till to-morrow. Tom is growing such a big baby, you will not know him when you come home. Now, my dear little Cally, good bye, be a very good boy to your uncle. All send you love and kisses.

Your own loving Mama.

✦ A4-(4315) To Isaac Baldwin McQuesten

Hamilton, Ontario   Asbury Park, New Jersey
                                      June 18, 1883

My own dear darling Hubby,

It does seem too bad that you and I are so far separated on our tenth wedding day; but still I feel thankful that we are all so very happy, having so much happiness in each other and though we have lost our little darling and my dear mother, still there is no sad or unlovely thought about them;[7] and we are thankful to have so many dear ones spared to us. Thank you so much for your kind telegram this morning. I hope you received my undying protestation in reply. Tell Tiny Cally received her letter and photo and was much pleased.

I am feeling particularly well, better than I have felt at all. To-morrow morning we expect Calvin [Dr. Calvin Brooks McQuesten] and then if I keep well we intend leaving here on Thursday morning for New York and leave New York on Monday morning by the Albany day-boat, leaving Albany on Tuesday morning. If Tuesday doesn't suit your plans for meeting, let me know. At present I am very well off, but if I find myself suddenly short will telegraph. Have done no shopping yet, really the noise and hustle of New York was too much for my head, I hope it will be stronger when I go back (my head I mean). Miss Fisher sends her kindest regards and congratulations.[8] Just as soon as I see Calvin it will be decided where we go in New York, and I will send you a P.C. [post card]. Give my kindest love to Papa [Baker]. Kind regards to Miss H. and Miss S. and Kisses to the darlings.[9]

                        Ever my dearest, yours alone
                        Mary B. McQuesten

[P.S.] Don't let them forget to send me a bit of the checked stuff to Calvin's address.

✦ A5-(4323) To Dr. Calvin Brooks McQuesten

New York City.   Hamilton, Ontario
                                      May 17, 1885

My Dear Calvin,

When Isaac wrote you yesterday, he was very anxious about your father as he seemed so very weak, but to-day he is much better, so that Isaac does not feel alarmed about him. He was going to write you, but I wished to write any way, so that would do.

I very seldom see your father, for if I do I have to face that awful O.L. and she always sits in the room, although she will not speak to me at all.[10] Besides after she broke her wrist, she had quite as awful-looking a female, as a companion. I really did pity that poor old man shut up with those two creatures, and not able to go out or rid himself of them in any way. I don't think now he minds them too much, as his mind is altogether gone; but they literally worried the sense of reason out of him.

Isaac tells me Dr. Henderson has gone, and you have changed your quarters, how do you like them? Where is Miss Mealing? We sent her a little book at Easter. You must write & tell me all about it, unless you pay us an early visit. Aura and Clara Sawyer are in Hamilton just-now, taking painting lessons. They secured a boarding place before they came, but they are here quite often.[11]

We're all very well, even Isaac is better just-now, since the warm weather came. Now I must close, it is bed-time. It is a busy time, spring sewing etc.

With kindest love
Mary B. McQuesten

✦ A6-(4327) To Dr. Calvin Brooks McQuesten

New York

Hespeler, Ontario
July 8, 1885

Dear Calvin,

I had resolved that I would never again mention the subject of Isaac's health but my anxiety about him is so great, that I must beg of you one favour and that is to tell me, if you would recommend him trying a specialist on nervous disease and who is the best.[12] My greatest difficulty is that Isaac does not feel he has a cent to spare except on necessities, and he has no faith in any man being able to help him. However if you could hold out any inducements as to the skill of any physician in New York, perhaps I could coax him. I asked you once, but you forgot to answer me if you thought there was any virtue in this "Compound oxygen" prepared by a Philadelphia firm. Will you be so very kind as to answer me as soon as you received this, for I am very anxious and if anything can be done the sooner the better.[13] The weather has been very hot to-day. With kind love.

Yours sincerely,
M. B. McQuesten

✦ A7-(3854) To Dr. Calvin Brooks McQuesten

Glen Tower, New York

WESTERN UNION TELEGRAPH COMPANY
Hamilton, Ont.
March 30, 1887

Father[14] died last night funeral Friday at 3pm do not come if you are not feeling well.

Mary B. McQuesten

✦ A8-(2520) To Dr. Calvin Brooks McQuesten
New York

WESTERN UNION TELEGRAPH COMPANY
Hamilton, March 7, 1888

Isaac Died This Morning. Come At Once.[15]

[Signed] James Chisholm[16]

✦ A9-(4343) To Hilda McQuesten
Toronto, Ontario   Hamilton, Ontario
                                    April 22, 1889[17]

My dear Hilda,

Thank you so much for writing, I would have written you before, but very busy. To-day, with Cally and Ruby's assistance and Tom's too, I have been taking all the books out of Grandpapa's room, preparing to begin house-cleaning to-morrow, for I want to have the upstairs done before you come back.[18] I am getting in a woman and man to help.[19] Have just finished a letter to poor Mary Lillie, for this morning I received a letter from Mrs. George Lillie telling of the death of old Mrs. Lillie.[20] I was greatly shocked after seeing her so lately.

It is very kind of dear Mrs. MacKay to say she enjoys your company. I trust you do anything you can to help her. Did Mary give Mrs. MacKay the note? I am waiting to hear about the cotton in case I get it you could bring it home in the bottom of the trunk. I think there would be room, you could put some things in a shawl strap. Edna missed you very much at first, and did not like it at all that she had not gone. She said she had not been at Mrs. MacKay's yet. I hope Mrs. Black did not disappoint you with your hats. I was very sorry to hear that Mrs. MacKay had to wait too long for you at the station. It was so tiring for her. I hope you will be able to read this letter, it is not a model letter for a mother to write her little daughter, but it is bed time and everyone has to be up early to-morrow, so I am writing as fast as possible. Give my kindest love to Mrs. MacKay and kind regards to Mr. MacKay & much love to yourself and Mary.

                        Your loving Mama,
                        M. B. McQuesten

✦ A10-(4367) To Hilda McQuesten
Hamilton, Ontario   6108 Walnut St.
                                    East Liberty, Pittsburgh, Penn.
                                    October 13, 1890

My dearest Hilda,

Many, many happy returns of your birthday! I am sorry I cannot be there to do something to make the day happier, but I hope you will be able to do something, and if there is any one you would like for tea, if Lizzie has not made any thing,[21] you can go to Crawford's and treat yourselves.[22] However cheer up and be as merry as you can, you are very quiet at home, but when I see the homes of so many children here in busy, dusty Pittsburgh, I feel we cannot thank God enough for such a beautiful home. Yesterday we went to church and Sabbath School, we took Edna with us up to the Bible class, they have a particularly fine teacher and it is quite wonderful to hear them recite all the books of the Bible; there are over 130 in the class. It poured when we came out of church, but Edna walked along under her umbrella. Miss Buchanan[23] wants us to stay for a meeting on Friday & we cannot start on Saturday, so if we hear no bad news from you children we will not start till Monday. Edna sends her love & I enclose a little present with my best love & kisses.

Your loving Mama,
M. B. McQuesten

✦ A11-(4387) To Hilda McQuesten

Hespeler, Ontario

Hamilton, Ontario
August 17, 1892

My dear Hilda,

   It was very thoughtful and kind of you to send me the postal card and the letter. I thought my eldest daughter [Mary] would have done so, not even a message has she sent me, since she left, but I trust she does not entirely forget her mother, though she shows so little attention.

   I would have written before but have been busy every hour. Ruby told you we had a little tea party for Elsie Buchanan Monday—very busy all day mending & going over Alice's [illegible] & my own. Yesterday, we sent Tom off to the Brant House in the morning, and Ruby went in the afternoon taking their tea with them; Edna did not wish to go, so I asked Mrs. Fletcher[24] to let her stay there, as I was going to Dundas. Mrs. Steele[25] had invited Mrs. Grant & me to an "At Home" at her house and to speak about mission work.[26] All the articles given for the box to India were laid out on the piano, and those from the Mission B. [Band] on a table. There were quite a number of ladies and we had tea etc! Mrs. Grant and I stayed till the evening.

   This morning I have been very busy sweeping & dusting getting ready for Miss Fisher, who is coming to stay a few days, then I may go at the dolls in earnest, for I have never touched them since.[27] Mrs. G. took home clothes to alter & Mrs. F. [Fletcher] is making chemises. Little Annie Young brought 3 dressed dolls & a box of little looking glasses have come. The person where Christie M. boarded came yesterday morning to tell me Katie M. was dead, she had lingered for six weeks & died after great suffering, on the 10th. Poor thing! Cally went off on Monday morning.

Am glad we are having such fine weather & trust Mrs. Haigh is not going to any more trouble than she can help.[28] We will expect you Saturday, & you can send your baggage up by Express man. I can pay him at the house. Did I give you those car tickets to bring you home let me know? Give my kindest love to Mrs. Haigh & all the others and I trust both my daughters are not forgetting to love and serve their saviour. With much love earnest prayer that God may keep you both in His care.

Ever your loving mother
M. B. McQuesten

✦ A12-(MCP 1-3b.16) To Calvin McQuesten

c/o "ZION" Divine Healing Mission "Whitehern", Hamilton
Corner Michigan Ave. and 12th St. Friday, July 25, 1896
Chicago, Illinois

My dear Calvin,

You must indeed have got into the clouds when you proposed <u>my</u> starting off to Chicago. You seem to have quite forgotten that I had to borrow the money that took <u>you</u> and that money was what I always set aside for my taxes.[29] Nothing could have induced me to break in upon that, but the almost certainty that you would be able to earn the money that would replace it. And I do not wish to discourage you but you must come home <u>well</u> before I would think of going. I am regaining my strength very slowly indeed, but as the weather is cooler I hope to get along faster. I am much exercised as to what you can do by next Monday, if you are not yet cured. If you think you had better stay longer you must let me know and I will see what I can do. It tries me so to write and makes me so nervous that I can't write any more. May God help you and strengthen your faith.

Your loving Mother
M. B. McQuesten

✦ A13-(MCP 1-3b.9) To Calvin McQuesten

c/o "ZION" Divine Healing Mission "Whitehern"
Corner Michigan Ave. and 12th St. Thursday, August 7, 1896
Chicago, Illinois

My dear Calvin,

Enclosed is the $10. which Mrs. F. in order to relieve me of further distress of mind offered to lend you.[30] I have none to lend or give you, <u>you must surely know this</u>. In my last letter I asked you if you could not get something to do in the Home to pay for your board. Now I am forced to speak plainly. If the spirit commands you to stay still another week you must rely on the spirit <u>not me</u>, to find you the means. The last money sent you was my water-rates for which I am now in debt to Mr. Hope and yet the Bible tells me "owe no man anything."[31] And I am so in debt I do not know which way to turn since you have been in such poor health I have kept things to myself as much as possible so as not to worry you. But you force me to speak when you ask me to lend you $75 to $100 dollars. Are you crazy?

Dr. Dowie, I think makes some very wild statements and I am very much afraid that it is just the excitement you are under that makes you feel better and that afterwards you will be weaker than ever. Your employment on the staff is not a certainty, we have heard nothing more about it, except that the word is still supposed—so that it would not be wise to borrow money from any of your friends because you see you have already to earn the $60 for the taxes. It grieves me to write such a discouraging letter but I can hide things no longer. May God help you in your constant prayer.

Your loving Mother
M. B. McQuesten

[P.S.] I think your ticket expires on Monday.

✦ A14-(4400) To Thomas Baker McQuesten

Hamilton, Ontario

The Sanitarium [sic] Company[32]
Clifton Springs, N.Y.
June 28, 1897

My dearest Tom,

By the time this reaches you, it will be your Birthday. As you know, I would fain be with you that morning, to wish you many happy returns of the day. May God's choicest blessings rest upon you; my own dear boy, and may you long be spared to us all in health and strength! But above all things, I pray, that you may ever be a faithful servant and soldier of the Lord Jesus Christ, never ashamed to own Him as your Captain and gladly defending His cause.

Here we find a great many Christian workers, and when you come to know them, they are all so agreeable. We have an old gentleman at the end of our table, who amuses us and entertains us very often. His table habits are particularly amusing, he rinses each strawberry in a tumbler of water and makes quite a study of his food. He was Consul General to Cuba, was in Cairo when Stanley[33] was on his way home and dined with him and the Khalive. I believe his specialty is geography, and evidently he thinks a great deal of himself. He is very polite certainly, but is nothing to a dear old man, who sits opposite to me. With him I made friends and found he was a veteran missionary from Siam. I cannot begin to tell you what trials he has undergone, it was the most pathetic story I ever heard, told without any boasting.

This is really a most beautiful place, the view from all sides is wonderfully lovely, I only wish you were all here. I have rebelled against some of the treatment, the cold bath and the sulphur water. We are up on the 5th

storey, but the elevators bring you up and down all the time and the view
is far finer. I am beginning to feel a great deal better. Yesterday however
Mrs. MacKay & I decided that we must not eat so many good things, I wish
Calvin & you could get my share. I take the salt-rub and do not object to it.
One stands in a little tub and is doused all over with hot water and then you
are rubbed all over with warm wet salt, which almost skins you, then doused
with cold, rubbed up and slapped and then you want to take a sleep.
Between resting and the various performances, one has very little time.

Now I must close, and send you a trifle, you know I thought of giving
you stamps, but could not discover whether you wanted them, so you can
spend the money as you like best. I do not suppose I can expect a reply from
you, as you are busy studying and I trust you are fixing your mind upon it. I
hope you are good to Edna and that she is well and happy with the rest of
you. With fondest love.

Your loving mother
M. B. McQuesten

✦ A15-(4415) To Calvin McQuesten

c/o Copp Clark Publishing Co.
Toronto, Ontario
"Whitehern"
November 12, 1898

My dear Calvin,

Received your letter last night and was glad to know you were keeping
well. I think your reviews are just wonderful. Mrs. Thomson thinks the
same,[34] she thinks they are more interesting than the books, in fact she has
a great admiration for you generally.[35]

Yesterday poor Peter Buchanan was buried, all the brothers and sisters
came up except Robert.[36] As the funeral was in the church, Mrs. Fletcher
and I went to it and a few other ladies, Mrs. Irving and poor Mrs. Levy.
Quite a number of gentlemen. On Wednesday evening about six o'clock,
the young man who attended Peter went up to his room with a letter and
found him standing in the middle of the floor. After he read it, he called,
"take hold of me, I am falling" he was laid on the bed and became immediately unconscious and was gone in three quarters of an hour. James looked
perfectly awful at the funeral, his face quite haunts me. I spoke to the sisters,
they did not go to the grave. Mrs. Robiti went right away back. Miss Jane
asked for you. Our new girl departs today, after being here a week, is a
delicate girl cannot stand the stairs. Have advertised in the Globe.[37]

The T.H. & B. is finally settled at cost of $1385. The first item cost was
in 1893. Mr. Chisholm would not take a cent except for disbursements.[38] Our
witness fee amounted to $64. I will show you all the items when you come.
Christopher Robinson charged $50. Mr. Thomson says he has charged them

as high as $200. I am borrowing $1000. at 5 per ann. Would not have required to borrow so much, if Webber had paid his interest, but some of the $600. I had deposited in Ham. Prov. [Hamilton Provincial Bank] had to go for taxes. Webber's mortgage is being foreclosed and property taken out of his hands.[39] Mr. C. [Chisholm] says I will not lose anything but I have to wait.

Do you never see poor Mrs. MacKay. Keep the tweed [?] till you come home. Would you like to get one of those light valises canvas with leather corners to bring home your things at Thanksgiving, they have them at Eaton's? Must close or I will lose the post. I have tried to get you a letter always in time for Saturday evening. With much love.

Your mother
M. B. McQ.

✦ A16-(4425) To Calvin McQuesten
c/o Copp Clark Publishing Co.
Toronto, Ontario

"Whitehern"
Monday Evening
January 23, 1899

Dear Calvin,

Mrs. Merrill has brought my rent, so I enclose $2.00, lest you should be short for the tea, and I will send you more, if you get the under-drawers.[40] We have had two students preaching for us these two Sabbaths that Dr. F. [Fletcher] has been ill. The first one was Mr. Findlay Mathewson, the last one, a Mr. Cameron, who said he knew you at our Collegiate.[41]

Be sure and go to see Mr. Dickson amongst your first visits.[42] It is most extraordinary that Mary has not heard one word from May Sutherland.[43] You would have thought she would have been sending a card at Xmas, if she had time for nothing more. There seems to be nothing more to say. With much love.

From your Mother
Mrs. McQuesten

✦ A17-(4436) To Calvin McQuesten
c/o Copp Clark Publishing Co.
Toronto, Ontario

"Whitehern"
January 26, [1901]

My dear dear Calvin,

Your paper reached me, and I know you must be always busy from the many articles contributed. It was really a very realistic report, that of the Victoria Mission and I thought you told it very well, and the Holy Door too was interesting.[44] Your remarks on the Queen's death were most touching and true. I was glad you sent me that "News" for I could not find in our

"Times" the full account of her death-bed. What a quick peaceful passing away was granted to her![45] My great regret is that not one of us was able to see her, and those great pageants of recent date, which can never be repeated. Miss Fisher saw Lord Roberts' reception in London and will probably see the Queen's Funeral but I wish you boys had been able to see something.[46]

We all feel troubled about the upsetting in your house. It breaks in upon your time so much, this changing and yet I fear that is what you will have to do.[47] Jessie Proudfoot knew some ladies who were at a Mrs. Suell's near your Church, and liked it very much, but I do not know her terms. I thought that was the name of the person Janie James was with on Church St. and did not like.[48] Now in the middle of the session it is so hard to find a place.

You may tell Tom, that I had a note from Mr. Gibson saying he would do what he could for Tom, but I now think I will not let him go surveying,[49] I have heard from several that it does not pay in any way.[50] Gordon MacKay has suffered from neuralgia in his back more or less ever since, the result of standing for hours up to the waist in water, & Mrs. Lyle does not think it good at all, so let Tom try and think of something else.[51]

I believe the Glassco affair was settled yesterday. He is going to some sanatorium, we heard.[52] Have to go out on business now, but thought I would write you a few lines, for I am troubled to think of you in such a comfortless home poor fellows. Mary has had tonsillitis all week, but is better. With much love my dear dear son.

Your loving Mother,
M. B. McQuesten

✦ A18-(4479) To Calvin McQuesten

c/o Copp Clark Publishing Co.

"Whitehern"
Toronto, Ontario
May 1, 1901

My dear dear son,

I wish you very many, very happy returns of the day, not only for your own sake, but for my sake. Your happiness and success is mine and you have always been a great help and comfort to me, and it is a great joy to me, that you are using your life to its very best advantage. Dr. McTavish[53] called on Saturday evening and he chatted a long time with us, and told me you took the C.E. meeting on the Sabbath before and gave a fine address, which of course pleased me very much. In Sabbath evening we had a most delightful preacher, the Rev. J. Idrisyn Jones, a Welsh Congregationalist, with a highly cultured voice and manner, and he preached the true Gospel in the sweetest, most winning manner. Mr. Chisholm was charmed with him, his middle name (Welsh) is a Celtic appellation given to his distinguished father and descends to the eldest son. He is to lecture on Friday evening on the British Empire and its supposed connection with the tribes of Israel. Dr. Fletcher introduced me to him as is characteristic.[54] Grandpapa is almost an Admiral now according to the good doctor,[55] and I am to take tea with Rev. Idrisyn Jones on Friday. Look out for him, if he comes to Toronto, he is charming.[56]

I wish you could see Ruby's Bible and the Hymnal, such a beautiful copy. Have not heard from Mrs. MacKay for a few days, but my present plans are to go down on Monday morning, the boat leaves here at 7 o'clock, but I do not expect you to meet me, will have nothing heavy to carry as am sending trunk. Good-bye for the present my dear boy, with best wishes and much love and earnest prayer that God's richest blessings may be yours.

Your loving mother
Mary B. McQuesten

✦ A19-(4500) To Calvin McQuesten

c/o Copp Clark Publishing Co.   "Whitehern"
July 13, 1901

My dear dear boy,

We received our weekly letter from Tom yesterday, so will enclose it, but I want you to return it, I suppose you received the last one, but I know you are always busy; I hope you are feeling rested after all the fatigue of Niagara and the Pan.[57]

We have been busy all week entertaining various people. Thursday Mrs. Davidson from Guelph, Mattie, and Miss MacKay, then the Lockes & Ken came up in the evening to have the long promised ice-cream which was to celebrate Edna's getting through with exams. Then last night Florrie Bell came to tea and in the evening Mrs. Gilbert and Bessie, Blanche and Maddie MacKay. Florrie Bell brought Mary a beautiful little brooch in form of a bird, but she does not look at all well. In the morning Ina and Muriel Hills suddenly appeared. The day before Jessie Brown, chattering as ever! Full of her experience at Philadelphia, so I have a feeling that we must always be ready, not knowing who may descend upon us.[58]

By the way, telephone Mrs. MacKay and find out if she received a letter from me enclosing five dollars. She may have gone to B.C. Would you like me to send you some money now toward the present for Mrs. Buchanan or later?[59] I can send it now if you like.

The garden is quite a show now with hollyhocks in all types and shades they are so beautiful beside the orange lilies and larkspurs, poppies, and the Yucca is most lovely. But sad to say the cherries are all worm eaten, it is so trying. Poor Tom misses the fruit. In a letter from him to Ruby, he says the food was abominable and just the two
[part of the letter is missing].

Have just received your letter.[60] I'm glad to know you are having such satisfaction in your bicycle, do hope no one will steal it. Poor Tom, I will be glad when exams are over. Whilst writing your letter Hilda went out and when she came back announced she had just had a tooth out. It had been talked of for some time and at last poor child, she went off quietly and got it over, the whole top had broken off, so Dr. Clark had to lance it right down to get hold of roots and took them out in <u>three</u> pieces, he lanced four times and put instruments away down, just think of it and she <u>took no gas</u>. Dr. Clark thought her courage wonderful.[61] She never screamed or made any fuss. Well, good-bye once more,

M. B. McQ.

✦ A20-(4521) To Calvin McQuesten

c/o <u>The Montreal Herald</u>[62]   "Whitehern"
Montreal, Quebec   January 23, 1902

My dear Cal,

Will begin my letter this evening, though really there is nothing to say. I posted "The Crisis" to you to-day and also a pair of fine hand-knitted socks given to Tom but too warm for him.[63] Yesterday we had a great fall of snow, but the weather has been beautifully mild this winter and has suited me well. Were you not shocked to see the notice of Gordon Clark's death from diphtheria?[64] Such a fearful trial for his father and mother! Wrote Mrs. Clark and Mrs. MacKay, but have not heard from the latter yet. Mrs. Mullin was in to-day,[65] she met Harry Evans the other day in Toronto, he is in newspaper work too, she understood, at Winnipeg, so I suppose he is with Sanford.

May Cameron was married the other day in Toronto to a Dr. White, who spent an evening here and played tennis once with you and Mary.[66] Hilda met him at a "tea" which Mrs. Lazier gave for them, and he inquired for you.[67] A very pleasant fellow. We hear May Mewburn is engaged to a Dr. Glen McDougal of Toronto who has received the appointment of physician to Boer prisoners at Bermuda at $6.00 per diem. May told Ruby about it, but at that time he had not received this position.[68]

Did we tell you about Jean Vincent's engagement?[69] It was a secret till now. Jean met the man at a wedding last October when she was bridesmaid and he groomsman, it was a case of love at first sight, he comes from Penn Yan, N.Y. state and is the wealthiest man in the place, having a [?] dry goods business. He is about thirty. He was here the other day and brought Mrs. V. a present of 15 yds of beautiful black silk, so he seems to be kind and we are very glad, for Jean is not fit for hard work and Mrs. V. is almost worn out. (Friday)

Have just heard from Mary. They were entertained at "afternoon tea" by T. B. McQ. [Tom] and his friends. Will enclose her letter, as you are so far away, anything from home interests. I am busy preparing my paper for the Conference next month,[70] I mentioned in my last letter, and think I have it well in hand now. Am so glad you are enjoying the snow-shoeing, there is nothing like out-door sport. It is pleasant for you to have Ken with you, to introduce you to his friends.[71]

It seems to me, you made a happy selection in going to Erskine, so many nice people. It seemed quite remarkable that Mr. Slater's sister should go there also, cannot make out her name. So Ida Welker is back, glad she received my letter, for M. [Mary] had sent her a lace collar in it.[72] The Rev. Mr. Young of St. John's lost a fine little boy of six of diphtheria. Edna is enjoying the skating she seems much stronger and works away at her lessons, her music and art school without any grumbling. She has a great amount of determination.

Did you get your book back from Mr. Robinson? I shall ask every letter till you say yes. If you have not, write him at once. Did you send Mr. Dickson a paper? He is one who would be interested. Have just heard from Ruby, she had a terrible time with a bad tooth and strange to say Hilda has had the same. R. was glad to have heard at last from you & Tom, I am afraid she has rather a dull time of it in Ottawa, though she never complains. Well how is the vaccination now! Uncle's took greatly. Tom's has not.[73] Well, dear I hope you are getting on comfortably and that the Montreal Herald is going ahead rapidly for the sake of the staff. By the way H. [Hilda] hears accounts of Sandwell's young lady, being a sad flirt.[74] With much love from all.

Your loving Mother
M. B. McQuesten

✦ A21-(4531) To Calvin McQuesten

c/o The Montreal Herald   "Whitehern"
                                               January 31, 1902

My dear dear boy,

Just to think this is the last day of January and one month of the new year is gone. Well, I am writing this taking my ease, for unfortunately last evening, I started out to take a little parcel over to Maud Shaw's for her to take to Ruby,[75] as she was going to Ottawa to-day, and at the foot of one stone step, in the dark I stepped on edge of plank and my foot rolled over (I had slippers on under my cardinals) the pain was very great and I could not touch my foot to the ground, so I had to crawl up stairs. The greater part of the night I suffered much, but it grew better. This morning to be on the safe side, I had Heurner examine it,[76] but there were not broken bones, so after about cooking my foot in hot water, he wrapped it up in cotton batting, so that it looks like the foot of a gouty old gentleman. However I am thankful it was no worse. The great trouble is it gives the girls more to do waiting on me.

Mary came home fortunately the day before and looks much the better of the rest. Tom wrote me a very sad report and Mary heard the same of the doings of Dr. Warden's son. He married Miss Gooderham, she is a great friend of Leila MacKay's, so I heard all about the wedding. At the time Mrs. MacKay wondered the girl fancied him he was in poor health and nothing to him. However we heard Dr. W. [Warden] was to supplement his salary in the bank. Well, it seems he lived beyond his means, took money from the bank, amounting to $40,000 then ran off. The other day his wife was found at her baby's grave, insane. Is it not perfectly distressing? I am very sorry for his father. To a man in his position to have such an awful trial. Mary understood from Ina Hills that Dr. Warden had paid back that sum, more than <u>twice</u> over. But surely this is an exaggeration. Dr. Warden might be ruined yet just by his sons. What are men like young Warden made of? They must be simple or weak minded, it does seem so insane. Where does the firm come in of going into debt? It is a terrible thing when an individual has not the resolution to live according to his means.[77]

Heurner told me this morning that Mrs. Dr. Wallace had died at the hospital after some operation, she was a daughter of Dr. Leslie.[78] Well I am glad you can enjoy the snow-shoeing, the weather has been <u>very</u> cold, so grateful it only lasted a few days. On one of the coldest—last Monday, <u>Mrs. Bell</u> came to see me, so we had a fine fire in the drawing room with five o'clock tea and enjoyed it very much. Poor Mr. Bell is worried to the death with the whole of them, even Herbie constantly wanting money and most rude when refused; last year used about $600. What would become of me with such a family![79]

Had a very nice long letter from Ida Welker. I think she & the Col. are glad to see you, whenever you call.[80] Well, my dearest child, I hope you have found a comfortable home, I should have thought you could have secured one, before giving notice as I would think they would be harder to find in the middle of the season. But you probably know, it is somewhat discouraging to have to spend years in boarding-rooms. That must be a remarkable family you mentioned, with all the sons. I do hope you will keep clear of gyps, and when you change, find some motherly person. I feel as if there was no one to look after you, only you could send a card to Ida. When Ken was there, I felt quite comforted, he is such a kind fellow. He sent us some pretty cards (postal) from Quebec.[81] It seems months since Xmas, wish you were not so far away. With love from all and much from,

Your loving Mother
M. B. McQuesten

✦ A22-(4535) To Calvin McQuesten

c/o The *Montreal Herald*   "Whitehern"
                                             February 5, 1902

My dear dear Calvin,

It is to be hoped you will not be caught like Naylor Briggs whom I told you about. I think he married the widow, with whom he lodged, so <u>beware</u>, <u>beware</u>. I do not know yet all your plans, but thought you intended to board with some French family. As you speak of giving $6.00 a month for room suppose you go elsewhere for meals, I am sorry to know you do this in the winter. Last Sabbath for instances, you could have taken a day's rest. Ruby in her letter was wishing for the good old days, when no snow ploughs cleaned the street, you could not be expected to go out. My foot is improving as fast as could be expected, but cannot walk on it yet. I am just as well in bed for it is so bitterly cold. Hope it will soon be milder, for cold is awful misery, but am not complaining for I <u>have</u> everything to make me comfortable.

[I] am sending you the will to look it over. There is just one flaw in it, the unmarried girls should have more than $400 when one or some are married, or if present income revenue permits, for I do not think $400 is very much & if two of them, say, got married, the other two ought to be able to see a little of the world by travelling, if they chose, after living so many years of economy. But with your young brains, if you will just think over if it is fair to you all. Of course, if anything happened to me just now, I scarcely know how the girls could live as we do & give Tom $350.[82] Mr. Chisholm's hundred dollars & Ruby have kept him this year;[83] of course the new roofs on homestead & Bold St. have been a heavy load. Wish I could be sure of you all having a good income, but I leave you all in our Heavenly Father's Hands who will never fail you.

Mrs. Fletcher told us that the story Dr. Fletcher heard of Dr. Warden's son was somewhat different. It was at the time of the MacEagle [sp?] Winnie [sp?] failure, young Warden in some way lost $27,000. His father was much incensed with the Gooderhams for some reason & sent his son away. The wife said to be in sanitarium with nervous prostration.[84]

Ruby tells me that Prof. Gordon of Kingston has two sons in Asylum and another one at Upper Canada, the fit of insanity came on & he ran away, & they do not know where he is.[85] Mrs. Bennett tells that Dr. Barclay's sons are very wild & drink terribly.[86] It is a sad world.

Ken [Trigge] sent newspaper with account of storm in Quebec etc. Was it not terrible. It snowed a good deal here, but nothing remarkable, only it is so cold. Jean Vincent wrote Hilda to-day from Penn-Yan [*sic*] her future home. She is delighted with everything and everybody, her fiance seems to have lots of money, her diamond ring from Tiffany's is a beautiful one.[87] You must take great care of will & send it back soon as you have had time to think it over; for it has been a long time on the way.

Anna Laidlaw took the girls to a concert last night.[88] We are very dull
this winter. Mr. Haddow is to lecture on "Jack Cannuck [*sic*] & his friends."[89]
Some of the young people were convulsed when Dr. Fletcher announced
it as John Canada, evidently thinking the title undignified for the pulpit.
Mr. Graham, of course, upset our girls nearly entirely.[90] By the way,
Mrs. Sutherland & the girls are much pleased with Arthur's wife "a sweet
dear little thing." Was not that a terrible thing of young Aleck McKeand
committing suicide or taking overdose of morphine at hotel in Buffalo. He
had no home poor fellow.[91]

Do hope you will not take cold. Is your room warm?

Your loving Mother
M. B. McQuesten

✦ A23-(4544) To Calvin McQuesten

Montreal, Quebec   "Whitehern"
                                                        [February 10, 1902]

Dear Cal,

Am enclosing you a letter from Mrs. Grant in reply to a question "How
much does it cost a single woman to live?"[92] After I wrote you it occurred to
me, that the whole arrangement of that will is a mistake.[93] To begin with the
present income is about $1700, out of that Tom could not receive $350 a
year and leave enough for girls to live on. Ruby has really paid his way, with
a little $40 from Mrs. MacKay last year & Mr. C.'s [Chisholm] this year. Of
course if the house could be sold that would save the taxes but they would
need it to make a home. So it seems to me that all the present income
must be left to the unmarried daughters. [94] You see the interest from present
investments is about $950. But of Montreal stock $400, and rent from
Bold St. after taxes, repairs, insurance are deducted is about $350. The taxes
on homestead are $226 & water rates $48, so that the girls home here is a
cheaper one. To think of our income one would think we should have
plenty, but of course during the last 3 yrs we have been paying for roofs,[95]
but it certainly is marvellous how much it takes to live even with greatest
economy. My foot makes very slow progress, I have borrowed Mrs. Davidson's crutches & so hop about the house, but am afraid it will be some time
before I can walk about.[96] Will write end of the week.

Your loving Mother
M. B. McQuesten

[P.S.] Return Mrs. G's letter, it is worth keeping.

✦ A24-(4549) To Calvin McQuesten

Montreal, Quebec   "Whitehern"
                                              February 10, 1902

My dear dear boy,

The two first topics just now are the Lancefield affair and the old mortgage. I suppose you see the Times everyday, let me know, <u>if you do not</u>. I think it is time that any person holding a position of trust should forfeit it if he is known to bet or gamble. L. always seemed to me a silly sort of man.[97]

I was also sent with a notice re mortgage by the law firm of Keir, Davidson & Paterson, Toronto; it seems strange to me that any government should do such a contemptibly small mean trick as even <u>try</u> to get the money so many years having lapsed. What have we to do with it. Fancy us having to pay out money to the government for no debt of ours, I'd like to see myself.[98]

Jean Vincent has just returned from visit at Penn Yan, the home of the young man. She is perfectly delighted with every thing they seem to be very nice & very wealthy people, Mrs. Vincent is just delighted, considers it an answer to prayer; so our Mary immediately suggested I should begin to pray for them.[99]

It did me good to read your description of your new quarters. You really seem to have been very fortunate, am so glad to know your room is warm, we have had such bitter cold weather, I hope poor Ruby is not freezing at that college. What troubles me about her too is that she never gets an invitation to any really nice home or has a chance to meet any one. Although she sees more than the girls at home do, it is terribly monotonous for them, tho' they never complain. However some day, something may turn up for them. Emily Colquhoun came in to tell the girls all the fun she had in Toronto this year, she met a Mr. Coats who was just leaving for Ottawa, she liked him & told him to be sure & call on Ruby.[100] By the paper, I see he left "The Globe" for Sabons Gazette. Did you know him? Maud Shaw had gone to Ottawa & had her veil & feathers sent down from Toronto for the presentation ceremony, when old Mrs. Shaw died. It was perfectly shocking the way those girls went on at the poor old woman, being so inconsiderate.

It is quite funny to think of all you fellows sticking together. It would have paid Mrs. Charles to feed you better. Every time I think of that old mortgage I boil with indignation. Do not feel as if I would ever vote (in influence) for the grit government, it does not make any difference whether they press the matter or not, I am done with them, they must be a low down contemptible lot, & precious hard up to stoop to raising money in any such unjust manner, even if the law permitted, it is most unjust, simply robbery. Cannot somebody find out who originated the idea? The thing should be shown up. Have not been able to hear what Mr. Chisholm thinks as he has been out every time Hilda went.

Well, I am still in bed I borrowed Mrs. Davidson's crutches & went downstairs, but every one said I would get better so much quicker if I kept quiet, that I took the advice as I am so afraid of not being able to go to Toronto on 25th. Tom writes that Mrs. MacKay is very poorly. [I] thought of going to St. Catharines with Leila [MacKay], who is quite cured now, but very weak.[101] So have given up all idea of staying there & will not be able to attend Student volunteer meetings, but will just go down for the day. James Buchanan & wife have been here for a few days the girls did not see her, but from those who did, she does not seem to be out of the ordinary in appearance. Mrs. Watson gave a 'tea' for them but she never invites us.

How is Ken getting along? Have asked this before. Has he been back in Montreal since he went on the Road?[102] Gordon Clark had got another diphtheria & was thought out of danger, when suddenly his heart failed. It occurred to me the other day that you are not so very far from the old homestead now (if it is not pulled down) how would you like to go there for your holidays? You could inquire price of ticket to Manchester N.H.[103] Had a long letter from Ida Welker. Every one who comes from Vancouver seems to have liked her so much. Am afraid it will be lonely in Montreal. It is an olden place. Well, take care of yourself dear, with love from all.

Your loving Mother
M. B. McQuesten

[P.S.] Did you get the book from Mr. R.?

✦ A25-(4582) To Calvin McQuesten

Montreal, Quebec

"Whitehern"
March 12, 1902

My dear dear Cal,

Well, I am glad to be able to write you once more, I intend to go about glasses some day, but must wait a little. In one of my letters to you, I suggested you might take a trip to the Homestead for your holidays and asked you to inquire about the railway fare. It cannot be very far from Montreal to Manchester N.H. So I told you to carefully save up your money for that and for clothes, but you took no notice. Your letter came a little late, for we could do nothing about Jack's present on Saturday afternoon, but H. went out as early as possible on Monday. We enclosed card in small envelope to Mrs. John Rioch.[104] On Sabbath went to church as it was communion, but felt somewhat shaky but am continuing to go out everyday, but find I can only go a short distance at a time, my heel is so very weak, it is not my <u>ankle</u> at all.

[I] Had a long letter from Miss Fisher from Rome, she is having a fine time. Was wishing you could be sent to report to Coronation,[105] but when I hear of the small-pox in London, would rather not. Was it not alarming to hear of the Varsity students? Tom is very thankful his vaccination took.[106] He sent me such an encouraging appreciative letter written on the 7th, the day of his father's death, that it cheered me very much. I was so pleased he remembered and he always has, it seems to be fixed on his mind.[107] He has applied to Dr. Bell[108] for position on Geological Survey and I have written Mr. Malloch[109] and Mr. Gibson. Hope he will get it but of course it is very doubtful. He says you get $45 a month for five months and there is nothing else to be heard of. Suppose you never hear of anything down there.[110] Poor Charlie Bell is in a sad fix, it was understood that a year ago Mr. Bell gave Mr. Pringle notice and Charlie was this year to have the place, now it turns out he never said a word to Pringle and Charlie is wild between his father and prospective mother-in-law, thinks his only hope is in these miserable plays he keeps writing. To do which he sits up through the night and drinks coffee to keep himself awake and of course in the most miserable health & his poor mother dragging herself downstairs to cook something he can eat.[111]

It is very satisfactory to me to think that you are in such comfortable quarters if you are ill and have a friend or two to look after you. Has Sandwell been getting any advance yet? Little Mr. Burns was inquiring for you, and wished to be most kindly remembered to you. Mary had a letter from Nellie Mullin this morning and she inquired for you & the widow.[112] She likes it very much at Johns Hopkins, but for the first six months they do cook & housing aids work to test their physical strength.[113] Mrs. MacKay writes that Leila leaves for Rome to-day (Thursday) and invites me down but will not go till after Easter. By the way is Ruby coming to you there, where will you put her? Should think it not very good time of the year to visit Montreal. Well, dear, I hope you are well & get encouragement some-times in your work. Everything gets very monotonous sometimes.

Tom writes that my paper was considered the best. Read at Conference but from member of our own board not a word, only have asked me to write another for annual meeting in London which I declined.[114] With love from all and very much from,

Your loving Mother
M. B. McQuesten

✦ A26-(4588) To Calvin McQuesten

Montreal, Quebec

St. Mary's, Ontario
July 1, 1902

My dear dear boy,

It seems such a long time since I wrote you and now that all are at home (I expect) you seem to be so alone, I felt I must write you a few lines. It seems to me months since I left home and I am counting the days till I get home. It seems too bad, for people are very kind and I am having a quiet rest, just the thing I needed, but still I want to be with the family, especially as I have not seen Ruby since Xmas, but Mrs. Irving would have been offended if I had not stayed two weeks, so I could say nothing, but will be home on Saturday. Unfortunately we have had cold wet weather. It poured on Sabbath so that we could not go to church in the morning but in the evening heard Mr. Wilson of India. You know Mr. Grant's church is Mr. Wilson's old charge. Then yesterday Mrs. Wilson addressed a ladies' meeting, of course I had to take some part, but it does not agree with me to have the least excitement and I rather regret having the quiet broken in upon.[115]

One draw-back to St. Mary's is that the hills which make the place so beautiful, make the walking so fatiguing, you can go no place without climbing a hill. Have just written poor Mrs. Watson. Isn't it most distressing? For I fancy Hope was the only one of the three younger ones worth anything at all.[116] Wasn't that place in Muskoka just about where you were? Just to think of the escape Tom Mewburn had. If that poor boy had some one now just to direct his thoughts to the mercy of God.[117] Last week was a terrible week for many.

What a wonderful thing is the King's recovery! And the more one hears of him the more we are lead to admire him. Have you read several articles about him in the Globe, showing him to be no ordinary man after all? I am sure there was a great deal of real sympathy with him, particularly as he had waited so long for the throne. Yesterday's Globe had a very thoughtful piece taken from some one who expresses the belief that this illness has drawn out the affection and esteem of his people far more than the gorgeous pageantry of the Coronation ceremony would have done, which I have no doubt is very true. And it will surely impress upon the minds of all, that there is no point of these gigantic extravagant displays and that men CANNOT plan and arrange everything at their own will. There is a higher power that can step in and bring all their plans to nought. It does seem as if the King at least, could never forget this warning voice, and I am sure it has made many stop and think.[118]

Well, it is dinner time, & post time. Was so sorry you lost your holiday. Hope to-day you are having some diversion. Have all your friends deserted you. I wonder if Ida W. [Welker] has any notion of coming to H. [Hamilton] this summer. Think I ought to write her. If you see her, you can give my love & tell her I am thinking about her & intend writing. The one comfort about this cool weather is, it will suit your work. With fondest love my darling son.

Your loving Mother
M. B. McQuesten

✦ A27-(4601) To Calvin McQuesten
Montreal, Quebec   "Whitehern"
                                                    July 4, 1902

My dear dear Cal,

Once more I am in the bosom of my family, came home on Friday evening and we have been groaning with heat ever since. I have such fine sleeps at St. Mary's, that I feel much better, though one is almost helpless in such weather. Tom feels the heat frightfully he is so full blooded, his face looks bursting. Have been writing Mrs. MacKay. Mary says Mr. M. seemed very far gone when she was there, he is in his 88th year.

"Drummond in Britain," your Tatler was fine.[119] Tom thought it the best yet, gave it to Mr. Chisholm, he says he likes to read your articles, they are so bright. Mr. Brierley may not be able to help it, but his dealings with you are certainly very dishonest in my opinion.[120] Have you sent your pieces to Mr. Colquhoun?[121] If you have when you come up, you can call & see him & tell him about them.

Now as to the canoe, I have tried to make up my mind to stand it, but simply cannot, the anxiety is more than I can stand, your time at home will be very brief and the girls want to have all the fun with you possible. We are planning various diversions and want to enjoy every moment of your stay, it will be all too short. I feel as if I could not let you out of my sight. Besides I know you need all your money.[122] Am afraid it scarcely pays to come up by boat as you only see "The Thousand Islands." Well, my dear, must close as it is very late and will write again soon, with fondest love.

                                        Your affectionate Mother
                                        M. B. McQuesten

✦ A28-(4635) To Calvin McQuesten
Montreal, Quebec   "Whitehern"
                                                    September 10, 1902

My dear dear boy,

It seems a very long time since I wrote you, when I did Ken [Trigge] was just here and his visit was the occasion of most trying experience for all concerned. Of course, I had to have a very plain talk with him and when I spoke to him of his not being an abstainer, he was very frank and open, but simply said that for him to be an abstainer meant that he must throw up his position and then I discovered that it was all far worse than I imagined. It is his business to be most agreeable to the firm's customers and to this end Mr. Beardmore gives him and instructs him to go to any expense in treating, asking men to lunch or dinner and when he does so of course he must drink or smoke with them. Well, of course, I said it was far worse than I had any idea, that I always heard a traveller's life was one of great temptation but I thought it meant that others would ask him to drink but in this case, <u>he</u> was asking others, in fact was making his living by tempting men to do wrong. What an awful position! So I said I could never consent. On explaining the state of affairs to H. [Hilda] she agreed with me, but it was a most distressing time and really made us ill. Ken felt so terribly, particularly as he said, there was nothing else he could do and all business is carried on in this way. But Hilda I must say was wonderfully brave and conscientious and though she had quite determined to take him, she withstood him and said no, she would not marry a man whose living was made in such a way. He himself said, that no one had ever put it before him as we had, that he was given liquor at home from when he was twelve years old and never knew it was any harm. But now, he said, he saw, that he was committing a sin every day of his life. But where to find another situation is the difficulty. It does seem a most iniquitous thing, this treating system, Ken had been pretty well disgusted I think with what he saw at Chateau Frontenac at Quebec. I do trust this may be a turning point in his life and that he may have strength to give it up and if only some good opening would present itself, I think he might become a really good man. I certainly spoke to him very strongly & he seemed impressed, but do not know what his parents will think. Think they will be very indignant with us. I would have certainly said no at the very beginning but had not the least idea of the business methods pursued, until I spoke to Ken about being a teetotaller. That Beardmore is one of the worst men he could be with, if he continues with him, he will be lost. What sort of business is Will Leslie in? Could he be any help to Ken? Of course I do not know what Ken means to do or whether he will try to make a change, he had such glowing prospects, it was a great blow to him, poor fellow. I am very very sorry, for I think he would have suited H. very well & she seemed quite heart broken but we must hope that it may all be overruled for their lasting good. All this fuss quite spoiled the last week of R. [Ruby's] visit, she went off on Monday morning and of course I felt blue for many days but live in hopes.[123]

I gave two or three of the Heralds to Colin Fletcher to read & the Doctor [Fletcher] came home and wanted to keep one to read which he had not finished, when I went for it yesterday of course he could not find it. Please try & get me another, August 30th, one of the most interesting, I was so provoked at losing it, I would not have taken it up to the Manse only I thought Colin had not seen any of your writings & he was quite interested in seeing them, but the Doctor is awfully stupid.[124]

The Tatler of today is very good too, that Eagle & the Serpent is a most remarkable thing, a keen satire, I should call it, especially that part where "people of brains are invited & reward immortality" that's pretty good.[125]

Had a card from Mrs. MacKay from Banff on their way home, can you believe it? They were to leave Toronto on August 16th & her card was written at Banff on September 5th & were leaving next day for Winnipeg. Did you ever know anything like them? That restless Donald? Well, dear, I wish you good success with your tale, but hope you are not working yourself to death & the hair off your head.

Perhaps you had better not say anything to Ken for a while till you see if he speaks to you about it. But I told him "I had just set to work & cross-questioned you, because I had to know how he lived," and you had said a great many kind things about him. What you may say about him, must write on a separate page, because the family always wants to hear your letters, and it would not be pleasant for H. to hear Ken discussed. With much love my dear dear boy.

Your loving Mother

M. B. McQuesten

✦ A29-(4647) To Calvin McQuesten

Montreal, Quebec   "Whitehern"

September 17, 1902

My dear dear boy,

This morning had a call from your old friend Nelson, he was hoping to see you, of course I told him all about you and he told me he had been doing Evangelistic work through Canada through the country I think. Had left Dowie some time ago. His address is Fergus. The friend who was with him (Brooks by name) as you were not here, would not give him time even to sit down (I had opened the door) but hurried him off.[126] I was sorry for I like his face and would like to have seen more of him. We received the paper yesterday, I am very glad you had the opportunity and such a good one of meeting the Premier[127] for the really most important event in connection with the Coronation was the meeting together of the Colonial Premiers.

In your letter, you were speaking of Ken's affair, well, you see on talking with me, he never for one moment thought it possible that he could give up drinking himself, he said, it would not be the thing at all to ask a man & take nothing yourself therefore we could not think of it. You see, I had thought he could make up his mind at least to give it up himself, but he did not even propose to promise that and then the more I thought of it, the more I feel convinced that it was all wrong, I do not see that any man is likely to become a Xtian who is engaged in such a business, for he is doing wrong to his fellow and no blessing can come to him. When Ken left me, he professed to see it, as I did. I wrote to Mrs. Trigge, regretting the result, but she has not answered me; they will probably be convinced that we treated Ken badly, by not saying what we did at first, but you see, I never knew till he told me, that the business involved him in such a practice. I thought he could be an abstainer, if he wished. Ken could not be in a worse place than he is with that man Beardmore, although I do not think Ken admires him as much as you think he does.

To-day Tom & I went up to the cemetery to prune the shrubs, for Frederick came down & showed Tom what to do with ours on the lawn, this is the time to do the spring shrubs! he says. I am glad to say H. does not seem to be fretting at all, but is quite cheerful, I think she felt so thoroughly convinced that she had done what was right. You know it is a terrible thing for a girl to take a man who is not decided in his principles. Tom and I also took a look at the collection of fowl at Dundurn; the most terrible set of mongrels you ever saw, Tom was wild with them, thought they would do for a comic article. Oh by-the-way about Thanksgiving, much as we would all delight to have you here, I feel sure you ought not, it is such a tiresome journey, that I would much rather think of you as taking a good sleep and resting yourself, even if you go to Ottawa, you are up half the night. I asked you before I think, is Mr. Leslie any good at helping on young men who want to do right? Am thinking of K. [Ken Trigge]. Must close, with much love from all.

Your loving Mother,
M. B. McQuesten

✦ A30-(4651) To Calvin McQuesten

Montreal, Quebec   "Whitehern"
                                             September 24, 1902

My dear, dear, boy,

Your letter was most satisfactory and your conversations with Leslie[128] & Johnson.[129] I consider it most Providential that you were able to have these, because in my own mind I felt it could not be true that all travellers must drink themselves. I quite believe they must offer refreshments, but it seemed to me, a man of any strength of mind need not take it himself. Of course Ken insisted he could not and I just saw at once that he did not want to. From your letter, you seem to think that I did not leave H. to settle it. Perhaps Ken made you think so. But this is just what I did. The first night he came, he took advantage of my absence to speak to her, though he was not to say a word for a year! But I have found out, he can twist things to suit himself. When H. told me, I was very much displeased because I wished to talk it over with him about this drink question and see what he would do, she poor weak child never said a word to him on the question, though I told her what you had said when you were here. So when I told her all that I had found out from Ken, she was thunderstruck & at once said "I would never do it!" and became at once just as determined as I was; so do not think I have coerced her, she entirely agreed with me, for she has an equal horror of these drinking men.

When Ken went away he professed to see the whole thing as we see it & I did not insist he should get out of the business but that he could become an abstainer himself. However, his parents did not support me, in my view, and he wrote H. that they did not think he could give it up, thought the matter should have been spoken of at first. I had plainly told Ken, that I never dreamed that his business compelled him to drink until he told me so himself so I could not have spoken sooner and I never thought people who are so strict about other things as the Brethren are, could countenance such a practice. I said, I postponed the thing for a year to test him to see what stuff he was made of & then I cross-questioned you and insisted upon being told just what sort of life he led. And thank God, I was led to do this. H. is not breaking her heart at all. I never thought she was very deeply in love, but because her friends were getting married, she thought it would be nice to have a beau too, & when he is here he seems able to get round her, you know she is very tender hearted but after when she read your letter, (I destroyed the one page), it all seemed to dawn upon her, & she came upstairs to me with her eyes blazing, & said "I am thoroughly angry, just furious and I'll give him, Ken, a piece of my mind." She seemed just to see the whole thing, he would give up her, before he would give up his glass. I never thought him good enough for her, & I am sure of it now, a poor weak chap and like people with very little brains, hard to convince. Mrs. Trigge has never replied to my letter. Do not know if she means to call, when up at Arthur's wedding. I hope to give her a piece of my mind, for I am boiling. To think of people professing to be Xtians and taking no stand against a vice which is the ruin, body & soul of millions, and at the same time with-drawing themselves from others, would not go into one of our churches, as it would look as if they countenanced us, Mr. T. told me this. At the same time giving her son liquor since he was twelve. Well, she will not get one of my fine daughters, I can tell her, for her son![130]

Yesterday an invitation to the Lyle wedding came for Hilda and Tom.[131] It has been a hard question to decide on the guests, the elders (of whom there are 16) the managers & trustees with other organizations in the church with their wives & the Warden connection swell the number to such an extent that just a few of Mary's friends could be asked, so we think it very friendly of them to ask any of us.

Nan [Turner] Gilmour is home, we hear that the Gilmours behaved very shabbily, the father took back the house he had given, also a cheque, saying it was a loan, there was no will, so they took every thing they could. Mrs. Gilmour never wrote to Nan for four weeks. Isn't it extraordinary the way people act?[132]

Did I tell you when home about the report of Dr. Wilkie taking Opium? Mrs. Ross says it is utterly untrue[133] & he is preparing when he has his plans laid to make an exposure of the whole thing. A lady missionary went to a ball, Mr. Wilkie thought it right to remonstrate, after that all was wrong.[134] Dear dear, whom can we trust? I do not know that you have heard all that I have in connection with dancing. You know in India amongst the natives, that only such girls who are all prostitutes dance at public parties. So it was a dreadful thing for a missionary to do. Do not breathe it, but it was Miss Sinclair of whom we all thought so much. What next? [135]

I was so pleased to hear of the stand Johnson takes, if there were only more like him. I think your writing on the passing of the sword was really beautiful and all you said about the magazines was so well put as if you knew what you were talking about.[136] When you do this work do you have just as much reporting to do or do they allow you time during the day's work for "The Tatler" because if they do not it is pure robbery.

Had a five minutes call from Col. McCrae, he asked for every member of the family, was sure Jack would be delighted to see you & asked if you saw him. Said the proprietor of the Star made $100,000 last year.[137] Tom went down for his 'Sup' on Saturday; got a room too on Alexander St. for $1.25 & same night went on to Desoronto for the firing competition on Monday, coming back that night, just one company with the officers went down & he is now with Martin Sergeant. It's too bad, but they kept them all day Sunday preparing the [?]. I do not know what is to be done with the volunteers persistent ignoring of the Sabbath. Tom did not like to refuse because unless they had the required number of men they could not compete, & they had hard work to get the men & we did not know they would have to work as they did.[138] With much love.

Your loving Mother
M. B. McQuesten

✦ A31-(4686) To Calvin McQuesten

Montreal, Quebec

"Whitehern"
October 30, 1902

My dear dear boy,

There is nothing of any account to relate. The weather has been so pleasant that I have been using it to make calls and on Monday walked as far as Locke and Hannah and home again, so you see how strong I am getting.[139] Yesterday I turned out my closet, which is a great achievement. After tea went over to T.H. & B station as Archie Mullin was going off and I wanted to bring his mother back with me. Archie goes to Baltimore to see Nellie and sails from New York on Saturday. Of course every one hoots at the idea of his having to go to Scotland in order to study but I trust he will make something of himself. Mrs. Mullin heard that Jean McIlwraith was making $50 a week in New York and I am going to find out how she does it. But of course she has been reading and working for years.

What I am convinced is your best course is to give your mind this winter to reading. If you can get your "Tatler" done in the day time, which you must do, then make a determined effort to read in the evening. I should think history would be of most practical value to you, but you probably know. And you must just feel contented to go on quietly on the present pay and use your spare time to store your mind before you could expect to start out in New York. If you think it over, you do well if you have sufficient to live comfortably whilst you fit yourself by storing your mind for better work. In all these books worth reading the authors are evidently widely read, so that it is absolutely necessary that you take time for this before you go further. Whatever course you pursue in the future you require to have a well-furnished mind so I would just settle down to this and not mind whether you get a higher salary or not. Though it would be very agreeable you would probably have to give more time and might not have so much time to yourself, which I believe is the most important thing for you now. There is going to be a steady demand for good writing.

Hedley has been very slow about packing those things for Ken [Trigge] but he promised to get things off this morning, he took them from here last week. You can tell Ken. When the pears reach you, [words missing from page] card & you will see "ready" open it. The other can be put in a cool dark place for a while. Have also found hat brush which I will send you. You left the soft shirt too, you will find it at bottom of pear basket.

Mrs. Scott was so pleased with your report of Gen Booth,[140] that she asked for some more of your writings.[141] Ruby & I both enjoyed "The Tatler" on the Canadian books. Who writes the "As seen by Her"? After looking at it again I see it is most quotes. I liked a piece in it by Margaret Hall on the way girls spoil young men.[142] Must close. Take care of yourself dear with fondest love.

Your loving Mother
M. B. McQuesten

✦ A32-(4713) To Calvin McQuesten

Montreal, Quebec   "Whitehern"
                                    December 3, 1902 (Wednesday)

My dear Cal,

Since you wrote, you have, I suppose, been to Quebec and back, but it is not a very good time of the year for travelling and I fancy you have winter with you. With us it is pleasant and mild with no snow. The girls worked hard last week counting "spots" tempted by the money. H. [Hilda] R. [Ruby] & Edna made a desperate effort, but each one got a different result so as Ruby had done hers with the greatest deliberation, they thought it best to send hers, but scarcely hope for a prize, for though the McQuesten family has much to be thankful for they have never had windfalls.

In Saturday's papers was published the enclosed protest against the Referendum and really it made my blood boil to think of these miserable men coming out publicly against the Act. Of course they would not approve of it, but they could keep quiet for of course it is far too stringent a law to pass.[143] However I got it on my mind that I must answer it so I got a Spectator & Herald to see their Editorials and I enclosed the Herald's which suited my purpose. So I wrote all three papers under the nom de plume of "courage" and am anxiously waiting to-night's paper to see if it is in. Of course I could have said, but was afraid to make it too long, for fear they might not put it in or people would not read it. It is not likely it will do any good, but it is so hard to keep quiet as Mrs. Mullin says when she sees these brilliant saloon windows she could just go up and write "HELL" upon them. Will send you paper if it is in.[144]

We are having special services every night this week up to the Communion, different ministers are speaking. Last night Mr. McGillivray from Newmarket, a brother of the one in London.[145] I was too tired to go out but Mary said he was splendid, I hope to hear him to-night. We are to hear different ministers also on Sabbath all this month, for at the annual meeting the Doctor [Fletcher] is to announce that he would like an assistant, but the elders & managers had to insist that they were to have the choosing.[146] The Doctor was surprised that we did not care for Gillies Eadie, but unless we get a first class man, we cannot keep up at all.[147] We have now to meet a deficit of $600.

Well my dear, as to Xmas presents we had no plans because we do not want to spend any money unnecessarily. I am thankful to say, that my money is lasting out wonderfully, but I have just to be careful, when only one house on Bold St. is rented. If you are not giving Ruby a book, you can go shares with me in a little scent and I think I'll get Edna a knife. If there is any thing you have in mind, just let me know and I might share in it too, because there are so many of us for you to think of and you must need all you have.[148]

On Thursday we have the Leper meeting here and a Dr. Carleton from India is to speak. Ruby is expecting Annie Anderson, a niece of Mrs. Ross, to visit us for a few days next week. Old Mrs. Moncur has had an attack of paralysis and they do not know whether she will linger or recover.[149]

Well, it seems impossible to think of anything else to say. Mabel Fairgrieve is being married to-day, the wedding is in their own house and just the relatives; last week they gave a large "tea" as a farewell. Well, good bye, dear, take care of yourself. H. has never got her photo back yet. Isn't he nasty?[150] With much love from all.

Your loving Mother
M. B. McQuesten

✦ A33-(4717) To Calvin McQuesten

Montreal, Quebec

"Whitehern"
Wednesday [December 10, 1902]

My dear dear boy,

It is so cold that my ideas seem frozen up and I have not time to reckon what day of the month it is. Yesterday was the Mission Band Sale and the girls had made and gathered a wonderful lot of pretty things. Mr. McPherson always gives the sugar, and this year Hilda and Ruby made it all. Such a tempting array of platters. The Mission Band was delighted with itself but the seniors did not do so well and our auxiliary is about $25 behind. It is thought our sale was injured by a big Scotch Lunch, which was held at the Central Church for two days and crowds flocked to it. It seems too contemptible, this lunch was given to pay for colored windows in the church. Miserable set always spending on themselves. And our church is getting so poor with a $600 deficit, and many people in it with means. In our own auxiliary I notice it, such carelessness in their method of giving, no wonder the church suffers.[151]

Well, I sent you the Herald with its reference to my letter, in one way it was courteous enough but underneath there was a bitter spirit it seems to me. Being charitable is one thing and speaking the truth is another. Sometimes we are called upon to speak the truth.[152]

So I am to be trotted to the Oculist, you sent far too much money, my dear boy, I hope it will not cost so much. You must just have robbed yourself. There are many calls at this time. It seems to me the weather is very cold for the season. I am hoping you will not get a cold. H. will write once more to Ken to either send or hand his photo to you. I would not like you to speak to him at all.

The temperance people here are not at all discouraged but some really jubilant with the results, you see both Toronto & Hamilton—the Cities— gave majorities and I think many who did not vote, would not vote against it. Do you know there were drunkards (poor things) who voted for it. One told Dr. F. [Fletcher] he did so in self-defence. They are a miserable godless drinking set in Montreal, and many like them here.[153]

Well, my dear, I am very thankful, we shall see you at Xmas, for one can never write about all they would like to talk about. We are expecting Annie Anderson, Mrs. Ross's niece, to-morrow. To-day we have the Annual meeting of Jewish Mission and the girls are going to assist at "Tea" at Mrs. Taylor's. I was asked to pour tea but would not forsake the Jews.[154] Now do not forget Mrs. Skeoch's address.

Your loving Mother
Mary B. McQuesten

[P.S.] I have found a good scheme for warming my feet, I just have a warm soap stone (whilst I am sitting) under my feet.

✦ A34-(4759) To Calvin McQuesten

Montreal, Quebec "Whitehern"
January 28, 1903

My dear dear boy,

You will, I fear think me very slow not to have followed your advice more quickly about selling the stock. But Mr. C. [Chisholm] did not help me in the matter, he advised me to go slowly and in the meantime am afraid it has gone down a little. To-day I had a long talk with Mr. Logie and he thought I had better sell, until I said that I could not quite see why I should sell, and in the end only have 21 shares, when I might use other money (which only brings in 5 percent) to buy up the new shares and at the rate given the stockholders it would give me 6 percent, and I would then have 23 shares in the bank.[155] Did you think of it in this way? I have $500 waiting in Ham. Prov. [Bank] for investment and as the call comes for paying in Mr. C. had said before he would lend me or we would manage someway to make amount up. Perhaps there is something still that I do not see. Of course selling now I would lose $20 off my dividend in June, unless they issue the new shares at once or very soon. I do not fancy the value will go down very much till after June 1st.

Ruby's letter on Saturday brought the unwelcome news of another scarlet fever patient but she had been taken to infirmary, so they were hoping there would be no other cases. I most sincerely trust so. To-day the streets are running with water and H. [Hilda] and I were tramping about making calls all the afternoon. Mrs. Mullin was here to-day for dinner, quite excited over an offer made to Robin. Through Dr. White, who married May Cameron, they are in Indianapolis,[156] the offer was for R. to take charge of some department in medicine, for which he was to receive $1500 to start and was to be sent abroad for 6 months or a year to study, so Robin has started off to see about it. But it is not to be mentioned until it is decided. Heurner has gone to Baltimore to learn something or other.

A letter from Tom to-day tells of a battle royal between the two old ladies at the boarding house, so that Tom had to hold on to Miss Maxwell to prevent bodily injury. I had a letter from Jessie Proudfoot, to whom I had written on the death of Mr. Proudfoot's brother the Rev. Dr. She said they had written each other every week.[157]

I should think you had been working hard, why Saturday's paper seemed full of your work, I should think they were trying what you can do, and I thought all your articles interesting but really I do not know how you are to keep up with this everlasting writing, it must be so wearing and not very satisfactory to yourself either, just writing scraps about various things, and yet this is what really makes up the newspaper.[158]

On Sabbath Afternoon we went to hear Eva Booth in Association Hall. She was very different in appearance from what I expected. Has most peculiar hair, short & curled round her face covering her ears, so that it looked just like a wig with staring, dark eyes and long nose like her father. She has a great flow of language, becomes very impassioned and would make a tragic actress. She also played on the harp. To me she was not a winning speaker, and had not a winning face or manner, she shrieked so much. I am sorry I did not hear the father.[159]

Well, I must close, my news is exhausted, except I heard Mat McKichan was here. I do hope you are not utterly worn out, I wish you had fallen upon some easier mode of making a living, but we do not live by chance and we know that our lives are ordered by a higher power, so that there is a purpose in them and it just remains for us to carefully & diligently seek divine guidance and follow its leading. The belief that we are so led is our greatest comfort and only support. Hoping you are well, with fondest love, my dear son.

Your loving mother
M. B. McQuesten

✦ A35-(4803) To Calvin McQuesten

Montreal, Quebec

"Whitehern"
February 12, 1903

My dear dear boy,

Have just received your card and glad to know you have managed the sale so well. I had been watching the papers and saw that five shares had been sold at 280. 2 shares and 3 shares, so I had hoped <u>those two</u> were mine, but perhaps I misunderstood and 275 is certainly a fine gain for me. I am seeing Mr. Chisholm to-day and will ask him as to the $79. Dear me! how rich we are getting! Mr. C. sold a property, the Lodge house, which was left in my hands some years, and of which we have been trying to get rid. The purchaser cannot pay cash but can give good security and will pay the interest which is a great improvement for Mr. C. has been so bothered keeping tenants in it. So that I almost feel afraid something will happen, I am feeling so easy in mind. Of course I have just been more than busy seeing to fitting up the other houses, but Mrs. Hill is willing to do part herself and is so pleasant to deal with. Mrs. Merrill left on Saturday night for New York. After that we had to keep up the fire for sake of paper and had a great deal of running about on that account as the luckless Vann had to have the mumps and though Ross promised to see to it, he thought I would send coal. Mrs. M. [Merrill] sent me no keys as promised, so I had to turn out Sabbath morning snow nearly up to my knees (but not cold) and go down Main near Walnut to get key from Ross and send a man with coal.[160] However, it did not hurt me, I am in such fine health.

Saw Mrs. Bell yesterday, she is quite alone except Mr. B. & Charlie no servants and Florri off in Toronto for more than two weeks, she was so discontented, her mother was glad to send her off. Herbie had been really ill with tonsilitis & high fever. Charlie Bell telephoned Florri, but she had never gone near him, nor even telephoned to inquire, though there is a telephone in Herbie's house. O how thankful I am for dear good children!

Monday Leckie came in to invite us to the celebration of Dr. Lyle's 25th Anniversary of his pastorate. We got talking and before we ended I had given him my ideas of the duties of a preacher <u>very plainly</u> and I was very much in earnest.[161] From Mrs. Mullin I learn, he was not altogether pleased. M. [Mary], H. [Hilda], Mrs. Mullin & I went to the affair on Tuesday evening. First we had programme of music by all their good singers, then Mr. Rutherford in an excellent address presented Dr L. [Lyle] with an illuminated one and a purse of over $600, to which Dr. L. replied in (to my mind) very bad taste, though quite intentional <u>on his part</u> he gave a long history of all he had done in the City, the church at large & his own church. He meant to show, I think how he had striven to fullfil his duty, but Oh dear it was just a blowing of his own trumpet.

Afterwards Leckie conducted Mrs. Lyle and Mrs. Hendrie to the platform (you should have seen the latter, she is the funniest figure and face I ever saw), and Mrs. Evel[162] made an address on behalf of ladies and Mrs. H. [Hendrie] presented Mrs. L. [Lyle] with a Persian Lamb Coat.[163] Then Mrs. Lyle gave a lovely address of thanks in which she quite eclipsed her husband. After that Dr. Fletcher gave a fine humorous speech which was a fine wind up. Lastly refreshments.

Well now dear, must close take great care of yourself. Have just to rush out, Mrs. Irving and Katie at the Manse.[164] Mrs. F. [Fletcher] said Mrs. I. [Irving] told her your letter to Mrs. Colin [Fletcher] was most beautiful and greatly appreciated by her, also the book you sent.[165] With much love dear dear boy.

Your loving mother
M. B. McQuesten

[P.S.] Miss Lawson of the mission always asks about you and says they are reaping the benefit of your work in the library to this day, it is so easy to keep it in order through your system. You are a dear boy! Mr. C. [Chisholm] says to do as you said and send me $79. He thought 275 fine.

✦ **A36-(4810) To Calvin McQuesten**

Montreal, Quebec   "Whitehern"
                                    February 26, 1903

My dear dear boy,

Well, Well! To think of my son going Fox-hunting! What next! I am thankful the fox escaped, that his death is not on your head.[166] I fancy you would have a good afternoon outing, but I should think you would be pretty tired. We renewed Mary Baldwin's [daughter] subscription, a dollar seemed so little and it might encourage the Herald a little. From Ruby's letter you must have had a pleasant out-time in Ottawa, only so very short. Those wretched trains are never on time. R. [Ruby] seemed to think you made yourself very entertaining, it was a pity the Robinsons lived so far out, it took up more time.

After I wrote you last week I think I had a touch of Grip and hurried along up to the Caroline St. mission to take the Mother's meeting on Friday, I tumbled down and between the two my poor old bones ached so much that I have not felt very smart. Was so provoked people will think I am always tumbling about. However it was well it was no worse.

Was reading in the Herald, the article on Mr. Steen I did not think you wrote it, for the writer (who was he?) got mixed up in his sentences quite badly. Just reading the article, I should think Mr. Steen had been advanced too rapidly, that he either lost his head, perhaps he was not conceited, but sometimes when men have got a little learning they take up new notions and lose themselves.

In Tom's letter to-day he tells of the Zetes' banquet on Saturday night some of the old members were present from Montreal, New York, and Condon, Governor of the Yukon, who was a nice chap, very fine looking in his evening clothes and made a very interesting speech on Alaskan boundary and told many interesting things. Tom thought the banquet better than Varsity dinner.[167]

Yes it was quite encouraging to make that extra share in Bk. of Montreal and selling the old Lodge property got back $100 of old interest. It all comes at a very opportune time. Hilda is off to Puritan Fair at Y.M.C.A., she is a puritan maiden dressed in grey <u>lining</u> dress with white fichu cap & cuffs. The Old Boys Carnival in August is to be great affair, they say you must try & get your holidays then. Have you got any one in City Editor's place that you like? Is Ken Trigge away or what is he doing now? Hope to write a more interesting letter next time, but very stupid to-day. With much love.

                                    Your loving Mother
                                    M. B. McQuesten

✦ A37-(4815) To Calvin McQuesten

Montreal, Quebec   "Whitehern"
                                     March 4, 1903

My dear dear Cal,

By this evening's post came a letter from Harry Whittemore saying that Reggie had been taken to Grace Hospital with appendicitis, the doctors were not decided as to an operation, but he asked for Hilda to go down to be with Reggie sometimes, as there was no one to sit with him. I do not know if I mentioned that Mrs. W. went to California a few weeks ago, some of the relatives I think had sent her the money for the trip. So it is very hard for the poor boys. I do trust he may not need the operation, poor fellow. Hilda of course starts off to-morrow.[168] We have been having an afternoon of callers, the two Mrs. Dr. Arnotts were here.[169] The young lady is a cousin of Mr. Riddlicombe's at Ottawa and a Miss Gilmour her cousin has just gone to school at Ottawa. Mrs. Fletcher and Mrs. Leitch[170] had been round calling on the bride Josie O'Brien Glassco, Mary & Hilda ran over also. Mrs. Bonnie Glassco was assisting, a very handsome woman they say. Bonnie does nothing you know, they just travel about living on her money. Now Cal, this is what you'll have to do, look out for a nice wife instead of grinding away your strength.

Tom writes that David Ross is in Toronto, getting together another party of students to sell Views, he is to be as manager and starts in the spring.[171] I cannot understand it at all, I thought the whole thing was a failure and when Annie Anderson was here she gave us to understand that David lived on his mother for ever so long and she was tired out going with him to her friends to buy the Views. Tom says David's eyes are so bad he cannot do anything else scarcely. It is very sad.

I do not know what we are to do about our assistant. Dr. Fletcher is determined to have some young man just to help in the visiting and he can do the preaching, this is his idea I am sure. He preached last Sabbath himself as he "wished to give us a good sermon before communion," you know he just thinks he can preach better than any of them and really I could hardly sit it out. After hearing these fresh bright young men it seems worse than ever. The first Sabbath we had a Mr. Wilson from Knox College a great many liked him, but I would not want him. A great many liked Anderson by far the best, but he is not strong enough. And I am afraid it is going to be a terrible try to pull our Church up again. People have so lost interest in it and I do not wonder. Hilda and Edna went to Knox to hear their new minister, Mr. Henry.[172] He is most original in his methods, but very fine and the Church is packed, crowds of young men. We heard that at Brandon where he was, the other churches were rather glad he left, for he took all the young men.

Do you ever see the new paper in Toronto? Is it still called the News? I never hear it mentioned. We had quite a little excitement on Saturday

Morning when the Palace Rink went up in a blaze, the fire had got well started before any alarm was given, so the firemen had just to water surrounding buildings well till it burned out.[173] It was a grand bonfire. I do wish St. Paul's [Church] would buy the land.

I have a warmer spot in my heart for the French people now that you have found them so friendly, it is a great help to a stranger. H. [Hilda] heard from Helen Gartshore, she said your letter made her mouth water for the fun.[174]

Well dear, I hope you are keeping well. Mary has got cold in her larynx, so she makes the most extraordinary sounds. The weather here is quite mild. Brownlow Sanders was asking for you to-day. Harold Thomson has enlisted in Rhodesian Mounted Police. With much love my dear dear boy.

Your loving mother
M. B. McQuesten

✦ A38-(4835) To Calvin McQuesten

Montreal, Quebec

"Whitehern"
March 13, 1903

My dear dear boy,

When I received your letter on Saturday I felt like sitting down and writing you immediately. You praise me far too much my dear and make far too little of yourself. Though I have had to manage on a limited income and had some reverses & difficulties to meet, I have never been worried with my children's bad conduct. That is the thing which would have killed me. You are not to abuse yourself and call yourself slow & stupid. You were <u>never either</u>, you were sadly handicapped physically, poor fellow, from the start, and met with some disappointments in your plans, but you bore it heroically and have had to push your way along without assistance from any one.[175] Your employers, who have hinted at your slowness, have simply used that as an excuse for not paying you your rightful reward. You have fallen into the hands of poor men, one would think unfortunately, but I cannot but believe in the guiding hand of a Heavenly Father, who is fitting you for some better work; though you may not have attained to a higher salary, you have certainly to a higher character and is not that the greatest thing in the world. I am always proud of you, for what you are. My only regret is, that you should be writing so little, that you do not see any prospect ahead of enjoying a home of your own for a long time and also that you do so much good work, for which you get no credit whatever. But still, we can only believe that is all a preparation for something in the future. But please, do not speak to me of your stupidness & slowness, for it is not true and makes me feel very badly.

Last night a meeting of the Congregation was called to appoint an assistant to Dr. F. [Fletcher] but the majority of the congregation did not

understand it was to be settled. However, Dr. F. had so managed the elders &
managers that they fell in with his opinion that as it was to be an arrangement for <u>only</u> two years till he retires, that they could not call any man in a
settled pastorate, but must call one of the four students we have heard &
because they might be picked up, it had to be settled at once. Numbers of
the people did not know one from the other, did not know their names
even. There were two Wilsons,[176] Martin[177] & Anderson. The best people of
the church wanted A. but some of these even did not vote for him because
they did not think him strong enough. Mr. C. [Chisholm] for one. But some
like Reggie & Winnie Glassco went for Wilson and Dr. F. was against him
from the first, said he was not strong enough & was not so <u>great</u>. In my heart
I believe he was too fine for the Doctor, for he is very close, <u>contemptibly</u> so.
Mr. Leitch voted against him & actually when it was decided, as the vote
was close, that if Wilson declined they should ask Anderson, Mr. L. was the
one man in the whole room who had his hand up against him. I shall not
fail to ask what he meant. But I should be very sorry to have Anderson wear
himself out in such a cause, [178] for it was very doubtful if any man can ever
bring the church up.I myself am so thoroughly sick of Dr. F. & the whole
thing that I can scarcely endure it. It is almost more than I can stand to
listen to him. He is dryness itself & is worse than ever and yet has such an
opinion of himself. He only needs help, he says, in the visiting. He can
manage the preaching and every one except the saintly Mr. Thomson[179] is
thoroughly weary of him.

Well, I delivered my conscience by rising & telling the meeting what I
thought we required and that I did not approve of taking any of these young
men, but if they were determined to do so, I said all I could for Anderson. It
was a very wet snowy Sunday that he preached & of course the Doctor had
never told <u>who</u> was to preach. If he had, nobody knew his name. Then too
Dr. Barclay was in Central, so that our church was very empty.[180] I wish you
would write Anderson and let him know that the best people of the church
wanted him and there is a great deal of dissatisfaction, for it is felt that the
thing was hurried on and scarcely any one thought that it was to be decided
at that meeting. At the same time let him know it would have been a great
pity for him to have taken such a broken down church close to two other
strong Churches & to have come to our hot trying city when he requires to
take a complete rest in the fresh country air.

I told you H. [Hilda] was called to the Whittemore's. Well, when
Dr. Temple operated he found an immense abscess, the worst he ever
saw, & gave very little hope. Of course they were all distracted & telegraphed
Mrs. W. H. sent me a letter by special delivery on Saturday & I was distressed to know whether I had better go down, but I felt useless. Monday
morning brought good news of satisfactory progress, & after to-day danger
would be passed. Dr. T. thought Mrs. W. was to arrive to-day.

I had such a fine letter from Tom on Saturday also far too laudatory, but nevertheless it is very sweet to get these letters & I ask no greater reward, there could be none, than that my children have found me a help.[181] Did you see in Tuesday's Globe that Tom got the medal for fencing against 5 crack players in the tournament at Varsity. He has also been made president of Political Science Club. That was a fine bit of news on "The Social Burden." All was most interesting & that extraordinary religion, it seems incredible.[182]

Must close. Have been so busy could not get your letter off in time for to-night's mail. Have got Mrs. James worked up to send Walter to Varsity, if she can get the money from home advanced from what should come to her. Walter was so clever at Collegiate, it seemed such a pity to have his talents wasted.[183] With very much love my dear dear boy.

Your loving mother
M. B. McQuesten

[P.S.] Wilson, who had preached last, got in by two votes over Anderson.[184] Had a letter from J. K. McQ. including this cutting, he was asking various questions about grandpapa McQ. as they were writing a history of the town.[185]

✦ A39-(4863) To Calvin McQuesten

Montreal, Quebec   "Whitehern"
                                     March 25, 1903

My dear dear boy,

Since I wrote last we have been having very remarkable weather. Thursday and Friday were so warm we scarcely know how to bear it. Actually we kept the doors and windows shut as it was cooler inside than out. But the last few days it has been regular March weather, very windy, yet not extremely cold. I do not know if you wrote Anderson or heard anything from him, we understand he is going to Winnipeg and do not know what [page torn] going to do.

Hilda came back from Toronto on Thursday, Reggie was getting on nicely, but it will be a terrible bill of expense, the nurse $18 a week and her board as she was a special nurse. But Reggie had saved up $100 fortunately. He is the best business man of the house, Frank and Holton both lazy and the former no brains. Frank has quite determined to throw up his place and go on a farm. So Henry is just distracted between them all, poor Mrs. W. [Whittemore] just a child among them.

It is really so quiet just now, there is nothing at all to tell, and I only wish that there were no such things as clothes, one gets so tired of seeing the new things in the shops and thinking what to get for the best. Hilda came home sick to death of Toronto, every one there dresses so much and such extravagance one wonders where they get the money. A Mr. Wm.

Murray—a cousin of the Bard's in Toronto died the other day;[186] he had been in New York and not feeling very well, went into a drug store & asked for something. As soon as he had taken it, he said he "felt it in his head and it was a pretty strong dose." After returning to his hotel was seized with vomiting; however he got home to Toronto, but did not recover. I am telling you this as a warning, it does not do to get doses from druggists. By the way are you looking after your teeth, you know when you were home last, you had let them go so that they were brown, now look to them & if they are not quite clean get a little charcoal & clean them off, do not neglect them. I suppose you are letting your poor hair go. Had a letter from Ida Welker with a little collar. She had not seen you for a long time.

Sometimes I get in a panic and wonder how you are ever to keep up this everlasting writing, nothing seems to me so wearisome as this, so hard on the brain. Do you ever on your rounds see anything else that might be easier? Tom Irving is at McGill do you ever see him? Mrs. Irving is still here, but Katie stays in Toronto she never calls for her here with Annie, and in Toronto there are a number of Scarboro people who knew her father and she enjoys going to see them.[187] Her chief amusement though is watching the Gamey business at the house. It seems abominable, that the Country should be forced by someone's trickery, to have its time and as a consequence money expended in such a way. Whoever is right or wrong, what a miserable dog Gamey is![188] But the most distressing thing to my mind is this charge against Hector MacDonald.[189] Isn't it pathetic to think of him after all his achievements? It seems incredible. He is not married, I think, Poor fellow! He is mentioned for his brave Soldierly Conduct in Afghanistan where Lord Roberts distinguished himself.

I found Lord Roberts' book very interesting in that way, it mentioned the names of so many since distinguished.[190] And it also gave one such a distinct idea of India's conditions before the mutiny and how she has been won for England really through the kind wise management of individual men, remarkable men, many of them Christian men of noble character and wonderful tact. One is filled with admiration of the men. Am reading "Donovan Pasha" now. Gilbert Parker[191] has a marvellous gift of putting before you a whole life in a few words, he seems to do in writing what Bengough[192] does, when by a few strokes he shows you a perfect likeness. Did I tell you I had read the "Blue Flower" and how much I was struck by "The Source."[193]

Well I cannot write any more as I have several other letters to write. Tom does not want to go on survey, he has some scheme in his head to take Editorship of Varsity which would bring him back September first, and so he proposes to go with his friend Grey up the Ottawa, Grey's Uncle has lumber interests, I believe and he would get paid but not so much I think as on survey.[194] He does not expect to come home at Easter except perhaps just over Sunday as the boats will be running then.

Well as it happens this is the third letter I have written without any reply to mine. One reached you after you wrote last week, you wrote M. [Mary] and so it is. Well dear take good care of yourself. We have great reasons to be thankful that none of us have been affected with serious illness. I think we sometimes forget this, the anxiety and distress of mind and expense are sometimes terrible. I. P. Buchanan sent E. [Edna] a Cornell Calendar, with himself in a group,[195] those Yanks are poor specimens in their sporting costumes reminded me of the Indian Famine Groups or as E. [Edna] said, the lepers.[196] With much love dear boy.

Your loving mother
M. B. McQuesten

[P.S.] "Tatler" was *very* good.[197]

✦ A40-(4902) To Calvin McQuesten

Montreal, Quebec   "Whitehern"
                                      April 22, 1903

My dear dear boy,

The event uppermost in my mind is the New Lieutenant-Governor and the Governess. Just think of it. Fancy the state and joyousness of Daisy Clark. Though I cannot for the life of me see where Mortimer's claim to preferment comes in. I cannot help thinking that no one could be found to take it. Some would not be bothered with it and some would not have the money. I thought of writing congratulations to Mr. C. but conscience prevented me. In this position, they are Expected simply to cater to the amusement of society and, at their age, I should think, they ought to be thinking more of things eternal. It is not as if Mr. C. were placed at the head of government, he is simply a figure head.[198] Fancy a man of his age an elder trotting round to all the society functions & what improvement is he on Sir Oliver, with whom so much fault was found by certain parties?[199] It will just suit Jean & Elsie.

It is keeping very cold and things growing slowly, there is a fine bunch of daffodils in the heart.[200] On Sabbath we had the assistant, in the morning. I was in despair, what he said was above the average, but he ran his words together and had so little life, it was no better than Dr. F. at his worst. In the evening he seemed more at home and spoke with much more animation, so that I quite liked him and hope he may improve as he knows us better. He is quite nice looking, medium height, dark, but has nothing of the voice or appearance of Anderson.

We are fixing up a neat wire fence between stable & clothes yard, we could not do without it any longer. Sutherland's horses got out the other day and made terrible havoc with the lawn. I think I told you Mr. Culham had gone to Baltimore ill, but the doctors say that he will probably be all right after some weeks. Do not know just what is the matter. Mary and Mrs. Leitch are going together to Guelph, they are to stay at Gracie Davidson's, though M. would have preferred taking her chances.

Edna saw Sandwell the other day with his lady love. The Choir gave an At Home to the congregation on Friday. M.& H. [Mary and Hilda] went, it was quite fine. The school-room decorated, quantities of flowers, refreshments including Charlotte Russe, and the various members of the choir sang. It is really terribly dull nothing is going on of any interest. I do not really care but it seems so very monotonous for the girls and yet how many would gladly change places. It must have been quite interesting to meet the little Jap. I was hoping he would give you some Japanese curiosity. I am posting you a book by J. M. Surrie it was rather amusing. It came among a lot for the hospital, so you can take care of it and bring it back with you in May.[201] Dr. & Mrs. Carter (Norah Ambrose) have bought Dr. Gulliver's house & practice, so are to settle here.

Tom says he is studying hard, but as he is interested in his study this year, he does not mind. Have just received from Ruby a little box of the Trailing Arbutus, it is a sweet little blossom but very small. Edna has a half-holiday on account of Sir Oliver's Funeral,[202] a luckless boy showed joy on the occasion and received severe rebuke from Mr. Asman, as being "disgusting." Poor Asman!

Well I must close, How do you get on at your house? Are there any changes. You never tell me any news of your fellow lodgers now. Did I tell you when H. [Hilda] was in Toronto she ran full tilt into Mrs. Trigge. As they were going up to Helen Gartshore's she spoke kindly & inquired for us. There is no knowing what Ken told her.[203] Well take care of yourself dear boy with much love from all.

Your loving mother
M. B. McQuesten

✦ A41-(4963) To Calvin McQuesten

Montreal, Quebec

"Whitehern"
Saturday, [May 23, 1903]

My dear dear boy,

Your final telegram has just come. It is too disappointing for any thing, and I am fine. You must be sick to death of these wretched strikes. For no matter what extra work you do, it is never recognized. I <u>do</u> think the reporters should combine, you have no more right to do work after hours than workmen do without extra pay. No wonder, men have to strike. Employers will take all they can out of their men, without any conscience. We were all looking forward to this holiday so much and had worked hard to get through house cleaning. So that I have my old friend a stiff-neck.[204] Poor

Edna has had neuralgia in her ear but is better to-day. Mrs. Whittemore and Reggie went off yesterday, we had a great time getting them off, Mrs. W. such a helpless person. Cannot tell particulars in a letter.

Hedley came up last <u>Monday</u> and took measure of book case and was to bring up crate and pack it, strange to say he has never come back, but I have sent Hilda to see him. Mrs. Mullin was wanting to see you, she wants to take Nellie and go up Saguenay sometime in August and would love to have you go at same time. I cannot say whether you have other plans or the exact time but think it is two last weeks of August.

Well my dear dear boy, I was quite heart-broken when your message came. I had been so longing to see you and have you rest and feed you, but we must believe it is for the best and trust you will get off very soon as you can have certainly a right to do. In some ways it is nicer to come on a day not a holiday.

We got our coal in on Tuesday had to pay 6.50 and 25cts more for rack ton carried in, but they say coal will advance 10 cts each month—it is a terrible price. Then we got all the downstairs whitewashed and wanted you to see how spic and span we are. Good-bye, poor dear boy.

Your loving mother
M. B. McQuesten

[P.S.] Great excitement last night about 10 o'clock. Fire at the Manse, neighbours opposite saw fire up in Mrs. F.'s [Fletcher's] bed-room, ran over where Mrs. F. was sitting with Mr. Colin [Fletcher] and others in the library. They ran up and the bed was on fire, they managed to smother it, but Capt Fairgrieve had sent in alarm and of course the reels tore up past us and we rushed up too. Mrs. F. thinks when she lit the gas, and put match in the little basket for burnt matches it was on fire and the basket fell on to the bed. It might have been far worse, insurance will make it all right. Did I tell you Tom works from six to six, sleeps 10 hours & thinks he must have gained 10 lbs.[205]

✦ A42-(4977) To Calvin McQuesten

Montreal Quebec   "Whitehern"
                                              June 16th 1903

My dear Cal,

It certainly was the most surprising thing for Tom to get a scholarship, it was so unexpected that the very idea quite upset me.[206] On Saturday the results had come out, but the Globe made a great mess of it and half the third year men were reported starred. The James saw it but did not like to tell us; that afternoon I went down to Mrs. Bell's and Mrs. B. congratulated me on Tom's passing and Herbie showed me the Mail which was all right and said from what Tom had told him he thought Tom might get a scholarship. I said, I was sure his writing would prevent it. When I came home Mrs. Mullin had been up to say they had seen the Globe but Heurner said it was evidently a mistake and Robin had telephoned that Tom had come out with flying colours. Well, I was so excited, I could hardly sleep and by Monday Morning was almost ill with suspense; but the news soon revived me, but when he had worked so hard wished for his sake he could have had the satisfaction of being first. However it may be the means of spurring him on more next year. Why I am specially pleased is, that when Mr. Chisholm and Ruby have helped him so much, I like them to see he has been doing his best and not acting like Charlie Locke, who is starred again simply because he wastes so much time.[207] But Tom said he enjoyed his work last year which argues well for his future. Tom had quite a number of congratulations, but when one came from Helen Gartshore also condoling on account of stars, I could stand it no longer and wrote to "Jimmie" Bubner to have it corrected. To-day I wrote Dr. Fletcher congratulating him on the brink of the moderatorship as Mr. Knowles termed it.[208]

Send copies of your Herald with the article on Dr. F. marked to him, Miss Lerned, Hopkinton and John McQuesten and Mrs. Fletcher here.[209] Miss Lerned thought so much of Dr. Fletcher, put your initials on this article and [send to] James Buchanan too.[210] Did you write John Duncan Clarke?[211] I have written Miss Lerned.

Have never heard a word from Tom but a card with his address and saying they are far from the post, so I thought the scholarship warranted a telegram as he might not get a paper for days.[212] When are you starting? Take any unframed photos you may have of the family with you. You could find out at Y.M.C.A. in Boston where you could get cheapest board. Do you need some extra money, you should see all you can. Let me know & I could send it to John McQuesten. With Much love.

Your mother
M. B. McQuesten

✦ A43-(5012) To Calvin McQuesten

Montreal, Quebec   "Whitehern"
                                    July 9, 1903

My dear dear Cal,

Your letter has just come with its generous enclosure and it was <u>most</u> acceptable. It will just pay Edna's board for the two weeks after she leaves the Gartshores.[213] We found out from Helen that very good boarding houses are there at $5.00 a week, so we have written to secure rooms for Mary for three weeks and Edna for two weeks. Mary gets so thin and tired out with the heat and work that I had determined to give her a change though I could really scarcely manage it.

In addition to the extra bills for Bold St. houses which I have yet to make up, I had $25 to pay for cement walks and sodding at Bold St. (Ruby brought home just enough for that). And also had to get my coal in April in order to secure reduced rates, but still it was high, making my coal bill $114 I have only paid $60 but the Capt. is very lenient. Then some of my money on mortgage came in and in re-investing I found by making a push and keeping some of my creditors waiting I could pay off a $1050 mortgage on Webber property held by North Scottish Life Ass. For I find if I do not watch carefully, I am tempted to use principal, if it comes in small sums & there were two or three odd sums waiting at Ham. Prov. for re-investment. I could only get 12 shares of the Ham. Prov. for which I paid $122 but as they pay 6 per cent I get 5 per cent on money invested and can get no more on mortgage. They always laugh at me, when I say that we shall be much better off next summer but if nothing happens to Mrs. Hill, it seems as if we must be, for to have one of the houses vacant a whole year is a very great loss,[214] & it takes me a while to catch up, having water-rates to pay too besides all the repainting & plumber's bills, the latter a hundred dollars & loss the same, besides $200 for electric light. I think it is just a wonder, we are as well off as we are. I am telling you all this to show how much help your ten dollars is.

I was so glad to hear of your delightful outing on the yacht. It is just the thing for you to get out in the fresh air. I am wondering how you stand the fearful heat of last two days. We are preparing a reception at the church for Dr. Fletcher. I spent all yesterday morning getting out invitations, the men had been so slow about it that yesterday Wednesday I found they had not been sent & Friday is the day. You see it is the first time moderator came to Hamilton and it is to be made a great affair. So the Mayor, clergy &c are to be invited.[215]

I feel so pleased every time I think of your trip, you seemed to see so much in the space of time and things turned out so providentially for you, it was fine to have that day's sail on ocean to refresh you, for you must have given your poor legs a hard time of it.

Edna got through her last exam yesterday, so fortunate just before extreme heat set in and she had perfect weather for exams and most of the study time, and she seems quite confident of having got through.[216]

We expect the Glasscos, McKays, and Sydney S. [Stevenson] for tea. So the girls have been very busy all day. I do trust it will be cooler to-morrow for Ladies insisted on having coffee and tea besides ice-cream and I am afraid no one will want hot drinks. I am afraid I rather upset Donald McPhie's plans,[217] he had an elaborate address of his own all prepared, and thought a formal written address to the Doctor unnecessary, but I did not think it would do at all and insisted a proper address must be prepared & presented by the elders and embossed afterwards, the same as when he was made a D.D.

Did you send Tom his paper? Forgot to say that Tom seems to have no time at all except Sunday and perhaps it would be a good opportunity for him to read Drummond,[218] that is if you can still think of sending it. Hedley has not yet sent his bill, but I will speak about it. You mention a picture by Robt. Browning, surely not the poet. Wasn't it fine to see all those paintings? Herbie Bell had to have his wound stitched yesterday, it had not healed up very quickly being a gangrenous one, but expect he will be all right soon. With many thanks for your loving thoughts and much love.

Your loving mother
M. B. McQuesten

✦ A44-(5084) To Calvin McQuesten

Montreal, Quebec

"Whitehern"
Monday Morning
[August 24,1903]

My dear Cal,

Your letter with its good news cheered us all up. I had been reading every day with great interest the reports of the Congress of Commerce and was quite anxious to know if you had been there, so was perfectly delighted to hear that you had been present at all the great functions. It really is worth a great deal to you, to be in Montreal just at this very exciting time for never before has there been so much to say between Canada and the Old Country as during the last year so that it is really a critical period and it seems as if everything said just now is really of great importance. I think it was quite a feather in your cap that you were sent to the banquet and I have been comparing your report with that of the Globe and it seems to me yours is by far the best report.[219] From the Globe one does not get such a fine impression of Sir Wilfrid's speech. Poor fellow! I am afraid that Railway will be the death of him. It <u>was</u> too bad the Englishmen did not speak but they had I suppose been talking all week.[220]

Tom writes me you have been offering him a pass down there and home. It will be lovely for him to see Montreal and a day or two with you. But how can you get him a pass home and come yourself for Labour Day? If it would interfere with your getting pass for yourself then let him come home by boat. Mrs. Mullin and Nellie are to take the Steamer Sparta on Tuesday evening which reaches Montreal on Thursday morning and will be that afternoon at Mrs. Irvine's Westmount, cannot remember the street, perhaps you know it. They are to take that Evening's boat for Quebec. You may not be able to see them, but am just telling you. All busy dressmaking, Ruby has only two more weeks at home. With much love dear, dear, boy.

Your loving mother
M. B. McQuesten

✦ A45-(5105) To Calvin McQuesten

Montreal, Quebec

Friday Night
[September 11, 1903]

My dearest boy,

　　Your letter had just reached me sent back from Toronto and I have just come back from there, having gone down for the day. Of course, dear, I am trying not to be anxious about you, but I am quite sure and have felt it for some time that you could not possibly have a more trying occupation, the very worst for your trouble. Then it may be too God's way of leading you into his service as you always longed to do. But what I want you to do is not to go back to the Herald Office, come right home, or if you think the sea air so good, go back to Cap a l'aigle, as it is such a reasonable place until I can consult those whom you mentioned. I can send you funds. But do not do another day's work. Would like to have you home, if you are to go so far away in October, but I know that Hamilton climate is not bracing so that you must do what is best. Think I will go to Toronto to-morrow as it is the last day of cheap fares and [see] Dr. Caven[221] and Dr. Warden.[222] Then I will talk with Dr. Lyle for he was up seeing the various stations on his way to assembly. Now please do no more work or you will lose the good of your holiday. I don't think you need regret the newspaper work for it is hard work for very little either money or praise. My heart is full of sympathy for you my dear boy, but we will Trust in God.[223]

Your loving mother,
M. B. McQuesten

1904-1908

❧

✦ A46-(MCP 3-5.7) To Thomas B. McQuesten

41 Isabella St., Toronto, Ontario

"Whitehern"
January 15, 1904

My dear dear boy,

　　Three weeks ago only to-day since Christmas and it seems like as many months. This week has been occupied with meetings till I feel sometimes like running away. Monday was invited by Mrs. Sanford with a few ladies to afternoon tea to meet a Miss McKinney who is here in the interests of a mission to India under the auspices of Lord Kinnaird, quite enjoyed the afternoon. I suppose you have been having a lot of snow like ourselves. This last snowstorm cost me a dollar. I am quite tired of it and the winter is only half over.

There really does not seem to be anything to say. Cal's letter on Monday had no special news, he thought the new horse was going to suit him. I had also a letter from Mrs. Jaffary thanking me for the book I sent her, and saying she thought Cal looked stronger but wondered how he stood all the hardships, but he never complained.

Hilda had an invitation to go down to Mrs. Stevenson's tomorrow Saturday by three o'clock train. I did not write you before for I knew you were busy, and you would probably hear from Sydney before Saturday. Sydney asked her to come on a Saturday so she could meet her.

Yesterday a gentleman called to see if I had ever an idea of selling this property. I said I might if I got a sufficient price to make it worth my while. The only thing about it is that it's so very large a house when we have to do our own work, and the servants' wages are quite beyond me. Of course, I could get no house at such a cheap rental as my taxes are, but a very small one, and it is rather hard to come down to an ordinary house after this large one. At the same time these new houses have many conveniences and are easier to heat, and if we are to do our own work, it is a great temptation to have a small convenient house, only it would be a trial to leave the old house if one were to remain in Hamilton. There was a time when I would have liked Toronto, but now I seem afraid of new people.

If you have any stockings to be darned, take them up to Tousie [Hilda]. Hope you are getting ahead of your work. Miss Fisher was greatly pleased with your photo. With much love dearie.

Your loving Mother
M. B. McQuesten

✦ A47-(MCP 1-3a.56) To Thomas B. McQuesten

22 Grosvenor Street   Whitehern
Toronto, Ontario   January 19, 1904

My dear dear boy

Your letter amused us greatly with its description of your office. I am very glad you are pleased and hope it will prove satisfactory. I went to St. Catharines on Tuesday morning, a lovely mild sunny day. We had a very pleasant party, Mrs. Lyle, Mrs. Wanzer, Mrs. Leitch, Mrs. Watson, Mrs. Dewar, Mrs. McCaftan. We reached the church at 10 o'clock, just in time for business meeting. The ladies gave us a very fine lunch, we began with [?]ter patties, and ended with Charlotte Russe and jelly. I do not like to enlarge on the food things as I would only make your mouth water. As it happened Mr. and Mrs. Webb of the Webb family of Toronto belonged to Mr. Ratcliffe's church and they managed the lunch. They used to attend the Northern Congregational Church and I used to see them there.[224] Mrs. Leitch and I came home by 5 o'clock train, as we did not want to stay overnight.

Dr. Fletcher had come in and taken tea with the girls, as he had another meeting at the church, so Mrs. F. had told him to come to us, it is so far up to their house. But I think the Dr. is very pleased at the way the church is treating him, they are giving him $500 a year and he is pastor Emeritus. With what the Dr. has, his income will be about $1000. He is buying the house, had to sell some stock and borrow some to pay for it.[225]

I was hearing about Gordon Gibson, he is still at Gravenhurst.[226] When he went there his lungs were badly affected and Mr. Gibson is in very delicate health, his heart is affected, his wife and family have been most anxious for some time to get him out of political life, but his party of course, begged him to hold on, so that it is really very unjust and untrue to say he resigned because he had to. People all have their trials and we really have reason for thankfulness that our only trial is shortness of funds. Poor Mrs. Laurie has had to give up her house entirely. Her brother said, if she would leave her husband altogether, he would send her an allowance, so they have gone to New York, one son, if not both has a position there and pays the rent of a flat. Naomi is to be married in June from her aunt's in Toronto. The ladies sent Mrs. F. [Fletcher] a cheque for $160 and more has come in since, so that will help to start things.

The Hendries are another unhappy miserable set, every one of them selfish to the backbone. Mr. Hendrie is in very poor health, has no use whatever for any member of the family unless he has been a success. So the luckless Jim who has been working up in a lumber camp, to keep him out of sight, had to stay at Mrs. Braithwaite's, and Murray Hendrie when in town stays at the Royal. So Mrs. H. is having a very hard time (with all her money).

I have been making inquiries about the black coals for the grate and Mrs. Bell tells me she got hers from Rice Lewis in Toronto. She said, she required 2 bags they were 75 cts a bag. Would you just go into Rice Lewis's and see about it. You know we have in the grate now 97 and 28 we had taken out, but the black coals are smaller, so you could find out size and tell me how many we would need. What we have are 2 cts a piece. Inquire right away because if you come up election day you could bring them with you. Two bags could come by express for 26 cts would not mind, they could tell perhaps how heavy they are.

We are all so sorry about the death of Mrs. Dr. McKelcan, she was one of the nicest and kindest of women, and it is so sad for her daughters. We are trying to read some of Gladstone's[227] life every night and intend copying some of his sayings, which are fine, and worth remembering. Must close, dearie, sorry to think you are all alone now in the house, it must be lonely. With much love

Your loving Mother
M. B. McQuesten

✦ A48-(MCP 3-5.11) To Thomas B. McQuesten

41 Isabella St., Toronto, Ontario   "Whitehern"

March 31, 1904

My dear dear boy,

This is a very dull day, chilly and damp, not calculated to raise one's spirits so that I scarcely know what I am going to say. Hilda heard from Sydney today that Miss Proudfoot was coming to live with them and would arrive this morning, I think so their house will be full.[228] Have not heard from Cal this week, think perhaps the storm in North-west delayed the mails, but I miss his letter so much.

On Sabbath I went over to Central Church, to hear Mr. Mackay the young minister of Crescent St. Church, Montreal. He did very well, but I do not care for the present-day style of preaching, it is neither helpful, nor instructive and does not satisfy one, for there is nothing in it to save sinners.[229] The musical service was so long that it was 12 o'clock before the minister began, and Edna and I were perfectly exhausted and our heads aching with the frightful noise of that organ. I really do not enjoy large churches, the minister is too far away and the service too ornamental.[230]

Monday went to a 'Tea' at Mrs. Thomson's, Tuesday was dinner at Miss Park's, a very fine one too, and yesterday was at Mrs. Bell's. Charlie and those insolent Gates' are now doing their best to have Herbert sent off to Paris this Spring, so that he cannot be here to be groomsman. You would really think, as his mother says, that he was a deformed hunchback, they speak of him in such a way. Arthur Trigge has bought a house on Markham St. and they expect to move in May. Heurner Mullin has gone to Baltimore for three weeks to visit the hospitals. Poor Bella Kerr has gone to New York to try and get a position. Jim's failure has left Mrs. Kerr with nothing.[231]

Winnie Gartshore is coming on Monday by train leaving Toronto at 1:15 CPR, If you wished you could send some socks or anything you wanted mended. O dear Me! Tomsie, it does seem such a long time since you were home. How glad I shall be when all this uncertainty is over about the wretched exams and you are home once more. Harry Whittemore and Florrie gave up their idea of coming to-morrow, it is as well, for the weather is not promising,

Be careful and not catch cold, do not leave off your over-coat too soon for the air is cold. It is often warm in the house, and one thinks it warm outside. Edna had not a cold all winter, and now has a miserable one. So hot in church on Sunday and very cold when we came out. Well, dearest boy, must close. With fondest love.

Your loving Mother

M. B. McQuesten

✦ A49-(5172) To Calvin McQuesten

Standoff, Alberta [232]   "Whitehern"
                                           May 9, 1904

My dear dear Cal,

I wish I had a typewriter for last week was so full that I can scarcely write it all. Before I forget, we read with interest your account of the Mormon leader, and it read well. I am sorry to think you are losing your power of writing you had such great hopes in that line when you went west, but of course if you are succeeding in the preaching it is an equally great power. But I would not let the writing go altogether, when opportunity offers to write up something.

Well, to go back, on Monday evening we had a very jolly Anniversary Tea.[233] Mr. & Mrs. Clark[234] of London and Dr. John Pringle were there, they are all extremely nice and pleasant and we had a lovely Tea of cold meats, salads, cake, tea & coffee, brown & white bread & butter. Dr. Pringle does not care much about the D.D. [Doctor of Divinity] does not think it very suitable but Mr. C. says it will do for "dog driver."[235]

Tuesday at noon I started off for our meetings and went straight to the church, St. James Square [Toronto].[236] We had our opening meeting in the afternoon and then I went up to Madison Ave. where I was billeted with Mrs. MacKay,[237] found them a delightful family three dear children the oldest seven and the youngest a little girl of two, two boys and a girl. They attend Dr. MacTavish's church. MacKay knew you and dined with you once at Mr. Leslie's in Montreal. I could not find out exactly his business but he had to go back every night. A Scotchman but with English manners very gentlemanly and he is very careful in bringing up the children, always has them playing in the morning! He wished to be remembered to you.

In the evening we had a conference, at which I proposed our bringing in a resolution of sympathy with the missionaries. We had determined to do this and I had written it before leaving home for several of us felt something had to be done to cheer the missionaries and with the unhappy feeling in the Board now over the Wilkie Case, we feel no certainty of anything, however everyone agreed.[238] On the Wednesday I had luncheon with Mrs. Henderson, her house was taken up with Mrs. Steele and a cousin, of course they asked for you.

In the afternoon I read my resolution, then I asked the audience to pass it by joining hands & singing one verse of "Blest be the tie &c." Then I said "We have with us to-day Dr. Oliver who has given 18 yrs of her life, and Miss Sinclair who has given 15 years,[239] and two other Missionaries who have given almost ten years in the service of this Society and we want them to carry back with them the brightest and happiest memories of this Annual Meeting and tell the missionaries when they go back how much we sympathize with them & how much we love them."[240] Then the audience clapped for which I was glad. I received many thanks for this effort, numbers came up afterwards & spoke, missionaries & their friends, Mrs. John Taylor's mother from Owen Sound amongst others.[241] Mr. Telfer was pleased too. After this Miss Sinclair gave simply a magnificent address, she was on her mettle and she did splendidly, she feels that so many are against her amongst the Toronto people, not so many as she thinks though.

In the evening I did not go to the Public meeting in Cook's Church but rested myself & Tom came over and spent the evening. He just looks the picture of health though his exams are on, he never looks the least worried. He told me that Prof. Hutton has not a friend among the Profs. I thought Ramsay Wright might be, but isn't at all, then Chancellor Moss is one of the Committee and Wm. Blake a fraternity man is to influence him and A. B. Aylesworth is to speak to Falconbridge to influence Moss also. It is most amusing to hear of all the wire-pulling. Then Tom saw Tietzel, who was most agreeable, gave him the glad hand like a true politician, said of course he knew him well and would write him a nice letter. He also met Falconbridge at lunch & would speak a word.[242]

The next day Thursday was our board meeting, I tried to get Miss Sinclair appointed as handling secretary for a few months but could not carry it. Then I had the question drawer. There were the usual questions about various matters, then came a set fishing Miss Sinclair to answer, such as "Will Miss Sinclair give who of the Famine girls in five years in the Board School were prepared to be qualified teachers. I, their number, II, their names, III, the place where they are now employed. Five different papers of questions and in each several questions as to details and one referring to the "Middle" School.[243] As I read them out, they struck me as very strange & Mrs. Shortreed too and we thought it absurd, but presently Miss Sinclair, after answering a number in the most remarkable way, said aloud this is a trap, and Mrs. Shortreed stopped it.[244] Mrs. Telfer asked me to lunch with her and I was so pleased to go they are so kind, but I heard so much from them, of how the advisory board of four keep things too much to themselves and through this Wilkie affair the Board is no longer a united one. She also told me when inquiring for you that Miss Grey was so delighted to receive your picture & a letter, it pleased her so much.

Then we finished that afternoon and as Mrs. Clark had very kindly asked me in the morning went down to Government House for dinner. There they were all just as cordial and kind as could be and I was shown the house and spent the evening and heard a great deal of the MacKays from Mrs. Clark.[245] They have left Dundas [St] and moved to a house in the Park just next north of the Proudfoot's old one.

Gordon [MacKay] was married a year ago last March by a Methodist Minister on Bathurst St. It was discovered when the Coachman took some things to St. Michael's Hospital for Gordon who was ill there; he was not in his room when nurse said he was downstairs with his wife she was ill there too. Of course when the men brought the news home Mrs. MacKay had to be told, she spoke to Gordon saying she must tell his father when he said, if she did his father would disinherit him & he would go out and blow his brains out. This was the final blow that broke Mr. MacKay's heart, and gave her the death blow. Mrs. Clark, however, made "William" tell Mr. MacKay and endeavoured to persuade him to speak to Gordon and have him live with his wife and make themselves fit. Mr. Clark made all the inquiries and found out if they were properly married and went to St. Michael's Hospital. The Mother Superior said she was not an educated person but I saw Mrs. Winchester since and she told me Mr. Winchester had gone to see her and she was a pretty little thing & he thought she had married him thinking to reform him. But as yet Mr. MacKay has said nothing and taken no steps, so Mrs. Clark thinks she can do no more, she feels very badly about them. She really is such a kind good woman, and it was quite a treat to see Government House, it is so beautiful with all the Clark's handsome things, and one is apt to get rusty as to table usages if one is always out of it. The next day I bade good-bye to Mrs. MacKay, my kind hostess. Mr. M. arranged to send all my belongings to the Station for me and I started off to see my friends.

Mrs. Whittemore has sold her house and may go to Parkdale. Then I went to Mrs. MacKay's, she has failed greatly since I saw her and can speak very little, had longed so to see me, the house is a fine one. Mrs. M. had been brought in the Ambulance. Leila could stay no longer and goes home next week. Mr. M. had a bad fall in the winter near his barn door, came in blood streaming from his head and hand. He was in bed for two days with ice to his head and his finger is still much swollen but of course Mrs. MacKay knows nothing of it, her arteries are all hardening which affects both her brain and kidney and her head cannot be raised at all. I cannot think she can last long.[246] Mr. M. had none of his old jokes. It is a very sad household to contemplate, some-thing [sic] Drummond is married too. Then I took the cars up to Mrs. Stevenson's & had lunch with her & Sydney. Miss Proudfoot is Sec. Treas. to a New Ladies' Club in Toronto so I took car down & saw her.[247]

Then I did a little shopping and went to an Afternoon Tea at Mrs. Shortreed's, Bloor St. East. There we had a great crowd of missionaries and our own ladies. Mrs. Telfer was telling Mrs. Hamilton what a fine work you were doing, Mrs. Jaffary was sure you would succeed, saw Mrs. Gregory too, but she never invited me to her house and paid any attention at all, rather strange I thought. Then Mrs. Henderson took me home with her to dinner, but I just had time for a plate of soup and then went off. Tom met me at the Station and reached home between 8 & 9. One day a Mrs. Anderson of St. James Square introduced herself and asked most kindly for you. Poor

Miss Tillie Robinson has completely broken down & is resigning from Fleming Revello,[248] I think she just needs a rest. Mr. McTavish looked worn out. Send you a "Globe" of one day, meetings hardly reported at all.

Well, I must close. Had Mr. Cunningham again preaching yesterday. He did not impress me at all, but I was very sleepy. I felt so well & strong at the meetings, better than for years. If I could get $15000 for our whole property will I take it [*sic*]. With fondest love in which all join.

Your loving mother
M. B. McQuesten

✦ A50-(5199) To Calvin McQuesten

Standoff, Alberta   "Whitehern"
                                                                  May 23, 1904

My dear dear Calvin,

When one has not got good news to tell, one does not enjoy letter writing. Perhaps you will have seen the News before this that the Rhodes Scholarship did not come to Tom. I can scarcely believe it and must say it has given me quite a shock. Though I endeavoured to prepare myself for the worst, still I could not help building on it, and I am afraid it is a very sore disappointment to Tom, have not heard a word from him since but of course he was just in the midst of his exams, that was one of the cruel things about it, to announce it just then. We cannot but believe it was a most unjust decision, 3/10 of the marks were given for Scholarship 2/10 for athletics and the rest for general character (Mr. C. [Chisholm] told me). We are quite sure that P. [Paterson] was not Tom's equal at all. Mr. C. said it was just another instance of favouring Toronto, he went down to the Senate meeting, where report of committee was brought in and Mr. Paterson was there, nobody could say anything and no one seemed inclined to. I have a feeling that Hutton, of course ruled it, Paterson would be his pet as having taken 4 yrs in Classics, he does not seem to have distinguished himself specially at it, and if Hutton pushed it, we have no confidence in Loudon, though he had professed himself in favour of Tom. Burwash was for another man and Moss did not know Tom at all, so Baker would be the only one. What makes me feel so sore is to think of the injustice of the whole thing. As far as I know all the members of the committee had not even seen the candidates, therefore they were in no position to judge. It makes me sick to think of it, though I know that God over rules all things and I put it into his hands and yet here I am fretting about it, it is so wrong of me, but it seems as if I can not forget it. Mrs. James tries to console us by telling us of the awful wickedness of Oxford, filled with bad women. But I would just have been too proud, I feel myself swelling at the prospect and I think Tom was almost sure of getting it. I feel so anxious as to how he comes out, after such a distracting time, poor old

chap, he has really had a hard year of it. To show you how these Toronto
men act, Mr. C. told me they actually object to Hamilton having two members on the Senate. Prof. MacCallum told Mr. C. he had voted for Snider
because he thought we should have only one representative & Mr. C. says
that those from a greater distance never attended more than once a year; so
that Hamilton men are really the only outsiders, it is all so terribly unjust
that one feels hopeless.[249]

Your letter written on May 15th we received on Saturday morning the
21st which seemed very quick. Mr. Pringle has only been here on his way
through several times, he is getting subscriptions for the Atlin Hospital. Oh
no he has not given up the Yukon. But I think he is disgusted with the wran-
gling over the Wilkie Case and fancy Wilkie going now to start mission
circles in the churches for his new mission. A copy of the Dominion Pres.
[Presbyterian] came to me, will send it. Isn't it terrible to think of them
keeping it up and taking King of Indore to task for his account of College
closing.[250] Miss Sinclair says she is "very tired of it all. Home Christians
have shown more uncharitableness in this matter than we ever did to each
other in India and I scarcely appreciate the 'I am holier than thou' attitude
of some of Dr. Wilkie's sympathizers." Indeed I came home perfectly sick of
Torontonians.

Mrs. Ross is not going to do anything just now but take a rest which she
much needs. I am going to send you a copy of the skeleton of a sermon
preached by Mr. Howitt. It was the last sermon Connie James heard and it
made a great impression on her mind, so to please Mrs. J. Mr. Howitt had it
all very nicely type written and put in shape. And I am sure you would find
them valuable. He is such a fine Bible Student.[251]

We have quite a nice class of Jews, yesterday we had two more young
Roumainians, very nice modest gentle lads. The three Roumainians are so
superior to the others & speak and read English fairly well. One Russian is a
fine tall man, most gentlemanly. In Russia he was in a soda water factory,
could not understand his broken English very well but thought he owned it,
he had to leave his wife & two little girls and now all he can do is to drive a
hay-wagon.

It is too bad about the Slide-out people, but it is their loss, you have
done your best.[252] We have not heard your letter yet for our Home Mission
meeting does not come till first Wednesday of June, it was just too late for
May meeting and when I saw Mrs. F. [Fletcher], she had only just received it.
She has been house cleaning since & we haven't met. It was quite interesting about Johnnie Woolf. I just noticed it in Presbyterian that Dr. Kilpatrick
is to write on the Mormons or rather a digest of his lectures on Mormonism
is to appear in Presbyterian.[253]

Up till last Friday we had very cool weather, but it has been very warm,
close and raining with thunder since. Annie Park & Mrs. Bell set off to-mor-

row to visit Hessi.[254] Ethel Atkinson's wedding is to be June 8th Hilda is going. Ethel's home is to be in California, but they will spend the summer in Muskoka.[255]

Look at "The News" of Saturday 21st on page 14 what they say at McGill about Rhodes Schp.[256] It seems as if something really ought to be done if one had some strong friend to take it up & fight it. We have been expecting Tom to-day, but he has not come yet. Suppose he has a lot of things to finish up. ⌐

Herbie Bell sails by the North German Lloyd first week of June. The doctor said if he did not get an Ocean voyage, he would end in the hospital with nervous prostration. Of course Mr. Bell & Florrie persist in saying it is all nonsense & Mrs. Bell had greatest difficulty in gathering enough money to send him. They are the most inhuman set. She has had no servant for weeks, is so ill she can scarcely stand on her feet but none of them believe her.[257] Well, I must close, with fondest love from all.

Your loving mother
M. B. McQuesten

✦ A51-(5233) To Calvin McQuesten

Standoff, Alberta   "Whitehern"
June 13, 1904

My dear dear Cal,

Your letter of the 4th came in this morning. Last week no letter came at all. We all got home from Toronto on Saturday.[258] On the Tuesday afternoon Mrs. MacKay let me have the carriage and I made a number of calls, amongst others at the Hills, where I found Mrs. Hills with one hand tied up, she told me for months she had been laid up with blood poisoning, the result of picking the dead flowers off a primula, which is poisonous to some, both her hands and her face were swollen up and she had a terrible time.

That evening took dinner with the Vander Smissen's. Edith is a quite handsome girl, has passed her first year at Varsity and tied with another girl for Blake Scholarship in French & German.[259] After dinner came in Prof. Milner and Dr. Walker, but did not see much of them as they went off to play cards. The next morning Mrs. MacKay proposed that Mary should come down if she could share my room, so I was only too glad, as I had been wishing she could come and see the pastoral play with us. Hilda was invited to stay with Mary Trigge.[260] So I sent off a letter by special delivery on Wednesday, and M. came down on boat with H.

Tom had already got seats for "As you like it" in the afternoon for himself and me, and then he got seats for them for "Midsummer's Night Dream" in the evening. It was great extravagance, but it was a great treat and sometimes one gets reckless and I just feel the girls will get behind the times, if I do not make an effort sometimes. Fortunately the weather was fine, and the play was perfectly beautiful. Ben Greet says that the Dean's garden so-called at Varsity is the best scene for these plays of all the places they have found. The platform slightly raised and covered with green is beneath two immense branching forest trees, the Sun shone and the birds sang and the singing of the foresters was perfectly beautiful. It was all too lovely for words. Rosalind is beautiful and Ben Greet as Jaques and Field as Touchstone were killing. Isn't Shakespeare wonderful. The quaintness and wisdom strike one so forcibly when you hear it well recited. Miss Mathison has such an exquisite voice. The girls said the "Midsummer's Night Dream" was lovely, the fairies were so lovely, they were orphans from "The Dorothy Dix" Home at Boston. Tom said it was very pretty most amazing but not so worth seeing as "As You Like It."[261]

The next day Friday was Convocation in the gymnasium; Mrs. Mullin, Mary Trigge & Sydney Stevenson came to go with us, we went early and got good seats. Am sending you a programme, all these Eminent Men for LLD, spoke and then introducees [sic] and I enjoyed hearing them but it was after four before they were through and by the time all was done, it was half-past five and it rather spoiled the Garden Party, for we waited for Tom and I think a great many had come & gone. At any rate scarcely any of Tom's friends were there. I spoke to Mr. Coyne, Prof. Loudon, Mrs. Dickson, Mr. and Mrs. Gregory, Mrs. Dr. Palmer, Dr. & Mrs. Richardson, Constance & Evelyn Henderson & young Kellogg, but that was all.[262] Prof. Hutton came up and spoke to Tom at some distance from me, I was quite pleased to watch the calm dignified expression on Tom's face, he never seemed to reply but just listened to what he had to say. I Believe about all he said was that Tom had "made a lot of trouble for them to decide." But Hutton evidently has a great deal of force and he just carried it by his determination. Loudon looks nothing beside him and you cannot hear him at all. Was so sorry McGregor Young was not at the Garden Party, was so anxious to meet him for he did more than any one else for Tom and is the finest looking man on the staff. Tom enjoyed the dinner at night very much.

This morning I met Sandwell he is leaving for the Old Country on Tuesday, he lost a sister some time ago, said he would write you upon return. Expects just to have a quiet time at home, spoke of it as a duty visit. He said Tom <u>should</u> have had that scholarship. He thought he had done awfully well, to do what he did, with the managership of Varsity, as the work for that is enormous.

At Convocation the funniest thing was that among the Pharmacists was just one girl, a very pretty one too, and the students sang with great gusto "Just one girl," then of course the Agriculturalists were greeted with the most amusing noises from the barn yard. Harold Lazier took his M.A. & L.L.B.[263]

Yesterday we had Mr. Cunningham and really we can scarcely listen to him, his sermons are nothing but essays, delivered in a very uninteresting manner, no Bible instruction whatever, nothing to arouse a sinner's attention, as young Howitt said to me afterwards. Arthur Howitt called on Tom in the afternoon and I had him for tea, and he went to church.[264] He is travelling for New York firm and is going out to the coast. Peter Taylor took his degree and has started for his field near Brandon, but none of the students think he will ever do at all and he is doubtful himself, he has no way "of giving the glad hand" as Tom says.[265] The Pastoral Players are to be at Highfield to-morrow so I am sending Edna with Mrs. Mullin to-morrow afternoon.[266] Am sure she will be enchanted with "As You Like It."

Ruby has been calling on Mrs. Ogilvie and heard that Mr. & Mrs. Skeoch had only been in Montreal for three weeks. After they came back from the old country Mr. S. was so ill they thought he would die but the doctors got him off for Trinidad & he was there all winter and is now much better. Mrs. Skeoch was asking for Ruby & wanted her for Easter, but was not at home. Ken Trigge seems just to be going down and down, but R. [Ruby] did not give particulars.[267]

The fire in Toronto was a very serious affair for Mr. MacKay. Gordon told me he lost $50,000. The firm rented the warehouse from him and he had also bought the building next so the loss fell on him, the Stock was really very small. Mr. MacKay told Maggie he felt as if he should go out of his mind, between it all, paying $35 a week for Willie at Deer Park & $18 to Mrs. MacKay's nurse and Gordon's marriage, and there was some trouble there for Mr. MacKay paid the doctor's bill for the wife at the hospital. Drummond is becoming like a child with constant smoking and drinking. Mrs. MacKay's mind is quite clear now which is a comfort, but she is very weak and can only talk a little, but would like me always with her so have promised to go back again with Ruby and stay a little while, but it is a very sad household and I do not know what to say to Mr. M. He has lost all his joking now, poor man.

It is really maddening to think of those rude stupid people letting that child spoil all your good sermons. I suppose if you stopped and said you could not speak unless they could listen you would offend them & do harm that way, but I cannot speak at all unless I can meet people's eyes. It is strange the mother would not have the sense to take it out, they are such ignorant people and I am sure have not the faintest idea of how much a sermon costs you. Do not suppose they appreciate a good sermon when they hear it, if you only had some friend who could speak for you.

Hilda has just come in from Grace Rioch's and her wedding is postponed, the man is ill again. It is too provoking to think how Mrs. Rioch and Grace could shut their eyes and not see what a poor sick old looking man he was, but she just seemed mad to get married. Poor Aleck Harvey, the last of that family was buried here yesterday. Well, I must close, we expect Ruby on the 25th. Do not work too hard, it is not wise. Mary had card from Herbie Bell, just starting on Steamer Cassels North German Lloyd.[268] Poor Tom is working away at the garden. With fondest love from us all.

Your loving mother
M. B. McQuesten

✦ A52-(5283) To Calvin McQuesten

Standoff, Alberta

5 Queen's Park, Toronto, Ont.
Monday, August 8, 1904

My dear dear boy,

As we are going home to-morrow, I must write your letter to-day.[269] Yesterday heard Dr. Parsons in the morning,[270] but it rained heavily in the evening so could not go out. Dr. P. is very much roused just now (no wonder) as to the views of many of our professors & preachers, whom he considers to be the tools of the devil, as prophesied there should be in the latter days.[271]

Ruby went over to Mrs. Henderson's Saturday to stay till to-day. That would be all she could stand, she thought, as Constance chatters away about herself so much. Mr. H. & Ernest have gone to England.[272] Velyien is to return with them & has a lectureship at the Medical College here for a year.

It was very sad about Prof. Campbell, but I think it a kind Providence for him, as his feelings had been so wounded, but he was to have gone to Queen's and Mrs. C. is left with almost nothing.[273] Miss Parsons took dinner with us yesterday & inquired for you. On Saturday morning Willie [MacKay], R. & I went through the Parliament Bldgs. and over to the University.

There we saw that collection of pictures by Paul Kane, 100 of them, very interesting of native Chiefs and camp scenes of the West in the Early days.[274] I was glad to have seen them for they were talked about a great deal last winter, they belonged to E. B. Osler, I do not know if he has presented them to Univ. or not. Then we went through the Library they have some fine portraits there. We saw the new one of Goldwin Smith[275] presented by Ross Robertson.[276]

One of the troubles of this house is keeping Willie entertained. Mr. M. [MacKay] does not at all understand that he is just in that condition of mind which leads on to insanity, and some congenial employment's the only thing that might save him, & how that is to be got is the question. Whether Mr. M. is as rich as supposed, I do not know, but he talks as if he were very hard up. One never knows, because so frequently old men get the notion that they are poor or going to be. And if Mr. M. would only give Willie sufficient money, it would be a great help. He is afraid to go outside the gate without a companion and he would like a paid one. It is a very pitiable case. Saturday evening in day-light, Drummond [MacKay] was brought home by a young man in a cab, helpless; the maids had to drag him up stairs and for a long time he could not be quieted. Fortunately I was not down-stairs at the time. But I will be so glad to get home. I can do nothing & it is all so deplorable. Gordon [MacKay] came up the other day in a cab, very much the worse. He has bought a house in Parkdale and he and his wife live there. They had been in New York, "Had the trip of his life" he said. Poor Mr. M. is hardly able to put one foot before the other. This afternoon we went for a drive and called at the Parsons and had afternoon Tea, and quite brightened Mr. M. up.[277]

When we came in found Miss Craig and she is very jolly. Ruby had come back from Mrs. H. [Henderson] after lunch & went with us, but has gone back there for dinner to meet some young people. After I commenced this letter yours came in; it was so interesting. And so glad you had the chance of meeting the other men at Presbytry meeting and that they were all so friendly. I do not understand how people can be Xtians and be so indifferent to other workers as these Anglicans are.[278]

It is Perfectly lovely to think of you being at Varsity again & so near us, though you must dread going to work again, but perhaps you may find it easier than you did & not find just the pass course so heavy.[279] The Y.M.C.A. secretary Rogers is going to be ordained, I see, though he took no course and if you find you cannot stand the study you could just go back to the preaching and in time I am sure, would make yourself so valuable you might be ordained too.

We are going down town in the morning & I will see about the Mounts at once.[280] I think it is fine to think of you having so much money to your credit. I <u>do</u> wish you could bring your horse with you, it would be so lovely for exercise, though the cars & automobiles might frighten it, but it would cost more to keep it than yourself. If only we had some of the MacKay's money! Must close, hope you will not fail to see Banff, borrow from some one & I will send it to you. With fondest love.

Your mother
M. B. McQuesten

[P.S.] Have run out of Ocean [?] post. Must compliment your handwriting it is so improved.

✦ A53-(MCP 1-1.25) To Thomas B. McQuesten

Carleton P.O. Carleton, Ont   "Whitehern"
August 18, 1904

My dearest boy,

The important thing of this week has been Edna's results. You may be sure there was great hurrahing when the Times came in on Monday with "honours" in French, Latin and Greek, though I think Edna rather hoped for a scholarship in Classics. There is a mistake somewhere as the papers state the

Governor General's Scholarship to Queen's for Classics and the girl who won it, did not take Greek, neither could she have taken it for general proficiency. I wrote registrar of Queen's inquiring as Thompson is in the North-West.[281]

Saturday's News had two of Cal's pictures, but the article was not to be seen. I hope it will appear next Saturday or Cal will be disappointed. He says he has some schemes for making something out of his photography. Have sent you several papers lately, as I thought you probably did not see any, and there were some interesting items.

The Japs are going ahead at a great rate. There is not doubt at all in the minds of Christian people that God is specially using them just now for the punishment of Russia for the treatment she has given His ancient people. When you think of it now all Europe has been afraid of Russia and suddenly there rose up this little people whom we used to laugh at, and who have completely vanquished her, and Russia acts as if she were paralized [sic].[282]

Mr. Singer came in last night to tell me about Wittenberg, the one I was trying to get work for. He had finally to go to Toronto and Mr. Singer says now he preaches with him, he is very eloquent and perfectly fearless and the other night addressed about 300 Jews.[283] Jean Ross came on Tuesday. Mr. Murray is back from the old country and took them all for a drive yesterday. We are all to go to Mrs. Fletcher's to-night and they come to us to-morrow. I mean Mrs. Ross and Margaret. We borrow Mrs. Davidson's chair for Margaret.

We are having cool weather, and a good deal of rain. We have not required any ice yet. Hilda came home on Monday, looking much better but she did not care for Walkerton or its people. Of course the Richardsons were very kind and Mr. [?] has been over very often but he seems very wretched and constantly suffering. I see that Dr. Osler has been appointed Regius Professor of Medicine at Oxford to succeed Sir John B. Sanderson. Herbie Bell writes that he has got quite fat, but tried some lessons in German and found he could do no study.

Perhaps you will not understand what this money is, about which there has been such an extra-ordinary decision in House of Lords. When the Free Church came out from the Old Kirk in Scotland, through Dr. Chalmers and Dr. Guthrie's eloquence and exertions a Sustentation Fund was raised to support the ministers who had left the Old Kirk, so that each one had about 300 pounds. When last year, or short time ago the Free Church & United Presbyterians joined & were called United Free Church, 24 of the Free would not join and these 24 stiff old Highlanders actually went to court to reap the Funds which had been vested in various properties. They lost it in Scotland and appealed to House of Lords, who really know nothing about it. One cannot imagine men of that sort to be Christians as to interfere with the whole progress of the Church to carry their views. It will never be tolerated.[284] Well dear, time is fast passing. I see you are paying great attention to the nourishment question. Try dear, not to neglect the study of your Bible. I hope you have a reference one, for one gets a great deal of light by comparing passages. I never could have believed it possible, that Prof. McFadyen could have got so far astray but I hear that he does not really believe in the Old Testament at all. He will soon be a Unitarian for he says God did not ordain the sacrifices among the Jews, that they just followed their heathen neighbours. I wonder the students had so little strength of mind as to be led away by him.[285] I see the Turbinia does not leave Toronto every <u>Friday</u> till 8:30 p.m. With fondest love.

Your mother

[M. B. McQuesten]

✦ A54-(MCP 3-5.57) To T. B. McQuesten, ESQ. B.A.

c/o G. H. Osler, Esq.	"Whitehern"
Beamsville, P.O. Ont.[286]	Thursday Evening
[Written on Envelope]	[Postmark] September 30, 1904
Keep till called for.	

My dearest boy,

Have just returned from Toronto to-night, and have secured rooms for you and Cal at 22 Grosvenor St. I had sent an advertisement to the Telegram for last Friday and Saturday, but none of the replies would answer. I went down Tuesday, unfortunately it rained Monday. Went to Varsity Y.M.C.A. and the Central one on McGill St. They told me it was almost an impossibility to find a single room, the secretary of Y.M.C. had been wanting one for himself. But after a steady house to house visitation of Czar, St. Joseph, St. Vincent, Grosvenor, Grenville & Wood Sts., I succeeded in getting two single rooms at Miss Oates, 22 Grosvenor, one on second story at $7.00 a month and one on third story at $5.00. Two respectable spinsters own the house and it's clean and warm, they assured me, but there is no gas in the bed-rooms and I am so afraid you will think them small, but rents have gone up and prices of rooms also and every place seemed filled, and I thought you would rather have a small room to yourself than share a room or bedroom with Cal.

Mrs. MacKay had failed very much, and scarcely knew me, takes very little notice now. I saw that unless I secured a room, you would be out in the cold, though I would have preferred to have had you choose your own. Cal was hoping to get here Saturday if his ticket reached him and I hope you will too.

(Friday Morning) Cal has just arrived, sporting large moustache. Hope you are quite well, have a wretched pen. With much love.

Your Mother

M. B. McQuesten

[P.S.] Enclosed is $5.00.

✦ A55-(MCP 2-4.52) To Thomas McQuesten

22 Grosvenor St.   "Whitehern"
Toronto, Ontario   May 18, 1905

My dearest boy,

Will begin a letter though I have been thinking perhaps to hear from you as to your success[287] and whether to expect you home this week. As you left so recently of course there is not much to tell. In either Monday or Tuesday "News" there was a capital article by W. A. Fraser on American and English Magazines and Novels. It gave the novel writers Mrs. Humphrey Ward, Anthony Hope [Hawkins], and others a fine dressing down, for their founding their tales on immoral characters and it was every word true. I wish the authors could read his article and I trust many young people may read it. People are becoming accustomed to read and speak of the vilest lives without being at all shocked. Just as everybody read "Trilby" and discussed it too, and young gentlemen presented it to young ladies. It was simply disgraceful.[288]

By a piece of good luck I got hold of Willie Stuart yesterday to cut the grass but he is engaged all the time by Mr. Ptolemy so I must look for someone else. This evening we saw Mrs. Mullin off at the station on her way to Baltimore. On Saturday the steamers Macassa and Modjeska[289] both commence running and time table is changed. They leave here at 8:30 a.m., 2 p.m., and 5:15 p.m—and Toronto at 9 a.m., 2 p.m. and 5:15 p.m., so you must remember that.

Well this is Friday morning and as have heard nothing by post will enclose your tickets in case you decide at last minute to come up. We are busy housecleaning. May God bless you! With much love.

Your Mother
M. B. McQuesten

✦ A56-(5333) To Calvin McQuesten

Staney Brae, Muskoka   "Whitehern"
                                  June 7, 1905

My dear dear Calvin,

Many and most hearty congratulations to you on successfully passing your examinations! You see I am writing on my best paper, as befitting the occasion. All the family join in the great rejoicing. This morning just as Tom was preparing to go out and see the Newspaper, Mrs. Mullin arrived to tell the good news. We all wanted to send a telegram, but concluded you would not receive it any sooner than a letter as it was not a matter of life and death, so Mrs. M. and we decided it was useless. Just to think of it Cal, through your

<u>third</u> year and <u>no sups!</u> Isn't it delightful? It will be such a weight off your mind. Am glad to know you are pleasantly situated, but we have not been having very favourable weather for Muskoka; we have had a great deal of rain with thunderstorms and very cool.[290] Tom is impatiently waiting to hear from that man Kerr, it seems strange he does not hear one way or the other.[291] Norman Fergus B. took dinner with us on Saturday, he took double first class honours at Queen's thus winning his M.A. as well as B.A., besides getting a gold medal. He is a very gentlemanly, good looking fellow. This is our "day", but the weather is not very favourable. You must have had quite a pleasant visit in Gravenhurst. I should think you <u>would</u> be sleepy after you got to Muskoka after all the running about and <u>thinking</u> you did here. I do not know what will become of you unless you stop thinking sometimes. Well, we shall see you next week, I suppose. Hilda goes to Sydney Stevenson on Monday. Hurrah! Calvin Hurrah! With much love from all.

Your loving mother
M. B. McQuesten

✦ A57-(5359) To Calvin McQuesten

Staney Brae,   "Whitehern"
Lake Joseph, Muskoka   July 17, 1905

My dearest Calvin,

Your enclosure reached me on Saturday and I was delighted to go out and pay some bills. It enabled me amongst other things to pay for the gas grate which was put in <u>before Xmas</u> which was quite a relief. It does seem perfectly astonishing where money goes. We have all just been trying to count it, what becomes of it, for sometimes it seems as if we should not be so close run and I should have plenty to help you boys, without your feeling troubled. Last year we had $1500 (besides my Montreal stock), as my Bold St. house needed no repair, and yet we were never closer run, and tried to be most economical. Yet when one compares the incomes of others, some require twice as much to live as well, and some have only half of it. We can only be deeply grateful for what we have, when we realize how much it takes to live.

On Saturday Tom brought Dr. Hutchison with him, I do not know if you have met him, a very nice pleasant little man, they went off this morning, the girls had to be up at five as the Turbinia leaves at 7. I am so thankful that you are in Muskoka this year, the warmest summer for many years, but fortunately the nights have been cool enough to be comfortable and our house is cool. To-day it is like a furnace outside. Mr. Ketchen is doing so well, he really preaches remarkably fine sermons, no mincing matters and so to the point.[292] I think that book of Gordon's is admirable. I found it very helpful.[293]

Nellie Mullin is here but have not seen much of her, she was here to tea one evening. Last week we picked our gooseberries and preserved and also the <u>cherries</u>, had great difficulty in getting them picked and they were not very good, a great many spoiled. On Saturday the Commercial Travellers were having a great celebration, and they had a procession, really a most clever and amusing affair. Cages of wild beasts I cannot write it. Must wait till we see you. Have not sufficient energy left in me to describe it. It was indeed a good thing Jamieson left Christian work as soon as he did, before he disgraced it.[294] He may be sadly lacking in common sense.

Well, excuse this apology for a letter, and hope to be more interesting next time. With much love from all.

Your loving mother
M. B. McQuesten

✦ A58-(5382) To Calvin McQuesten

Staney Brae,   "Whitehern"
Lake Joseph, Muskoka   August 15, 1905

My dearest Calvin,

I was so delighted to hear of your great success on the Anniversary Sabbath. It was really <u>most</u> gratifying and I was particularly glad to know, you had opposed so successfully the chartering of the Islander. They did that the summer we were in Port Carling and we all decided it was a very wrong thing of the church to do, to countenance a Sunday Excursion. I really think it was a very large sum to raise. You must indeed find it almost impossible to get any quiet time at all. This is probably the very worst month, if you stay in September you would get more quiet. Mr. Mack says it would not do to use salts of sorrel, it would rot your shoes to pieces. Shall we send you some pipe clay. On Friday we had Mary Trigge, Mrs. Locke and Helen, Mrs. Mullin and Nellie for a farewell tea to Mrs. Locke, they are going to Toronto to live with Arthur Trigge.[295] Helen will go nursing so Hilda's last friend is gone.

Joe Thomson's wedding is next Saturday, as Lady Taylor is not well, it is to be a quiet one in the house.[296] Mrs. Thomson is very sorry as she will feel quite alone at the wedding, none of her own friends being there, Joe wanted it in the church and to have the Highlanders with himself in Highland uniform. Our girls are much disappointed. Mrs. T. [Thomson] does not like to <u>repeat</u> <u>Laura's</u> opinions of the marriage. L. of course is still away.[297] Your rates are very high. Nellie Mullin and Anna Laidlaw were at a place upon the Lake of Bays where they were very comfortable at $5.00 a week single rooms.

I am afraid Edna is not very comfortable with John [Baker] because of his incessant arguing against the Bible.[298] Lorrie's sister was there and told Edna Lorrie had been much disappointed in John, his violent temper and the way she has to work are very trying. I am regretting I sent her, every-thing irritates her.[299]

Tom was in Newmarket last week and tried to find out some of the old land marks. The Registrar, with whom Tom had business, knew of Grandpapa. Tom went back there on Monday. Warm close weather last week but Sabbath night came in such a chill I was rather upset.

We had Logie Macdonnell, on Sabbath evening, he managed to give a sort of an address on a Psalm without mentioning the name of Jesus Christ. In fact not a word of the gospel in it. It is almost impossible to conceive of a preacher being really a converted man, who has so little conception of his duty and opportunity in the pulpit. They can never have grasped the thought of a lost soul, or they could not stand up in a pulpit and talk such twaddle. It is really terrible to think of the church in the hands of such men. Certainly Dr. Lyle has been most unfortunate in his assistants.[300] Mr. Ketchen is so different, he is so earnest, wears himself out indeed.

What a lot of people you meet in Muskoka, it is most interesting. You are very gay indeed with all your aquatic events. I noticed the names of the Van Nostrands and Williamsons. Helen Locke said the Dicksons speak so highly of you. Mrs. Hill gets her butter and eggs from them and Mrs. D. is so kind and nice and often brings over hot Johnny cake. They would not have room for Edna would they? It rained all night and so far to-day. Well, dear, there is nothing more worth saying. With much love from all.

Your loving mother
M. B. McQuesten

[P.S.] We had quite an original and amusing letter from Dr. Hutchison, the writing ten degrees worse than yours, so I feel encouraged.[301]

✦ A59-(5426) To Calvin McQuesten

Knox College

"Whitehern"
Tuesday, 8:20 a.m.
October 10, 1905.

Dearest Cal,

Just a line. We telephoned Dr. Clark <u>yesterday morning</u>. E. [Edna] had not slept all night. He came in the afternoon E. took to him at once and believed in him, he said she was at a very critical point wished he had seen her a month ago. <u>Ordered</u> a nurse and that she should be put in warm pack at night and on no account any sleeping medicine. We hurried all over for nurse, in "Gods" great goodness He directed us through Miss Turnbull of Central Church, to a relative here on holiday from Montreal, a graduate from Edinboro, a specialist in nervous cases. Miss Hutton a middle-aged warm hearted motherly soul, who just suited E. exactly, knew just how to take to her, very cheerful and amusing. Think she got to sleep shortly after two. Before that the trains excelled themselves.[302] Dr. C. also prescribed fresh air and good nourishment so must get her out of the City at once. Will make inquires about place at Waterdown where the Douglas Buchanans stayed.[303, 304]

Your loving mother
M. B. McQuesten

[P.S.] Last night we could not thank God enough for the help given us. Tom took the *Horace*.[305]

✦ A60-(5464) To Calvin McQuesten

Standoff, Alberta   372 Assinaboine Ave.[306]
                                                     Winnipeg, Manitoba
                                                     May 17, 1906

My dearest Calvin,

Our meetings are over finished this afternoon. It was assigned to me to give the closing words, so the weight is now off my mind. As you are my own, you would like to know how I did. Well, it seemed to me, as if I were inspired for it, for my memory was so aided, that what I had prepared came to me without having to glance but a little at my notes. Any thing to equal the kind words of praise given me especially by the Western Women you cannot imagine. They all said I had helped them so much, it was more touching than I can say.[307]

We were all invited on Tuesday to Mrs. Colin Campbell's for tea, and Mrs. Campbell invited me to come to her to-morrow and stay till Monday, they have a magnificent house. Then on Tuesday we are arranging a party to go out to see some of the schools. We had a great number of the missionaries in the West at the meeting and among them Dr. & Mrs. Gilbart, they both asked most specially for you, and I expect to visit them at Rolling River, as we make our tour; She, Miss Clark of Toronto, is a dear little woman but <u>so</u> delicate.[308]

On Wednesday afternoon we were invited by Lady McMillan to Government House;[309] then this afternoon we were at Mrs. J. M. Aikins, Solicitor of C.P.R., magnificent house. They are Methodists of course, but these Winnipeg people have feted us royally. Chas. Gordon asked for you to-day. Winnipeg is a beautiful city and I am in such a lovely family. It does seem such a long time since I heard from you. Our only draw-back has been the weather since Tuesday, extremely warm, then thunderstorms, which took a great deal out of us, cool to-day but threats of rain.

Rev. John Taylor and wife arrived and was to have spoken at last night's meeting, but word came of the death of his mother and they went right on, was introduced to her mother, Mrs. Copeland. If only I <u>could</u> remember all the people I have met. Just before I left a letter came from Geills McCrae

Kilgour[310] to Miss McLean who was visiting Mattie Davidson, with a message for you to stay a few days at Brandon. Well dear, I must close. My heart is full of thanksgiving for all the way by which I have come. Do hope you are in good spirits. With fondest love.

Your loving Mother
M. B. McQuesten

✦ A61-(5470) To Calvin McQuesten

Standoff, Alberta

372 Assinaboine Ave,
Winnipeg
May 21, 1906

My dearest boy,

It does seem so very long since I heard from you and I trust to hear before I start for home which will be about June 9th if all goes well. To-morrow morning Mrs. Steele, Mrs. McLagan[311] and I start for Minnedosa, where Dr. Gilbart is to meet us and drive about 16 miles to his reserve at Rolling River. Then we expect to be in Birtle for the 24th. After that I am not very clear as to our movements, but will be at File Hills June 3rd and after that will go to Regina. We can do all this for about $22 as we go single fare. I do hope the weather will be fine or I do not know how we shall manage. On Friday I went to Hon. Colin Campbell's and stayed till to-day.[312] They have a new house built in Colonial style, with every thing very fine and in the newest style. Mrs. C. is extremely warm-hearted and kind and all my newspapers have been posted at the Attorney-General's expense.

On Saturday had my first experience of an Automobile ride and do not want another—decided that only a childish man could enjoy it. Amongst the visitors on Sabbath was a Dr. Fred Young who said you were at Varsity with him. He seemed very nice and interested in you and has got on here very well. In the evening we heard Ralph Connor again.

In the letter from Hilda to-day she tells me Sydney Stevenson is with her; the story of Hart's life and death is a very sad one she says. She also tells me that poor Annie Ward has died, it must have been sudden, for she was at Montreal. I am very very sorry not to be at home when Edna gets there but really I must use all my opportunities for seeing the West.[313] Every one is so kind and I am feeling very well. I do hope you are keeping well; the weather is very changeable, for the most part cold and windy. On Friday after the meetings it was fearfully cold & windy but I was afraid to waste a day, so we took the street-cars to Kildonan. We had to cross a wide stretch of mud to reach the gate of cemetery, but managed to keep our rubbers on. Most interesting. The monuments of Rev. John Blach and wives, Rev. Dr. Robertson, Rev. Jas and Mrs. Nisbet, Rev. Dr. and Mrs. King and son and many other old and revered Presbyterians. On my way back we carried a stick according to the old custom to scrape the mud off our rubbers before taking the cars. Afterwards went to a tea at Mrs. Sifton's, mother of the Hon. Clifford, meet Lady Schultz every where, she is most agreeable. Must close with fondest love and hoping to hear you are well. Mr. McMillan suggests you should look out for inspectorship, I suppose he means of school in Alberta. Just as he was speaking we were interrupted.

Your loving Mother
M. B. McQuesten

✦ A62-(5487) To Calvin McQuesten

Standoff, Alberta

372 Assinaboine Ave
Winnipeg, Manitoba
June 7, 1906

Dearest Calvin,

Reached here this morning at 7 o'clock and most thankful to be here. I think I wrote you from File Hills, well on Monday, after the Sabbath, (Communion Service) with the Indians, Mr. Heron, principal of Regina School drove Mrs. Steele and myself over to Regina, a distance of 86 miles. We started about 10 o'clock Monday morning a beautiful summer morning, and the scenery as we passed through the ravines and down into the Qu'Appelle Valley was most lovely, the river widens out into a lake and 4 miles from the Fort is the great Catholic School under Father Huguenard, a most vigourous, unscrupulous French priest, who sticks at nothing to bring in the Indians, and who is the greatest difficulty to our missionaries. At the Fort we took lunch with Gus Laing and his wife (a very nice looking young women).[314] You see Mrs. Steele belonged to his father's congregation; he inquired most kindly for you and they were both very kind, he is very much improved.

It began to threaten rain but we started off about 4 o'clock and reached the house of the Indian farm instructor just in time for tea and to escape a heavy thunderstorm. They were hospitable people and Mrs. Davidson a very kind woman, and Mr. Heron says they are glad to see ladies, they see so few.[315] Mrs. Steele and I shared a small room, we had driven that day 35 miles and we were up in the morning for 7:30 breakfast.

We started off to get the Interpreter and visit the Reserves—Pasquah's, MusCoetung's [sic], and Piapot's. The interpreter, Stevenson, is a half-breed married to a squaw, we had to wait in their house, whilst he got ready. Most providentially for me, the day before he had brought home a new covered buggy and Mr. Heron arranged I was to drive with him. He is a very kind good Xtian man, has been many years on the Reserve and could tell me a great deal, but unfortunately it came on to rain, and poured so that we had to give up seeing the Indians and take most direct route. So we drove 16 miles in the rain to another farm instructor's. Where we found the wife, a very nice little Scotchwoman with two little children (she had come out a bride). She gave us a very good lunch and Mr. Heron pleased her by taking the children's photos, she had been anxious to send their pictures home and had never had the chance. How I pity these nice little women! By this time the rain had stopped. Stevenson left us and we had a delightful afternoon to drive to Regina. We were not tired, the prairie roads are so soft and quiet; we stopped by a stream, rested the horses and ate our own tea, and felt all right till we reached the Regina roads. Then we suffered. Muddy, rough, if the horses went off a walk, we were shaken to pieces. However we finally reached the school, which is 4 miles beyond Regina. We had driven 51 miles. Mr. Heron said, it was an astonishment to him, the way we had stood it. Mrs. Steele and I had a room at the Principal's house, Mr. H. gave us his room, he is a bachelor and boards at the school. It is wretchedly out of repair, built by the government and like a barracks inside and out. It is to be decided by the Assembly whether the Church continues to carry it on; it has not paid so far, but in the face of what the Catholic Church is doing with the Indians, it would be a very wrong thing for the Church to give it up. Mr. Heron has only been there a year, give him time and he will bring it into shape for he is an extremely fine man,[316] very manly (went to S. Africa with Strathcona's Horse and was one of the 130 men who were fit for service at the close of the war) and very spiritually minded, 6' ft 4" in height, but delicate, such a pity![317]

Well, the morning after our arrival, we were thoroughly tired it was pouring rain, we had to go out in it to reach the College for breakfast and I could give no ideas of the wind (Regina is celebrated for it worse than Winnipeg) accordingly it is impossible to keep the floors clean, and boys' feet are always muddy and it lies in lumps all over the halls, the dining-room and the school-rooms. Just a sickening place. My plan was to leave Regina that evening for Winnipeg. Mrs. Steele was to remain with a cousin, Mrs. Shaw a sister of Mrs. Jaffary's.[318] So in the afternoon Dr. Shaw drove out for Mrs. Steele, he had a covered buggy with a span, so I was providentially brought into the station without being wet, through indescribable seas of mud. In the meantime poor Mrs. Shortreed, ill with a cold, had arrived with her daughter. They were driven in later, in an uncovered Democrat and of course very wet. They were going a few miles on train to Sintaluta and then drive 8 miles to Hurricane Hills, how Mrs. S. would stand it I do not know. In the meantime when my train came in, it was pouring in torrents, we had to make a rush and to reach the Tourist, one must go through a pond of mud or force the dining car porter to let us on, he had just turned down several, when I reached him and insisted that I must get on there, a gentleman backed me up, so he was helpless. On looking into the 'Tourist' felt I could not venture it, so went into a Pullman, no lower berth vacant. However after I had taken my dinner (the first swell dinner since I left home and I had no provisions at all with me and was too tired to go without) I returned to the sleeper and a young lady said, you are going to have my lower berth, it would be a shame for you to climb up. Wasn't it sweet of her? So I had a most comfortable night and reached here this morning, it was not raining and I got up nicely to Mrs. Bryce's,[319] but now it is pouring rain again and my plan is to go out to Tenlon Hospital this evening Saturday in the morning; starting for home on Saturday morning but laying off at Kenora, to visit our Cecilia Jeffery School on Lake of the Woods, said to be a beautiful trip. Then I go on Monday night to catch boat at Fort William and expect to reach home on Thursday 14th. [320]

So glad to receive your first letter at Regina (Mrs. Bryce sent it on) and another dated May 23rd and Macleod P.O. 29th was here when I arrived to-day. Very glad to know, you are feeling better and have a horse; hope it will be just what you like. Sorry to hear Mr. Jaffary is leaving Macleod. Had letter from Ruby also, says E. [Edna] feeling better and brighter all the time, she will be home now. Am so glad according to my suggestion R. [Ruby] is arranging with Miss Middleton to go to Quebec as soon as her holidays arrive. They are going down the Ottawa by Steamer, and she has written to a boarding-house Miss Robinson knows so I hope nothing will prevent their having a lovely time.[321]

If you have any suggestions as to things or places worth seeing be sure and write her immediately as your letters are so long in coming. The only thing I dread now is having to give an account of my travels, but suppose I shall get through.

I do feel so thankful for the encouraging report of yourself and Edna.[322] God is so good to us and I could not but thank Him for the many ways in which my various journeys have been made easier for me. With fondest love, Calvin dear.

Your loving Mother
M. B. McQuesten

✦ A63-(5512) To Calvin McQuesten
Macleod, Alberta

[Written at top of letter A63-5512]. Nellie James has just brought home your red mittens. Thought you'd enjoy R's letter. Cannot find your box number.

"Whitehern"
June 21st 1906

My dearest Calvin,

I was very glad indeed to hear you were feeling so much like yourself, but very sorry indeed about the Jaffarys. It is certainly most trying to have them go away for I quite understand how you feel, somehow or other it is so difficult to feel quite at home with perfect strangers and one meets so few congenial people. We had a letter from Ruby to-day enclosing me one from person with whom we were to stay on Gatineau and she has to give us up as she cannot get servants, so we are quite upset again.

You will be shocked to hear that Central Church was completely burned out last night. You can imagine our consternation, I was awakened about one o'clock by a glare in my window and a sound like an explosion of an automobile. I looked out and just on the road near our small gate was this explosive light, like natural gas coming out of the front and burning. Then over at McKay's door, it seemed as if people were throwing firecrackers on the street. No one seemed to be on the streets, till at last two young men came along and I heard them say "it is a live wire, they couldn't get in at McKay's so went down the street.[323] Shortly after the fire reels all rushed up and I wondered why, when they stopped in front of the church, and we saw just a little smoke coming out, they broke in the glass doors, and out poured the smoke, then there was an explosion and the whole inside seemed to be a mass of flames it must have been burning for hours. The fire-men worked hard and turned on tremendous streams of water, and so confined the fire to the church, but it is completely burned out, it really was a sad sight. I hear there is only $29,000 insurance, but it is just another instance of danger of electricity. One never knows, what freak it may take.[324]

I am just bothered trying to get my report of the West into shape, there are so many interruptions and we are to have an evening meeting for all. Tom was up on Saturday, but do not expect him this week, he is practising for the rowing races with the Argonauts. Mrs. McKenzie of Staney Brae wrote Mary a kind letter saying she was to have your room for $6 [I] would like to go there too, but thought at first, that it would be monotonous for the whole family to go to one place and now would not like to propose it, as she could not afford to give us all such low rates. Colin Fletcher was very ill with peritonitis, but is much better. Hilda is going to the Gartshores first then Mrs. Collins and then Bessie Richardson's.[325] Hilda did not visit Mrs. Collins. Edna is very cheerful & well & if the girls had not to do the work, we would both rather stay at home. With much love.

Your loving mother
M. B. McQuesten

✦ A64-(5596) To Calvin McQuesten
MacLeod, Alberta

Bayview Farm, Dorset, Ont.
August 13, 1906

My dearest Cal,

We were glad to hear from you on Saturday. I missed your letter a week before, but just knew you were out of reach of P.O. We were not able to get to Dorset to church yesterday morning, but in the evening, R. [Ruby] and I went with a young man and his sister to the Methodist Church. Service does not begin till 7.30, so it was nine when we started to row back in the dark, but it was a clear starlight night, though no moon and they made a bon-fire on our shore so we got home alright. We heard a most remarkable sermon from a young Englishman with a broad dialect though he did not drop his h's. Sometimes we did not know at all what he was talking about, he used very flowery and original language and it was a marvel to me how he talked so long and voluminously about nothing and not a word of the Bible in it or a particle of gospel teaching. I am almost wild with the preachers. Before he began he announced that he was physically tired after an 8 miles walk from his last service but his tongue was not weary apparently, his prayers were equally remarkable, but perhaps I am too matter of fact and practical to appreciate the imaginative.

It was very cold yesterday morning but it is warming up again. We have now got in the next room to us a fat doctor from Berlin with his wife and child, the latter has taken away the peace of our house. I am thankful we had so many weeks of quiet. We have been here nearly five weeks, so the holidays are fast flying. I am sorry for the girls; for me there is no place like home. I fancy Mary's sleep has been disturbed too for she speaks of having gone out to the boat house to sleep and being much quieter. If we could fill our house here with our own party, it would be perfect, the situation is so lovely and the table so good. Hilda is in Walkerton now they are so kind to her always. Tom is a naughty boy not to write you, but I think he is not a good hand at writing letters. To make up for my stupid letters will enclose the family ones. It is a good thing I think to be getting fat, if one's nerves are to rest Dr A. says one must be fat. With much love from us all.

Your loving mother
M. B. McQuesten

[P.S.] By the papers see that Central Church has determined to build on cor-ner of Hannah and Caroline.

✦ A65-(5622) To Calvin McQuesten

Macleod, Alberta   Bayview Farm, Dorset P.O.
                                    August 20, 1906

My dearest Cal,

I was glad to see by weather probs that it was cooler in Alberta, for you would feel the heat very trying; it was extremely warm here on Saturday but is somewhat cooler. On Wednesday we had a great surprise in the shape of David Ross. His story at first was that he had been at home with a sore leg and before going back to his surveying job on the C.P.R. had come up to recruit. At first I quite enjoyed his visit, he got a canoe and we went out paddling and one day I actually started to paddle having got on a stream so shallow that we were in danger of grounding. But alas! it was all a sham.

Would you believe it he had come to propose to Ruby! It was last night she told me, and you can imagine I scarcely slept a wink all night. It was a complete surprise to her too, for she had never dreamed of it, he is only 24, Tom's age, is three years younger than R. Of course I know that he is a fine tempered Christian lad, and as R. says they have much in common, she is fond of all the Rosses, but we both think he must wait a while till his prospects are more settled.

I feel rather cross with him thinking about it at all with his mother and sisters all working for a living, but of course he tells R. that he would not be ready for two years. He is working with the head engineer on the new double track of the C.P.R. between Fort William and Winnipeg, gets $100 a month and expects soon $125. Has a man working his homestead, which is 50 miles north of Regina: his plan is to build a home there for his mother and Jean, they expect also to have Bessie's children to bring up. But it seems to me that R. ought to do better than this, she is a very attractive girl and it has always been a grievous disappointment that she never seems to meet any one worth looking at.

Then too I do not know whether David's view of things is to be trusted, the Rosses are as a family easily satisfied (I fancy) for they have been brought up very plainly and what D. might consider a very comfortable home I would not at all. R. is not worldly wise enough either. He looks such a boy too and has a weak face, sometimes I feel angry at his presumption; he speaks of the wife of one of the engineers, the only lady living in a car and I believe they both think this would not be so bad, poor simpletons. The more I think of it the less I favour it. Sometimes I know I am thoroughly irked, for R. suggests that they might do much home mission work there and I know that is true but it seems as if R. were fitted to take a fine place in a higher sphere. When you write me about this do so on a separate sheet. In the meantime D. is to be told to wait till his prospects have developed.[326] Edna is writing. Write to Hamilton next time. With much love from all.

Your mother

M. B. McQuesten

✦ A66-(5630) To Calvin McQuesten

Macleod, Alberta

Bayview Farm, Dorset, P.O.
August 27, 1906

My dearest Cal,

All being well this is my last letter from here. We start home on Thursday and just think of poor us the boat leaves at half past five, and the mornings lately have been misty and chilly for rain has been threatening and falling since Saturday. It was very trying to have another wet Sabbath yesterday; one cannot read all day. Ruby received some very interesting views of

Portsmouth from Dr. McDonald (her Ottawa friend) he was travelling abroad and it seemed so fortunate that he sent views from there for all the places. I was most glad to see views of Southsea (where he was staying) and Portsmouth.[327] He really has been very kind to R. he sent her a green tie from Ireland and she wrote thanking him when he replied sending the views.

We had a great thunderstorm here yesterday and the thunder reverberates round the hills and we see such beautiful rainbows. I wonder if I mentioned seeing about three weeks ago a fine display of Northern Lights and a wonderful circle of light just like a bow reaching completely over the heavens from Dorset shore to ours. Later in the Times Mary saw an article by R. Marsh, it was a moon-bow and as fine as he had seen in Labrador.

Every one, including the Misses Shaw went out of our house last week, so we have fine quiet sleeps for the first time, for this early departure and late arrival of steamers is the great trouble of this place and it is a serious one for a bad sleeper like myself.

David Ross went off on Thursday, he is such a restless jump-about, it was quite a relief. I feel thoroughly cross, every time I think of him, speaking to any girl before he had any settled living at all with his mother a poor worn out looking woman. It is a crazy idea too, that they have of Mrs. Ross and Jean settling out on a homestead 50 miles north of Regina on which a house has to be built.[328] But then I am afraid, I am too worldly wise, it troubles me very much too, to think that I am.

Have the August Westminister but am waiting for family to read it, and will send it, unfortunately it was left out on the verandah and got wet. Did I mention to you that Percy Robertson failed again in his examinations, his mother told me, the evening before I left home, her trials with him, and she is determined not to send him back to college.[329] I just feel sorry for her, denying herself and he simply pleasing himself; she is far too amiable. Irwin Proctor had been no help to him, having lots of money and it seemed too bad he should have got through. Mrs. P. thought he would not, for he had been wasting his time.[330] Dear me! I am thankful my sons never gave me such anxiety, it would have been the hardest trial and is, that a mother can endure. It was very sad the drowning of that young McQueen. Will send the Presbyterian of last week after the family has read, there are one or two interesting items. Mr. McGillivray in China had such a narrow escape.[331] Now that the Jaffarys are gone you would not see church papers. Cannot you persuade the McNeils to take it, it would do the young men good to keep in touch with the church.

Will send the family letters so you can know what they are doing. Had a letter from Mrs. Bell from St. Joseph's Hospital, she went back from Muskoka to get the house ready with a servant before Mr. Bell got back from sea-side, and Herbert is to be home this week; she felt ill but she as usual made desperate effort and made red currant jelly, then telephoned for doctor as she was only able to move. So was taken in ambulance and Heurner Mullin (Dr. Malloch being away) attended; it was inflammation of the bowels, but she escaped an operation. You will be glad of cooler weather but the warm weather is best for this region, but you always liked the cold and it would be more bracing.

It was fortunate Convocation Hall was ready for B.M. Association meetings. Think when I return, I shall have Tom pay his and your subscription to the fund. Do not like the bills coming and sometime you can pay me back. With much love from all.

Your loving mother
M. B. McQuesten

✦ A67-(5654) To Calvin McQuesten

Macleod, Alberta

"Whitehern"
September 17, 1906

My dearest Calvin,

I am thankful to say, the weather turned cooler middle of last week, but it continues very dry. We are still in a state of confusion, as it is so difficult to find any one to do what one wants. Last Thursday Tom started to paint the spare bed-room, but Ross had only sufficient paint to do the windows, and not until this morning could I get any more sent to finish the job. But this morning I got up at seven and went down and managed to get it sent. The men took up two bed-room carpets <u>Monday</u> and came <u>after</u> <u>tea</u> Saturday to put them down, but only Mary's could go down as the painting was not finished. It is all so dry and dusty too that cleaning seems useless. Tom is taking his holidays at home, but there is really no fun going, it is a dull season.

Yesterday, Communion Sabbath, we had very fine sermons from Mr. Ketchen, but he is looking so thin and ill that we all feel very troubled about him. He had nearly two month's holidays but seems to have gained very little. It does seem so trying both for him and us. Ruby went off on Tuesday and she writes back of feeling so fine and well and fit for her work, and that she is going to have an easier time this year, as arranged at present.

Heurner Mullin met me the other day and was inquiring about your field, he simply said he had a patient, whom you knew too, that he would like to get out there, he may be writing you. I am wondering if it could be Willie Johnson but he could not preach could he? Mr. A. I. Mackenzie is very low, not expected to live many hours and Mr. Carscallen died yesterday.

You say you have worried often about the girls, and I have too. Though I know it has been very wrong, for I feel that if I had attained to the perfect condition of Christian faith, I should feel quite at rest, believing that God plans all things for us with Divine wisdom. I confess that having brought up the family as nearly as possible to the way I thought pleasing to Him, I had fully anticipated that He would provide for them. Well, when I come to think it over, there has been much of self-seeking in my service, I am afraid, and most certainly, we do not know what is really best for us. Hilda says from what she has seen of her friends' married life, she would not be married for anything. I am afraid M. [Mary] is not fitted for it at all, she has not head enough and there would be trouble. Altogether it does not do for one to plan or worry, for we do not know what may come. It does seem sometimes, as if it had been a great cross to have been burdened with this property during the best years of our lives, and just when we seem most to need money, but then we do not know.[332] Saw Miss Buchanan (Jane) at church last night, she had just been spending 6 weeks in the Adirondacks, she apparently has a much better time than any married lady.[333]

When Tom left the office for his Holidays, he received $25 of a bonus, which cheered him up very much and on the strength of which he took Hilda to lunch at the King Edward, she had gone down to the boat. Helen Gartshore was here a short time last week she is preparing to go again to New Zealand. Mrs. Gartshore's sister's husband is very ill cannot recover and is all alone there. It seems almost too much self-denial for her father to let her go, as Mr. Gartshore is really in very poor health, he had a severe attack while Hilda was there and is any thing but well, and when he is ill it is Helen who writes his letters, he ought to have a partner and is trying to find one. I do not know if I ever said how thoroughly Mary enjoyed herself at Staney Brae and they were all so kind; she was like a different creature when she came home, it was very fortunate we were not in the city this summer and the heat kept on so long. Think it is coming on again.

Well, Cal dear, there seems nothing more for me to say I hope you have had cooler weather and are getting cheered up. Edna is getting up her spirits wonderfully and you will probably. With much love from all.

Your loving mother
M. B. McQuesten

✦ A68-(5665) To Calvin McQuesten

MacLeod, Alberta   "Whitehern"
                                             Hamilton, October 1, 1906

My dearest Calvin,

It was good news to hear that you had gone to Lethbridge. I am very grateful to Mrs. Lait for taking you out. A change does one a great deal of good, particularly too if you can get a little good grub, and I am sure you must be sick to death of Western fare. I always think of you when I see the fruit going to waste, for I am bothered to death as usual how to get rid of the pears. By degrees we are getting the house settled, if we could only get help when we want it, would be done long ago. Our dining room carpet was so very shabby, I had to do something, so Tom found what is called a Moravian rug, it looks like a Turkish but is quite cheap and this put down as a crumb cloth makes the dining room look quite fine. I am thankful to say the curtains are all up. I wonder if I told you about the rug before, it seems as if I did. This is a very troublesome time too about the clothing. I get quite distracted arranging what rack one is to have for coats and hats, you have no idea what a problem it is to dress <u>five</u> women, <u>no</u> two alike, and get colours that are becoming.

But all these troubles drop out of sight in comparison with the terrible ending of poor Harold Thomson. On Wednesday we were much shocked by the news in the Times that Harold C. Thomson had shot himself at Vernon B.C. Word had been received from Chief of police there and to inquire for relatives; then Thursday night's Times was the enclosed but it was not correct in names. Ernest died years ago and Alfred, not Charles, was at the funeral. I am so confused with so many things but think my letter of last week was written the evening of Mrs. Sanders funeral and that I told you about that. Mary did not let me send the paper at first, she kept hoping it was a mistake, but I am afraid it is too true. Whatever can have happened to him? There was always something a little mysterious to me about H. [Harold]. He certainly had ability of some sort and why he should be always wandering about I could not understand. He smoked a great deal I wonder if he drank. Such a nice chap he was, and such good manners. I am thankful his poor mother and aunt did not live to know it, but I am truly sorry for Alfred he is such a fine gentlemanly man and to have this dreadful thing put in the papers.[334]

Just in the middle of this your letter from Mr. Lait's Manse reached us, it is all very well, but I know you were never attracted to a bachelor's life. Poor Calvin, I do hope dear that some day you will have a comfortable home of your own, I feel quite sure there are some bright days in store for you yet, and in the meantime your health is improving which is a great matter. I know one gets discouraged sometimes, I do myself, but that is the worst of a nervous temperament like we have, one gets tired and then blue. I was just thinking, when I read of poor Harold, it is only faith in God that keeps others from taking the same step. There is so much that is discouraging, that really the people who have no God to rest upon, must get desperate indeed.

On Tuesday I went to Toronto and after Dr. Capon had attended to my tooth, went up to Mrs. MacKay's where I had lunch. She is very dull now, knew my name and asked for the children but it seemed to me, she had less life than ever before and could scarcely speak, so I only stayed a short time. Tom called for me and left me at Eaton's and after looking about came home. We are having delightful weather now, and I start off to Chippawa to-morrow taking the 1.55 p.m. train to the Falls and going by trolley to Chippawa; Think it a fine opportunity to see that country.

Saturday, it had teemed rain all day and in the evening Dr. Lyle dropped in. We were talking about the University—he thought it very strange that the Univ. Council appointed had been wholly from Toronto, and it a Provincial institution. It is true, I am sure, that the doctor has more knowledge of educational matters than most of them;[335] he thinks that Prof. Falconer is the man for the president. He does not know Mr. Colquhoun (though he had heard him greatly praised) but he mentioned Prof. F.'s name to two of the council and they actually asked the doctor, what side of politics Prof. F. was on.[336] Isn't it disgusting.

Tommy Cook's baby was baptized yesterday and Mr. Ketchen preached a sermon on baptism and suffer little children &c. His remarks on baptism were of the briefest, he always seems afraid of these doctrinal subjects. Well dear, I must close. Have been on the run all day and must now rest before going out again. With much love from all.

Your loving mother

M. B. McQuesten

[P.S.] Tom brought home your books and as he was in a hurry, I said I would see to them, so posted them last week with some Presbyterians.

✦ A69-(5709) To Calvin McQuesten

MacLeod, Alberta

"Whitehern"

November 5, 1906

My dear Calvin,

I have been quite worried ever since I last wrote you, that I had ever said a word to you about that account with Methodist Book-room: I am afraid you will be worrying, that I know it. I had quite a nice note from Dr. Briggs, saying he had heard from A. C. Cameron who had said you had not been able to push the sale of books but would see to it when you returned this fall. Then he had seen Mr. McKay of Univ. Y.M.C.A. and he would be able to reduce amount shortly. In the meantime I was not to trouble about it. But what does trouble me is that when you come back to Varsity, instead of having nothing on your mind but studies, you will be trying to get rid of these books. Would Dr. Briggs not take any of them back? Or is there any one there who would take your place in the Bible Study department and try to dispose of the books?[337]

Had a letter from Tom to-day. His visit to St. Mary's was very unfortunate as to weather, it rained so heavily on the Saturday could not go out at all and there was a blizzard on Sabbath. He saw Mrs. Irving and Katie, they are in a comfortable little cottage. This is foot-ball season. A great match on Saturday in Toronto between Tigers and Argonauts. Tigers winning. Stuart Macdonald was down and saw Tom there. I see the Ottawa beat Varsity by one. Too bad.

Ruby is to give the Bible Reading at the Ottawa Presbyterial to-morrow. She is a brave one. We were at a grand "Tea" at Mrs. Gordon Henderson's on Saturday.[338] She bought "Idylwild" and it has been entirely redecorated under the Superintendence of Miss Evans.[339] It is very artistic and in the drawing room the lighting is entirely hidden but somehow there is no house I think looks finer than our own when it is in order unless Mrs. Thomson's.[340] We have been having Miss Honeycomb and had to make up my mind to treat Hilda in particular and all of them to a new machine, the old one had been quite trying for sometime though we are sorry to give it up.[341]

To-morrow we are having a small "Tea" for Mrs. Buchanan, it is somewhat of a trouble but last time she was here, I was invited to Auchmar to a nice little tea and we do not like to live always to ourselves.[342]

Edna is so much better in every way, though she gets very easily tired and I feel as if I could not worry much about anything after what we went through last winter. Her recovery was such a great mercy, so be sure and not worry. Another good thing interest on money rising. Quite a large mortgage is just due and it is being re-invested at once at a higher rate. We are having quite mild weather again. Yesterday in the morning we were addressed by Rev. Mr. Dulcos on behalf of French Canadian Mission. Do think it a shame that the Point aux Trembles School has been so neglected; it could have been such a power for good.[343] So much has been laid out on Queen's.

Last Wednesday night I gave an address at Knox and as they have no minister Dr. Fletcher presided, there were not a great many out, doubtless they would not think me worth listening to, at the same time I have a feeling there are very few men there, who are of much value and it is left entirely on the minister to attract a crowd. There seem to be no elders worth any thing. Poor little Prof. Johnson thought my address ought to be published for the information of the church.

The Bells for St. Paul's church have arrived, eleven in number. Each one has been presented. One by the Ladies' Aid, another by S.S. The largest given by James R. Moodie in memory of his father, another in memory of his little girl. One by Wm. Vallance, one by Jas. Thomson one by David Kidd in memory of his father, one by the choir. Cannot remember the others; they are all sitting in a row at the church door and are quite the object of interest to the passers by.[344]

On Saturday night the street car men went on strike, so no cars are running. The Company never kept its word to the men, so we do not blame them. Mary and I were thinking of going to Toronto some day but must wait, we could not walk to the wharf. The Spectator had on its bulletin, "Every body walks including father."

There are a great many weddings this month. Mr. Eastwood to a daughter of Senator (Willie) Gibson.[345] Roy Moodie to a Miss Farmer, and Eleanor

Malloch on the 15th to Mr. Calvin of Kingston. Hilda and Edna have gone to a social evening at the church, they are having one every two weeks.

Century has commenced a ten cent show every Saturday night just to attract the crowds off the street. Last night had Frank Yeigh, next time Jim Fax. It is a good idea I think. Well, Cal dear must close. Glad to hear you were visiting some of your old friends. With much love from all.

Your loving mother
M. B. McQuesten

✦ A70-(MCP 2-4.34) To Thomas B. McQuesten

22 Grosvenor St.   "Whitehern"
Toronto, Ontario   November 12, 1906

My dearest Tom,

I shall be in Guelph Wednesday and Thursday and be fully occupied with Mrs. Taylor to-morrow. Am writing you a few lines to let you know of my safe arrival on Friday night. Nellie James came on the boat, so we walked up together and were home before eight, the streets being quite quiet.

Saturday morning, Hilda heard people talking in the Market, that if when the cars were started by non-union men, the people would patronize them, the men would lose their case. So I felt moved to write a letter to the paper. H. said you would not be pleased with me at all, especially was she annoyed at my own signature, but a great many have told me, they were glad I spoke out, so I do not feel worried about it. Of course, I knew, it would probably do no special good, but I satisfied my conscience. You see there is almost universal sympathy with the men, for after being kept weeks in arbitration, the company did not comply with the terms.[346]

Well, we are being treated at intervals to music by the Chimes. Cannot say, that I fancy them a great deal, do not think the pleasure at all worth the money; besides we are too close. Outside the noise is terrible and you can imagine what it is like, when our bell begins and the Church of Ascension also.[347] This afternoon was at Mrs. Fletcher's at a small Tea for Miss Buchanan and Elsie very kindly had the man drive me home. To-morrow she is going to drive me to station to meet Mrs. Taylor. Ruby writes that Eleanor Ross is ill with pneumonia, but hopes it is not serious.

On the Steamer was a lady and her daughter, whom I have not seen for years. A niece of old Thos. Carlyle, she is a nice chatty body and it helped to pass the time. We are to worship in Association Hall, while the church is being renovated. Not a great deal is to be done, just the walls. It seems a pity the managers could not have decided when people were away in the summer; the school room will not hold the people at all, last Sabbath morning it was wet and there were 600 people out. With kindest love,

M. B. McQuesten

[P.S.] You might as well let us have the latch key, when you are not at home. Did I happen to give you the Hamilton, Prov. Book to carry for me anytime? <u>Cannot</u> find it.

✦ A71-(5744) To Calvin McQuesten

MacLeod, Alberta   "Whitehern"
December 3, 1906

My dearest Cal,

By the time this reaches you, you will not mind a short letter, seeing we have entered December. Your letter, telling of your congregations reached me on Saturday. It is certainly unspeakably trying to deal with such people. If people have not been started right and kept right for the first few years at least of their life, it is a very difficult matter to do anything with them. Habit is a wonderfully strong thing and people who have never had the habit of attending Church are almost beyond reach, it seems to me. This morning every thing is covered with snow, as Mr. Thomson says, "the Earth is dressed as a bride," it is difficult for me to see any thing but snow-clearing. On Thursday I went again to Dr. Capon, walking to and from the boat. I have only to go once more; this week the steamer stops. We are thankful the cars are running again with the old men. I received a great many compliments on my letter, which has re-assured me.[348]

Tom wrote me that old Mrs. Rains had died, and had been buried on the Saturday, but it was not in the papers. "Old Mrs. Drouillard went over to the house on Monday expecting to be regaled with a funeral. Imagine her disappointment when she found the bird had flown." He's a bad boy that! At present he is busy for Xmas Exams.

Yesterday morning we had the new preacher of Knox—Mr. Nelson— preaching, he has a rich brogue and he simply convulsed the people, clever too, but such a mixture, on the whole did not like it at all, got no good whatever. In the evening Mr. Ketchen preached to St. Andrew's Society their annual Sermon. He just did finely. He is never afraid to speak plainly and faithfully and yet is never offensive or vulgar.

Some of my moneys have been paid in, so I have been re-investing and have been much gratified to find that I have not broken in so very much on my principle, considering the Expense of E's [Edna] illness. I have only used $825 of my principal since beginning and the rate of interest having risen my income will only be $20 a year less; so it seems to me we have all done remarkably well. Of course next Spring I have a heavy fee for Tom,[349] but that can soon be caught up.

Must close, have not heard yet about Cookbooks, will probably hear next time. I wrote you about it, in case letter is lost will say, the one Hilda liked so much is called "A little Cook-Book for a little girl" with picture of little girl outside, otherwise it is very useful for a woman, more so than big expensive ones,

75 cts. is price.[350] The last news from Ottawa is Mrs. Needham has typhoid fever, light case, Eleanor R. [Ross] recovering.[351] With much love from all.

> Your Mother
> M. B. McQuesten

✦ A72-(5765) To Calvin McQuesten

[22 Sewweud, Toronto]

> "Whitehern"
> Hamilton, Ontario
> January 15 [1907]

My dear Calvin,

There is really nothing at all going on except meetings and last week, we had such a number and I have not yet recovered, and simply dread going to one to-day, the W.H.M.S. But I seem to have been dragged into it. Elsie Buchanan was forced into being President and the Evening meetings are to be discontinued they are to be in the afternoon now, for after Mrs. Fletcher declined and Mrs. Marsh went away no other lady would face a general meeting.

I do not want them to look to me, because I find, I cannot stand too much in the way of being responsible. We have so much material to help us in the W.F.M.S. meetings, but it is not so in the Homework.[352] If one had Mrs. Ross's gift in giving Bible Readings, it would be a great help, but it is very difficult for me now to fix my attention sufficiently on my subject as to make a study of it, my mind wanders so much.

We had a great snow-storm on Friday night and it cost me a dollar to get it off. I had a letter from Dr. Gilbart last week, which I will send in the parcel, it is so sad about poor Mrs. Gilbart, it was far too hard a life for her.[353]

Well, I have just returned from our W.H.M.S. meeting. We had quite a large turn out, having the meeting at 4:30, we had a number of teachers, and others who have never before come to anything. I always feel quite ashamed of the way in which I have to fight myself, the W.F.M.S. has so long been the chief thing with me that I know I am jealous of any other society coming in, so I am constantly reasoning with myself and fighting the feeling.

Isn't it terrible this Earthquake in Jamaica? They seem to be coming all over. When we came home we found a message left by Edna, that she had gone to take tea with Mrs. Mullin. Last night we had Lorna Culham for tea, she teaches Domestic Science at one of the schools.

I am glad you have friends to go to on Sabbath. I often wonder that Tom does not keep up with his friends more. I hope to write a more interesting letter next time, but am somewhat stupid myself just now. With much love to Tom and yourself from all.

> Your loving mother
> M. B. McQuesten

[P.S.] We got off the parcel to-night.

✦ A73-(5788) To Calvin McQuesten

Toronto, Ontario "Whitehern"
February19,1907

My dearest Cal,

It is indeed a crisis in our family history this learning of the old house.[354] But the more I look at it, the more I feel that after the March was over, we would really be more comfortable elsewhere, it is not so bad here when the double windows are on and the snow on the ground, but when we returned last summer from Muskoka, the dust and noise seemed almost unbearable. The garden is really only pretty till after the rose season. Of course, it is not finally settled whether the place is sold or not but one cannot help, indeed, must plan. You and Tom think we should go to the old country. Well, I have considered it from every side, and I am afraid it would not be wise. To begin with, I could not make up my mind to stay a year or two from you boys, then it would be monotonous for the whole family to go together and I cannot help thinking that bye and bye we shall be able to manage a little travelling too. Hilda cannot bear the thought of it at all. You see we cannot afford to fritter away one cent of our means, for it will just give us sufficient to live on and no more, this is one of the reasons Tom thinks I should take it now or I will never have it to go travelling. But I think we will. For one thing if we were an ordinary house we could rent it furnished you see, I have need of a little house to get rested, invest my money and get returns, and I have not the courage to go among strangers where I should have to pay cash down for everything and the thought of being homeless makes me so nervous, that I can scarcely bear it at all. When I think over, where best to settle, Mary is sick of Hamilton, and yet I do not know where we would be better. I would go to Toronto, if I thought the girls would have any greater opportunities, for I doubt if living costs much more, and property is very high here.

Building here at present seems out of the question, but a carpenter told Mr. Chisholm that the prices would almost prohibit building, and he thought the men would get tired of it and perhaps by August things would go down. I would not like too small a house, for we have beautiful things to make a handsome home and the thousand dollars spent just now in travelling would make the difference between a poor and a comfortable house, then too I would like it in good locality. My preference would be Aberdeen Ave. about Highfield and am going to inquire price of lots. Am a little afraid they may be too high. In the meantime we could go to Oakville for the summer. Thomas Pulham [?] told Edna yesterday of another house which we could rent furnished for the summer. Tom would perhaps remember it, one we admired with nice whole verandah. Suppose you or Tom when you have a spare time run in and see Jack Lyle[355] and ask him if that material in Mr. Hendrie Jun.'s house is more or less expensive than brick, I do detest brick.

That was a good letter of Prof. Kilpatrick in the Globe.[356] It is dreadful to have such miserable specimens of men as Hon. Frank Oliver in the Government.[357] I heard all about his origin one day. He could have at least kept quiet, for he was not answerable for P.M. K. and he [knew] the Professor was right. Mary Haunsford was in the other day and offered if we moved to come in and help us pack up, she is a faithful soul. Well I must close, in the meantime we must pray earnestly that we may be guided into what is truly best for us. With much love to you both.

> Your loving mother
> M. B. McQuesten

✦ A74-(5794) To Calvin McQuesten

Toronto, Ontario

"Whitehern"
February 26, 1907

My dear Calvin,

We have heard nothing further and neither has Mr. Chisholm, we met Joe Thomson to-day and he said the matter was not settled, had heard the Husbands[358] were asking only $13,000; and also had heard on direct authority that Railway was going to expropriate our property. I really do not believe anything I hear, for a report was going that Central was offering their corner for $1600, which is perfect nonsense. They ask $20,000. Unless I get a good round sum, I could not leave here at all and Mr. C. [Chisholm] is sure the Railway is bringing a spur line for freight by North East end.[359]

For myself I just feel as I did about the Rhodes' Scholarship, I felt quite unable to judge what would be <u>really</u> the best thing.[360] So I put it into the Lord's hands to direct the whole matter, and it is a great comfort to me to feel that I can put this business also into the hands of One who Knows the future, and can make no mistake; otherwise I could not stand the strain at all.

I really do not wonder that Mrs. Ross would speak of Prof. McFadyen's work as "poisonous," it seems the exact word to use. Jean Ross (Ruby tells me) heard him read a chapter of Genesis one Sabbath morning and then close the Book and say "Of course you may read this to children but what grown person could believe such as this?" I would like to ask him why he read it. If he thinks so, Genesis is not suitable reading for the Pulpit.[361] Dr. Jordan of Brampton is the same, I fancy.[362] Think I told you of hearing him the other morning at St. Paul's. Such a very poor effort! You forgot to tell me if you received the Record of Xtian Work, when you are through please return it.[363] This week we have been trying to make calls. Yesterday saw Mrs. Chas. Robertson. Percy has been home ill for days got run down and took grip: she does not know what to do with him. He just likes to play, would play the Mandolin all day, has no particular fancy for any calling. I feel very sorry for his mother. She had to give up keeping a servant and just herself to do everything, and I do not think he appreciates it one bit. Well, I am thankful I was never afflicted with lazy children. Must close, with love from all.

Your loving mother
M. B. McQuesten

✦ A75-(MCP 2-4.37a) To Thomas Baker McQuesten

c/o Messrs. Royce & Henderson   "Whitehern"
Barristers, Molson Buildings   March 7, 1907
King St. West., Toronto, Ontario

My own darling boy,

This is just a little letter to yourself, you know you are the only one who remembers to write me on this day and to me your letter is just the sweetest gift and always cheers me up so much that instead of feeling sad I always feel particularly cheerful.[364] Last night my mind was so full of plans that I did not get to sleep till this morning, so I was having my breakfast in bed and feeling very stupid when your dear letter came. You do not know just what a help and strength you have been to your mother. I am so very nervous and anxious minded that if you had been anything else but what you are I would certainly have broken down. If you had been a lazy idle good for nothing, selfish and unsympathetic, it seems to me I would have died, for people do die of broken hearts. And it is really terrible the number of selfish men, sons who are positively cruel to their mothers and sisters through self indulgence without apparently any thought of it.

To one of my disposition and views it would seem to me life would have been impossible. As it is you were strong and vigorous and unlike son Cal, physically fit to go into any kind of a rollicking life and so have been led into many things altogether ruinous but thank God, you did hear His voice, I am sure, speaking to you, and you have been enabled to live a pure life and thus have been an unspeakable strength to me.

Many times, I have had grave anxiety as to whether my standard of right has been <u>too</u> puritanical and has shut out the girls from any opportunities, but yet I could not forget that "We are not to do evil that good may come," and I believed that it is only when obeying God, that we receive His help, and I always felt far too weak to go into anything without His approval. And as I look back and read my Bible, it still seems to me the only Safe Course. The only anxious thought I have for you dearie is, lest you should by mixing continually with those who have really scarcely a thought of God, you should grow formal in serving Him and not be spiritually minded. Sometimes you seem a little hard and unsympathetic with people and you know we ought to have "the mind that was in Christ." For this we both need to strive and pray earnestly if we are really to attain to what our Saviour expects of us. With fondest love, my dear son Tom, and earnest prayers.

Ever your loving Mother,
M. B. McQuesten

✦ A76-(5800) To Calvin McQuesten

Toronto, Ontario

"Whitehern"
Hamilton, March 13, 1907

My dearest Calvin,

Our house question is not yet finally settled for when I submitted the offer of the Club to Mr. C. [Chisholm] he thought I should be assured of more than $750 as they proposed, that they should take it for six months at $900 and another month if they wanted as proposed. So that proposition was sent Monday afternoon and we have not yet heard. It may have been wiser, but I would almost rather have settled it and taken the chance, for I am so tired of indecision and am afraid of missing Oakville houses. Page's Cottages are so very small and close to each other. Think it a very good suggestion about photographing rooms and will try to have it done.[365] It was very sad indeed about Gradie's young lady. Tom's friends are very unfortunate. We hear the Commercial Club is leasing the 8th story of the Bank of Hamilton and paying a rental of between 4 & $5000. The girls are planning to hear Dr. Grenfell to-night.[366] Yesterday we had a call from Mr. Judson, Mr. Bone's successor, a very excellent little man, I am sure. Sabbath Evening Mr. Ketchen gave a sermon on "Gambling" which was very good, and did not skirt the question. Hamilton is said to have a very bad reputation in that line. The dearth of news is great. I hope you will get on satisfactorily with your exam this week. Sorry for Miss Oates![367] Tom is a first class bed-maker, I know by experience. Hope to have something more definite to write later. With much love.

Your loving mother
M. B. McQuesten

✦ A77-(5820) To Thomas McQuesten

Toronto, Ontario

"Whitehern"
Monday Morning
[April 22, 1907]

My dearest Tomity,

Just a line to express my sympathy I am sure you are just worn out with this endless study; and do try and get some nourishing meals. Go to the King Edward or any place where you can get a really good lunch or dinner, we can easily afford it <u>now</u> when our house is rented and such good prospects from Bold St. You were so thin and looked so weary when you were home I was really troubled. You cannot do justice to yourself at the exams if you are only half fed.[368] And then dearie, put your trust in God, acknowledge your own weakness and throw yourself on His Almighty strength and He will bring you through.

We are all feeling in good spirits and it seems wonderful how a kind Providence just at this time when we most need it is raising up this help for us.[369] With fondest love, my dearest boy.

Your loving mother
M. B. McQuesten

✦ A78-(5854) To Calvin McQuesten

Glenhurst, Saskatchewan

Oakville
May 30, 1907

My dearest Calvin,

I was just delighted to receive your letter and card last evening; it was the greatest relief to my mind, for it was so stormy on the Lake here, that I was somewhat anxious and feared at least you were having a miserable time. The fare on those boats is very excellent, and I am so glad you were able to enjoy it. It was perhaps trying not to have a free Sabbath, but you do not know the good you may have done, there are so few sermons with any thing in them and the old gentleman's encomium would cheer you.

We had a great storm of thunder lightning and rain, on Sabbath evening came on just as we were starting, so that Edna and Hilda fled into the English Church, but Tom and I pushed on to encourage Dr. McNair.[370] On Tuesday went up to H. [Hamilton] to inspect Bold St. houses, everything getting on well and the porch just what I like, suits the houses exactly.

Many of the club regret they could not buy our house, but a railway man warned Hugh Baker that the railway would have to have our property eventually.[371] It does seem such a strain. However we are just going to enjoy ourselves. Have heard nothing more whether Tom is settled or not. If he were, think I should have heard.

I am very indignant with these Oakville Presbyterians last night at Prayer meeting three people beside ourselves, Mrs. McNair and her servant. The Manse is so large, that Mrs. McNair has to keep a servant and the grounds so large, Mr. McNair has to have help with it. The church is in debt, they seem to have no system of envelope giving and I would like to shake them.

The family is forcing me into taking these grand furs and I feel as if I were too extravagant and yet I think it may not be in the long run, as that beautiful stole is reduced just because the skins were purchased last winter and they were "doing the best they could for an old customer." So I shall be a great swell.[372]

Well, Calvin dear, by this time I trust you will have found a place to lay your head. I earnestly pray that some comfortable home may be opened to you. With much love from all.

Your loving mother
M. B. McQuesten

✦ **A79-(5868) To Calvin McQuesten**
Glenhurst, Saskatchewan

Oakville, Ontario
June 1, 1907

My dear dear boy,

Tom said he would write the particulars about your exams which he could explain better than I can. All I know is, you're to be allowed to take your M.A. next year.[373]

Mary and I had a fine time in Toronto last week. Maggie [MacKay] wrote to come on the Thursday so I went with Tom to the opening of Convocation Hall. I was so glad to have the opportunity, it is a most beautiful building, simply perfect for the purpose. The interior is very fine and when lit up the crimson cloth lends such a fine effect. We had good seats and saw the unveiling of Vice Chancellor Moss' painting or rather portrait. Then we heard Prof. Hutton, but he has got into an unfortunate sing song.[374] Sir Wm. Meredith was perfectly natural and gave a resume of University affairs, which was very good.[375] Grey came in escorting Miss Elliott.[376]

Then on Friday morning I went shopping. Mary came by boat and little Mary Taylor went with us to Convocation, we had a good seat in front of one of the galleries.[377] It was a sight worth seeing as the students came in, a space allotted to each department, the ladies coming first; the students occupied the first tier and the effect was excellent. I was so glad that Tom was able to represent the family on that opening day. It was a fortunate coincidence. Unfortunately Tom had to rush for boat races a soon as he got his degree which came near the first, so we had to make our way to the garden party by ourselves, except that I fell in with Dr. Ellis, who took us in. There were not many we know, but fortunately I knew Prof. McCallum and he got a waiter to bring us refreshments and he attended to us well. Met John King who told me Tom had done remarkably well at his exams and that all the men at Osgoode liked Tom very much indeed. We enjoyed the outing altogether very much, weather delightful, the finest we have had and Maggie made us so comfortable feeding us on the very best.

Do you know in Mrs. Mackay's first will she left you $500 but her relatives evidently worked on her at the last when she was weak. They got all her jewellery even some that had belonged to the Gordons.[378] Tom has been engaged by Mr. Henderson to take charge of office at $75 a month until he finds what suits him.[379] Masten had not decided just what to do.[380]

We had Mrs. James with us for ten days, came to us completely used up but by keeping her in bed and proper diet she became perfectly well and went off to day in fine spirits.[381] She quite dreaded, I think going up to Sparrow Lake. The weather keeps so cold; yesterday and to day, strong east winds and so cold, we are afraid to go out by front door. I am preparing to speak at a meeting at St. David's on Thursday evening so I have to go into Hamilton to take the train to Niagara Falls and so on. Hilda heard last night the reason of Mr. Cavers here leaving the Presbyterian Church, Mrs. C. you heard me speak of as a Miss McMillan. It seems that Dr. McNair was calling on him and it was after a sermon preached by the doctor. No one knows the exact particulars, but the fact remains that the doctor knocked Mr. C. down, to the universal joy of the community. The wonder was how he did it, as Mr. C. was a big man. Even his son-in-law was perfectly delighted and the Marlatts whooped, Kenneth said.[382]

We have also heard from Mrs. Culhain that our Tom is engaged and that the whole thing is settled, to <u>whom</u> is not mentioned,[383] also that the only girl Tom ever really cared for was Annie Fletcher.[384]

I was interested to read how the Western ministers stirred up the Assembly. Young Gordon seems to have done well.[385] Well Cal dear I must close as I have things to do. Trust you have found some sort of a comfortable home and your horse to be alright. Am quite anxious to hear just where you are. What paper do you get? I have forgotten. With best love from all.

Your loving Mother
M. B. McQuesten

✦ A80-(5898) To Calvin McQuesten

Glenhurst, Sask. Oakville
July 5, 1907

My Dearest Calvin,

I was just delighted to hear from your letter this morning that you had at last found a home. It is a kind Providence that opened this home for you; and I am so thankful your health is so good, it makes everything light; and good congregations too. It is all so encouraging, and I am sure when you are feeling well, you will be able to give them something worth hearing and that will do them good.

I have just been reading a magnificent address by J. A. Macdonald to the students at Northfield.[386] I am just proud of him, he is really a very able fellow. I read it aloud to the family and it thrilled one. I saw him and Mrs. McD. [sic] at Convocation, she is a dear little woman.

Nellie James arrived last night, so glad to have her, she is always so cheery. Willie has given up his position at Knox & Co., he could not stand the heavy work and their meanness any longer.[387] Jim Stuart is back there again, they offer him $60 a month to go to Toronto. What is that to keep a wife and children in Toronto? Willie has nothing in view. Some of their men just left them without giving any notice. You see men will not go through all the heavy labour of moving for employers who are thoroughly mean; and they have been doing a very large business. We wonder at their moving.

The bills for Bold St. improvements are coming in and though large, think they can be met in course of time without taking more of my principal than $500 of the money coming from the club. I cannot forget the wonderful provision made for us this year. I am so glad to get Bold St. in such shape as to obtain the increased rental but I would have been very loath to use over a $1000 of my principal; and then to think the Club was sent along to provide the extra money; just the year when Tom needed $200 in one sum and Edna needed to be in the country. It all seems just such a wonderful and kind provision of our Heavenly Father. And this place is so delightful and not too quiet.

We had a call, a P.P.C. as he called it, from Robt. Buchanan.[388] He is going off on this tour of the world with some of the laymen, visiting the mission fields, but he is going to take views and give illustrated lectures on Canada. If you could have heard him on all the things he intends doing, and the way he has been working the C.P.R. and the G.T.R., specially eulogizing these R.R. [He] had Col. Davis to report this part in full, sent the paper to the officials etc. and now hopes for passes. Our brains fairly reeled with his projects. I had to write a letter introducing him to Mr. Nosse at Ottawa, from whom he hopes to get some introductions.

I saw the reference to Dr. Primrose, it must have been a slip of reporter from Dr. Peters. Dr. Primrose was at Convocation, I heard a lady pointing him out on platform (I do not know him). We had Mr. McGregor of Presbyterian last Sabbath, a good discourse, but such a sing-song delivery that I really did not understand half of it, and felt too tired to try.[389] Ruby is writing you, so she will report her own doings. With much love to all.

Your loving Mother
M. B. McQuesten

✦ A81-(5984) To Calvin McQuesten

Milden, Saskatchewan

Oakville, Ontario
September 13, 1907

My dearest Calvin,

It was certainly most gratifying, that after such a sore temptation manfully overcome you should find my letter waiting for you at Glenhurst. Letters mean so much more, when one is amongst strangers and so far distant that there is only a weekly mail. I see you are still determined to take that Hamilton Mission, it still seems to me most unwise. You have besides your Knox Coll. work that last subject to overtake and you meditate I believe writing for your M.A. There is nothing like having the Sabbath Day for rest and to start every Monday morning not only unrested, but more tired is a fatal mistake, we have all suffered enough in the past, for your persistent taking of your own way.

We expect to be here till after Christmas, and I hope so. I need a long rest, as I had not been picking up as fast as I would like, I went in to see Dr. Caven on Wednesday, so he examined me, told me not to see visitors, not to talk to people and gave me a prescription to take for three weeks, stop a week and then come back to him.[390] So I feel encouraged and thankful to have this fine resting place and no worries. It was just the result of overstrain.

Tom has secured your room at Miss Oates' and his own also. He seems overflowing with spirits when he comes home, the relief I think from exams and having a little extra money. Busy getting his dress suit and topper for the wedding on Monday.[391] H. [Hilda] at first thought she would not go, as it would be too many from one family, but after Mrs. F.'s [Fletcher] letter she could leave your big trunk with Miss Oates.

I do not know if you bought a return ticket from here to Toronto. We have got a ten trip ticket and I can send it to Miss Oates for you in case you need it, it saves 45 cts on a return. May God bless you and give you a safe journey home! Love from all.

Your loving mother
M. B. McQuesten

[P.S.1] Grey's young lady is from the East some place.[392]
[P.S.2] I feel, I did not say enough about or rather <u>against</u> your taking that Knox mission. After all we have gone through, it does seem very wrong of you to persist in this thing. I thought you had a lesson you would never forget. If you attend to your work for Knox College, you could do it so well that you might win distinction which would pay far better in the long run for you might get a reputation which would be worth a great deal in the future.

We are going to be in a better position than I have ever been since your father died. My income from Bold St. alone is to be $75 a month from Jan[uary] and Tom has often said he was going to help you through. So be wise and obey your mother. I shall be very indignant if you do not, it would be <u>so</u> much better to give your <u>whole mind</u> to your work. That is the reason the old countrymen have excelled as professors, because they could not run around as our students do, but had to stick to their work. Now just think it over. <u>There is not the slightest occasion or need for you to do this.</u>

M. B. McQ

✦ A82-(5990) To Calvin McQuesten

Glenhurst, Saskatchewan

Oakville
September 21, 1907

My dearest Calvin,

To begin where I left off. Tom arrived home on Saturday night a week ago with all his new toffery. He was very much set up indeed with his fine Prince Albert, silk hat, grey tie and gloves and patent leather boots. When arrayed he was quite imposing. Well, Monday Hilda, Ruby, Edna and he started off at 1 o'clock for the Fletcher wedding, it was an oppressively hot day but good for the girls' thin dresses. When Tom reached Mrs. Fletcher, she asked him if he would make the speech for the bridesmaids none of the ushers was equal to it, so Tom had to do his best on the spur of the moment. The Bard wrote us since that they "all thought Tom very happy in his little speech, and looked important enough to be an Attorney-General with at the same time all needed geniality."[393] He certainly did look very fine in his dress suit and I was glad he was able to take his part and assist Mrs. Fletcher. It was an immense wedding but they all thought it very dull, Colin [Fletcher] and Mrs. Colin hardly spoke, the Murrays all very quiet and Dr. Lyle too, all seemed too tired to be jolly and of course poor old Dr. F. was feeling very badly.[394]

Tom went straight back to Toronto, so have not seen him since, but have heard from him from North Bay. He and Mr. Kerr were expecting to go on to Herron Bay. Before leaving Toronto he had seen Masten and on Tom's return he goes in with him at $1000 a year, I feel most sincerely thankful.[395] He had an offer too from Angus McMurchy solicitor for C.P.R. but he preferred the work in the other office.

Then on Thursday Hilda & Ruby set off for the Whittemore wedding, they were to stay at Mr. MacKay's till to-day, so they are not home yet, it was an evening wedding at the Haworth's house in Rosedale, only the girls were asked. I sent both Annie F. [Fletcher] and Florrie H. [Haworth] a chaffing dish.

I was sorry to see by your letter received yesterday, you were not starting till first of October, that will not give you any days at home, be sure and do not manage to preach the first Sabbath you get here. You have done that sort of thing too often, that is, preached when you were tired.

You would notice the sad ending of poor Jamieson it was very distressing. How much they must all have endured and suffered, it is terrible to think! You must excuse this letter, I have had a number of business letters to answer and am very tired. Being in Oakville necessitates so much writing.

You have had so much trouble getting your letters I shall just send this to Glenhurst. As I said before if you have time to go up to Miss Oates, before coming on to Oakville, you can get the "Ten trip" ticket we have for Oakville. With much love from all.

Your loving mother
M. B. McQuesten

166

✦ A83-(6012) To Calvin McQuesten

Toronto "Whitehern"
Monday Night, [January 20 1908]

My dearest Calvin,

Was very glad to receive your letter today. Indeed it is just wonderful how much I have been able to do and have slept so well at night. This has been the secret of my keeping up so well. Yesterday of course I could not go out but dozed most of the day. In the mornings feel very tired, but manage to start again. Of course I do no work, but it is the constant looking after others. Twice I went over to the [Hamilton] Club, after missing things and to-day at last John the Carpenter is to finish boarding up the kitchen and stopping up the electric light holes. There are just as many little things that one has to get right. Friday Rachel worked away and got the kitchen's pantry & cellar clean. Today another woman got the stairs and halls cleaned and the big dining room. The dirt you know has been terrible. Since I wrote you I had Matthew's men up, before seeing Patterson again and decided it would be best to let Watkin's man do it. They had the best oak all ready seasoned and would put a border 20 1/2 in. besides windows all round for $35, it would then be entirely finished. I could see no special use in a floor all over and after Patterson's work was done, then Ross would have to finish it.

Then about the library, there was more than enough paper but it cannot be quite finished till Ross sees Tom and consults about colouring of ceiling: to get the right shade it would be necessary to paint ceiling, as it is so old they cannot get the colouring in Calsomine. The new carpet in grandpa's room is lovely. Edna is perfectly delighted with the colour of her room. All the bedroom carpets are down. The drawing room set came home to-day and perfectly gorgeous. All the people from Matthews say they never saw anything like them. Then our new bathroom and bath and Ross found a lovely border and put the same round little room next and Calsomined the room in green so all that paint is fresh. Finally I got to the root of what made the awful smell downstairs. The club's porter was over and I just got at him. There were 5 kegs of rotten oysters in the coal room and he had to open them and was sick enough himself as was the painter first day he went to furnace. Then in the ice under refrigerator was a lot of rotten fish. I felt better after I knew just what it was, so we have tried carbolic acid, but it is not gone yet, but to-day I got another stuff from Parke and hope to get it out finally. But with it all think we have reason to be very thankful that no real injury has been done to the house. They certainly did very stupid things taking down brackets etc. when there was no need and making trouble but these are trifles.[396]

Hilda was very sick for one day and very miserable for a day or two after, but she is picking up by degrees. Then our baize [*sic*] door being off made us rather cold last week but it is so mild now, we do not feel it. Who do you think is my latest retainer for clearing snow & ice? Aleck Gourlay![397] Poor unfortunate! most thoughtful to do any jobs.

Today we were surprised by a visit from Herbert Bell, he leaves tonight for New York and sails for Plymouth, where his mother joins him and they go to Frieburg in Germany 30 miles from Switzerland. It seems he contracted lung trouble from a chap who roomed with him at Philadelphia, at the time this fellow's doctor feared he had bronchitis, but it was worse than that. So when H. returned in Sept. he had to go right to a sanitarium which is considered the headquarters of treatment for tuberculosis. He lived in a tent, was fed to bursting, exercised and treated till he was considered practically new. He has been a short time in North Carolina. Then the doctors ordered him to be in a climate of a certain altitude. So it was decided he should go to Freiburg. There is a university and he could go on with German. I am so pleased that his mother goes with him; she is nearly worn out at Florrie's. Their new house could not be got dried, in spite of stoves & all possible means. They all narrowly escaped pneumonia. Herbie was so sorry not to see Tom. Well, you may come up and see it as soon as we are really settled. I would not have Tom come this week, if it were not for setting up library and unless he can get away at one o'clock he also had better wait till he can. Well, I must close with much love to you both.

Your loving mother
M. B. McQuesten

[P.S.] Miss Ramsay's coming did not trouble me. She is coming up again this week, as she is going to do Mrs. Gartshore. I am very pleased, for she could not possibly do it without; the hair was all wrong, too much of it and wrong shade.[398]

✦ A84-(6053) To Calvin McQuesten

Glenhurst, Saskatchewan "Whitehern"
March 6, 1908

My dearest Calvin,

It was quite a surprise to receive a letter from Tom at Cobalt. Sorry it is the winter season, but I see by this morning's Globe Mr. Masten is a director in a Mining Co. there, so Tom will doubtless have many opportunities of going.[399]

This week I have been quite gay, on Wednesday went to Mrs. Walter MacDonald's to meet a few old friends at 5 oclock. Then yesterday I took tea and spent the evening at May Stevens to meet her mother, Miss Somerset and Mrs. Mullin. I thought it would be better to do this and get my mind off the house and bills. I find many have suffered from this palpitation, "nervous heart" as it is called and got quite over it in time.[400] I hope you do not feel disappointed about the M. A. Bremner promised Tom you should have it this year, although you had not got the B.A. last year, though it is more convenient not to pay the $20 <u>this</u> year.[401] I have heard from Mr. Baker but as he is very busy invites me to write to him, which is a nuisance, as it is a long story. Hilda is making marmalade to-day, a double quantity.

A letter from Hon. J. M. Gibson to the Presbytery proposing to absorb Locke St. church with all the Funds collected for it into Central has made great excitement in church circles. I am extremely sorry about Dr. and Mrs. Lyle, sure they are worried to death, taking this great new church upon their shoulders, no prospect of selling the old one, people criticizing Jack's work.[402] The whole Lees connection gone to St. Paul's, old Lees was the largest giver in the church and many others will leave,[403] when the church finally goes, so that altogether it is a very heavy burden for Dr. Lyle, and then for the <u>great</u> Central Church to propose to swallow up the Funds collected in poor little St. <u>James</u> (as it is now called) it was most unfortunate.[404] Altogether John Knox of St. Paul's who is treasurer of the Locke St. Fund declared he and others would withdraw their subscriptions if St. James did not unite with Central, so it is a fine muddle all round. Mrs. Fletcher says that St. James' Church is as far away from the new Central, as the latter is from ours.[405]

Dr. F. [Fletcher] said that he did not know what to do with Dr. Lyle, he was just so worried and in addition <u>Jack</u> will <u>not</u> put in his tender for Knox College, but thinks it should just be given to him. Silly fellow! Dr. L. is very much incensed with the actions of the Central Managers and Mr. Gibson's letter, which was full of misstatements and spoke of their "<u>having</u> been <u>fooled</u> by the Presbyters." Such an expression! As clerk of the Pres. [Presbytery] Dr. F. refused to put the letter on record. You see the whole matter had come before Presbytery and it had been settled where they were to build and no mention made of uniting with St. James. Mrs. Thomson says Mr. G. [Gibson] is "spoiled" and was "<u>always</u> bad tempered."

Now I must get you to get me some more prescriptions filled at Mr. Jeffrey's. The pellets are for taking at night and the other in the morning, when one's liver is sluggish so you can get a supply for yourself too. I want double the quantity of each for myself and you can get the same. The number on the box of tablets is 188981, but enclose prescription for the other, if you get it in proper can just put it in my bottle. If Tom does not come up to-morrow it will do the next week. We are expecting Mary Taylor on Monday and you could send a parcel of clothes up with her if you telephoned and found out what train she was coming by and Mary will meet her here. The telephone is not in her name, but you can call up "Inquiry" and ask for the phone at 44 Isabella St. This is surprising that Tom is not coming up and the clothes would be ready for him to take back next week. Glad to know you are keeping well, with much love to you both.

Your loving Mother
M. B. McQuesten

[P.S.1] Want the prescription here returned.

[P.S.2] [On a separate page]   **"Private"**

In case Tom should not come home to-morrow and go to Sudbury next week, I want to give you both a warning as to being careful when you are travelling about using <u>certain places</u>, especially those in connection with wayside stations, to which dirty people may have access. Mrs. M. yesterday told me some amazing things which is well for all to know. Her niece in Montreal had gone out to the coast with her husband and they both con-tracted a most dreadful trouble, very difficult to cure and it seems Archie and all the staff of the Bank of Hamilton had a terrible time with the same at the time the Bank was being enlarged, because the foreign workmen were admitted to the same W.C. They are small things called crabs (not bed bugs or body lice) with many legs which worm themselves into the flesh and cause fearful irritation and pain to get them off. Heurner directed Archie to rub himself all over with coal oil and then gave him something to put on the parts which stung frightfully.[406] He decided the safest thing to do was, when compelled to use these public places, to be careful to rub the seat as hard as possible with paper. Keep a careful outlook.

✦ A85-(6063) To Calvin McQuesten

Toronto, Ontario   "Whitehern"
                                    March 11, 1908

My dearest Calvin,

On Saturday morning when I received your sweet letter of sympa-thy,[407] I wanted to write immediately and thank you, but have been much occupied ever since. You need never reproach yourself for not having been able to help me financially, it was from no fault of yours. You always did the very utmost your health would permit, more than it permitted some-times. Then your character has been a great strength to me and as the oldest son you cannot estimate what it may have meant to the family espe-cially Tom, a great deal depends on the stand taken by the older ones of a family if they are careless and show themselves heedless of the teaching and wishes of their parents, the young are always sure to do the same, and the family is lost. Isn't it just wonderful to look back over the twenty years since your father was so suddenly taken from us and think of the serious illnesses of different members of the family and how we were brought through them all and now look at the comfort and luxury in which we are now living![408] To me it is a constant wonder for which I am never suffi-ciently grateful.

You are really the only one who endures hardships, but I hope you will be feeling comfortable in your shades. I am so provoked, that we had no idea that we could have sent twice as much with the bale. You had said something about a certain amount having to go, but it did not occur to me, I could send things in a separate bundle, or I would have sent a stock of groceries. Another year we will know better.

Am glad you will be home in a few days.[409] I would enclose a couple of dollars to bring you home for next Sabbath, but am very hurrying to get bills paid. However I am much stronger and they do not bother me as they did. Went out to the Communion on Sabbath morning. Wish you could have been here, there is no service like ours with Mr. Ketchen and Dr. L. [Lyle] calling past.

Poor old Dr. Black was absent for first time in years, fell the Sabbath before on the ice, cut his forehead, was taken into a doctor's and after 12 stitches had been put in walked home—87 years of age.[410] Must close, with much love.

Your loving Mother
M. B. McQuesten

✦ A86- (MCP 3-5.4) To Thomas B. McQuesten

c/o Masten, Starr & Spence, Barristers   "Whitehern" Monday Morning,
Canada Life Bldg., Toronto   [Postmark] May 16, 1908

My Dearest Boy,

I had fully intended to write you on Saturday, but in the afternoon I was taken for a little drive. My old friend Mrs. Bell was again staying with her niece Mrs. Poole at Mrs. Frank Malloch's house. Mary went up to see her and explain I could not, so Mrs. Poole said when she was taking her Aunt out, they would call for me. It was such a lovely afternoon and we drove through Dundurn and saw the tulips. I could not help regretting you were not here then and yesterday. It was such a fine warm day for sitting on the verandah, the trees are just in their first green and there were so many birds; the weather was so cold and wet last week, there was not much advance. The little prune is just coming out. I only hope we shall have such fine weather this week when you come.

The reason I wanted a little monetary help was that this week the 21st I have to meet Ross's note and I just wanted enough to keep me going. If you could just send me $5.00 or $2.00 now, it is all I require, and I might need another five before end of month. On the 30th the McPhie Int. comes in. I do not want to take any from you more than I can help, as I have to send Ruby away and have no money to do so. I shall be obliged to accept your kind offer for that. Dr. Arnott thinks Ancaster a very good locality as it is high and dry, they do not think so much of Muskoka now.[411]

Heard from Cal Thursday, he seems to be thoroughly enjoying life. I can assure you E. [Edna] thoroughly enjoyed the luncheon, I was glad you took her, she has seen so little and admires everything so much, she did not let us know when she was coming and came bravely up by herself, her suitcase is very light. E. says hyacinths in your park are fine. With much love dearie.

Your loving mother.

[M. B. McQuesten]

✦ A87-(6135) To Calvin McQuesten

Glenhurst, Saskatchewan

"Whitehern"

May 22, 1908

My dearest Calvin,

As Tom comes home to-morrow for the Queen's Birth-day, am writing you whilst I have a quick time. The great event for that day is the unveiling of the Queen's statue. All we are able to see now is the old lion lying at the base. He is a fine old fellow and it seems to me very true to nature, not the time honoured one which appears with the unicorn and is really much handsomer, but like the beast in its natural state as I remember seeing it in Central Park. This one is in green bronze and reclines against the flag, its head raised as if watching.[412] The tulips are blazing in the Gore too. I saw all this as I went down to-day to the second-hand store to look again to look for your stove. I found one which I thought too good to lose; it was a Burrows Stuart the Jewel and that is one of the best, it was as good as new, a great bargain Wright said for $6.50 and I thought the right size taking an 18 in. stick. It ought to sell for good price when you are through with it, as you will probably be able to recommend it. On the way up went to Osborne's and got a small barrel to put the preserves in and next week will try to get them packed and start the whole thing off.

We have had endless rain but to-day it cleared and was lovely. Mr. Chisholm advised me to raise stable rent to $12.00, I was afraid but the men are willing to give it if I clear the loft completely, which I am quite glad to do. I have (through my interest coming in) just cleared off $200 of Ross's bill, so I only owe him thirty; I had paid Watkins $100, but I still owe him a hundred besides a lot of smaller accounts which I hope to pay with McPhie Int. this month. In time we shall get them off and our house is in good shape for a long time all but the verandah, the club took every vestige of paint off and it looks very bad. I think I'll have to let Gourlay put a coat on the floor.[413]

Mr. McPhie has organized the young girls of the church with a committee to put flowers in the church, last Sabbath it was "Pickle" Glassco's and Edna's turn. Hilda and E. [Edna] went to the market and got carnations beauties for 25cts a dozen (the manager allows 75cts a Sunday) and they mean to get garden flowers when possible, but it has been so cold and wet nothing was to be got. Well E. went up with "Pickle" to their house and as it turned out Dot had the measles (though they did not know it till next day) and poor Edna came out with a rash on Monday, as she had not all the symptoms and we did not want to keep away from people, we had to send for the doctor who said she had German Measles, and quite harmless. She was alright next day but it was so much more on doctor bill and gave Edna one day and night of many chills and then fever, her face stung so much.

Ruby is going twice a week to the doctor to have her throat healed she got so very worse and coughed too, that I at last took her down and doctor said it was Bronchitis, and she must come twice a week to have it sprayed, and when the warm weather comes, we hope she will get rid of it. We are trying to find a place at Ancaster to send her, it is high and dry there. I am not worrying but because her general health is so greatly improved and she says she feels a different person. But what does irritate me is, that it was all brought on by her determination to stay at Ottawa; and I do not think she realizes at all, that she brought on this heart trouble with me. I never had that at all until after I discovered she had carried out her own way with that young man and broken her word to me.[414] However in your letter do not say anything about her throat.[415, 416]

(Saturday morning) I wish you could see the garden now, as you enter the gate you see in front of you the plum covered with pink and the bridal wreath (it is really a spirea) in front and round the heart are large clumps of yellow tulips alternating with clumps of narcissus these are backed by the syringas whose foliage is now light green, the borders too have clumps of narcissus and the crown imperials, though they are fading a little now, the japonica is out too, but is nothing to Mrs. Husband's, hers (2) are magnificent but she has nothing else.[417] The grass borders are so green and lovely and all the lawn, the snow came so early last year and there was no ice, that the grass all over is particularly fine. The larch is beautiful just now too in its fresh green. Tom is so pleased to have been able to see the place in spring for the first time in many years. Your turn is long in coming. Am ashamed to say I forgot to look for the folding egg cases. It just went out of my head. Colin Fletcher is doing very well. Mr. Murray was in yesterday and said nothing had been the matter but the one thing. We hear that poor little Mrs. Baillie (Topsy McCoy) is dying, blood poison, her little baby is three weeks old. Poor child! it seems so sad. Mary has just been to market. Spring lamb at $2.75 hind quarter. Do not hanker after it at all cold wet spring bad for lambs. In reply to mine of sympathy Mrs. Hendrie wrote me an extremely nice letter and sent me an ebony hat brooch with handsome silver "M" as a memento of her father. Wasn't it nice of her?[418] All at present. With much love from all.

Your loving Mother
M. B. McQuesten

✦ **A88-(6173) To Calvin McQuesten**
Glenhurst, Saskatchewan   "Whitehern"
                                                     July 2, 1908

My dearest Calvin,

This morning we got Ruby started off she went by the ten o'clock train and will take lunch with Mrs. Whittemore and then leave Toronto at 1:00. Helen Locke was just returning from her holidays on this morning's train, otherwise she and Helen would not have seen each other at all, it seemed quite a coincidence.

I wrote you last in great haste after Ruby had been to the doctors in Toronto. She really seems perfectly well and I cannot help feeling thoroughly cross with Dr. Arnott for giving me such a fright and I really think a good rest and change at Ancaster would have been quite sufficient, but I did not like to disappoint Ruby and I also felt if she should happen to have any return of trouble I would blame myself. Besides the doctors in Toronto said she needed a good change, so poor Tom again came to the rescue with $90 towards her expenses. The tickets to Laggan cost just the same $80 as to Calgary, so she will be able to see Lake Louise and I don't know what more. She goes by boat from Owen Sound. Florrie Whittemore is on the outlook for a boarding place for her. Now that I have no anxiety about her health, I am feeling much better, the money is of small importance, although I scarcely see how I am to get through.

I wish indeed you could have seen the catalpas, they were a great sight, and the roses were so fine and so many of them, it is doubtful if there were any prettier sights, the catalpas form such a magnificent background people just stopped and gazed. The grass has kept so green too, and now the poppies are out.

Tom had his birth-day celebrated as usual, he has always been lucky in being home for a birth-day tea as next day is Dominion Day. When we were cleaning out the loft we came upon an old chair of your father's which had been broken and I got Gentle to repair it, so we just gave it to Tom for his present; as he will never lie down, it just suits him to stretch out in. He was fortunate enough to have business to do, so his expenses up were paid. He has had to bring up some large sum of money to Mr. Gibson in connection with some deal and was introduced by Mr. G. to Mr. Dewar of the Bank of Commerce, so he is getting to be known a little by people.[419]

Mrs. Colin Fletcher came in to-day with Mr. Irving[420] who had come over the holiday to see Colin [Fletcher].[421] He [Colin] is not exactly on his feet again, he is at Dr. [Donald] Fletcher's but the wound is not healed yet and Mrs. Colin seems a little doubtful as to his being altogether well again.

Ruby went to see the Uncle before she left, he says he has had a good many attacks lately she says he seems to think a great deal of you. I was thinking perhaps you might find time to write him, poor old chap. Tom thinks he ought by all means keep on right side of him, 49 Main St. is his address. I am afraid summer is over before you get the preserves, they are all jam so will keep till another year if you had a place to leave them.

Prof. McLaren had a slight stroke, he fell coming home from church, but recovered quickly.[422] Edna is well indeed and active, has taken to visiting Aged Women's Home, taking roses to them. One of 105 years interests her very much. Capt Fairgrieve is in his office to-day first time for months, and I luckily happened in, so he offered to put in all my coal now, as the price is now at lowest and let me pay in October for which I am very thankful. Well, Calvin dear I must close, with much love from all.

Your loving Mother.
M. B. McQuesten

✦ A89-(6252) To Calvin McQuesten

Glenhurst, Saskatchewan

[Note written at top] Have just had an invitation to go to Sparrow Lake with Edna am going for two weeks.

"Whitehern," Hamilton,
August 11, 1908

My dearest Calvin,

When we received your letter yesterday telling of your finding good water in your well, we were all most thankful. We had never known you had to go such a distance for your water. You must have had a very trying time, it seems to us and never let us know the discomforts you were suffering. In that heat you must have suffered greatly in your shack. I just pity you, but I hope there will be no return of the intense heat. For the last week we have had very pleasant weather. Last night there was great excitement over the home coming of Bobby Kerr, all the belles in finery and whistles blowing for hours, a great procession headed by the Mayor.[423] This is a great time for athletics, but I fancy all sensible people think there is far too much of it and these Olympian games a race-track with men instead of horses. I hope something will be done to stop these long distance races.

I fancy Ruby will have told you all about her trip to Laggan. As to her going to Macleod I do not see how she could go round in the way you describe. People do not mind the preacher visiting them, but they feel differently about a young lady seeing their household amusements; she does not like sharing her bed with anyone, either. Of course I know your idea, to keep her longer in the country at less expense to us, but I do not see how she can do this, Hilda is going to write Grace Rioch, perhaps she may invite her.

Last Sabbath Dr. Jordan of Queens was again preaching.[424] From the reports given by the family, he was giving some Higher Criticism, which seemed most reasonable. Tom was greatly taken with him.

Mrs. Mullin is now enjoying herself at the White Mountains. Had a letter from her and one from Mrs. Fletcher from Winnipeg who is very proud of being a grannie. Mr. & Mrs. Colin [Fletcher] have gone home. I am glad you have the tomatoes so hard to have no fruit in warm weather. Will you be able to store any preserves if you have too much where it will not freeze? The time is flying on now. With much love from all.

Your loving Mother
M. B. McQuesten

[P.S.] Wish you had a crop this year as it promises to be so good.

✦ A90-(6318) To Calvin McQuesten

c/o Knox College, Toronto, Ontario   "Whitehern"
Tuesday, December 1, [1908]

Dearest Cal,

As my coming depends on the weather could not let you know exact day, besides it would not be worth your while as I rush immediately to Dr. Capon. It looks as if to-morrow would be fine so just telephone to Mr. MacKay's at 2 o'clock and see if I have come. If you have any clothes bring them with you, I am bringing you a couple of shirts. Tom ran in yesterday, said he had been so unsettled. He had not seen you at all. It is about decided now that he shall go in with Mr. Chisholm in April, but does not quite know what to do in the meantime, he seems to have a horror of staying longer than he is wanted though Mr. Masten is quite agreeable just now, when he sees Tom is making arrangements to leave; not that he makes any complaint of Tom's work but business is not brisk. It is a difficult matter to decide as to Tom's final start, but he thinks, and I think, perhaps it is as good a place as anywhere else here in Hamilton where Mr. C. would give him a chance, and he has a certain standing and could enjoy the home. It takes time to get a practice and we are not sure there is any special advantage in Toronto.

I had always thought perhaps some special opening would come, but at the same time on the other hand hope that here I may get him interested in some good work besides his business. In Toronto he will be old before he begins anything and in a smaller place too one's influence tells more.[425] It is a matter for earnest prayer by us all, for it is a critical time. We have had such lovely mild weather but I am afraid winter is coming now.

With much love
Your mother

1909-1934

ॐ

✦ A91-(6336) To Calvin McQuesten
c/o Knox College, Toronto

[Written at top of letter] I wonder where the key of Tom's trunk is, you need not return Constance's letter. Photos in parcel. Tom's letter just came as well, will send it soon.

"Whitehern"
January 24, 1909

My dearest Cal,

The box and trunk arrived in good shape. I hope to send off your parcel to-morrow. The weather keeps wonderfully mild and the snow keeps off, which saves the snow cleaning for me, but it is hard on the unemployed. Had two letters from Ruby which you can send on to Tom, but return the photos to me, they might get lost at Elk Lake. It is a week to-day since I heard from Tom, but suppose the mails are uncertain. Isn't Ruby fortunate in finding such a comfortable home? She certainly has a very comfortable time of it. Hilda went up with Mrs. Mullin Monday and spent the night. Nellie is neither better nor worse, at the end of the 21 days, as hoped, the fever did not go down, so now it will have to run again for 21 days, and there is nothing to prevent running another 21 days. R. had a nice letter from Constance Kellogg. Will enclose it too. It is very sad about the brother.

Hasn't this shipwreck of the Republic been a most thrilling affair?[426] Isn't this wireless telegraphy like something miraculous! This is a great triumph for Marconi.[427] Poor Mrs. Woods is such a delicate person and too nervous to drive behind a horse even, so just imagine her. It is a mercy Mr. W. was with her. And poor Miss George (our W.F.M.S. treasurer) will hear enough about her comb. I am sorry for Mrs. Caven, who, I am sure, has enough to do looking after that nervous husband of hers.[428]

I am glad you went to the Dicksons, they were always so friendly. Lately there has been nothing but weddings amongst "Society" people. Now that you have your meals by ticket you can call Sundays on Maggie for dinner when you are at a loss.[429]

Yesterday was our Presbyterial annual of the W.F.M.S. As Mrs. Steele is away I had to take the morning business meeting, but got Mrs. Lyle to take the afternoon meeting. We had invited R. P. MacKay to speak for we had never yet succeeded in hearing his account of what he saw of our missionaries' work in the East, so I wrote him that we were particularly anxious to hear of our own missionaries and would you believe it, he gave a great account of a large gathering of the American Meth. [*sic*] Episcopalian mission and of the Ep. with social, and never mentioned our missionaries' names or a word about the work, except a little reference to a Xmas tree in our Widows' Home. Mr. Lyle and I were so exasperated we could hardly contain ourselves. Was there nothing to be seen of their work? It really looked so badly that I was more than sorry I had ever asked him. He looked worn out and dropping with sleep. It was fortunate I happened to write just the week before as he had forgotten and thought meeting was in the evening. I wish we could send some bright woman over to bring back our account.[430] Mrs. McGillvray would do finely if she were a good speaker, but she has a very poor voice and no animation, otherwise she is exceedingly observant and clever and can write well.[431]

I am very indignant too about another thing. You know I had to keep at Mr. Ketchen before we got Prof. Kilpatrick for our anniversary sermons and I told him if he could not get him, to try for Prof. Kennedy. Well, we got Prof. Kilpatrick last year. This year when I inquired who do you think, they had fixed upon but Hossack?[432] Mr. Leitch had voted against it, but Dr. Fletcher and Mr. Milne wanted him. Prof. Kennedy's name never mentioned. Can you understand people having a man like Prof. Kennedy within reach and no desire to hear him?[433] As for Mr. Ketchen he seems to have nothing in his mind but his sermons. Sunday morning Mr. Gray of Dundas preached for us and came in by Radial, but Mr. Ketchen did not look at time-table and reckoned on a 10:10 trolley car.[434] There is none on Sabbath, so he did not reach Dundas till 12 o'clock. If the ministers went on Saturday night, there would be none of this confusion on Sunday mornings. Mr. Ketchen is inviting some of the young men in to have a smoke with him. Am thoroughly disgusted with these men. Well, I must close, glad if you can get nicer meals at Varsity, it is fortunate you can make a change. With much love from all.

Your loving mother
M. B. McQuesten

✦ A92-(6343) To Calvin McQuesten

c/o Knox College, Toronto, Ontario　　　　"Whitehern", Hamilton
February 2, 1909

My dearest Calvin,

Indeed I was most interested and delighted to hear about your Greek critical exercise. I always am so glad to hear of your worth being appreciated. Between it all I am in great danger of being too much uplifted, for Mrs. Fletcher came across the church after service on Sabbath, to tell that Mr. Cunningham had been up and said "his people had listened spell-bound to you" and that you had a style of your own which he much liked. Then Mr. Paulin of St. Giles[435] had told her you gave a most brilliant speech at the dinner to the Principal, so that some said, they had no need to bring J. A. Macdonald when they had you. So you see my dear, your star is in the ascendant, and I have been cheering myself by looking back and thinking no doubt the time you spent in the newspaper work will always be of great value to you. You had an opportunity of hearing some fine speakers and it is quite an education.

I am enclosing R's letter, she seems to be getting on finely, I am wondering if it is a nuisance to you to send on her letter to Tom and his to her, as you may not want to write them every week. I may send you down some common envelopes and stamps to help along and you could just send on without writing, as I am sure you are very busy. Time flies so. Glad you heard Mr. Pringle, like him so much.[436] So poor Mrs. Sawyer is gone at last, died on the same day as Rolland Hills last year.[437]

We had our Auxiliary meeting to-day, a very good meeting. Mrs. Symington[438] and Mrs. Thomson read very good papers, especially the latter. Miss Fisher took tea with us yesterday, she goes back to Toronto on Thursday. Dr. and Mrs. Caven, after their experience do not feel like an ocean voyage immediately, so are going to Florida.[439] A great many terrible things are happening all the time.

Edna and I take the greatest satisfaction in going to Mr. Howitt's Bible Class on Friday mornings. He is taking up Genesis, and it is a treat. I had a bill from Dr. Arnott with message that he was going away for six months. His father & mother and wife are going too. By the time he returns, he will have been a year out of his office. Well, Cal dear, I must close. With much love from all.

Your loving Mother
M. B. McQuesten

[P.S.] We have the greatest satisfaction in the new man we got for ashes and snow cleaning. He is very civil and quick, does the work in half the time Gourlay did.

✦ A93-(6347) To Calvin McQuesten

c/o Knox College, Toronto, Ontario   "Whitehern"
February 9, 1909

My dear Calvin,

As your clothes arrived on Saturday evening we are wondering if you are likely to be in Tom's neighbourhood shortly or if we are to send them. I have been congratulating myself on the mild weather, but to-day is a regular old-timer and I find my courage sinking rapidly. I regret to say that the "parson" is under a very serious charge namely of appropriating funds given in trust. As his sister Edna was anxious about a certain sum ($2.50) entrusted to her brother Thomas, I wrote him, whereupon he replied that the aforesaid sum had been left with his brother Calvin, before he left for Elk Lake. Well

Cal dear it probably slipped your mind, but I was thinking, as you will probably be needing help from me by next month, you had better keep the money (hope you have not lost it) and I will pay Edna. Tom has never said a word about what his board is, you have seen all his letters. It is scarcely worth while to send on Ruby's letter of this week, you might keep it till we get next week's and send Tom both.

I have been reading the Queen's letters, she certainly, as a girl of seventeen, had a great deal of ability and of the fear of God. Her uncle the King of the Belgians incidently had so much wisdom and common sense and was such a fine man in every way. Strange that he should have had a son like the present Belgian King. He must have taken after his French mother's side of the house. It is really a good thing to read for it refreshes one's mind on so much of her early reign and interests me particularly as I used to hear your grandpapa speak of so many of the mentioned. Old Wm. IV and Queen Adelaide.[440]

Yesterday Mrs. Thomson called for me in a cab and we called on old Mr. Gordon, everyone else in the house was out and he was in his room.[441] Mrs. Thomson found him upstairs but his asthma and heart so bad could hardly speak.

These are very quiet days inside and a blizzard outside, so am afraid to go out. Did you see that poor Mr. Woods of Woods' Fair fell downstairs and so injured his spine, there was no hope of recovery?[442] So sorry he was such a kind man to his family. Well, I cannot think of anything else to say. All join in best love.

Your loving Mother
M. B. McQuesten

✦ A94-(6363) To Calvin McQuesten
Knox College, Toronto

[Written at top of letter] Did you notice in last Presbyterian Feb. 25 & week before also Charles Gordon's account of Evangelistic work in the West if you did not see it, tell Tom to send it to you as I am sending it to him Feb. 25th is the best.

"Whitehern"
February 27, 1909
Dearest Calvin,

Indeed that terrible murder gave everyone a shock, because one felt it might have happened to any one. The man must have been in an insane frenzy and there seems to be so many insane people going about one never knows when they will be encountered. Of course every [one] declares, they will never let a tramp inside the house and the hardware people have exhausted their stock of chain bolts for doors. The tramps declare (in the paper to-night) that the Kinrades never turned any one away without help so they would not have touched them.[443]

Well, Calvin, I am quite disappointed that you should not have a day or two with us after your exams, but I suppose it cannot be helped. Now you must let us know, if there is anything you wish to take with you in the eatable line. Can you take a cake or anything? Then what about the new nightgowns? Can you get them or will I ask Maggie to write to get them for you?[444] I can give you some money. And if you leave paying of board till end of term, that means you have to take meals at Knox. If they are not good do not take them, I can manage someway to let you have some money.

I am sending you R.'s letter. I really feel provoked at the doctors persisting in my keeping her out there during cold winter, I am sure it was not the climate at all for her. I know the effect of a cold winter upon me was always to make me feel very weak in the spring, and as to her face it will never be well <u>there</u>. One would really think it did not matter to us how long she stayed. However I have told her, she can stay for March (I had suggested she should come at end of her half month the 21st) but she must come at end of her month April 6th. I had hoped she would be home here before you left. I have told her, she need never expect her face to be well there.

Laura Hostetter finally arrived home on Wednesday night, but of course had taken cold on the way and was in bed since so we have not seen, but Mrs. Thomson is delighted to see her free of asthma and able to lie down asleep like other people.[445]

Edna was out when your Valentines came, so Mary put hers into E.'s envelope, she was simply charmed with it and would have been most disappointed with Cupid. You do not speak of getting any, too bad if you were forgotten. You can send on cuttings with R.'s letter to Tom. So the Methodists are having another squabble. Lots of things for the newspapers now-a-days. Heard from Maggie White, Mrs. Senkler home and feeling very badly, we hear that now Mr. Hammond is dead Ontario Bank affairs will be settled, but they kept quiet not wishing to disturb him.[446] Be sure & tell us what you need. With love.

Your Mother
[M. B. McQuesten]

✦ A95-(6391) To Calvin McQuesten

Glenhurst, Saskatchewan

"Whitehern"
April 20, 1909

My dearest Cal,

I was just beginning to wonder what you were doing when your letter came in yesterday. It quite cheered me to think of your having thoughtful friends like the school-teacher to look after you. I think we will have to send him something good in your barrel. H. is going to start the cake very soon.

I have at last been told of your sad experience in February. Poor you! To think of all you have gone through and just when you were starting in to do something for exams, that this dreadful thing should have come upon you, and what you must have suffered! Poor dear child! Your life has been a strange Providence but perhaps it was sent to save you from straining your hairs for a scholarship, and we must be thankful you recovered in time to pass your exams, that was the chief thing.[447]

There is quite an excitement over the doings of the Railway, they are buying on south-side of Hunter between James and John. Gave Stanley Mills $40,000 for their corner on John & Hunter! There is talk of a great Union Station. This uncertainty seems always to block sale of our property, which we had suggested for the new Public Library.[448] So we await developments. Mrs. Mullin lent me "Sowing Seeds in Danny." It is certainly a most comical refreshing book. So glad you found your little horse alright. Enclose Tom's last he will come home June 1st, there is no use wasting time where you cannot get paid for your work. Aside from the experience, it would have paid far better to have stayed with Masten till April 1st.

To-day's Globe says nothing but letters can be taken now to Elk Lake, roads broken up, only can be carried by men on foot.[449] So Turkey is in a turmoil, it is a good thing to get the old Sultan out, if those terrible Moham-medans had not come down upon the poor Xtians and missionaries.[450] I sup-pose you get the Globe. We have been very busy. Ruby feels better of the rest at home. All join in much love.

Your loving mother
M. B. McQuesten

✦ A96-(6419) To Calvin McQuesten

Glenhurst, Saskatchewan

"Whitehern"
May 15, 1909

My dearest Calvin,

Your letter of May 3rd only reached me yesterday. It did seem such a long time since we had heard, but I just thought it was the fault of the mail service. It just seemed too bad that your ordination should have been performed in just such a hole in corner sort of style. Does Dr. Carmichael ever appear when expected![451] I had hoped by the paper you were to have something of a service. It does seem poor Calvin as if you were kept in the background a good deal, but we do not know what you may do some-day.[452]

We had a long cold time too but this last week have had some warm days. To-day I have been trotting more or less since 7:30 am after the gardeners, they are very trying they arrive here without their proper implements and then I have to see after them and put them into their hands. Various things in the beds spread over and got out of order. So I had to have them reset. I only invested in one new thing an Irish juniper. The place opposite is not to be a factory but a storehouse, which is a comfort. I am really not worrying about the railway it is all so un-certain. The trees are coming out beautifully even the plum and peach tree and the little cherry; for a couple of months now is the loveliest time for our place. We hear that Mrs. Scott is ill of pneumonia. H. is going to inquire after her. We have been busy getting our curtains done and spring things ready. Dr. McTavish is to be with us at Assembly. Would have liked to have taken two more, but did not feel I could just afford to hire help and the girls could not cook for so many for nearly two weeks. Mrs. Hendrie is to give a garden party for the Assembly. I was glad to see Tom's name mentioned in the account of Elk Lake church in this week's Pres. [Presbyterian].[453]

Was greatly shocked to see in to-days Globe of this motion to do away with the clause Against the Catholics in the King's oath. Isn't it terrible to think of Mr. Asquith favouring it?[454] He can have no religion and indirectly his wife has none and is a simpleton, as you perhaps saw, she had entertained a company at <u>Downing St.</u> with a display of new dresses on models brought from Paris. What we have come to! People are so ignorant now-a-days of right and wrong that one is never safe.[455]

Yesterday afternoon I opened the door to your friend Norman MacEachern, Mary also came in. We chatted quite a while and daresay would like him on better acquaintance but we had to do most of the talking. He goes next week, so we have no opportunity of entertaining him. He apologized for not calling before, but had been very busy, so many sick people and there are 1100 members in Knox. He goes now to Crescent St. Montreal. Wish I could hear him preach, it seems an undertaking for him to go to so lay a church.[456]

We want to get your barrel off next week and will remember tin, shredded wheat. In yesterday's letter you have not mentioned where to send it, so unless we hear again will send to Saskatoon as before, unless I can find out here if we can send to Zealandia. Thursday was a lovely day and Mrs. Thomson took me driving to make calls; and Mrs. Joe [Thomson] went too, but every one was out except Mrs. Fletcher and Ann the baby is just lovely the picture of her mother, and a dear little child. Mrs. Lyle was away, she & Dr. have gone to New York to Harry's wedding. The house on the outside is painfully plain and ugly. I believe Jack designed it for two stories and his father thought there would be no room for family at Xmas, and added a story, with the result you saw. Certainly the present day houses taken altogether are very ugly, and unfinished. Well I must close as H. is waiting to post this. With much love from all.

Your loving mother

M. B.McQuesten

✦ A97-(6446) To Calvin McQuesten

Glenhurst, Saskatchewan   "Whitehern"
June 11, 1909

My dearest Calvin,

Yours of the 28th only arrived to-day. I wonder if you get all my letters, for the card telling me to send your barrel to Fessier reached me in good time and I have said so more then once. I hope you have got the soup tablets. I posted you before we sent barrel & <u>box</u> which left here on 21st.

It would not be possible for me to begin a discussion on the change of Coronation Oath. Anything that yields one iota to the R.C. Church is a terrible mistake. Their Religion <u>is</u> "superstitions" and idolatrous and a religion that supports the vile practices, which it does, should be opposed in every possible way. What do you think those nunneries and orphanages in Montreal are for? And on Wednesday Mary James brought a Mr. Cooper in for dinner.[457] He is engaged in Mission work in Brazil and he is collecting for an orphanage there, because of the number of illegitimate children of the Catholic priests. I have read of it, but he says it is beyond description. There they do not care enough to hide it, but in U.S. and our country and Britain, the nunneries and orphanages are maintained for the benefit of the priests. He said, it made him sick to hear Protestants speaking of them as sincere when it is an altogether false religion. In Mexico the Virgin is an idol and she is worshipped all over the world by catholics as divine. When Rome has us in her clutches and a Catholic on our throne, then the charitable people will bemoan the progress of Romanism. I know there was a paragraph in the Globe, expressing just your sentiments. Of course the Liberal party has always kept itself in power by the Catholic vote, when I was a child, my father used to speak of the Globe truckling to the Catholics. They look upon us as poor fools. It was good to hear Dr. Pringle at the Assembly giving the government a good setting out, he did not spare them. Dr. Fletcher looked almost aghast. You will remember if it had not been for one of those laws, there would have been the elevation of the mass and the people bowing down in the streets of London, and it will come yet, if you begin meddling with the old laws. People are not so well grounded in Christian doctrine as they used to be and very few know what they believe.[458]

Well we had such fine times at the Assembly, we went as often as we could. On Sabbath we had Principal Forrest from Halifax.[459] A good man and interesting but not an able preacher like Principal Patrick whom we heard in the Evening on "I am not ashamed of the Gospel" XXX [sic] the power of God much salvation. He is very fine in every way, fine voice, speaks entirely without notes, keeps close to his subject, in illustrations no poetry, extremely earnest, people never took their eyes off him (it was in King St. Methodist) and he made the most direct individual appeals with considerable action, bringing home <u>salvation</u>, What it is, the signs of its possession, its effects. It was very fine indeed.[460]

Then the subject of the Church Union at the Assembly.[461] Unfortunately did not hear opening by Principal P. [Patrick] & Dr. Duval,[462] which were said to be very fine and Principal MacKay against Union did extremely well but effect was spoiled by having to stop as it was time to adjourn.[463] When we went in the Evening he was not able just to take it up again so well. Dr. Robert Campbell[464] the clerk, supported him but spoke in such a way that he roused Principal Forrest who rose up and shook his fist whilst the Assembly cheered them on and seemed to enjoy it immensely. I was surprised to hear Principal F. speak in such a nasty sneering tone in reply to Principal McKay. I went back next morning to hear the end. Old Dr. Sedgewick[465] opposed the union, a very clever old chap who warned them, that the first thing they knew, they would be under a "stationing committee" and it almost made him weep to think of Principal Patrick in such a position. Then as Paul said, Galatians, he said "Oh foolish Presbyterians, who hath bewitched you." But Principal P. had made them think they were like Alice-in-Wonderland. There was a great laughing, but it was carried to send the question down to the people. Which in my judgement will mean a terrible lot of discussion & ill feeling and as our Speaker said it will take 10 to 15 years for the congregation to recover. The Western men were the strongest against it.

Another night we had Moral reform, Dr. Pidgeon spoke remarkably well on this.[466] And then Charles Gordon reported on Evangelism.[467] He then introduced MacGregor to tell of Chapineau meetings at Orillia (he seemed such a good fellow without any conceit)[468] and then a Mr. McKinnon of Minnedosa Presbytery such a good fellow too,[469] and then Dr. Kilpatrick told of his Experience in the Kootenay. I never heard anyone like the Professor such a beautiful spirit so humble and childlike in a way, and all so finely expressed, I could give you no idea of it and the impression made, people were so moved by it all and stirred to the heart. Then Principal Gordon of Queen's wound up in a most admirable way, saying among other things it had been the finest meeting ever held at our Assembly in Canada.[470] Dr. Kilpatrick finally urged the young men "Out with you to the West and leave the old men here in Ontario." Last night we had a call from Mr. Byers, I always liked him and he is nicer than ever and become quite chatty telling us many interesting things. He wants to be in Canada again but I think has no church.[471] One afternoon Mrs. Fletcher gave a small tea for some of the ministers, Fred Anderson was there and inquiring for you; he looked well but thin and finds the excitement of speaking affects his digestion, should think this new position would not be a good thing. Colin Fletcher looks better than for years. James Little was asking for you too.[472] Must close, Tom is still away up north. To-day is warm, the first for a week. With much love From all.

Your loving Mother
M. B. McQuesten

✦ A98-(6460) To Calvin McQuesten

Glenhurst, Saskatchewan "Whitehern"
June 28, 1909

My dearest Calvin,

Do hope this letter will not miss the night mail but I was not able to get my letter off on Saturday as I generally do. Your letters are coming on finely now, as they just come in a week, yours of the 18th reaching here the 25th. I was so glad to know the supplies had reached you so soon, weeks quicker than last year, I think but H. is terribly anxious about the packing, she didn't have such good stuff for packing and was afraid of the box. Tom just started to his office a week ago Saturday that was on the 19th. It really seems scarcely possible that he can be there, but it is certainly going to mean a great difference to us.[473] Mr. Chisholm goes off with his sister to the old country this week.[474]

We have had extremely warm weather for over a week the roses are out in full great quantities of all colours, last week the gardener cut the hedge and put every thing in apple-pie order and it certainly is a most beautiful garden, it is such a long time since you saw it. The grass edges to the flower borders are so particularily trim looking on the gravel walk. The strawberries are in great plenty, but the weather is so hot, afraid they will not last as what we got on Saturday were almost too dead ripe. Last week the young men gave Mr. Ketchen a surprise party to which an invitation was sent to Tom gotten up by Mr. Grow &c. It was printed and at the bottom "Bring your pipe"! You can imagine my wrath. A smelling concert at the Manse! Mr. Maw would not to go to it and others were disgruntled but what can be done when the Minister smokes.

Will send you the paper. Rev. Jos. Nite Cory (brother of John) of B.C. preached yesterday morning.[475] Isn't it too bad that Prof. Kennedy is going?[476] What did you think of Prof. Seyas[477] proposition to have Prof. McFadyen take his place and get someone else for Prof. McF.'s place?

On Friday evening Tom, H. [Hilda] & I took the cars up to see Mrs. Mullin and then walked home, but it was the most tiresome jaunt, when we reach the place, we have to mount those steep steps and when we get inside have to go upstairs to sit, either in the sitting-room or on the back verandah and then there is not a chair big enough for Tom, so altogether it is not a joy. I hope by this time the Presbyterians have reached you, I thought you would rather see the papers from April, as you would be back here for October. I often wonder how you stand the heat in your little shack, it is a mercy you have your screen door up.

Did you notice May Mewburn's marriage at Port Arthur on 15th,[478] Ruby has heard nothing since she left May when M. was in very poor health, and it always made her very ill to travel but she had intended coming to Toronto early in Spring for shopping. So perhaps it was thought wise for her not to go home again.

Thanks for the paper, it was most interesting to see they were moving mail to Glenhurst. Poor little Laura has been very miserable with asthma, it came on again before she left La Coma. You would notice her little bottle of marmalade tied up with blue ribbon "true blue." It is just a pity of poor little Laura and Mrs. T. [Thomson] too, so disappointed to find her in such poor health.[479]

It is just so warm I cannot think. Tom will take this out to post. It is after dinner and he is fanning himself on the sofa. The British Ladies are getting the idea of Canada as ..... [*sic*] snows well melted out of them. In my last letter we were just expecting Maggie [MacKay] White but she never came at all have not heard from her. Well Cal hope you will not get sunstroke. Will give Tom his letter on 30th. With much love from all.

Your loving mother
M. B. McQuesten

✦ A99-(6483) To Calvin McQuesten

Glenhurst, Saskatchewan   "Whitehern"
                                        Friday July 23, [1909]

Dearest Calvin,

Your last week's letter which you thought would be late reached on the Monday. It was too bad you should be called away from the picnic when you really could not be in time to be of any use and so missed the opportunity of becoming acquainted with the people, which I know you are anxious to do. Maggie [MacKay] White at last came to-day, she reached here by the Turbinia at 10.30 this a.m. and we took her round, unfortunately she arrived this afternoon and though Hilda took her up the incline it was too foggy to see anything and she has just left for 5.30 boat.[480]

It seems that Dr. Senkler came down after Leila and stayed for five weeks. He invited Gordon [MacKay] and his wife to lunch at King Edward and made Leila go, though she was in grief with the result that Gordon was induced to sign a cheque to Leila for $31,000 in exchange for stock to that amount in the warehouse. You see there was $125,000 left by Uncle Edward to the MacKay children and put into the business, this the Ontario Bank cannot touch, and the boys have the interest of that, and Mr. MacKay too about a year before his death suddenly took into his head to take out insurance of $30,000 between Willie and Gordon, so they have that. Providence looked out for them in spite of their sins, for there is no telling when Ontario Bk. affairs will be settled. Leila also, in spite of the direction of the will, took upon herself to divide up the furniture getting what she wanted for herself, letting Gordon have a very good share, but giving a very poor share to Willie, he felt much aggrieved but had not the courage to stand up for himself, though they did have a pitch battle and poor Willie was of course thoroughly ill whilst he was there.

On the way home Dr. Senkler took ill with Rheumatic fever at Salt
Lake City and the altitude so affected his head, he nearly died and had to be
taken out in a special car to Portland Oregon. They have dismissed Small
and the cook, they had been together robbing the house for years. Mary wept
rivers, but Maggie thinks Drummond was almost afraid of her, though she
had always been very kind and waited on him most devotedly and giving
him Catholic books to read. Drummond says if he were anything he would be
a R.C. and the other day was quite indignant with the Orangemen's band. I
think it is most probable the priests had Mary put up to taking him in with
his money. At present the Smiths have got him in Muskoka, though he is
very tired of them. He had taken a great fancy to a nurse in the hospital,
when he was there; a little Grace [illegible] a friend of the Gartshores a grand
niece of Mr. Woodhouse. Poor little Grace would be horrified I am sure.[481]

In to-day's Globe we see that our City Engineer proposes that the tracks
in the tunnel be lowered and the trains come in through a subway. The
C.N.R. to come in this way too and he thinks the two tracks quite sufficient.
It seems too good to be true if this could be carried, that we should be
delivered from those trains on Hunter St. Tom has just come in to say that
Eddie of St. Mary's has sent him a pass to go to Tilsonburg to stay over till
Monday. Eddie going too.

The MacKay's do not know what to do for a house. Maggie cannot find
anything that would suit. Willie needs a little ground and where he could be
private. The University would buy it but would only give $7000 and Mr. Mc.
paid $16000 for it. So they scarcely know what to do. Willie suggested to
Maggie to look here, but really houses are very scarce here.

Miss Fisher and her friend Mrs. Wood of Toronto came to see us the
other evening, (they are living in the Logie house for the summer). Mrs. W.
is almost quite blond but very pretty and most interesting, having travelled a
good deal. Her dog is quite a noted beast, a little Pomeranian, brown and
tan with a fox head, long hair and fine tail like a spitz dog, it was given to
her in England and is a brother of the Queen's dog and of a dog which is said
to have been beside the Queen when she died; worth $300 as puppies and
the father worth 1000 pounds.

(Saturday Morning) Your letter to Ruby has just come, and was full of
interest. Indeed you did well to give such a good tea to that young couple I
hope they'll return it with a good fee. I wish you could have been at more
weddings to make you feel easier. It was very sad about the poor young girl.
You have various experiences. I had just been going to ask when the baptisms
were coming off. Peter & Douglas came back here after their two weeks in
Muskoka and have been hanging around here for two weeks, to add to the
prosaic style of the Event. This was to cheer up Mrs. Williams Helms.[482]
Well, I must close with much love from all.

Your loving mother
M. B. McQuesten

✦ A100-(6509) To Calvin McQuesten
Glenhurst, Saskatchewan   "Whitehern"
                                     August 30, 1909

My dear Calvin,

After I wrote you on Saturday, it occurred to me, Supposing you had a chance to sell your homestead when you were ready to leave there would be the $500 mortgage on it. If you once put it on, then you would almost have to keep it till you paid that off and what would your taxes be? Your belated letter came this morning and your question me as to my summer outing and I had been expecting it and I feel that I owe it to you to spend the money you sent me in that way and yet I need it so much for other purposes that I did not like to spend it on a trip.

So I think I must just at last tell that we have been under extra expense for Ruby. Before going further I want to tell you so that you will not be alarmed that she is now we believe out of danger and getting on rapidly. Well, when Ruby reached Toronto from Winnipeg she went to Dr. Caven and he advised her to go to a Sanatorium at Gravenhurst under a Dr. Parfitt in whom he had the greatest confidence. This was a new place started in March. Dr. C. said for her just to go for two or three months, and there she could learn how to take care of herself.[483] I suppose he did not wish to discourage her, but he must have known that it takes at least a year to make a cure. Of course this gave us all a terrible shock and we decided as you were so far from home, it was useless to tell you, and we would wait till you came home and by that time she would be better. After she had rested there for two weeks and Heurner attended to her, her fever was lower and Mrs. Mullin and Hilda were up with her, they were delighted with the doctor, the nurses and everything about the place, and Ruby was quite happy too. The present system is to keep the patient perfectly quiet and feed them well. By the blessing of God Ruby never went back. And when Tom went to see her in June on his way from Elk Lake, the doctor said the disease had been checked, at first he was afraid it was in her throat but it was not. Then two weeks later Hilda went to see her. About the first of July she was moved into a tent a fine large one with floor and comfortably furnished, R. said she felt better immediately; the nurse says she is getting fat and she enjoys her food thoroughly and eats well. Her card on Friday says "I must touch wood, have been feeling especially well these last few days and my temperature is "out of sight" so we feel she is getting on finely. The doctor also uses the new treatment of injecting tuberculin into the back to destroy the germ, the effect of this is to increase the temperature, but evidently now since it was "out of sight," it has had a fine effect upon her. Dr. Parfitt himself nearly died of it and was given up but fought it out and is now a strong fine looking man, he is a very fine man too and takes the greatest care of his patients. His wife also is a fine woman and so is Mrs. Fournier the head of the house. It is called "The Minnawaska" and was an Hotel which was bought with 14 acres of land, it is fitted up with steam heating &c and very comfortable, they have excellent food, and we can but feel grateful to God that such a place was ready when we needed it. Crawford Pawis is up there and though he seemed very ill, the doctor thinks he will be moving round by the spring, it is quite wonderful the cures we hear of. Gordon Gates was there but there was no hope of him from the first, it had gone on too long, so he was brought home.[484] Whilst there he was very kind sending Ruby papers and magazines and made his sister come to see her, and Miss Gates came to see me after she returned and sent garden roses while we had them. The poor sister said he was her child companion. They always went every place together for they did not go into society. Dr. P. [Parfitt] said Calgary was too windy not a place for R. at all.[485] I must tell you that Jean Black McKeracher is in the Manse at Gravenhurst and she wrote inviting any of the family that wanted to go up and stay with her, so H. did and found Mr. McK. so kind & nice and most hospitable, so I am sure if you could stop off on your way home, you could just stay overnight with him and you could get meals at the sanitorium for 25cts. Jean will probably be here in October, but you could introduce yourself and get your meals at the san. Mr. McK. & all the Blacks have been so nice and kind in visiting Ruby.[486]

"The Minnewaska" is not far from the Manse, within the limits of Gravenhurst. I cannot tell you how thankful we are for the good hope we have, for it was a disappointment when she came home from Calgary and had to be sent right off again.[487] Now I think the very hot weather is over, really cold to-day. You see I could hardly go to a place by myself and it takes the two girls to keep the house going.

Maggie [MacKay] asked me to Toronto, but think I will wait till you are back here before I go, it would be nicer to go out for little walks with you. Tom helps all he can and he wants to get your answers to his questions before deciding. Of course if one risks nothing one wins nothing. We pray that you may be guided. R. will be writing you now as I have told the tale. With much love.

Your mother
[M. B. McQuesten]

✦ A101-(6636) To Calvin McQuesten

Knox College, Toronto

"Whitehern"
Saturday [February 12, 1910]

My dear Calvin,

I was very glad to hear you were keeping well and resisting temptation though it is very trying to always have to be careful, but Tom says those debates are not worth your spending any strength on for the few who hear them. Isn't that a fine Editorial in the British Weekly? Such a fine setting out of the whole case, the condition of things in Germany and America too! It seems to me "Protection" has been settled for awhile. Haven't had any papers since, those three came together. Very glad they sent the one with the Editorial.[488]

Do not know that I have written since Hilda and Edna had the upset, they took Connie Turnbull with them on Tuesday and had had a fine drive, which is such a treat for Connie, as she has seen very little of the city. When on their way home, they came down Queen St. and at Aberdeen Ave. their runner caught on car rail and over they went, they were not hurt but it was so sudden H. let go the lines, the horse trotted off. But the Bard and Charlie[489] saw them and assisted them to gather up their things, everything was dumped on the road two soap stones etc. and it was a thawing day and they were covered with mud or slush rather and were sent in to Martha to get cleaned up, whilst the brothers looked after the horse, it was caught on Aberdeen Ave. near James and brought back. Then to Hilda's intense disquiet Charlie was anxious to drive them home, "just as if she couldn't drive or the horse had run away." O it was very mortifying! But these things often occur now-a-days with these tracks the snow is cleared off them and left high on the sides. Emily Colquhoun said her mother was turned out at the Federal Life corner and a whole lot of groceries spilled out too. I saw one yesterday, groceries too spilled out at Club corner. The next day I drove them and we went away East, saw St. Giles church and all those new streets. It is certainly the thing for Edna, it makes her sleep and eat finely.

Charles the office boy was trying for a prize offered by Spectator for essay on "The Whale." Tom had given him books to help and to-day we hear he has got it, a gold watch. Tom had threatened Gordon Southam[490] with bodily injury if he didn't give it to him. Had a card from Mrs. Bell written on the 1st she was sailing the next Sabbath, had been seeming ill for three weeks and would be so glad to get home; she should reach New York very soon now. I see by paper over 500 children sent in essays. I understand the prize was given by "Tindell and Tobey" clothiers here, and essays were said to be most comical; there was a prize for the country as well as city and one for those under thirteen.

Ruby's letter seems very cheerful. Isn't Mrs. Young wonderfully kind? It seems as if we ought to hear soon of her sitting up. This is the marmalade season and H. has been busy at it all day. The James' never succeed so we coaxed them to let us make it for them, though Mrs. J. would pay for materials. I went out this morning, though the snow was up to my knees to get R.'s valentine, which took the shape of a red heart box full of red candies in hearts etc. such as Crawfords gets up very nicely.[491] The snow seems to be endless, but it is a beautiful winter and we have no beggars, so much work made by the snow. Well, I must close. With love from all and much love from myself.

Your loving mother
M. B. McQuesten

[P.S.] That must have been a funny little place you were at, but every dollar counts.

✦ A102-(6676) To Calvin McQuesten
Knox College

[Note at top] Be sure to put the ticket in the coat you are going to wear

"Whitehern"
Wednesday [March 30, 1910]

Dear Calvin,

You certainly are having warm weather for your exams,[492] it is so trying so dry and smoky like August, we want rain so much. Am afraid the [Halley's] comet is going to burn us up. We have just got the double windows off. The snowdrops have been out some time. The crocuses are very bright and some violets; waiting for a man to take off the manure These wretched gardeners are just a nuisance, no comfort with them. Our visitors are leaving us to-day we enjoyed having them very much, Mai Mathewson is a very nice girl and of course Nell, is always herself.[493]

We are very busy hurrying up our sewing, for when Tom was up at Gravenhurst, he talked with the doctor and found a cottage close to the Minnewaska and when he told me I decided to take it at once. The Dr. thought R. [Ruby] needed a change and to have her own people. So Hilda is to take charge and I am to be there as much as possible. Say nothing if you write, as we have not told Edna or Mary yet. It is $15 a month and we have to take it for eight mos. This is all just now, will expect you Saturday night. Get down to boat as early as you can, if you expect to get a seat inside. Boat leaves at 5. Have your overcoat.

With love your mother.
[M. B. McQuesten]

✦ A103-(9058) To Calvin McQuesten

449 Ninth St.   "Whitehern"
Edmonton, Alberta   December 19, 1910

My dearest Calvin,

Just a few lines to wish you a very merry Christmas and a happy New Year and may you see many of them in the enjoyment of health and every blessing. It seems and is a kind Providence that gave you Lorna's home to keep Christmas and it will be a pleasure to her too when she is so far from home to have one of her childhood's friends with her, for there are none just the same. I am glad to know too from your letter of the 13th received this minute that you are still more than satisfied with your position and so happy in your work; though I feel that you will just be overwhelmed with engagements, but I pray daily you may have strength to bear it.

Dr. McQueen <u>may</u> have called upon you to speak as an afterthought, but it was not fair or thoughtful, perhaps I should not say it, but ministers <u>can</u> do mean tricks and the older man is often jealous of the younger.[494] However as you have charge of the prayer-meeting, I trust you will make much of it, for that is where the church is failing to-day. I wonder what kind of a man Mr. Dowling was and how he was liked. You got the impression he was sick of his position, did not get sufficient preaching, but other work.[495] Whatever you do try to keep quiet and do not run yourself to death. You are very like myself in temperament.

I am sorry but Saturday we posted some parcels to <u>you</u> at <u>Lorna's address</u> not her care. Look at <u>both</u> sides of tags. I cannot quite understand how a <u>flat</u> cuff case can be so good as your travelling collar box as they come home rolled from the laundry. Ruby's present is to help you to go quietly about it, if you take into your head to get up early or go to bed late.

Would love to send Mrs. Jaffary something but have so many calls. Have just heard from John Baker, the turkey is coming. As the time draws on I feel more and more sorry you are not to be with us. We are planning to have our dinner up at the Cottage. Ruby is enjoying so much seeing our various purchases, we take everything up to show her, even to the smallest card, before we send them.[496] Will send you John's letter when she has read it.

You may have to wait till your birth-day for the [ink stain]. Did not just think to wait long enough for your reply. You know I get utterly bewildered at this season of the year; there is just so much to plan for and the constant running up to the Cottage and thinking what Ruby can eat is very wearing. Tho' I think I have got wonderfully strengthened to hear things without fretting.

Well Calvin dear, good luck to you and may the future hold many blessings in store for you. I should think you would need to spend some of your money on furs for yourself and lined overcoat. You might get it cheaper through his friend ["Shiner"?]. Have not found out yet about where skins are prepared, but am almost sure they are sent to England. Remember hearing Mrs. Proctor say she had been sent a beautiful skin, but it cost her the price of a muff to get it made. This is not a proper Xmas letter at all and would not do for a [?] of a letter from a mother to a son, but cannot compose my mind at all, as I am just flying out. With much love and best wishes from all.

Your loving mother
M. B. McQuesten

[P.S.] Edna remarkably well, a great comfort.[497]

✦ A104-(6736) To Calvin McQuesten

Staney Brae, Muskoka

Bayfield
July 25, 1911

My dearest Calvin,

Just inclosing [*sic*] these letters for your entertainment We are having a very windy time which set in yesterday morning, not so very cold but a high wind, so that we can go out very little, so thankful to be going home on Thursday.

You are really most enterprising at Staney Brae glad to hear of your doing something to amuse yourself. It really is so tiresome if one cannot get up something. Edna is very well indeed and endeavours to cheer me up. All she can.[498] It does not do for me to have nothing to do, I have decided this is the trouble, at home there is always something to occupy my mind. Hope you have bed clothes enough I had to send home for blankets. Glad to know you are feeling so well. With much love.

Your loving mother
M. B. McQuesten

[P.S.] The next British Weekly you receive is full of interesting things, what the ministers say of coronation. It seems too bad that Dr. Thornton should have been moderator this year and so got into it instead of a worthier.[499] Please keep the paper, would like it again.

✦ A105-(6738) To Calvin McQuesten

Staney Brae, Muskoka

"Whitehern"
Hamilton, August 3, 1911

My dearest Calvin,

I have been trying to write you ever since I came home, but when I was not on the go, I was too sleepy to do any thing or it was too warm, altho' on the whole the weather has been pleasant except that it feels so dry. It threatens continually and it is quite oppressive for awhile, but passes off. On

Sabbath went twice to St. Paul to hear Mr. Sillars of Edinboro' whom I
quite liked for his old fashioned style, but the young did not like at all.[500]

Then Monday Tom took Hilda and myself down to Tuckett's Farm on
the way to the Beach to see the Aviation meet. I had demurred at first, but
was glad I went, as we had an excellent view of McCurdy's Machine and saw
him make a most successful flight. Tom had been down on Saturday to see
him and was given two passes. It was a wonderful thing, the engine is just in
the centre McCurdy sits in front, strapped in, then there are like two pairs of
wings and a tail. Two mechanics are with him, they start the engine and are
obliged to hold the machine down by main force, till all is ready, when the
aeroplane runs along the ground on four wheels, the distance of our grounds
when it rises beautifully just like a bird and circles in the air, rising and
falling as directed, came down once so close over our heads, we were rather
frightened and the noise is terrific, but it certainly is a most interesting and
wonderful achievement.[501] Willard's machine had been injured so did not
see it and there was some fuss with the Englishman but McCurdy is greatly
elated with his machine.[502] Coming home there was such a crowd we had a
great time getting the cars, but the policemen lifted us on and we got home
alright.

Then Tuesday Hilda and I took 10.40 boat to Toronto, her nose I determined must have treatment, so we went to Hiscott Institute on College St.
and the head of it said, after treatment it would be alright in about five
weeks which I hope will be the case, as it has been a sore trial.[503] It was very
warm and close in Toronto, but pleasant on this boat. When I came home
from Bayville I was distressed to find Mary in bed with ulcerated sore throat
and she had got so nervous about herself however she was much better by
next day and able to take a little nourishment so she was able to come down
to dinner on Sunday. We got her ready and she went off to Chippewa
yesterday afternoon.

After that I had a visit from Mrs. Jos. Henderson. The wife of little
Mr. Henderson here, the caretaker, died last week and Mr. Jos. H. had come
up to the funeral, but she [Mrs. Henderson] had waited and came yesterday
to see the family and to see us; she was very nice and kind.[504] Is much
perturbed lest the Union should carry. Principal Patrick very ill. There
certainly would be fearful confusion and beyond human brains to right it
it seems to me.

You would see all about the Asylum horror in the *Globe*. We never
heard or saw any thing of it, till postman told Edna, reference to it was in
Globe, but nothing alarming. Mattie Davidson came home this week after
a stay in Preston which she enjoyed very much. Tom is going down on
Saturday to stay till Monday—Wednesday if he could with "Strap Watson."
Our lawn is in most beautiful shape, the grass so green and most of the
evergreens have done well and some of the hydrangeas.

Tell me how to send the money. The papers give glowing accounts of the crops near Saskatoon. We saw in a Clinton paper that Jean Ross was married in Rochester, and a letter from Mrs. Ferguson to me from Formosa mentioned the wedding day as June 24th and <u>Mrs.</u> <u>McKay</u> greatly delighted—Doubtless![505] Well, I must close. I am sure you could have a very pleasant time at Staney Brae. With much love.

Your affectionate Mother

M. B. McQuesten

✦ A106-(6746) To Calvin McQuesten

Staney Brae, Muskoka

"Whitehern"

August 11, 1911

My dearest Calvin.

Am obliged to use a pad, as am out of any but best paper and it is too warm to go out. Tom came home with good news last night; his salary is raised from July 1st to $100 a month. Mr. C. said they cleared last year $12000 of this Mr. C. gets 3/5, Mr. L. 2/5; next year they expect to make more and then Tom is to have a "<u>very</u> substantial increase." This is very encouraging and Tom certainly deserves it from the way he treats us.[506]

Well yesterday afternoon H. E. [Hilda, Edna] and myself actually went to the matinee at the Temple Theatre, (formerly Bennett's). Isn't it terrible? The Thomsons going to-day. Well, we went to see the Kinemacolor pictures of the Coronation and London scenes I <u>do</u> hope you will have a chance some day of seeing them. They were perfectly wonderful, coloured, said to be taken just as they were. You seemed to see the whole thing before you, it was just marvellous [sic]. Must tell you when I see you, we were just lost in wonder. There you saw the King and Queen bowing etc. The Lord Mayor presenting, the addressing, bowing, then being helped on his horse, his voluminous robes being much in the way, then riding off. In fact we were being raced along all the time at such a rate I was quite out of breath. The Peers and Peeresses hurrying into Westminster Abbey holding up their robes here most comical and so natural, elderly gentlemen looking much "fussed". They concluded by showing spring flowers coming into bloom, <u>very</u> wonderful.[507]

I do not hear of any vacant churches except those I noticed in Presbyterian, Kincardine and St. Thomas. Before we went away Mrs. Steele came in. Mr. Gray, she said, was not at all a good visitor and she wondered if he would not be expected to do a great deal of that, as he was only to preach once a day. Then he was no use at all either in his own house or in other peoples' in making a pleasant evening with young people. They had so many years of always "considering" Mr. Gray and he still needs it, that they would like to get one in good health.[508] The Steeles will be away in Vancouver till

Oct.1st.[509] I hope you received the Globe, they promised to begin last
Saturday. I am going down to Chippewa on Saturday to see what sort of a
place Mary is in, her two weeks will be up on Wednesday and I want to see
if it is a good place for her. Can go for week end for $1.40.

Edna was pleased to hear from you, she is very well indeed, stands heat
better than any of us. Are your rooms all taken. Hilda is off to Toronto to-
day with Jean MacLaren, thinks her nose improving a good deal and has
gone for another treatment. Fortunately for us us [*sic*], the nights cool off,
very nicely. We had a Mr. Sillars from Edinboro' preaching, think I told you
about it. Mr. Thomson came in last evening, just delighted with him and
not at all pleased I think, that our young people were not enthusiastic. He
wants to settle in this country as he has daughters here and is much taken
with the West, he is far too old for it. Well, I must close, glad you are not
having to preach this hot summer. Have not yet heard from you how to
send the money or when. With much love.

Your affectionate mother
M. B. McQuesten

[P.S.] As Tom was away with Strap Watson last Sabbath, he did not get
British Weekly read.

✦ A107-(6752) To Calvin McQuesten

Staney Brae, Muskoka   Chippewa
                                   August 17, 1911

My dearest Calvin,

Here I am still. When I came down on Saturday it was with the
intention of just seeing how Mary was and returning. When Mary left home,
she was looking so weak and miserable and feeling so nervous about herself
after having the ulcerated sore throat, that she had made me nervous. But I
found her very well and picking up rapidly. I myself had got so worn out with
the heat noise of the city, that I could not resist the temptation of staying on
myself, as the place exactly suits me. It is a very comfortable house with
nicely furnished airy rooms and a pleasant lawn where our hammock is hung
under the apple trees. Then we are perfectly quiet, no other boarders and
just Miss Davidson, the lady of the house, (who lives alone since her
mother's death), a nice lady-like person, who gives us very nice meals and
plenty of milk. Mary brings up my breakfast and we are much at home. For
which the charge is only $5.00 a week. So I feel it would be foolish not to
stay and try to get up my strength till September.

We take lovely trips on the trolley. I was tired and afternoons warm so
we have not gone far yet, but we mean to. So far we have gone after tea
down to Victoria Park. It is most beautiful, I can give you no idea of the
flowers, they are just in masses. Just now there are the tall phlox in all

shades of pink and those golden glow daisies, these are against a background of shrubs evergreens and trees and amongst them those lovely Japan lilies, some with gold spots and stripes and others turn caps with pink and brown, beautiful begonias with immense flowers some double in all colours. Such pretty picturesque buildings too for the lavatories and the "Refectory" where you can get ice-cream etc., and rustic seats every where. It is a wondrously beautiful spot, the soft spray from the Falls keeping everything so fresh and green.

Before I left home Tom had succeeded in getting on as one of the reporters at the election for which he is to get $10 a day for four days, so he was much pleased. Have written him to send you the money. I hear that E. is most happy and well, so I am quite care-free, not for many years have I felt so and must try to build myself up, and thank God with all my heart.

Just at tea time yesterday we had a terrific thunderstorm. I never saw the lightning so close, and it struck twice quite near us and set fire to a barn not far away; it seems of late years the storms are very severe here. Miss Davidson wonders, if it is the electric works so near that attracts the lightning. In the afternoon we had gone to an auxiliary meeting one of the ladies had a cousin visiting her, who is a missionary at Sante Fe, New Mexico, and she gave us an account of her work and then we had ice-cream and cake, both delicious. Mary is having the time of her life reading stories and sleeping as much as she likes. The weather is very comfortable, warm of course in the sun, but I do not like it chilly in the summer, it does not agree with me. Chippewa itself seems full of large old deserted houses. Well, the time passes and September will be here all too soon. Hope you are still enjoying Staney Brae. With much love from us both. Your affectionate mother,

M. B. McQuesten

✦ A108-(8817) To Calvin McQuesten
"The Manse"
Bracebridge, Ontario

[Written at top] I telephoned at once to Bobby R about your folders, Shearer seems to know nothing about it, but is writing you & sending samples. Stupid I think. I never saw [?].

"Whitehern"
Friday, April [1], 1912

Dearest Cal,

You ought to see the array of fine furniture that is nearly ready. All the things at Gentle's got finished last night at 11:45 owing to most strenuous endeavours. It was just pouring rain all yesterday and this morning too, so I got Hill the Mover to bring them down early. [Hockaday?] is a fine packer and we expect to get them down to the station to-morrow, hoping they will reach you by Thursday or rather Wednesday night. You see we had planned you should telephone us when they arrived, but if they do not reach you in time of course Hilda would not like to start. On one packing box you will notice written on the directions a crate opener, if you can borrow something to open it. Perhaps I can get it put in with your cot bed that is going up. You could cut the strings with your penknife, there is a splendid hammer and a lot of Uncle's tools going up. Got your letter to-day in time to run out and buy a small rug in green for bed-room, same kind as in our dining-room, ["ex"?] matting no odour.[510]

If your floors need washing get whatever woman you get to bring her own cloths or buy 1-1/2 yards of flanelette [sic], a pail & perhaps a scrubbing brush, the softest kind and not too large, she must not use the brush on your painted floors. Some soap too. I wonder if we could mark the names on, if you could get the men who take up the furniture to carry the heavy pieces into whatever room they are for, such as the desk, bureau, side-board and the bed-steads. I think the bed-stead you got at Burrows is the handsomest to go with the fine bureau. If I think of any thing else will write Mrs. [?]. Small table is really not a kitchen one, but we'll cover it with white oil-cloth.

Tom received your letter with cheque. Hilda is in [Toronto?] today. I have Chisholm here doing his best to get the paint off bath-room window, we want to put on the window pane, too.[511] I got your grape vine, it is lovely, but I got a [figured?] white for hall on account of the brown letters [sic]. I have just put it in the bureau drawer where the lace curtains are just at front in brown paper. Hope no one will grab it or they'll spoil it. Mary is greatly delighted with her [?] new garments and hats. The forks replated have just come home will get spoons & knives later before it goes. Perhaps after H. gets up, you can get your cot bed set up for her to sleep on and get your breakfasts & tea and go to hotel for dinner. H. I am sure you would like, she will know in which case are bed clothes. Next week I start on Tuesday to Lynden for a meeting then return to Copetown & stay with Miss Inksetter. Wednesday to West Flamboro and Thursday to Kirkwall, had an extremely nice letter from Mrs. [?] (some [?] wrote it) asking me to stay all night at the Manse. Hope to survive but my mind will be relieved when the furniture is got off to-morrow. Do not tire yourself by thinking too much. With much love.

Your mother
[M. B. McQuesten]

✦ A109-(8867) To Calvin McQuesten [page edged in black]

"The Manse"   "Whitehern"
Bracebridge, Ontario   April 12, 1912

My dearest Cal,

This is a dull heavy morning, and I seem equally dull; we have been on the continual go this week, and I am just tired. Altho' the 9th was the date when darling Ruby left us, it was more present to me on Sunday, I seemed to go over it all again. It was indeed a loss to us all never to be repaired, but I do not grieve about it now, she just seems to have gone a little before. I think the greatest loss was really to yourself, she would have been such a help to you, and I always planned that she would be with you at first; I used to fancy her, charming the people. But God plans for the best.[512]

On Wednesday I went to Burlington to address the Auxiliary, Mrs. Thomson went with me. They seemed pleased with my address, but Mrs. Thomson was dreadfully depressed to see the few in numbers (this was their old church)[513] and if you believe it Mrs. Symington was not there, tho' she is Treasurer of our Presbyterial and Mrs. Thomson says Willie takes no part in the church tho' one of our elders. Mrs. James had a letter from Willie and he thinks your manse can be made very homelike and you recited splendidly and were much appreciated.

It is good to hear the people are so friendly asking you to tea. (Are there any girls in those families?) Edna was much pleased with the Easter card, most interesting as yours always are. Sorry not to be able to write more now but must dress to go with Mrs. James to lunch at Mrs. [?]. Find out if there are any doors for the space between the two rooms. Hope you did not catch cold on that wretched drive, and it does not look as if it would be better next Sunday. Am sure you did well; you were nervous because tired with running about, the first Sunday too. With much love.

Your mother
M. B. McQuesten

✦ A110-(8848) To Calvin McQuesten

"The Manse"   "Whitehern"
Bracebridge, Ontario   April 19, 1912

My dearest Calvin,

Your letters are very cheerful and you seem to be getting on as well as possible, but I am sure you are busy every moment of time. It is well you have the fresh air to help you. We seem to be very busy here too. The painters have been two weeks here, getting off the old paint took a week from the porch and front door, a fearful job altho' they worked well. Our minds were greatly relieved by hearing Miss Honeycomb could come on

Monday. We were beginning to despair of her.[514] Am glad you were treated to maple syrup; as we will have no preserves, think it would be well to get 2 gals, if there was too much for you we could bring some down here.

We saw the pictures at Thomson's yesterday, but none of us could tell if we saw them all and Thomson hadn't put them down. I'll tell you what we saw and perhaps you can remember—Livingston the large engraving from Saturday night, Ruby's little watercolour on the river, the blue one and a brown sepia and Edna's ships.[515] Were there any photos?

Have scarcely been able to talk or think of any thing but the "Titanic." Such an appalling thing! Men seem of late years to have gone crazy on speed; to gain an hour or two they sacrifice any thing, it is just a craze which seems to have seized this generation.[516]

Heard D. C. McGee on the Social Service, on Monday p.m.[517] It was very good indeed. We got a very pretty covering for the sofa, it will go with any thing, but I think we'll put it in the living room. I got a picture frame at Burton's, Gentle is doing it up and Browns will put a glass in it, it will do for third bedroom over a dressing table which Hilda will rig up, perhaps with uncle's kitchen table. I think you said there was a table in your [?]. What colour is your rattan chair? I did not know if we should buy any more here, for $2.50 seemed very reasonable, of course I do not know its kind. Well, Calvin dear, next time I hope to write something more worth while, but seem stupid to-day. There are so many things on hand to distract my mind I thought it was a most encouraging thing to hear of people who would walk a mile to church.

But that afternoon meeting makes a long day for you but it will not be so bad when the roads are better. Do you need any money? The weather continues quite cold with us, but the crocus and scilla are showing themselves, but we have very few of them. Do you see any sign of a garden about The Manse? Sweet peas should be planted early. It was a good plan to start the tennis lawn. One needs to get hold of the young people in some way. Well, I must close. Do not work too hard. Your cot is just the size of one in my room. Have got the green denim and will make it here. With love from all.

Ever your loving mother
M. B. McQuesten

✦ **A111-(6780) To Thomas Baker McQuesten**

Whitehern, Hamilton

On board the Steamer,
Princess Mary[518]
June 30, 1912

My dearest Tom,

I cannot forget this is your birthday and feel how thankful I should be that God has so mercifully spared you to me for thirty years. It seems scarcely possible that you can have attained such an age and it makes me feel rather sad to think your youth is passing away and we can be only young once. But in these 30 yrs you have been a great joy and blessing and strength to all in times of great sorrow, and we pray God that he will mercifully spare you as long as my life lasts. That sounds selfish does it not? I can scarcely realize this is the Sabbath day, it is a very quiet set of people on board. It is a bright sunny afternoon M. [Mary] & Grace Weir[519] are sitting out on deck, but we have a fine observation salon with large windows and I sit inside; we are passing through large islands with beautiful snow capped mountains rising up in the background all round we have just passed the steamer Princess Sophia with I suppose the Hendersons[520] and Mrs. McLagan on board.[521] We have a lovely state-room, think it is one of the bridal suite and a fine steamer, but the meals are not very good, but we will not suffer. There is hardly any motion on the boat. With much love, my dearest child.

Your loving mother

[P.S.] Have just heard this can be posted at Prince Rupert Township. Do not send this on (night & go back by GTP line). Before leaving Vancouver after our meetings were over and we were going to Alberni and Victoria I drew $125, that paid bill at Glencoe Lodge and gave the funds for the trips. Then you see on my return I drew the $300 for Alaska trip ($160 each) and will need balance for trip through Rockies etc. $9 each extra for Lake Superior Steamer, that is less tho' than sleeper and meals on train. So our trip will have cost $425 plus about $175 for our fares etc. to Vancouver, $600 for two. Seems quite a sum but think we have seen a great deal and in great comfort and have purchased a few things for our Christmas presents which are all to the good.[522] So glad your roses have been so successful would be sorry if you had no success for all your time.

With much love.
Your mother

[P.S.] Do not be alarmed if you receive a telegram announcing our safe arrival back at Vancouver, but I may not get an opportunity to do so and it may cost too much.

✦ A112-(8792) TO MR. NASMITH [Naismith]

[Bracebridge, Ontario] "The Manse," Bracebridge[523]
September 18, 1912

Dear Mr. Nasmith,[524]

You will be sorry to know that Mr. McQuesten has been very ill, since we saw you and a supply for Sabbath is coming from Toronto. The Sunday we were out, he had been very busy in the congregation all week and was tired that day, so that he was much exhausted when he returned from Monck and had to preach again;[525] the having to use his voice when tired being the very worst thing for a preacher. Accordingly on following Monday that is next day he was seized with a most irritating cough, which increased so much and was so incessant day and night, that we thought he would choke. He has not had a night's sleep since; last night he was better and managed to get some sleep. His throat and tongue were coated but now they are better, so we hope he will gain strength and recover. I am telling you all this, because it is only right the people at Monck should realize how much it costs a minister to keep up this service. Mr. McQuesten understood it was maintained for the sake of some old people. As you know there are no old people attending; and I would like to ask if the people at Monck could not make up their minds to join the Bracebridge Congregation. Do you not think the young people especially would enjoy worshipping in a larger church with good music and meeting the other young people? It would bring more brightness into their lives and create a greater interest in the work of the whole church at large.

It seems to me, if they would honestly consider the question, they can come into Bracebridge during the week for the benefit of their bodies, why can they not come in on the Sabbath day for the benefit of their souls. From what I hear every minister who has been here has suffered from this heavy charge of two congregations and the doctor says it will be weeks before Mr. McQuesten's voice will be in a condition to use it. As you must know Mr. McQuesten started out to do his very best for you, he is in debt now for a horse and buggy to enable him to overtake your work and the whole thing has been too much. So I trust the people of Monck will give their very earnest consideration to the whole question. My son is the last one to shirk work, he was never lazy, but he certainly cannot continue as he has been doing. Now please understand I am writing this letter without his knowledge, he is too ill for me to disturb with any talking, but I felt that you must consider this matter very seriously without loss of time, and that it was only right that I should acquaint you with your minister's condition. I trust that all I have said will receive your kindest consideration.

I am, very sincerely yours
M. B. McQuesten

✦ A113-(8787) To Calvin McQuesten

Bracebridge, Ontario   "Whitehern"
                                        December 9, 1912

My dearest Calvin,

It seems a long time since I wrote, but I am sure Edna would tell you all the news. Last week I had to give reminiscences of the early days of our W.F.M.S for our own Aux. and St. Paul's, celebrating our 25th annual meeting. I had the old secretary's book beginning in 1876 and everyone seemed to think what I made of it most interesting.

To-day Janie James came in, she unexpectedly ran up on Saturday to see this great Palestine exhibition which has been in the Drill Shed for two weeks. The Howitts met her and kept her till to-day.[526] She said the Exhibition was fine, but we had heard so very little praise of it from any one and the Drill Shed was so miserably cold we heard, that we gave up the idea of going particularly as we were very busy with Honeycomb[527] and I never felt just able to go and stand about in the cold. It is going on to Vancouver and will be in Toronto in May. Janie is not looking very fit. She looks as if she had not been fed up.

Mrs. Fletcher took tea with us last week. She thinks the doctor very far gone, but I think he'll last a good while yet, which is not to be desired, for he requires so much waiting on and no one but Mrs. F. will do.[528] I think you must have been feeling lonely when you had to go down to see the McKerachers; it is a good thing you have them so near, for I am sure you must need some one outside the congregation to speak to.

You do not say anything about your health. I hope you are keeping free of cold and not feeling yourself getting too tired. We have been having windy cold weather for two days. I hope you have not suffered. I am anxious how you are going to stand driving in the cold after preaching. Has Dr. Parfitt's bill come yet?[529] Be sure and let me know. Do not buy Dr. Jowetts' Yale lectures.[530]

Mary is going to Toronto to-morrow, has at last given in to consult Dr. Graham [Chambers?] about her face.[531] With much love.

Your affectionate mother
M. B. McQuesten

✦ A114-(9013) To Calvin McQuesten

"The Manse"   "Whitehern" Tuesday 7:15 a.m.,
Bracebridge, Ontario   January 7, 1913

Dearest Calvin,

There was great excitement here last night. You would have enjoyed it immensely. We did not hear if Tom had got in till after eight o'clock,[532] but quite early we knew that Allan was in.[533] You can imagine the telephone ringing all morning. Mattie D. and Hilda started off in Stanley Mills' car the first thing in the morning worrying out their women voters, and I can assure you the tension here was very great. They and Mary had been going for days, house to house canvassing, even Edna went to some and it is said the women's work put Allan in, but it was only MacNab St. women who worked. The miserable Baptists led by New went for Bailey and St. Paul's was not active except John Knox. Mrs. David Gillies did great work and the dirty Herald actually alluded to her by name. It seems she would not take the Herald and told them as a reason that she had two respectable maids in the house. I telephoned her my appreciation of her work and also Mrs. Evans who said that "My son was the fore-front of the whole thing."[534] He certainly planned and worked up the whole thing, until he made it a live issue. It was he that had the women organized and that miserable Newton Galbraith[535] telephoned Mrs. Evans and accused her of working for Allan, because she had Cataract Power Stock. We were most sorry that Mr. Milne[536] did not get in as Controller but Morris, Cooper got in and Gardner will follow and we think Bird[537] will do. He is the most simple looking creature, a clerk in Grafton's but a <u>Catholic</u>, but it is too bad.

We are also sorry that the By-law to take off 27 licenses from hotels failed, tho' the one for shops carried. But 27 would mean taking it from some of the better hotels and the liquor men spent $20,000 on the elections. It was disgraceful too; the manufacturers came out in a long list as opposed to the reduction.[538] Well, I must run, if I am to make my toilet before breakfast but I want to have this posted for morning mail. Heard from Miss Fisher who was much concerned to hear of your illness and wished me to convey to you her best wishes for New Year.

With much love
Your Mother

[P.S.] There is a letter from Saskatchewan we are posting.

✦ A115-(8756) To Calvin McQuesten

"The Manse"	"Whitehern"
Bracebridge, Ontario	March 17, 1914

My dearest Calvin,

I received your two letters since I wrote you and note all you say. First of all I want to say that anyone who knows anything of nervous prostration would know that your health could only be restored by <u>months</u> of rest and they would feel that a small uncertain congregation could not stand it, but it was most unChristian and cruel to give no expression of appreciation of your services, of gratitude for all you had done, or of regret at losing you. I wonder you did not leave them on the spot, and I wish with all my heart you had realized your condition and resigned of your own free will before it came to that.

There is one side of this question which you do not seem to be looking at. After you had taken six months' rest, what sort of congregation would you come back to? How could your friends keep it going with no regular minister and a section of the church—and hitherto the most active—against them? You would return, you would [?] have the attraction of being a new man, it would be a tremendous strain, because you would be on your mettle, to reorganize, and by the end of 5 or 6 mos. you would be a wreck, and your friends would be disappointed & sick of it. You have no right to take any such period of rest from a people with whom you have been such a [?].

Now I want you to look back. You have not been a minister for two years till April. In your first year you took your month's holiday, you exchanged pulpits and through illness you were absent <u>ten</u> weeks. In your second year you took your month's holidays in July then there were exchanges and in less than five months, counting from August1st you were used up. When you came home at Christmas, you were quite worn out. Now we all knew you had used yourself up in a good cause and perhaps it seemed your duty to do it, but on the other hand the actual work of the church comes first, and when your strength is limited one can understand that the patience of the managers or elders might be exhausted, but if they had not been common [?] unsympathetic men, they could not have expressed it in such a cold-blooded way. Now as to Dr. Mc[G?yle] and Mr. [Kinsey?], the doctor is [not rich?] and has always seemed too busy to do anything in the church, it would be impossible for a doctor. Mr. [Kinsey?] may be liberal, I never saw him but once in the church, he could not help you in the prayer-meeting or in the S.S. [Sunday school]. Who will superintend in the S.S.? What will you do when Mrs. Thompson and Mrs. Bastedo leave the Ladies' Aid Auxiliaries?

I have a feeling you think me chiefly anxious as to your monetary support, no indeed, I want to be sure who is going to support you in the work of the church, do the Laymen's work? Have you any guarantee that these new people who, you think, will come in, will be able to do so? I cannot imagine who these business men are, to whom you refer, and I thought I had found out all the Presbyterians; if they had been worth any thing, surely they would have come to the church, even tho' they would not take office with these bad men, I have very little confidence in that sort of Christian myself. In the summer and as long as fine weather lasts the lake is such an attraction, that it seems impossible to overcome it and all the work must be crowded into the winter months.

But to go back, the chief point is, that it would be wrong for you to ask for six months' rest, it would be asking too much of your supporters to leave them with the burden of keeping up the church, and that you have not the temperament to endure the severe mental and physical strain of re-organizing and working up a scattered congregation, who are really as a whole most indifferent.

I feel so afraid of wounding your feelings but my dearest son, you know how anxious I am for your best interests and I feel I must lay the truth of the circumstances before you, no one but myself could do it, your best friends cannot venture to speak plainly and I am so afraid of your being led away into a great mistake by people who like you, patting you on the back to encourage you and afterwards be absolutely useless. So just let them know that after careful consideration you feel it would not be fair or wise to ask for such a prolonged rest. I do hope you will see it as I do. Surely Bracebridge is not the only church in the country and it would be too much altogether to ask them to wait so many months whilst the church goes to pieces.[539] With fondest love.

Your loving mother
M. B. McQuesten

[P.S.] Sent your jersey to-day.

✦ A116-(6801) To Thomas Baker McQuesten
Whitehern, Hamilton, Ontario

[Written at top] We had a pretty card from Mrs. Bell, Freiburg [?]: "Cal gave an excellent exposition at prayer-meeting, which was much appreciated by the few." St. Mary's
Saturday Night, July 27, 1914.

My dearest Tom,

Edna and I came back from London this morning. I only went yesterday morning. Mai Copeland has a beautiful house, very handsomely furnished Turkish rugs etc. We were taken out to Spring Bank quite a beautiful drive by the River Thames; but what entertained us most was the hearing David Lloyd George.[540] Asquith and Winston Churchill speak on the budget. Wasn't that a marvellous thing![541] It really seemed magical. They have a particularly fine victrola. The only drawback was the extreme heat and we were thankful to get back to St. Mary's, it is just a different atmosphere, so fresh; and cool after four o'clock. It did Edna much good tho. She is much obliged for Punch, the man who had tried the six sea sick remedies is awfully funny. We hear that Olive Harris is to marry Rev. John McNeil, Walmer Road Baptist. H. says it does not matter about the eggs floating, but she used to fill each crock and put on the lid, and perhaps the 30 dozen would not fill all. You should not put in any cracked ones. I shall inquire whether express charges were really paid here, as I had instructed them to do so. In case you were not in when delivered. It was just like poor Alice to worry she cannot count, and the cherries came just when we expected they would.

Mrs. Maxwell has just been in and told us of a nice quiet house we can get. So when weather permits, we may try it. A very nice girl here gave a very pleasant tea to introduce H. to the girls. Expect to hear from Mary Monday. Am afraid you will have suffered from the heat these days; it must have been fearful in the cities.

Your loving mother
M. B. McQuesten

✦ A117-(6805) To Thomas Baker McQuesten
Whitehern, Hamilton, Ontario

[Written at top] No hurry for money, but when rent comes in think you had better send $60. Chisholm is coming up but think I could not wait so long, but you could send me $25 bal with Lizzie.

St. Mary's
July 30, 1914

My dearest Tom,

We have been having some pleasant cool days. I am alone this evening H. and E. were invited out to play croquet and Cal as usual is playing bowls. It would do you good to see how well E. is, she is so happy and in such good health. This afternoon we had a call from Mrs. [?], Lorne's mother, she is a very pleasant person Lorne and his wife have been away on some newspaper excursion up the lakes, so have not seen them yet.

Affairs in Europe and indeed all over seem in a desperate condition, indeed the newspaper is full of horrors. I do hope Britain will keep out of it, war is too serious a matter, but I pity the Servians [sic].[542] Am glad Mary had left Austria, she is in Florence and will be in house by Saturday, if all is well.[543] Am very sorry about Aleck Logie, his unfortunate parents.[544] Edna appreciates very much your kindness in sending Punch. A good take-off that of the hat. By the way Stevenson is not to lift the carpet in Mary's room to put in heater. If he can would like it placed in corner opposite the door, where blue chair is. H. thinks it would warm room better. How are you getting on by yourself? Saw the instantaneous heater in Mrs. Copeland's bath-room. It would be very convenient in the summer.

I noticed poor Mrs Taylor is dead, the poor old husband will be very lonely. Mrs. [?] said if ever you wished to come, up, there would be a room for you there, but Mr. Hunter next door has a room. There really is nothing for me to relate. E. was particularly with the people at the country cottage wearing their fancy dress costumes. No wonder the country man was "struck of a heap."

208

Take care of yourself Tomity dear. Over in the Anglican church lawn is a summer hyacinth, which we are waiting to see in bloom. All one end of church covered with trumpet creeper. A great many of them here and fine climates. Well I must close.

Your loving mother
M. B. McQuesten

✦ A118-(9153) To Calvin McQuesten

Buckingham, Quebec[545] "Whitehern"
March 26, 1915

My dearest Calvin,

Edna was glad to receive your letter yesterday. I am sure your sketch of Edward Blake would be very interesting and it is well you were prepared to give something so useful and interesting to young Canada on a St. Patrick's occasion as a reminiscence of that statesman.[546]

Poor Mr. Ketchen is having a terrible time with 'Grip.' He went up to see his father and the minister of the place had come out to call, when going away Mr. K. stood a long time out at the door talking with the unhappy result, suffered terribly in his ears, now in his throat and has not slept for nights. He came home in the meantime and went to Toronto to preach for Harper Gray, but was obliged to give up and come home. Mr. Gray is tired out and resting out at Dundas.[547]

I am so thankful to have got through the winter so well and feel much better than usual. Have been busy this week getting various things done. Wednesday, had Peter up for a general clearing up of the barn and burning up rubbish. Glad to get it done while stuff was dry, it rained that night. It has turned out very cold to-day.

Mary has gone down to secure tickets for Stephen Leacock, who is to give an entertainment of his own writings next Thursday for the Belgian Fund, I believe he is going through the country giving his services.[548]

It is so distressing about Gourlay Colquhoun his poor brother just walks around at night. It seems so strange that two men have told of his body being found in the trenches with seven wounds and yet no official report. The slaughter of officers is so fearful.[549] Did you read Lloyd George's great speech at Bangor. It seems to me sometimes that the war was sent to bring men to their senses about the liquor traffic,[550] for the selfish callous heartlessness of the liquor sellers and others was <u>fiendish</u>, as poor Mrs. Colquhoun says, it was just the devil's own work.

Am sending you a most interesting cutting, the words of the late American ambassador to Petrograd and the Duke of Connaught's remarks.[551] I <u>do</u> wish I could remember the things I read. Punch is good this time, see last page.

We expect Hilda home to-morrow night, she has been away two weeks and has been on the go continually to various old friends. What do you think of Tom's suggestion as to trip? I see the railways are holding out inducements to go to San Francisco by various ways. When you are in Ottawa next, you could inquire about them. One way suggested is by G. T. Pacific to Prince Rupert and down to Vancouver and on by water. It sounds fine. If I contributed a hundred or more could you manage it? You can spend quite a bit at one of these ordinary resorts and have nothing much in return. One cannot go to Europe this year. Your letter has just come in. You might make the inquiries all the same. You would have to judge what would rest you most and I know it is a long train journey; still food is good, and we found it warm only one or two days and quite comfortable at the Coast. Only $60 from Vancouver to Skagway and return. Then I should think there would be reduced rates for the Exposition, and I understand, there was to be an agreement amongst hotels to prevent over-charging. I know <u>my</u> trip enlarged my vision very much and gave me something to think and talk about. To-day our Ladies' Aid has a sale for Sick, Poor and Red Cross. Well, I think my news is exhausted. Sorry there is no trolley. Don't forget the two eldest girls have had fine trips and I would like to give you one if you would enjoy it. Well, good-bye, much love from all.

Your loving mother
[M. B. McQuesten]

✦ A119-(6828) To Calvin McQuesten

Buckingham, Quebec "Whitehern"
April 30, 1915

My dearest Calvin,

Very many very happy returns of the day! May-day is a lovely day for a birth-day. I am sorry to think that none of us is with you, or you with us to celebrate it. And am very disappointed that the present I had intended for you will not arrive as I had hoped. I wrote some weeks ago to the Upper Can. Tract about a book and they did not answer, then I wrote Hodder and Houghton in Toronto, they hadn't it in stock. Then finally heard from U.C.T that they had it and after sending P.O. and directions, this morning received the enclosed.[552] I was so annoyed, and disappointed, for a present is not worth half as much when it does not arrive on <u>the</u> day; and Tom wants to share in the present, which I did not want, as I liked to send it myself.

To-day the men have succeeded in cutting the grass, tho' it rained off and on, the grass in the garden should have been cut two weeks ago, the Kentucky Blue Grass yields such a tremendously heavy crop. The shrubs are fine this year the winter season was so mild, forsythia very good and japonica, flowering, prune hurrying out too, as well as tulips. Poor Peter has been beating rugs and labouring at cleaning the verandah all day. So now we feel that we have got into pretty good order and will be ready for next week.

Dr. Drummond phoned me last night suggesting that we use the Moderator to have a brief prayer service at noon at our meeting on Wednesday for the Empire and soldiers etc. and I think it is a good idea.[553] Dr. H. you know is to preach our Anniversary sermons on Sunday and will be in the city until after our Wednesday evening public meeting.

O dear Yes! The war is so terrible and all these young Canadians cut off in the prime of life and their mothers left to mourn them all their days. I feel so distressed, because I am afraid until there is a recognition of sin and repentance as God requires of His ancient people, there will be no help from Him.[554] Just look at those people in England, the clergy refusing to give up their indulgence. The only hope is that He will have mercy for the sake of the few, who serve Him. We were greatly amused with Maj Hunter's cable, it makes one laugh every time you think of it. Poor Col. Logie had to get a knock too, but think it will not be serious.[555] Am afraid, this has been a scribble but E. is seated waiting for it, to go to the post.

Last Sunday was a most trying day, that heavy moist heat. It would be very hard on you, but I think Dr. G.'s life might be more interesting than an ordinary sermon, any way, 12.20 is not too long.[556] Well, Calvin dear, the time is flying on and soon summer will be here, I trust to-morrow will be a happy day and that you will have a good day on Sabbath. With fondest love and many good wishes.

Your loving mother
M. B. McQuesten

✦ A120-(6853) To Calvin McQuesten

Buckingham, Quebec "Whitehern"
May 24 [1915]

My dearest Calvin,

I had intended writing so that this letter would reach you to-morrow, but was just so stupid and sleepy, that it was impossible; but to-night am feeling brighter.

I reached home by 6 o'clock on Saturday night leaving Montreal at 9 a.m., it is really a fine train. Mrs. Colin Fletcher and I went and came together I cannot enter into particulars about our meetings. We had one tussle with the "Home" party and baffled them, for which we were thankful! Fortunately our Prov. Board is almost a unit.[557] On the Wednesday I managed to get in a drive with three others from 5:15. We went up the mountain passing through McGill ground and seeing the residences of many notables on up to the "Look out" point. Just as we reached there and got under cover, it began to pour in torrents, so we had to wait, but we had a fine view and the rain stopped. We passed that magnificent statue to Sir Etienne Cartier, a superb thing not yet completed on account of the war.[558]

Then on Friday morning I ordered a car for 9.30; took Mrs. Colin F. and two other minister's wives for two hours and a half. We drove out through Westmount and partway up mountain and away back again to the French quarter and then to Bonsecours Church and market, then to Chateau de Ramezay, Notre Dame (but they would not let us into the garden) and then to St. James. It was really a great treat for us all. Of course the time was too short for the Chateau but we got a good idea of it. I wonder when you last saw St. James, if those beautiful mural paintings had been put in, they are around the two wings and are scenes in the early days of the Romish priests in Canada, one presented by the French Government, they are most beautiful. Then that magnificent bronze canopy over the altar!

Then at 2.30 that day St. Paul's ladies treated us to a trip to Pointe au Tremble. We enjoyed that very much, had refreshments and were addressed by the Principal and a Dr. Kelley, it is really appalling to hear how the Catholics are gaining ground and the Protestants losing, the priests are even persuading the young men not to go to the war, but to stay at home and have families, getting hold of the farms and sending these children whose parents are unknown—as soon as old enough—out in batches to settle in the west.

Our ladies suggested a collection and $153 were given a friend of Mrs. Hays of Ottawa, Miss Margaret McKellar giving a $50 cheque.[559] Altogether I got a very good idea of Montreal. We met scarcely any of the ladies and they did not entertain as far as we knew, but I fancy the war has affected them very much.

By the way, did you ever receive a life membership from the Bible Society? The Agent was preaching here some months ago and I gave $100. He wrote saying I should have two life memberships so I sent in your name for one. You ought to get also their monthly "The Bible in the World." If you do not, let me know, for it has some very interesting news in it.

We heard that the son of Rev. A. H. had been terribly treated in the war. At our meetings we have been praying that the "accursed thing" strong drink may be cast out, feeling that something is hindering our progress in the war.

I am afraid you will be lonely without Hilda. The weather keeps so cold. Poor old Mr. Black was kneeling at his bedside when he died.

With much love
Your mother

✦ A121-(6951) To Calvin McQuesten

Buckingham, Quebec   "Whitehern"
                                                February 11, 1916

My dearest Calvin,

By this time I trust Miss Smith is beginning to be a little settled, and as she was only to reach you on Wednesday evening, you would not have time to write me yesterday, but I did not like to leave my letter till to-morrow, as you would not get till Monday, but I am quite anxious to hear how Miss Smith strikes you. Kind remembrance to her.[560] Mary Taylor has been with us going on two weeks, but we are glad to have her, she is so amusing and does not tire Edna.

You were telling me in one of your letters of Mr. Winchester's address at Ottawa without a word on missions.[561] Our ladies were much disgusted with Mr. McPhail[562] at our Pres. Annual, held at Caledonia. He appeared in Khaki and gave them to understand that missions must take a secondary place this year in givings; the very sentiments we are trying to fight. However, our Missionary from India and Mrs. Joseph Thomson didn't let it pass, but gave him a setting down. I think he must be as erratic as his wife.

I had a note from our Prov. Sec. telling me, that after considerable work, they have discovered, that in 1915, our W.M.S. in Ontario, raised more than $5000 above the amount raised by the two societies in the year before amalgamation in spite of the war demands. We think this very satisfactory, so that we meet all our claims and pay back a large sum, due to the old W.F.M.S, which advanced $50,000 at low interest to the new Society.[563]

We have had scarcely any snow, till the last day or two, when it has been snowing pretty steadily. You would get a shock like we did over the Ottawa fire. The recruiting in Hamilton is terrible, scarcely a man would be left, one thinks.

When Miss R. was with you,[564] I suppose in the cold weather you had to do the buying, but I hope Miss Smith is stronger and will do the marketing and Post so as to save you time, let her know you would like her to. In this cold weather, she can market in the afternoon for next day. You were rather short of sheets, but I have just been getting from Toronto through Maggie White two pieces wholesale.

We hear that the men at Knox Coll. are having a bad time, they are being urged to enlist, at every opportunity, at prayers, they are told there are no fields for them in the West, this comes from H.M. Com. I am sure Col. McCrae has to do with that, he is very busy at Guelph recruiting. This war is a fearful thing. I hope you are keeping well, so afraid you will be tired now.

                                        Your loving mother
                                        [M. B. McQuesten]

✦ **A122-(6967) To Calvin McQuesten**

Buckingham, Quebec   "Whitehern"
                                                March 10, 1916

My dearest Calvin,

When I reached home from Toronto on Wednesday afternoon I found your very kind letter awaiting me and one also from Ethel MacLaren to Edna. She writes very nice letters, and we were greatly pleased to hear her account of the snow-shoe party, she seems to have enjoyed it immensely and the wind-up at the Manse and liked Miss Smith very much.[565] It must be a great satisfaction to you as it is to me, to be able to entertain a little. It pleases people you know, and I always felt if you were not able to invite them there, they would not be satisfied.

On Monday I took the noon train to Toronto, it was snowing and blowing considerably, when I arrived, but was able to reach Mrs. Robertson's on Euclid Ave. But as the afternoon went on, the storm increased to a blizzard with thunder and lightning, so I was obliged to send for a taxi to take me over to William Mackay's and had to wait a long time for it the travelling was so heavy. The next day however was fine, when we had an all day session.

Then I had planned to see the Temperance procession on the Wednesday, but it was at an awkward time 1:45 to 2 p.m. I was tired from the previous day and had no place of view where I could go and wait, for these things are generally uncertain, so I had to give it up. But I was quite disappointed, especially now since it seems to have been quite a sight. We are of course boiling with indignation at those soldiers. It is all very well to blame the Liquor men for urging them on, that was to expected, but they should have known better, and these recruiting sergeants are far too smart. The poor young lads have no peace at all, if they are tall for their age, they pretend not to believe them. To think that we have to support men like those convalescent soldiers and their conduct shielded. Col. Denison actually said the procession should not have passed that way. I am afraid there are a great many undesirables amongst the soldiers. Gen. Logie has all he can do.

Edna has not forgotten about the things for the lawn and wants to know if you have a nursery near Ottawa where you could get hydrangeas and lilacs etc. Also the length of space opposite verandah. Your letter has just come in. H. once met she thinks this Mr. Cameron and he had such a nice wife. We hear that part of the congregation wishes to get rid of J. P. not caring for his preaching, but others want him to return after war is over. Mr. Lees moved to this effect in Presbytery the other day, so things seem unsettled.[566] I first called up Mrs. Strong who says she thinks Mr. P. wants to go, but some are trying to have him return, they are to bring it up again at May Presbytery and she thinks Mr. P. wishes to keep on the church as long as 86th are here.

How long that will be is uncertain. Mr. K. thinks he will be very unwise not to give up altogether, as there are really a large number not wishing him to stay. It seems to me it would not do for you, as a friend of P.'s to write too soon. When I hear of any decision will let you know. Cunningham, the photographer is there, but do not think they have any outstanding men. I do not know them. [illegible] A. M. McKenzie 129 Fairleigh Ave. S. But as things are say nothing for awhile.[567]

You are certainly quite gay when you go to Ottawa, but it must be a treat after Ottawa [*sic*]. Am sorry Marion Robinson could never take any interest in church work. The love of theatricals has always the effect of making every thing else seem slow.[568] Must close now with love from all.

Your affectionate mother

M. B. McQuesten

[P.S.] Poor Louise, John Becker's wife died last Saturday.

✦ A123-(6975) To Calvin McQuesten

Buckingham, Quebec
"Whitehern"
St. Patrick's Day
[March 17, 1916]

My dearest Calvin,

This is a bitterly cold day and it has been very cold for days. I hope the March wind will not get into your throat. Mary has been busy for days preparing for a St. Patrick's Day party for her S.S. Class. She has been making cakes and cookies in shamrocks with green icing and they are to have green and white ice-cream etc. Your cards arrived this morning, the rhyme on Edna's was very interesting. I never heard that reason for the date.

To-morrow there is to be a great parade and Mayor Walters not satisfied with the 8000 men in our city, proposed to bring in the men from Brantford and other places asking people for $3000 to pay their expenses and imposing on the churches to give them supper; so McNab St. ladies are preparing to feed 125 men. We are all very indignant with him when there are so many funds for the starving people of Europe, why should he start this waste of money just to get up a procession.[569] It is intended to stimulate enlistment, but the 8000 would have made a good showing, without going to all this expense. We are getting quite tired of the way men do things; up at Central School they are arranging to give coffee to a thousand men, and I do not know where else at all the schools I hear. I myself think they should recruit men to do the work in the West, on the farms; and around here they do not know what they are going to do for help.[570] I am afraid, I cannot get this letter finished in time for the post, have been so interrupted. Thank Mrs. Deverney[?] for the card she sent me, it was kind of her to remember me.

Well, Mary's girls have arrived, and seem to be having a merry time in the drawing-room. They came dressed in dresses of green crinkly paper and they were really very pretty, this was the idea of the two Irish girls, they are such nice girls, the others are the two Gentles and Vera Straus. Hilda and I went down town this afternoon and I do not want to go out again till it gets warmer only 3 above zero. Yesterday we managed to make a wedding call on Alice Macdonald Martin, on Mrs. Walker and Mrs. Macdonald now I shall stay in for a few days.

(Saturday morning) We were so glad to get your letters this morning, and to hear of Miss S.'s intention to entertain Ladies' Aid. I really think it was a special Providence that led us to Miss Smith. Had a note from Mrs. Henderson, who had been hearing from Mrs. Brown how well pleased Miss S. is, finds the ladies so kind, and likes her position so much. They are so pleased that she is not in a menial position, but in one equal to what she has been accustomed. I am sure you are doing good work with the children and parents like that. Ethel Maclaren was telling me about the favours for each class for regular attendance, which seemed to be bringing out children. Well, certainly the hope of the country is the children and they get very little fine bringing up at home. Mrs. Smith of St. Catharines told me, she was doing all she could to urge the teachings of the Bible and was to give an address in Buffalo on the subject.

Tom has been having a time in the Council fighting United Gas and fuel on behalf of the Natural Gas to prevent the City entering into a monopoly. He did not win out, but Dr. Malloch stopped him on the street and complimented him on the stand he had taken. He has also won in quite an intricate law case, which has been hanging on for a year. So by degrees, I think, he will make a place for himself.

I think this is the day you were going to Ottawa; so you manage to get some sanity, which is a good thing when you live in Buckingham. We'll send for flower catalogue. Edna and I are going down to Mrs. Dr. Leslie's to see the great parade. For awhile I could not bear to look at the soldiers, but now I think, the war will be pretty much over before these reach the front.

Take good care of yourself give kind regards to Miss S. and with love from all.

Your affectionate mother
M. B. McQuesten

✦ A124-(9180) To Calvin McQuesten

Buckingham, Quebec   "Whitehern"
                                                 Hamilton, April 7, 1916

My dearest Calvin,

It was very good of you to write Edna, such a hearty invitation. She is really very well and has just now come in from gathering up a lot of papers in the back yard. She was pleased with a letter from Ethel McLaren giving her Winnipeg address, it was so friendly of her.[571] E. is particularly excited just now on the subject of bird houses. Some of the schools have had a display in connection with Manual Training of 200 of these houses; they are shown in "Mills" window and are very attractive. They go on sale tomorrow, so we are to start out first thing to get some for the encouragement particularly of the wrens.

I went to Toronto by noon train Monday, spent the afternoon with our President and Lee going over various things before Tuesday Board meeting. Then went over to William MacKay's. He is particularly well now and does all he can to make my visit pleasant. Spent all day Tuesday at the meeting. Then on Wednesday morning went down town for short time, and Mrs. Steele came in to have a chat about various things. You see when the fall returns came in by mid of Jan., we found ourselves $27,355 behind. The [Wish?] had fallen behind and so many, particularly the [Banks?] had given their money, we suppose to Red Cross &c. Now we are called upon all over the Provinces to have a special Easter offering. Mrs. Steele has had a talk with Dr. Grinch[572] and we are very pleased that he agrees with us in not having any more hospitals built in the West. Our contention has been that the municipalities should do that, not the church. Then we are not going to take up the Social Service work as was suggested by some. We believe that is not the work of denominations.[573]

On Monday just before I left, Elsie Buchanan called and I then discovered that she has been at Auchmar for nine months, but did not come to church as she did not wish to go to meetings. Have since learned that she brought up ten girls from the Refuge, two babies and Miss [Hatte?] who has also taken the son of a special friend of one of our ministers Rev. Jack. He has, or is threatened with tubercular trouble. How it is financed I do not know.[574] Well, to go back, Wednesday afternoon (in Toronto) I took Maggie [MacKay] White to see the "Travelogue" in Massey Hall.[575] These are very fine moving pictures, which are drawing immense crowds. We were anxious to see the Dardanelles, which were to be shown in the Evening, but found all seats had been taken three weeks ago and there were only rush seats; as I could not undertake to stand an hour or more, we had to content ourselves with seeing London and Paris in the afternoon, the pictures are very beautifully coloured and quite worth seeing. Then I took the 5 o'clock train for home and was not too tired for I am feeling better this spring than for a long time. Before taking my train, met Mary coming off hers, she is to visit Mary Taylor for a few days.

Edna thinks she is not clear about <u>where</u> lilacs might grow. My idea is that in order not to break in on the lawn, you might put a japonica and lilacs between the lawn and the road leading from big gate to the back. Then if you could widen the border at the verandah we could put in as many hydrangeas as space permits and scarlet geraniums in front of them, for of course this year, they will not be much, and the pansies were pretty too. The dwarf double lilacs are lovely but Tom found Fonthill near Welland the only good place to get them, and I am afraid they might be too dry when they reached you. Perhaps Graham could advise you about them, whether they are satisfactory down there and if they can be got. The old fashioned tall mauve and white lilacs are always sweet in the spring. The Persian is beautiful but requires a good deal of room. Will leave it to your discretion, but will foot the bill, as we think it a nice idea for each occupant of the Manse to leave some improvement behind him. You spoke of raspberries, be careful to order a sweet variety, some are <u>very</u> sour. I would not order Tree Hydrangeas, but Hydrangea <u>paniculata</u>.

MacNab St. is getting very busy for the men are starting out to give Mr. K. [Ketchen] an auto and also a presentation to Mr. Chisholm, who has been over 25 yrs Treasurer. The weather is quite cold, snowing to-day, our Xmas roses came out under the bell glass we put over them, and the snow drops have been out for a week.

(Saturday morning could not finish letter yesterday). We have purchased six bird houses they are quaint little ones covered with bark. Would send you one, but they are quite heavy, and would go to pieces if not well packed. Last night H. and I went to Bible Society Annual Meeting. Mr. Sedgewick[576] and Dean Owen[577] gave excellent addresses, as it was in the Tabernacle we had a full congregation. Hope you are getting good food that you relish, and taking care. With love from all.

Your affectionate Mother
M. B. McQuesten

✦ A125-(MCP 1-3b.15) To Calvin McQuesten

c/o Foote's Bay P.O., Ontario   Oakville
                                       August 19, 1918

My dear Calvin,

I was sorry not to have managed my letter to you on Saturday, but it was first of all put out of my head by a phone from Tom, that he would be down for dinner as he had to be back before six. It turned out Cauchon is to visit him for a few days.[578] He brought us down a lot of pink and yellow tomatoes, very acceptable, as we have none here yet or to buy, tho' they are selling in

Hamilton Market quite reasonably. We have been getting excellent blueberries, which all the family like. As usual you seem to be very busy; you certainly did well to get some berries and raise money for bottles and [?]. The berries have been so dear do not know how fruit is going to be managed for soldiers.

The heat was terrible in the city at that time, but did not last, fortunately, and has been very pleasant since. The Blacks went home, but left the chair with the Rutherfords for use of invalid sister and for me when wanted. So Friday being a cool day, H. [Hilda] and E. [Edna] took me up in it to Mrs. Munro's for it is quite a distance, and we had quite a pleasant time. As to my health, am just as well as usual. To-day H., E. and I are going up to Hamilton to see what Glassco will make a coat for. They advertise reduced prices for Aug. and Edna <u>has</u> to have a <u>warm</u> coat, she is quite decided herself, which is a great help. It is a lovely day and I am glad of a change. Wind being Easterly, lake has been quite grand for some days. Have just had card from Mrs. Mullin, she had finished up her packing and taken up her final abode at Y.W.C.A. and will visit us this week.

Tom made a rather distressing discovery in the garden. Alick told him melons were no good near cucumbers so he had to pull up cucumbers. Ours here have done well, have had all we could use. Had a lovely cabbage on Saturday, and have plenty to come, tho' there's a general complaint that they are not heading. Edna has found a companion for a short time, called Francis Carroll, a cousin of the Pentecosts, Catholics [*sic*], but she is a nice gentle girl. The family took a cottage near by & have a motor. Cool weather again, had to build coal fire yesterday. Am sending you the papers, when everyone has read it put it in your trunk. Alice asked us to save them. This year Mrs. Wm. Woods at Rockton is getting my eggs for me, but I have to hunt round for butter. Mrs. Clarke is not able to be of help to make it, as usual. Had a letter from Maggie White with sad news. Her <u>fine</u> brother of the Salvation Army has been taken to Gravenhurst. Between his own work and serving as a Chaplain at Base Hospital in Toronto has been utterly worn out; he is at Military Hospital, Gravenhurst. But what seemed an almost more tragic happening was the death of their "dear" wee doggie, Tip, killed Aug. 2 on the R.R.—he was the idol of the Lake Shore—Mr. MacKay cried like a child.[579] I have not space for further vapourings and must close as we are to have early dinner and take 1:30 car. So very sorry to see in Thursday's Globe, the death of "Bob" Henderson's wife, Tom's friend in whose office he was, the first child was born few days ago.[580] So hard. Take care of yourself, with much love from all.

Your affectionate Mother,
M. B. McQuesten

✦ A126-(8734) To Calvin McQuesten

Room 307. East House
Knox College, Toronto.

[Written at top of letter] Do not trouble to write. Saturday so near.

"Whitehern"
Hamilton, October 20, 1920

My dearest Calvin,

Just a few lines to let you know that E. [Edna] has been quite herself and has taken to her knitting. I was sorry not to say good-bye, but did not realize the time or I would have been downstairs for I know you were so hurried and could not take time to come up. Sorry you tired yourself going away down to Ontario Ave. Dr. A. told you, in your case there was always a cause.[581] Surely there has been a cause for Edna too for at least two years tho' we did not know it. Her complaint had been coming on for a very long time at the very centre of the nervous system.[582] So try and not think of us and stay away as much as possible. It is not good for you to be here and it only adds to my anxiety, for unless you have a free mind you cannot possibly do any literary work. For this purpose you took your room and it would not be honest to all those who wanted it and those who secured it for you, for you to be engaging in outside work.[583] So just settle down and try [?] yourself. I am able to pray and have got back my faith that all will be well. With much love.

Your affectionate Mother
M. B. McQuesten

[Written down right side] H. is packing your trunk.

✦ A127-(24 APRIL 1923) The *Hamilton Spectator* report of Mrs. McQuesten's Speech on Church Union

[The Hamilton newspapers of April, May and June 1923 provide accounts of the many church meetings held to discuss the proposed Union of the Presbyterian, Methodist, and Congregational Churches in Canada. A special women's meeting of the Women's League of the Presbytery was advertised for 23 April 1923, at 3 p.m. On 24 April, *The Hamilton Spectator* reported on the afternoon meeting under the headline:]

"Women Score Union:"

Rev. Dr. Brown [from the West] made a stirring speech.[584] He paid a glowing tribute to the work of women in the church, declaring that they were conservative regarding their home and religion, which explained their suspicions of church union.... He declared that the general assembly was not the whole church—that the people were the church, and that the men were not sportsmen or they would give women a voice in the assembly. Rev. Mr. McClung protested one of Rev. Dr. Brown's statements "Is a man going to make such statements to an audience of women and not be challenged?" he asked.[585] A lady at the front retorted "not by a man at a women's meeting." Mrs. McQuesten made the most impassioned speech of the meeting, and in fighting terms denounced the Men of union. She urged doing as Rev. Dr. Brown had informed the meeting had been done in Montreal: that is, having agents send out literature and canvassing every household. She laid special stress on the serious condition of the foreign missions. One reason for this was, perhaps, she said that last year after the women had collected the foreign mission money, the men had attempted to dictate that it should not be spent in that way. The idea of merging the Presbyterian Church into obscurity was a proposal both insolent and impudent, she said. Mrs. McQuesten asserted that it was time to stop the nonsense of government of the church by men. They had time to go to the Canadian Club banquette, to the golf clubs and other places, but when asked to attend important church meetings, they are too busy. "If we women can't get into the general assembly and have a vote, we are going to show them that we can do something to block this church union."[586]

✦ A128-(8719) To Calvin and Mary McQuesten

Whitehern, Jackson St. West, Grand Hotel London[587]
Hamilton, Ontario August 13, 1924

Dear Calvin and Mary,

Touring Devonshire, Cornwall, St. Ives Penzance, Land's End—Cornish Cream in great abundance. I always groan when I think of you two poor things left at home and <u>poor</u> Edna. Cal did tell me of his visit to Edna, it comforted me very much. She could not help but feel sore at our going off and leaving her for the whole summer. Have treated myself to a lorgnette and black feather boa and going out today to get SOROSIS boots[588] ... [page(s) missing?].

✦ A129-(8716) To Calvin and Mary McQuesten

Whitehern, Jackson St. West, St. Enoch Station Hotel
Hamilton, Ontario Glasgow, Scotland
  September 1, 1924

Dearest Calvin and Mary,

Have a few minutes waiting for Hilda's return. Coming here from Braemar. Tom fell in with Hugh Edwards, Welshman, who writes for B.W., very friendly, on way to preach here and speak at celebration of Covenanters.[589] Offered to call for us and take us so we were taken out to a hillside (so as to be more realistic tho' raining). Pipes played lament etc. We were honoured with seats on a small covered platform, adorned with heather. After

Mr. Edwards' speech came Rev. Jas. Barr of great repute an orator on the Covenanters. An immense rugged man, who roared and aroused great enthusiasm. Chairman insisted on Tom, as Canadian Barrister, speaking and tho' protesting he did <u>very</u> well. Afterwards Mr. E. came to tea with us and took us to church where he was preaching. Packed to the doors. Chairs were carried in for us to sit under the pulpit. Came back to hotel to find Mrs. Kay and Mrs. MacLean waiting for us. This P.M. going on to a coast town whence we sail for Belfast joining our ship afterwards there on 6th. Much love to you.

Your affectionate Mother
M. B. McQuesten

[P.S.] The coast town is called Strathcona. Had invitation to go for a day to Eleanor Johns on Sept. 3, but too late for us; she had rented her house for summer months.

✦ A130-(7018) To Calvin McQuesten

Gaspe, Quebec[590]

"Whitehern"
Saturday, June 23, 1928

My dearest Calvin,

Received your letter posted at Quebec <u>yesterday</u>. Very prompt. As your places are so frequently changed it has been a little difficult so that one B.W. and N.O. have gone to Carleton, but no callous Globe has gone or is going there too. Nothing special in it to-day if any thing occurs will cut it out or send paper.

Last night Tom made a speech by Radio for Liberal candidate. On Thursday we attended at most delightful garden party at Mrs. Charles Bull's on the Mountain. She had asked about four hundred, a large Marquee on the lawn. So many of the antiques like myself who never meet, that they all enjoyed it immensely. The situation is somewhat awkward; but Tom got <u>Mr. Welby</u> to drive us in our splendid new car,[591] as Tom was not yet able to drive; it needed good driving, for there was a jam of cars. The view is not very good there are too many bushes which ought to be cut out. No fine flowers yet. Our garden is magnificent Lady Duff Gordon and Therese are beyond description and all the others with profusion of yellow lilies, lupins, iris. The cool wet weather has been most favourable; but an anxious season for garden parties, however on Thursday it held up. We have decided that if day (next Thursday) for <u>our</u> Ladies' Aid G.P. is wet, the house is to be "thrown open." This lifts a burden of anxiety off all concerned.

I was glad to know cheque with letter reached in good time. Back gate repaired and one coat paint on. Tom has engaged young man for a month to teach car driving.[592] Hilda took first lesson yesterday a.m. Raining to-day. H. sees no difficulty with practice.

Have had a few strawberries off our own patch. They are 38 cts a basket to-day, but as weather is cool, not such a craving for them. I am really wonderfully well, and report of Edna much better, she went to church and enjoyed it. Mary was very doubtful of your boat trip as she had such wretched accommodation, poor food and noisy nights because of stopping at places by the way.

Had a visit from Emily Colquhoun McCarthy and husband Wed. Eve. he is very likeable, seems to know so much about china and admired everything greatly. Thursday Sydney Stevenson came for lunch and Jessie [Proudfoot] has car with chauffeur and drove her up; she has just returned from Egypt, Palestine and so on, but she has never tried to call on me, but went to Wood's house as she has always done, there can only be [?] Wilson, housekeeper now.[593] Take care of yourself, much love from all.

Your affectionate mother
[M. B. McQuesten]

✦ A131-(7037) To Calvin McQuesten

[Gaspe, Quebec]   "Whitehern"
                                         Hamilton, July 12, 1928

Dearest Calvin

Your letter came <u>this</u> morning telling of your proposed plan for a trip to Barbadoes [*sic*]. It is very tempting The only difficulty in my mind is whether it would be <u>safe</u> for you to take such long holidays. Can you get leave of absence from your employers? I know you would be greatly worried if you lost your job; the only sort of work you like or can do.[594] But I am sure you have thought of all this and are probably arranging for it. I am afraid Barbadoes will be extremely warm, but the Captain could tell you. You must tell me, what money you would require. Tom is willing to help, only he would not like you to risk your position, just because you would feel so badly if you did, for it would be a serious loss to you for more reasons than one. You will not misunderstand me. Will seek God's guidance about whole matter.[595] With much love.

Your affectionate mother
M. B. McQuesten

P.S. Give me address of [?] [?] for "Sunday at Home."

✦ **A132-(MCP 2-4.89) To James Chisholm**[596]
[Post Office Box 36, Hamilton, Ontario]   ["Whitehern"]
[Late December 1928]

[Dear Mr. Chisholm]

I regret exceedingly that my writing to you has been so delayed, but the paralysing bout of Grippe on head and pen hand has made it impossible. Your splendid Christmas gift came that morning just as I had fallen a victim. After M. advised me a few weeks before of your generous intention there was much questioning in my mind as to the reasonableness of such a large gift which I could hardly reconcile; but your beautiful letter cleared away the doubt and I had a radiance over the whole matter and the assurance that the giving gave real pleasure to you made the acceptance an entire pleasure for me. Your remembrance of my dear husband and all he had brought you was very sweet to me. The years have flown and so few now remember him at all. He did many kind and unselfish deeds, but so few seem to speak of them. Scarcely an old friend is left. So I shall treasure your letter and put it with other [val?]ued papers for the family to read in future.

But there is another side dear Mr. Chisholm to this matter. I·and my family are under deep obligations to you. When I was left with six young children, with no business knowledge, with some property but little money, what would I have done if you had not treated [me] like a brother, managing my affairs to the best advantage with the utmost carefulness and making no charge for services through all those long years, but giving me every dollar. Those things can never be forgotten.

You and I have suffered many sore trials but we have faith to believe that our Heavenly Father doeth all things well and "All things work together for good and those that love God" and so believe it, we will rest in the Lord, and pray that His [illegible] may [illegible] to look on you and you will be spared to carry on your beneficent life!

Very sincerely
M. B. McQuesten

✦ **A133-(7074) To Calvin McQuesten**
Gaspe, Quebec   "Whitehern"
                              Hamilton, August 5, 1929

My dear Calvin,

Your most interesting letter came this morning and we were all glad to know you had been so well entertained in various ways. It was really quite an event to see the Memorial service to poor Count De Lesseps, I always felt sorry to think of him being buried in that far away spot, as if his family had no interest in him.[597] Then it was a pleasant thing to see the French ship. How late your strawberries are! Sorry H. forgot to send little fan back, but first time she is returning your socks, it must go. As it is Civic Holiday we are having quite a quiet day no workmen in or out. The fence is about finished, that was the most noise, the incessant hammering, which is over and the filing of the plummer [sic] but I think it must be nearly over. Duncan C. [Chisholm] is to try his hand on first coat of paint to give him work, under Festner's supervision.

We were very thankful to have a phone message from Mrs. Dayment, Alice's friend saying she would see Alice to-day and would be pleased to take her for a few days to her house and then take her to Dunnville. This is a great relief for us. It has been almost too cool for me but is getting warmer now at noon. The flowers in front look splendid, making a fine ray pattern. Archie is a good weeder, very careful and painstaking, but the vegetables did not recover from early drought and cold, they are scarce and dear in the market, peas were too poor to eat, cabbages are nice. Tomatoes poor. Quantities of raspberries of all kinds in market. Had a letter from Janie James. Mother had fallen on the rocks, but was recovering, she did not break any bones.

That was a splendid booklet of Gaspe with a great deal of information. Tom was surprised at the number of people all that old history is very interesting. The stocks and salpiglossis have done very well, snapdragons coming on too. Last report of Edna excellent. Must close now with best love from all, so glad if you have pleasant society.

Your affectionate Mother
M. B. McQuesten

✦ A134-(7085) To Calvin McQuesten

Foote's Bay, Muskoka

[Written at top] Sent on New Outlook yesterday

"Whitehern"
Hamilton, July 8 [1930]

My dear Calvin,

Yesterday Mr. C. [Chisholm] was operated on and a tube inserted to draw off pus of which there was a great deal from an ulcer back of appendix, but latter is not removed yet. He had a good night and doctor well satisfied.[598]

Last evening Tom took us all to see the Rock Garden and also approach to McMaster.[599] It is all beyond description simply amazing. At Gage Park 120,000 seedlings were grown and used, the rock work is marvellous.[600] We are having great speeches, but none on Radio since Dunning.[601] But in this morning's "Globe" there [sic] Hon. Frank Oliver speaking in the West has given a great exposure of the Wheat Pool, which ought to help things.[602] On the front page the Globe has actually come out quite well, of course taking praise to itself. I am doing well with my reading with my ette [sic] glass and the whole "Globe."[603]

The lady senator too I think is helping letting [*sic*] the women of cheaper tea and china.[604] I surveyed the front garden last night, the Phlox D. is perfectly beautiful and the blue petunias round the Heart extremely fine. Another good shower last night, so that every thing is in profusion. Take care of yourself, with much love.

Your mother
M. B. McQuesten

✦ A135-(7095) To Calvin McQuesten

Foote's Bay, Muskoka   "Whitehern"
                                                        July 15, 1930

My dear Calvin

This is the 16th tho' I started yesterday. We seem to be so busy all the time. On Friday Tom drove Mary and me to Guelph and then on to Preston. It was a perfect day and E. [Edna] very happy. Laura had had a visit from Joe and Margaret which did not seem to cheer her for Miss Paterson says she frets all the time and they do not know what to do for her. She was told that Mary and Jean were with the Hendersons and Laura crying herself sick.[605] L. had actually written a splendid reference and Mary had gone to Daisy Rousseau who is laid up with her broken leg. She came with her baggage but almost immediately after disappeared probably preferred to booze with the Hendersons.[606]

This Daylight S. [saving time] gives us splendid evenings, so hearing from Mrs. Whittemore from Oakville, she was going home, we went down to see her on Monday evening.[607] After being so well on Saturday, that he was going home, Mr. C. [Chisholm] took cold and pleurisy, but is much better again and will go soon.[608] I spent yesterday afternoon with Mrs. Bell was in good spirits filled with her grandson's Gerald's achievements and great talents tho H. and her family are getting all the money they can. Mrs. B. will be here till end of Aug. Anne gone on trip abroad. Herbert in quietness writing a book which seems endless. The garden is magnificent every thing has grown so well, I can see very well now, the brilliant borders in front, from my window, such lovely phlox and snap dragons and wonderful salpiglossis. Then the Lilium regalia very fine.

Did I tell you I heard the King and Prince of Wales on the Radio from London? Did you read in Globe Harry O'Brien's great letter for the Government? He had voted for 15 years (I think) for Conservative but would vote now for Liberal not a party question now but for the Empire. This Patriotic vote gives a fine opportunity for the women too to spread themselves.[609] The Diamond Jubilee at Winnipeg gave King and Lapointe a great opportunity in spite of the heat.

Marshal brought a fine lot of raspberries this morning wish you could be home in fruit season. Fruit is very dear. Kenneth is busy in H's room will be through to-day I think.

Whidden amazed at the flowers at McMaster,[610] cannot take any more students. Have had such good rains and not too warm, so that I feel very well. How lovely to see those ducks! Tom says the scraps are not eaten. A good thing for them! H. is much engaged taking Lizzie C. to the Hospital as often as she can. Posted B.W. yesterday. Glad you have some congenial interesting guests. Take good care of yourself, the time seems to be flying. Stay longer than the month if you can. With love from all.

Your affectionate Mother

M. B. McQuesten

✦ A136-(7111) To Calvin McQuesten

Muskoka, Ontario

"Whitehern"

Hamilton, July 29, 1930.

[Written at top] Mr. C. [Chisholm] doing well, voted.

Dearest Calvin

Only a few lines, we are so thankful for a cool morning. Yesterday a terrible day 100 in the shade and then the great disappointment of the Election. It is really maddening, how could men vote against King and Dunning. I think the C. [Conservatives] were very anxious and got out every voter they possibly could. H. [Hilda] was scrutineering up at Dominion St., now Chilton Place, beside Mewburn's[611] and there they dragged in poor old Mrs. Watson over 90, blind, so she had to be sworn in. So weak she could hardly stand. We heard the reports on Radio till midnight. A great shock.[612] Well, we will see what they will do with the unemployed next winter. Our butter-man and people in the market saying "We must have a change ignoring the fact that it was the drought last summer, they deserve another. It made no difference what the Gov. had done for them, they <u>must</u> have a change. To serve the public is a thankless job. Take as long a holiday as you can. I have been sleeping well in spite of heat. With much love.

Your mother

M. B. McQuesten

✦ A137-(7116) To Calvin McQuesten

[Somewhere in England]

"Whitehern"

Hamilton, May 12, 1931

Dearest Calvin,

Have just phoned the P.O. and find the English Mail leaves at 5 o'clock to-morrow morning. We received the card from Montreal and Quebec in due time and this a.m. Mrs. Todd's note and yours written on Sat. which I suppose were posted on at Farther Point. Rejoiced to hear you are so comfortably placed on the steamer, lovely to have a window, (we had just a port-hole) and away from noise too so you will just have a splendid rest and be ready for the grand tour.

We are having lovely showery weather some good rains, for which I am truly thankful for Tom's sake. So glad you had friends in Montreal to give you a good send off, Mr. J. to take you to the Steamer was a great help. Mrs. Todd's note said "We the three Todds want to tell you how happy we are to have Uncle Calvin for a fellow voyager etc." The family were amused at the warmhearted little girl who threw her arms round your neck, and Tom said he was a handsome boy. Well it certainly is pleasant to have friends on the voyage and Mrs. T. is very kind. Nice of Canon Daw to see you off; they drove him home. Phoned last night to Miss N. who said E. [Edna] was very well physically, but so restless; wanting to get up, which I think is quite natural. The garden in front is beautiful beyond description. The pink sublatum [sic] phlox, the Arabis, the daffodils, the Prunus Trilobi, Forsythia and Japonica, never saw the latter so fine, just a magnificent display & grass so green; then in the back, the triliums are a great show with hyacinths, tulip & honesty coming on & fruit trees in bloom.

Tom is delighted with the Rock Garden[613] and the flowering shrubs and trees at Gage Park. The Globe has on its front page the first report from their new lady correspondent. In the Mirror I read that the Painter Wyllie's funeral service was at St. Thomas's at Portsmouth taken there from the Point Tower House (?) [sic] where he lived. After the service sea scouts rowed it back up the harbour to Rochester Castle (?) [sic] where he was buried beside his daughter next the Castle Wall. We never saw the castle or Tower House.[614] I also read in M. a great description of the New Zoo. 500 acres in the country about 35 miles from London called Whitsnade, where wild animals are to be in large enclosures but not in cages and birds. Refreshment booths. The finest of the animals are still to be kept in the London Zoo, so I think it would not be worth while for you to spend time going there. It would mean too much walking after you got there. Opened on May 23rd. Would send the Globe's Lady Cor.'s account of Westminster Parliament but not worth.[615] Well, there seems to be nothing more to say except much love from all the family. Take good care of yourself, my dear.

Your affectionate Mother
M. B. McQuesten

✦ A138-(7136) To Calvin McQuesten

[On vacation in England]   "Whitehern"
                                            Wednesday, June 3, [1931]

Dearest Calvin

Your splendid letter about the Wales trip came this morning. Wed. seems to be the day your letters come. It seemed quite wonderful how you made friends by the one who gave you such a fine view, the Welsh mountains. I had sometimes read of terrible accidents to climbers on Snowdon. May was very cold in London, I saw by the "Mirror," not so cold here. Our garden is most lovely now with iris, tree peonies etc. and the laburnum. Tom took me to Gage Park, very beautiful at the East side where the little stream runs and banks lined with iris and the pink hawthorn too in various parts and tree peonies.

Tom, Norman and Fred Marshall starting to-morrow for a few days fishing up to some new place. Nellie James was to spend to-day (King's Birthday) with Edna. We were up on Sat. She looked better then I have seen her for a long time and was in happy mood. Hope you received the cheque. You must not try to write me such long letters, for I want you to rest all you can; but just keep a note book of specially interesting places or things, which will recall to you what you saw, after you come home. Mr. Child saw Tom other day and was speaking of you, said "he was very fond of you." I noticed in the Mirror a picture of a Marvellous stairway of Indo-China, which has been built an exact copy in the Exhibition at Paris being held there all this summer.

Dr. Drummond has been brought home, but is not expected to last long. I sent him some lilies of the valley with honeysuckle. I think it a fine idea to grow the fruit on wires at back of borders. We did not see the gardens at Windsor and [illegible] where Queen Victoria and Prince Consort are buried only half a mile from Windsor.[616] We did not see wither we had to hurry too much, when we had a hired motor waiting. As before found out from P.O. that Mail closes at 6 this evening. So far you seem to have been very fortunate in what you have seen. Hope Lancaster Hotel is really comfortable. With much love from all.

                                            Your affectionate mother
                                            M. B. McQuesten

✦ A139-(MCP 2-3b.40) To Calvin McQuesten

c/o Bank of Montreal   "Whitehern"
Waterloo Place, London, England   June 18, 1931

Dearest Calvin,

I am so glad you sent me the "Itinerary" so that I know where you are; so to-day you are in Paris and last Sunday you were in Rome, a good day for it, I would think. We are just going along as usual, we hear quite good reports of Edna, planning to go up on Saturday. The garden is magnificent, never saw so many roses; all the old kinds in the back have such quantities and in front too, and the rose bed very fine Oriental Poppies in great quantities. Your route is rather a puzzle but I suppose you are coming down again from York to S. England.

Poor Duncan Chisholm died yesterday, we heard St. Andrew's Society looking after him.[617] Holton W. called last week as usual pursuing the Soft Ball clubs, had been to Kitchener. I hope your strength is holding out and that you are not being raced to death. I think you missed some bad weather by going to Italy but you missed Ascot. I am really keeping very well, the weather very comfortable. You will find quite a bunch of letters at the Bank, I fancy. Take good care of yourself.[618] Have just read in Sat. H. that Saint Dunstan is buried at Canterbury.[619] With much love.

Your affectionate Mother
M. B. McQuesten

✦ A140-(MCP 3-5.71) To Thomas B. McQuesten

["Whitehern, Hamilton"]

[Greeting Card illustrated with Garden scene and house]

Hamilton, June 30, 1932

Wishing My dearest son Tom, Many Happy Returns on his Birthday, June 30, 1932. I would like to select a handsome present as a keepsake, on this your fiftieth Birthday and if you can think of anything you would really like and could use, I will be most happy to add to this.[620]

God Bless Your Birthday
And
Grant you Many Happy Days
The Lord bless thee, and keep thee; the Lord make His face
Shine upon thee, and be gracious unto thee.—Num. 6, 24-25.
The old sweet message, "God bless you!"
I send from my heart today,
May he ever guide, strengthen and keep you
As you journey along life's way.
Kate Hopkins.

My darling Tomsy on your fiftieth Birthday
From: Your Mother, June 30th 1932.

✦ **A141-(MCP 3-5.70) To Thomas McQuesten**

c/o Mr. Frank Broom   "Whitehern"

Kearney, Ontario   September 8, 1933

Darling Tomsie,

Just a few lines to urge you to stay away as long as possible. The heat keeps on nearly 90, but the house keeps cool and I am very well and comfortable. We had a phone from Mrs. Ketchen, Joe Thomson had phoned Dr. K. that Laura had died and would be buried at Burlington to-morrow (Sat. Morning).[621] Such a mercy! Hilda is motoring Cal & Mary and Mrs. Fletcher down. Archie was on hand Thursday morning, he does not like the Americans. [I] Found account of young Ferguson's wedding in the Globe. The bright boy had won scholarships for Research work at Washington—Graduate of Toronto Univer., and wife also, but they sail on Sept. 16th for Cambridge. We are bringing Miss Buchanan and Elsie with Mrs. Fletcher for a cup of tea and see the garden as she wished to do, this afternoon. On Wed. night had a thunder storm and splendid rain for <u>hours</u>. Bold St. houses look splendid, passed them last evening all lighted up. The top room of West house a brilliant red lamp looked most attractive. So just stay as long as you can, for I am very well and bearing up as well as could be expected in your absence.[622] With fondest love.

Your Mother

M. B. McQuesten

✦ **A142-(7156) Bereavement card from McQuesten family**

[Mary Baker McQuesten, deceased December 7, 1934][623]

The family of Mrs. McQuesten
acknowledge with grateful appreciation
your kindness and sympathy
in their bereavement.
"Whitehern,"

Hamilton, December, 1934

✦ **A143-(Excerpts from Mary's will)**
Last will and testament of Mary Baker McQuesten[624]

I ALSO DESIRE [sic] to mention with loving thankfulness my appreciation of my children's loyalty, unselfishness and self denial as evinced in their loving service to myself and to each other without which under the Divine Blessing the Homestead could not have been maintained.

I ALSO DESIRE [sic] to record my deep sense of gratitude to Mr. James Chisholm, who has ever been my kind and valued friend and wise counsellor, and whom I can never repay for all his thoughtful care and unwearying assistance in the management of my affairs, but can only commend him to the faithful regard and loving esteem of my sons and daughters.

✦ A144-(Eulogy, 10 December 1934)
A Fitting Eulogy to a Christian Life

Rev. Beverley Ketchen pays Tribute to Late Mrs. McQuesten
[At her funeral, MacNab St. Presbyterian Church]

It would be utterly impossible at any time, but especially here where fitting simplicity demands brevity, to pay anything like an adequate tribute to the memory of the brilliant and gracious lady whose passing has brought us together in sorrow and sympathy today. And indeed I know that any attempt at an elaborate eulogy would be utterly out of accord with her own refined tastes and wishes. But Mrs. McQuesten was too prominent a figure in the church life and the public life of Canada to be laid away without some vocal recognition of her outstanding character and work and influence.

When I came here nearly thirty years ago, it was she who put my first gown on me and her address on that occasion was a very memorable and impressive deliverance.[625] These thirty years of intimate association have greatly endeared her to me, as one of the brightest most courageous and most charming Christian ladies it has ever been my privilege to know.

Mrs. McQuesten was brought to this church as a very young bride and for nearly three score years and ten she has been one of the most conspicuous Christian workers and spiritual forces, not only in this congregation and community, but in the church at large.

It is hardly necessary here to give any detailed account of her untiring labours in connection with the women's missionary activities. As long as any of you can remember, her name has been almost a household word in the Presbyterian homes of Canada.

One of Founders

One of the founders of that wonderful, dynamic organization known as the Women's Missionary society, Mrs. McQuesten was for twenty-five years president of the auxiliary in this congregation, and for more than half a century has been very actively and prominently identified with the general work. Her knowledge, her rare constructive ability and the force of her earnest prayer-life being invaluable. One might say that missionary work was her 'ruling passion,' but she was never, even in the midst of her most strenuous missionary activities, a Mrs. Jellaby [sic].[626] She never neglected her primary duties in the home. She was a very devoted mother.

Naturally, she was honoured by the women of the church with election to the presidency of the provincial society, and in her latest years she has been a very highly esteemed and valued honorary president. To the very last, although growing physical infirmities curtailed her activities in that direction, her interest remained as keen and alert as ever, for neither her brilliant mind nor her indomitable spirit ever showed the slightest sign of infirmity. And while for some time she has not been able to mingle in the councils of the church, her prayers were doubtless bearing rich fruits, which, now that the day has broken and the shadows have fled away, must gladden her ardent spirit.

As I have said, Mrs. McQuesten came to this church as a very young and strikingly beautiful bride, and although her life has not been one of luxurious ease, but has had its full share of troubles and burdens, and responsibilities and cares, that singular loveliness was in her face to the last.

Steadfast Courage

The spirited daughter of a commander in the Royal Navy, she knew how to weather stormy seas and how to fight a good fight, and I should attribute her rare and steadfast courage to her unshakeable faith in God, her daily communion with Him, who gave her the strength and guidance and help she needed from day to day through the years, and the unfailingly loyalty and devotion of her family. Not many finer things are ever seen on earth than the romantic tenderness of that devotion, which she so well deserved, and we are glad that before the end she enjoyed the thrill of a mother's pride and joy, through the distinction in her son.

Mrs. McQuesten had a real Puritanical sense of right and wrong. Her uncompromising conscience would not countenance anything that was not utterly honourable. But with all that inflexible integrity were blended a very great kindliness and the graciousness of a true lady. She was an aristocrat by birth and breeding; she was an aristocrat intellectually and spiritually, too.

Lavender and Old Lace

Many of you who knew her only in public life saw, perhaps, only the brilliant side of her, admired the remarkable mind and realized the force and influence of an exceptionally strong personality. But it was in the home that she was at her best, where her wit sparkled most and where her gentleness overshadowed her cleverness. To see her in the home or about the beautiful garden that she loved so much was to think inevitably of lavender and old lace. How fitting it is that her body should be surrounded here by these beautiful flowers, but we believe that her spirit is now surrounded by beauties greater far, in that "land of pure delight" and "land of everlasting spring and never-withering flowers."

The editor of the Herald very fittingly spoke of her love of beauty, and referred to her as being in great measure the inspiration of the notable beauty spots in our city. Thus indirectly she has rendered a great and lasting civic service, of which, our parks will be beautiful monuments for all time. And that same inspirational influence is yet to be felt more widely through the services political and otherwise, of those who inherited from her so much.

No eye hath ever seen, nor ear heard, neither hath it ever entered into the heart of any one to conceive the service she has rendered even more indirectly still through her constant, earnest, faithful intercessions at the Throne of Grace.

It was a very great privilege to know her. Her memory will ever be cherished with reverence and affection, and we rejoice to think of the exceeding great reward which the grateful Master must have prepared for her.

Mary Baker McQuesten (circa 1925)

Dr. Calvin McQuesten
(1801-85)

Elizabeth (Fuller) McQuesten
(?-1897)
Third wife of Dr. Calvin McQuesten

Dr. Calvin Brooks McQuesten
(1837-1912), son of Dr. Calvin
McQuesten and brother of Isaac

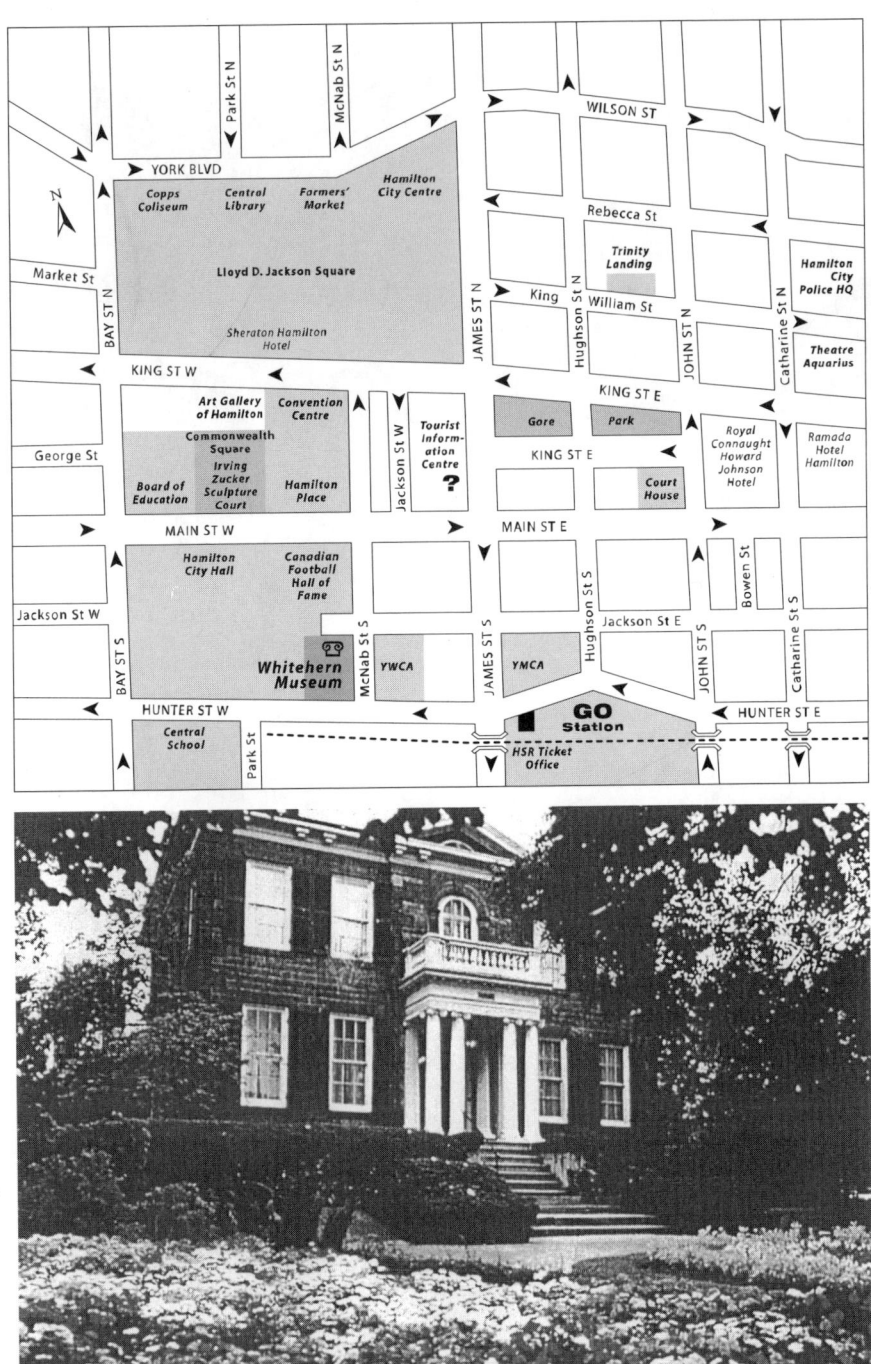

Downtown Hamilton and Whitehern Historic House and Garden
41 Jackson St. W., Hamilton, Ontario

Whitehern and McQuesten family (circa 1895)
Dining room and library at Whitehern

Notes

ë**.

Any letter number that is not preceded by an "A" can likely be viewed on the Web site www.whitehern.ca.

Notes for Part One

1 Rev. Thomas Baker's correspondence at Whitehern, dated from 1809 to 1887, includes military service records, church papers, sermons, and family letters (Farmer, *CMQPW*, Sec. 7; and many sermons on microfilm, MCP 1-1.29).
2 The detailed invoice for Mary Baker's trousseau is included on p. xx.
3 Isaac's condition suggests manic depression or bipolar disorder for which there is "strong evidence for hereditary predisposition." The extreme form leads to psychosis. The lesser forms manifest moody behaviour in which the "up" phase can result in "feats of great achievement and creativity" (*EHB* 722-27). Several members of the family suffered these symptoms in varying degrees, including both parents, Isaac and Mary, and two of their children, Calvin and Edna.
4 Mary called it "nervous prostration" and described it as a weakness "at the very centre of the nervous system" (A126-8734).
5 The "Nina Vivian" columns are (Box 13-060 to 085). The "Father" articles are (Box 13-001 to 059).
6 Calvin's two book manuscripts are entitled: *The King of Fighting Men* (Box 04-028 to 033) and *The Healing Ministry of Jesus in His Day and Ours* (Box 14-078 to 081)
7 Thomas collaborated with his friends Noulan Cauchon, H. B. Dunington-Grubb, John Macintosh Lyle, and many others in his projects (MCP 1-3b.15; A84-6053). John Lyle, one of Canada's foremost architects, was celebrated in a recent lecture by architect Bruce Kuwabara as part of Hamilton's growing impulse toward urban renewal (Art Gallery of Hamilton, 21 October 1999).

Notes for Part Two

1 I have included a selection of excerpts from Mary's missionary society addresses at the end of Part Two.
2 Ania Latoszek, former curator of Whitehern, provides an analysis of the WFMS in "The Women's Foreign Missionary Society Auxiliary of the MacNab Street Church (1887-1907)—A Preparation for Change" (1993 unpublished).
3 Brouwer adds that at least Lucy Maud Montgomery, a Presbyterian minister's wife, "rejoiced at the unification." Montgomery stated, "I think these missionary society meetings will be the death of me ... I have to attend all three every month." She also noted that she had a "surfeit of meetings" and found them "deadly dull" (Brouwer 51-52).

4 I am aware, of course, of the postcolonial research that has exposed some of these missionary efforts as harmful to the targeted people, but this was not known at that time. Mary's letters are valuable for a cultural study of the movement and demonstrate the moral, philosophical, and political motivation behind the missionary efforts.

5 Christians. Mary often uses this abbreviation.

6 Mary would likely have completed the quotations from scripture in her speech but did not write these into her notes.

7 Mary often uses this abbreviation "&c" for "etc."

8 Date established by Mary's letter to Calvin (Box 12-340, 30 January 1913, approximate date).

9 The following excerpts are taken from some of the Mary's addresses that are largely illegible.

10 William Carey was a pioneer English missionary in 1793 (Brouwer 11).

11 Although the address is illegible this closing statement provides an example of Mary's sermon-like conclusions.

Notes for Part Three

1 I use "Victorian" throughout in the sense of its continued influence into the twentieth century. In *The Mind of Ontario*, Royce MacGillivray comments: "Explanation is needed for the late introduction of Victorianism to Ontario, and for its late departure.... The educated Presbyterian clergy with their Scottish associations and the attachment to rationalism appropriate to their intellectually-oriented religion, prolonged, no doubt unconsciously, the dominance of the Scottish Enlightenment." One of the reasons he offers is that it promoted a settled way of life rather than the disorder and fluidity of pioneering conditions. It provided a network of congregations for the dissemination of ideas, moral standards, literacy, higher education, family values, and the work ethic (51-52).

2 A selection of excerpts from Mary's missionary society addresses is included at the end of Part Two.

Notes for Part Four
1873-1903

1 Dr. Calvin Brooks McQuesten (1837-1912) was Isaac Baldwin McQuesten's half-brother. He was practising medicine in New York and had declined to attend Isaac and Mary's wedding because of a conflict over Isaac's management of their father's (Dr. Calvin McQuesten's) estate. In spite of Mary's special pleading Dr. Calvin did not attend the wedding. The relationship was mended when the brothers were forced to form a united front against their stepmother (Elizabeth Fuller McQuesten) to counter her demands on their aging father. Dr. Calvin Brooks lived in New York until 1908 when he moved to Hamilton, to 49 Main Street, near Whitehern (A7-3854; A2-4283; A6-4327; A88-6173).

2 The wedding took place on 18 June 1873. The detailed dressmaker's bill for Mary Baker's trousseau is included here following the wedding photo on p. xx (3885). Also Rev. Baker was charged $4.00 for the rental of two wedding carriages (4060).

3 The baby "Tiny" (Mary) was nine months old and the first of seven children. At the time of this letter Mary was five months pregnant with her second child, Calvin, born 1 May 1876. He was born with a withered hand and some paralysis on his left side. It is not know what medication Mary took for relief of symptoms. Isaac had reported the birth of their first child to his half-brother Dr. Calvin Brooks on 21 March 1874: "The show is over and well over, thank goodness.... Mary felt splendidly and took a couple of glasses of grape wine; about 4 a.m. Friday, she had a "stomach ache that that confounded wine must have given me." It drained out her internals. About

8:30 a.m. she suggested it might be well for the nurse to call in, as possibly it might be something else. She was in some pain. Dr. Mullin came in ... and about 11:30 a.m. it was all over. The real pain only lasted about an hour and a half. She has been first rate since, and the Dr. and father say the child—a girl—though small is quite healthy. Our calculations were about ten days or a fortnight astray"(2440).

Wine appears to have been an acceptable beverage even though Mary objected to alcohol. Isaac made wine and cider in the home from Whitehern's large orchard, as his father had done before him. In June 1907, Edna (daughter) mentions taking "a bottle of old port wine to Annie Fletcher" (minister's daughter) in hospital and, in 1908: "another bottle of dandelion wine ... I had a swig to keep out the cold" (5832, 6043). During the Temperance Referendum of December 1902, which was defeated, Mary's objection was to the "saloons" and drunkenness, no doubt influenced by Isaac's tragic experience with alcoholism (A32-4713).

4 The Crystal Palace in Hamilton was begun in 1858 and opened 1860 by Edward, Prince of Wales. It was designed for provincial exhibitions of commercial goods in competition with Toronto. Built of wood and glass, it stood on twenty-two acres in what is now Victoria Park. It was condemned in 1891 and the buildings sold (*DHB* 1. 26, 28, 188). Albert H. Hills (1816-1878), Hamilton architect and civil engineer, designed the Crystal Palace and modelled it on the structure built in London for the Great Exhibition of 1851. Hills designed many Hamilton buildings, including Knox Presbyterian Church (1846), the Royal Hotel (1857), and the Custom House. He had an office in his home on Charles Street, near Whitehern. His son Lucien was also a Hamilton architect (*DHB* 1:103). For the Hills family, see A19-4500.

5 Four of the McQuesten children are mentioned in the letter: Calvin, six years old, was being treated by his uncle Dr. Calvin Brooks McQuesten in New York for the congenital defect in his left hand and weakness on his left side (A2-4283). Tiny (Mary) was eight years old and Hilda was five. Thomas was three months old. Ruby is not mentioned in the letter but was two years and eight months old. Edna was not born until 1885.

The Donald MacKays were close family friends in Toronto and are frequently mentioned in the letters. Mrs. Maddie (or Mattie) MacKay (nee Gordon) (18??-March 1907) operated a small private school in Toronto and took the McQuesten children for a time after Isaac's death. It may have been a childcare arrangement. She also accompanied Mary to Clifton Springs, New York, when Mary had a breakdown in 1897 and required rest and treatment (A14-4400). Mary visited them regularly in Toronto. Her letters describe the many problems the MacKays had with their declining health and with their children's behaviour and handling of money.

The MacKays were very wealthy. Mr. Donald MacKay (1813-1909) (A27-4601) was president of Gordon, MacKay & Co., Wholesale & Dry Goods, Haberdashery and Woolens, at the corner of Front and Bay streets in Toronto in 1904. In 1900 they lived at "Dundonald," 591 Yonge Street, and in 1904 they moved from Dundas Street to 5 Queen's Park Crescent where they resided until 1909 (A49-5172). Their sons, J. Drummond MacKay (on the Board of Directors) and J. Gordon MacKay (salesman) lived at the same address in 1900 (Tyrell 78). In 1904, J. Gordon MacKay lived at 485 Marion Avenue, Toronto (*Toronto Street and Business Directories*). The MacKay children were Gordon, Drummond, William, Leila, Maggie, and Blanche. Leila married Dr. Senkler, Maggie married a Mr. White, and Drummond married a Miss Smith.

Mary's relationship with the MacKays went back to the Gerrard Street congregation in Toronto, where the Bakers, MacKays, Gordons and Clarks attended, and "Uncle Donald MacKay" appears to have been a neighbour. The MacKay/Gordon/Clark familial relationship is apparent in the letters. Mrs. MacKay was a Gordon (A79-5868). Mrs. Mary Gordon (nee Robertson) was the mother of Rev. Dr. Charles William Gordon (pseudonym, Ralph Connor) (A57-5359) and she gave an address to the MacNab WFMS in 1885. The MacKays were also likely related to Helen "Daisy" Clark (nee Gordon), wife of Sir Mortimer Clark (A40-4902), the lieutenant-governor of Ontario in 1903. (A9-4343; A14-4400; A15-4415; A17-4436; A18-4479; A19-4500; A20-4521; A21-4531; A23-4544; A24-4549; A25-4582; A27-4601; A28-4635; A49-5172; A51-5233; A52-5283; A57-5359; A68-5665; A79-5868; A80-5898; A91-6336; A94-6363; A98-6460; A99-6483; A100-6509; A121-6951; A124-9180).

6 Katie was likely a servant.

7 The year 1882 was a very difficult one for Mary. Her mother, Mrs. Mary-Jane (McIllwaine) Baker died on 13 August 1882, of the newly diagnosed disease, diabetes (3597). Mary's son, Thomas Baker McQuesten, was born on 30 June 1882. Her daughter, Muriel, 22 months old, died on 27 August 1882. Also, Mary had had six children in ten years, was exhausted, and had gone to Asbury Park for a rest.

8 Miss C. Fisher was a relative on the McQuesten side. Isaac's paternal grandmother was Margaret Fisher (1760-1833). Miss Fisher lived in London, England, and travelled a great deal. Mary may have visited Miss Fisher when she was in New Jersey or may have received a letter. Miss Fisher corresponded regularly and visited occasionally (A11-4387; A17-4436; A25-4582).

9 Miss Henwood and Miss Stanton were housemaids at Whitehern (4309).

10 "O.L." (Old Lady) refers to Elizabeth Fuller McQuesten who was Dr. Calvin McQuesten's third wife and stepmother to Isaac and Calvin. She had a very poor relationship with both sons that had worsened over time. They were engaged in a legal struggle over Dr. Calvin McQuesten's estate, in which she was thwarted, and after his death on 20 October 1885, she was granted a dower and went back to the United States (234; Best 2-6).

11 The Sawyer family was widely dispersed between New England, Hamilton, Montreal, and Muscatine, Iowa. Aura, Clara, Ida, and the Colonel [Stein?] are mentioned in Mary's letters. They lived in Montreal in 1902 (A92-6343). The Sawyers were cousins related to Dr. Calvin McQuesten through his sister, Sally Barber (McQuesten), who married Stephen Sawyer in 1824. Dr. Calvin and Stephen were partners in business in New England and Muscatine, Iowa. The Sawyer family lived at 264 MacNab Street between 1844 and 1857. Dr. Calvin gradually sold off his Hamilton foundry interest to his nephews, Luther, Stephen, and Samuel Sawyer. It eventually became the Sawyer-Massey Company (DHB 1:146; DHB 2.139-40; Leona Bean McQuiston [sic] 84).

12 Mary's anxiety was compounded by the fact that she was also six months pregnant with their seventh child, Margaret Edna McQuesten, born 23 October 1885, just three days after the death of Isaac's father, Dr. Calvin McQuesten, and on the day of his funeral. At that time Isaac's mishandling of the estate became evident. Bankruptcy was looming for him and his brother and he and Mary had a large family and a large home to maintain. Between April and August 1886, Mary required rest and treatment for depression. Isaac wrote to her on 23 August 1886: "Home these dark, short evenings is almost worse than no home at all without a wife ... it makes me sadder to think of a sweet, pure little one like you having to lie on a bed of pain when you don't deserve it, & I have all well when I ought to have something like sciatica in every part of my body" (2495).

13 The cause of Mary's great anxiety is further explained in a letter from Isaac to his half-brother, Calvin, written on his return from treatment at Guelph on 1 October 1887. Isaac had been suffering from alcoholism and severe depression, had frequent break-downs, and spent several periods in the Guelph Sanatorium. This is the last extant letter from Isaac to his brother and it describes his condition as an "unhealthful excitement, and afterwards came the reaction," periods of "sluggishness" and insomnia. He is very frank about his guilt and despair over his "responsibility" in the use of "stimulants" and the "heinousness of sin." Isaac also provides a cryptic message about a "mystery" and a possibly violent course of action that he was contemplating: "I am fully aware that I and I only am to blame as far as responsibility. Nor think that I will allow feelings to permit me to do a foolish thing that could benefit nobody, and sim-

ply injure all concerned. And while I cannot tell what the exact step to be taken—as yet—is, or what it will result in, I will not be party to right being subservient to any other motive. Don't think I am making any mystery now. I am not. But I want you simply to be prepared, when such occasion may occur, to quickly and calmly use your best judgement, and not by my leaving the possible consideration of steps that may not be necessitated, until such time or action has to be taken, then be flurried by being taken unexpectedly. All I want you to understand is that if it becomes necessary to deal decidedly with a man who is not a fool, you will be prepared to act without rashness; and further that I will not pursue a course of temporizing simply because I do not want to fairly face what may not be pleasant.... I have made no attempt at concealment and have so informed those who have spoken with me. It may be very painful and humiliating, but nothing is gained by an attempt at evading it.... And it is these sudden impulses that I must look out for. It is one long continuous want or craving" (2511, 1 October 1887).

14 Rev. Thomas Baker, Mary's father.
15 The *Hamilton Daily Spectator*'s obituary for I. B. McQuesten, M.A., Thursday, 8 March 1888, stated: "The deceased was enjoying the usual health until evening, but was taken sick about midnight.... Mrs. McQuesten left him reading in the library and went to bed. About midnight she heard a fall, and on going downstairs found her husband lying in an insensible condition. In a glass in the room was the remains of a sleeping draught which the deceased was in the habit of taking occasionally, and it is supposed that in his latterly feeble state of health the dose proved too much for him. Dr. Mullin was immediately summoned and stayed with him until morning by which time he had partially recovered consciousness, but shortly after he relapsed into insensibility and died in a few minutes.... He was 41 years of age at the time of his death."

There were many rumours circulating at the time, especially since Isaac's death was accompanied by bankruptcy. He had been frank about his alcoholism, and his death was attributed to alcohol and a sleeping draught. But whether it was suicide or accident is impossible to establish, and Isaac was given an elaborate and honourable funeral. There were conflicting reports as to the cause of death. The *Globe* obituary, 8 March 1888 stated: "Your reporter was walking with the deceased gentleman last evening and he was in the best of health and spirits and spoke freely of the future and of his increasing law business. The deceased was taken ill at his home about midnight, and although two physicians were in constant attendance upon him, he never rallied, but died about 9 o'clock this morning. Death is attributed to disease of the heart."

The identity of the "reporter" is unknown. Dr. Fletcher, in his sermon at MacNab Street Presbyterian Church on 12 March 1888, stated: "During his illness—for it is not generally known, he suffered from congestion of the lungs—he spoke to his pastor affectionately and earnestly of spiritual things."

16 James Chisholm (1858-1944), Isaac's law partner, handled Isaac's estate and tried to salvage what he could from the bankruptcy. He also assisted Mary with any legal matters (Best 5). He managed to preserve a few investments, Whitehern, and the Bold Street houses, which were rented but badly in need of repair (A16-4425). Isaac had had the forethought to place Whitehern in trust for Mary. When the estate was settled, Isaac's assets were $10,000, and his liabilities $92,000. His brother Calvin's losses were $80,000, and even the estate of Mary's father had been depleted (A7-3854; Best 5).

For the future, Mary's income would be approximately $1,700 per year, with which she had to maintain Whitehern and raise her six children, who were between the ages of fourteen and two when Isaac died (A23-4544). "The residue of the estate was hardly enough to feed, clothe and educate her children, particularly so since [Mary] Baker struggled to maintain a semblance of her former social standing" (*DHB* 3; 5). Chisholm also gave some financial assistance to Tom for his university education, became his mentor, and took him in as a junior law partner in 1909 (A23-4544; 6458). In 1928, when Chisholm was seventy years old, he gave Mary a substantial gift of money (see A132-MCP2-4.89; *DHB* 3:33). Mary acknowledged his kindness in her will (see A143 excerpts from will).

Mary thought very highly of Chisholm and paid him a public tribute in her address at the MacNab Church Diamond Jubilee Service in 1927: "His face impressed itself on me almost more than anyone in the Congregation; he had a very fine head with snow white hair; he was a Highlander and when you were introduced to him, a wealth of kindness shone out of his bright eyes; and I appreciated his warm greeting" (Annual Report of MacNab Street Presbyterian Church, 1927, 43). Chisholm married Anne M. Stewart in 1889; she died of tuberculosis in 1890. They had no children and he never remarried. He devoted his life to law, the MacNab Church, where he was treasurer for twenty-five years, the Liberal party, and the 91st Highlanders (Argyll and Sutherland). He and his partner Alexander Logie (A34-4759) (and others) had worked relentlessly between 1880 and 1903 to establish the Highland Regiment in which they served during World War Two. He was a member of the Scottish Rite. Col. Chisholm lived at 77 Claremont Drive and became a Hamilton character, seen daily, an "amazingly alert soldierly figure with his cane, swinging along" to the Hamilton Club or the Armories (*DHB* 3:28-33; A15-4415; A18-4479; A22-4535; A23-4544; A24-4549; A27-4601; A34-4759; A35-4803; A38-4835; A42-4977; A73-5788; A74-5794; A87-6135; A98-6460; A116-6801; A134-7085; A124-9180; A143 excerpts from Mary's will).

17 We have found no letters in Mary's hand between Isaac's death in March 1888 and April 1889. There are many letters of condolence in a commemorative journal at Whitehern.

18 Mary's daughters, Mary and Hilda, were visiting a close family friend, Mrs. MacKay, who operated a small private school in Toronto. Mary was fifteen and Hilda was eleven years of age. Cally, Ruby, and Tom were thirteen, ten, and seven years of age, respectively. Edna, four years of age, is also mentioned in the letter. Earlier in April, Mary had been at Mrs. MacKay's with Tom, and Mrs. Grant (a friend) had been looking after the other children at home. For MacKay see A3-4297n.

19 Because of financial constraints, keeping servants was a problem, and it is difficult to establish when Mary was forced to give up servants. This letter suggests that Mary had no live-in servants at this time and that she hired help as needed for the heavier work. The two servants mentioned in letter of June 1883 are not mentioned again (A4-4315), although "Lizzie" in the letter of 13 October 1890, may have been a servant (A10-4367). There is very little mention of servants in Mary's letters after Isaac's death. The census for 1891 lists two servants at Whitehern, but this may not be accurate. As the two eldest daughters became capable, they assumed many of the household duties, and Mary often comments on their heavy workload (A21-4531). In 1892 Mary describes doing the housework herself while her daughters are away, and she asked her friend Mrs. Fletcher to babysit Edna (A11-4387). In 1898 Mary had dismissed a girl and planned to advertise (A15-4415). In January 1904 Mary notes that "we have to do our own work, and the servant's wages are quite beyond me," and in August "we shall all have to work like Trojans." In 1906 she is "exhausted" by the housework. In 1909 Mary cannot "afford" to hire help (A46-MCP3-5.7; MCP3-5.33; A55-MCP2-4.52; A68-5665; A96-6419; 4847).

20 "Old Mrs. Lillie" was the wife of Dr. Adam Lillie who died in 1869. They had been missionaries to India. He was a minister in Brantford and had been a professor at the Congregational Theological Institute in Montreal for thirty years. He and Mary's father, Thomas Baker, were friends for forty years, and Rev. Baker preached a lengthy eulogy in his honour.

21 Lizzie may have been a servant at Whitehern. For note on servants, see A9-4343.

22 Crawford's Confectionery Store was near Whitehern, on King Street, between James and MacNab streets. It was a restaurant and bake shop famous for wedding cakes and

cream puffs, and had a tea room in the rear of the store where ladies held afternoon tea parties. It was owned by two brothers, William and George Crawford (HPL, *King Street Scrapbook*, *Hamilton Spectator* article by Fred Howe, 10 February 1962; A101-6636; 6436).

23 Miss H. Elsie J. Buchanan (?-1951) and Mary were attending a WFMS conference in Pittsburgh. Mary was secretary of the WFMS at this time. They may have been staying with Elsie's brother, James Isaac Buchanan, a successful Pittsburgh businessman and millionaire. Miss Elsie Buchanan was a charter member of the WFMS in 1876 and held the office of secretary for a number of years until 1884 and from 1893 to 1895. In June 1890 she travelled to Washington for a WFMS meeting and delivered an account to her auxiliary in Hamilton (Latoszek 6, and notes). Her obituary states that she was a "woman of cultivated tastes and charm of manner." Her mother, Agnes, was also a member of the WFMS (Latoszek 4, 11, 25). Miss Elsie Buchanan was one of the eleven children of Agnes Robert (Jarvie) Buchanan (1826-96) and Hon. Isaac Buchanan (1810-83), an entrepreneur, industrialist, and "a merchant prince, politician and Hamilton promoter." He was a "pamphleteer," a prolific and influential writer of political tracts. The family business was Buchanan, Hope & Co. He was elected to represent Hamilton as an independent in the Assembly in the late 1850s and early 1860s. "Like many committed Protestants of that era, he was intensely anti-Roman Catholic ... and anti-French Canadian" and had a distrust of the clergy (*DHB* 1:31-36). He and his family founded the "Hamilton Education Movement" (Johnston 220) and assisted in the formation of Knox College in 1858. He gave financial aid to Hamilton's MacNab Street Church and laid the cornerstone in 1856. An ardent supporter of the "Free Kirk," he announced that "he would contribute two hundred and fifty dollars to every congregation in Upper Canada that within a stated time would build a church and name it Knox," which was accepted by Dundas, Galt, Guelph, Acton, St. Catharines and Hamilton. His son, James Isaac Buchanan, also donated money for the choir-room addition and the vestry-study at MacNab Church (*DHB* 2:49; Campbell 100; *POH* 77-8,137; *Wee Kirks* 67; A11-4387; A15-4415; A19-4500; A24-4549; A59-5426; A69-5709; A124-9180; 8740).

24 For Fletcher family, see A18-4479.

25 In 1896, Mrs. J. Emily Steele of Dundas was elected president of the presbyterial for the Hamilton and district auxiliaries to the WFMS. She was the daughter of Catherine Ewart who had inspired the Ewart Missionary Training Home for women missionaries and deaconesses. She attended the Winnipeg conference with Mary in 1906. In 1911 she was elected president of the national body of the WFMS and moved to Toronto to facilitate the work of attempting to get women's formal representation at the Board and conference level, but the men resisted (Brouwer 40-41). In these gender wars Mrs. Steele and Mary worked closely together and in 1912 they attended the Vancouver Assembly together. During the assemblies of 1914 the WFMS was coerced into joining with the home missions to form the Women's Missionary Society (WMS). Their spirit had been broken and they felt that they had become just a "fund raising arm" of the church, but they continued in an auxiliary relationship with the Home and Foreign boards (Brouwer 51). Emily Steele continued as president and many other members of the executive joined her (Brouwer 27, 40, 41, 50-2, 87; A49-5172; A61-5470; A62-5487; A106-6746; A124-9180).

26 Mrs. Robert Grant was elected second vice-president at the formation of the Mac-Nab Street Church auxiliary in 1887 (Latoszek 25). Mary was secretary at that time and became president in 1893, the office she held until 1914.

27 For Miss Fisher, see A4-4315.

28 Mrs. Haigh was likely the wife of Rev. George Haigh in Hespeler, a friend of Rev. Thomas Baker (3812). In a letter to Calvin of 29 May 1906, daughter Mary noted that "Maud Haigh had left for Winnipeg," likely as a member of the missionary inspection group along with Mary (5477).

29 Calvin had fallen under the influence of Rev. John Alexander Dowie and his "Zion" Divine Healing Mission. He joined the Dowieites for healing in 1896 after he suffered an emotional collapse brought on by the stress of examinations after his first year at University of Toronto. He failed mathematics and English and was forced to transfer from Honours Classics to a Pass program (MCP1-3b.68). The Dowie influence had a profound and long-lasting effect on Calvin and his diary entry of 1933 refers to his "rebirth in 1896."

John Alexander Dowie was born in Scotland in 1847 and came to the United States in 1888 by way of Australia. He formed one of the most successful faith healing ministries in the United States. He declared that he was "Elijah the Restorer" and wore "High-Priestly robes." In 1896 his ministry headquarters was a seven-storey building on a city block in Chicago, and by 1901 he owned 6,000 acres of land near Chicago where he built his "Zion City." He and his wife fell into financial ruin when they "began to indulge in secular activities" such as personal mansion building and Paris vacations. He was deposed in 1906 and died almost bankrupt in 1907. Dowie's work has become of interest to the healing revivalists and millenialists of the present day and his sermons were published in 1996 (*CBD* 437; *The Biographical Dictionary* online 5 pp. 4 October 1998, Keyword: Dowie, John Alexander). In 1901 Dowie spoke to a crowd of 10,000 and "devoted much of his time to abusing the press and concluded that he might start a daily paper in Chicago" (*Evening News*, Toronto, 23 January 1901). An article in the *Montreal Herald* of 6 December 1902 carried the title "John Alexander Dowie, Merchant Prince of Faith Healing, makes $15,000,000 in Ten Years." A Montreal branch of the Dowieites was formed, and on 10 June 1903 another *Herald* article noted "the rather peculiar state of affairs" in which the "Queen Street Baptist Colored Church" was attempting to raise the funds to get rid of the Dowieites with whom they were sharing the church. It is not known if Calvin attended this church in Montreal; however, he may have written these articles as he was a journalist with each paper at the time of publication.

30 Probably Mrs. Donald Fletcher, wife of the minister at MacNab Church (see A18-4479).

31 Likely, Adam Henry Hope, lawyer, one of the three sons of the Hon. Adam Hope (1813-1882), a Hamilton merchant in wholesale hardware goods and a senator in 1877. Adam Henry Hope married Hattie Sawyer, daughter of Luther D. Sawyer, nephew of Dr. Calvin McQuesten (for Sawyer, see A5-4323). In 1904 Adam Hope began selling the Electric House Cleaning Machine. The Hope family lived at 323 Bay Street South and were members of the MacNab Street Church (Tyrell 143; *DHB* 1:105, 146; *DHB* 2:140).

32 Mary suffered a breakdown and was at the "Sanitarium" for rest and treatment. She was accompanied by her friend Mrs. MacKay from Toronto (A3-4297).

33 Sir Henry Morton Stanley (1841-1904) was in Cairo in 1870 for the opening of the Suez Canal, and then went on to "find Livingstone" in Africa (*CBD* 1387).

34 Calvin had taken a job in journalism with the Copp Clark Publishing Company in Toronto, which he held from November 1898 to July 1901. His reviews and articles were unsigned and so difficult to identify. The column "Books and Magazines" in the 3 November 1898 edition of the *Evening News* is likely his. It reviews *McClure's*, *North American Review*, *The Gentlewoman*, and the *Ledger Monthly*.

Calvin also wrote a daily column for the *News*, beginning 2 January 1901: "A Corner for Women Readers: Conducted by Nina Vivian." This pseudonym he likely adapted from "Vivian," the English vaudeville "comique" of indefinite gender who played in Hamilton during the 1890s (see A37-4815n). The column featured a wide range of women's cultural concerns: politics, religion, literature, art, poetry, humour, food, fashion, and social events. The first column included two articles with a feminist slant: "The Czarina and Women's Clubs" applauded her reform movement, and "French Women as Lawyers" paid tribute to "Toronto's own woman lawyer, Miss Clara

Brett Martin" and to France's two women lawyers. I have found no evidence that Calvin's mother or the family knew about his writing of these columns (Box 13-060 to 085). He disclosed the fact when he ran for alderman in Hamilton in 1946 and was courting the women's vote.

35   Mrs. Anne Laurence (VanEvery) Thomson (1837-1926), widow of Robert Charteris Thomson (dates unknown), lumber merchant, lived at "Amisfield," 1 Duke Street, near Whitehern. The home had been purchased by Robert in 1887, but had been previously owned by his father, William Thomson (1796-1866) and his mother Jean (Charteris) Thomson (1799-1887). There were several branches of the large Thomson family in Hamilton and they are frequently mentioned in the letters.

Robert C. Thomson's widow, Mrs. Anne LaurenceThomson, purchased "Amisfield" and the contents from the estate in 1902 (4623). She lived there with her son Joseph James Charteris Thomson (Joe or J. J. C.) (1864-?) (HPL, Special Collections, Burkholder article). Mrs. Thomson also had a large family living with her as she notes in 1903: "all of my young children are on my hands yet" (5026). Mrs. Thomson wrote A Little Book of Verse (1914) which is in the Whitehern library. Miss Laura Hostetter (likely a relative) lived with them. Their summer home was in Burlington (Tyrell 157). They were members of MacNab Church and Mrs. Thomson was a member of the WFMS. Joseph married Margaret (Mary) Wardlaw Taylor in August 1905, the youngest daughter of Sir Thomas Wardlaw Taylor and Lady Margaret (Vallance)Taylor (see Taylor, A58-5382). Joseph's wife was also a member of the WFMS (Latoszek 5; Campbell 171; HPL, Pamplet File Weaver "Amisfield"). Joseph was president of R.Thomson & Co. G. Laurence Thomson also lived at "Amisfield" in 1907 (A37-4815; A38-4835; A58-5382; A68-5665; A69-5709; A71-5744; A74-5794; A84-6053; A92-6343; A93-6347; A94-6363; A96-6419; A106-6746; A121-6951; A110-8848; A109-8867).

Other Thomsons mentioned in the letters are four brothers who were likely cousins of the "Amisfield" Thomsons: Harold C., Ernest, Alfred, and Charles, (see A68-5665n). For Mr. and Mrs. James C. Thomson and James A., see A38-4835n.

36   Peter Toronto Buchanan (1844?-1898) was the eldest of the eleven children of Hon. Isaac Buchanan (1810-83), a prominent Ontario industrialist and politician. Peter had been in the family business—Buchanan, Hope & Company (DHB 1.34-36; A10-4367).

37   For a note on servants at Whitehern, see A9-4343.

38   James Chisholm, Isaac's former law partner, fought endless battles with the T.H. & B. Railroad after the City granted them permission in 1895 to run their new line along Hunter Street directly between MacNab Church and Whitehern. It created noise and dust and devalued both properties. The expropriation was a hotly debated issue in Hamilton and it caused the McQuesten family and the church a great deal of anxiety (DHB 3:29; Best 37-38). For Chisholm, see A8-2520.

39   Perhaps, John A. Webber (1861-1944), son of Esan Webber, a building contractor in Hamilton. Mary may have held a mortgage in his name (DHB 3:223).

40   Probably the rent from 1 and 3 Bold Street, the attached houses that Mary and Isaac had shared with her parents, the Bakers. They were badly in need of repair which would be expensive, so were vacant for periods of time and, as Mary slowly made the repairs, she was able to rent them out as boarding houses to a Mrs. Merrill and a Mrs. Hill (A16-4425; A22-4535; A23-4544; A35-4803; A43-5012; A57-5359; A77-5820; A78-5854; A80-5898; A81-5984; 2364; 3763; 3959; 3964; 4067; 4098; 4769; 4771; 4885; 5436).

41   The student preachers were likely from Knox College in Toronto. A Finlay Matheson and a Hugh Dallas Cameron graduated from Knox in 1899 (BDKC 146, 31). The Hamilton Collegiate Institute was the high school attended by the McQuesten children. It was located at Caroline and Main streets (Johnston 220).

42   Possibly Dr. James R. Dickson, Mary's father's old friend (3121).

43 May Sutherland was a friend and Mary (daughter) repaid the visit in January 1902 at 66 Bloor Street West, Toronto. These Sutherlands may have been related to Mr. and Mrs. John William Sutherland (nee Graham) 120 Duke Street, near Whitehern. Miss Leslie S. and Miss Graham lived with them (Tyrell 156; *DHB* 3:42, 71, 150, 165; A22-4535;A40-4902). James William Sutherland (1860-1942) soft drink manufacturer, also lived near Whitehern at 14 Duke Street, had two children and attended Mac-Nab Church, but I have been unable to establish a definite family relationship between them (*DHB* 3:203).

44 Calvin's article, "Victoria Missionary Conference," appeared in the *Toronto Evening News*, on 21 January 1901. It outlines the various sessions and addresses from the mission fields, such as the Indian missions of Manitoba and the Northwest, giving an account of "the redmen," and "Pagan Indians" of British Columbia. The address on "China, our territorial trust" describes the missionary enterprise "in that portion of the great empire." I was unable to find the article on "The Holy Door." Calvin sent the papers home with his articles marked and they were circulated among family and friends, but most are no longer extant. His articles are not signed and so are difficult to recognize.

45 Queen Victoria died on 22 January 1901. Calvin's articles for the week provide an account of the Queen's deathbed. On 26 January 1901, Calvin wrote a "Tribute to the Queen" in which he reviewed the London newspapers' tributes to her. On the same date his article "Queen City of the West Mourns the Dead Queen" describes Toronto as a city in mourning, the various buildings draped in black and purple streamers representing the grief, admiration, and love felt for her, "everything being done on a very elaborate scale" (*Evening News*, Toronto).

William Murray, "The Bard," commented on Calvin's article: "Saturday's 'News,' 'Last Tribute to the Queen' on p. 4. It is 'pithy, painted and true' and has the high tone about it which we expect from all McQuestens. Bye & Bye, I hope you will drift into the management of one of our Hamilton sheets, and as the right arm of the Church, do something elevating for the city of your birth" (7290). For Murray, see A101-6636.

In the same newspaper on 28 January, an article noted that the women of Hamilton had organized and collected donations for a statue of the Queen. In a letter on 22 May 1908, Mary describes the statue "draped and ready for unveiling for the Queen's birthday" (A87-6135). The statue stands in Gore Park today. The inscription reads "QUEEN VICTORIA 1819-1901. QUEEN AND EMPRESS. A MODEL WIFE & MOTHER." Below the lion at her feet, it reads: "MANY CHILDREN OF OUR CHILDREN SAY SHE WROUGHT HER PEOPLE LASTING GOOD." On the North side, it reads: "THE WOMEN OF HAMILTON IN AFFECTIONATE ADMIRATION HAVE RAISED THIS MONUMENT."

46 Frederick Sleigh Roberts, Earl of Kandahar, Pretoria, and Waterford (1832-1914) became field marshal and commander-in-chief in Ireland in 1895. He published *The Rise of Wellington* (1895) and *Forty-One Years in India* (1895). He assumed the chief command of the 2nd Boer War in 1899, came home in 1901, and was created an earl (*CBD* 1248). These books are not in the Whitehern library.

The letter is likely a reference to the ceremony of the earldom. The *Toronto Evening News* carried two articles on Lord Roberts: on 2 January 1901, "An Earldom for Lord Roberts" and the "Conqueror of Boer Republics," and one on 26 January, "Roberts' Last Visit to the Queen," which is a moving account of Roberts' shock and grief at her feebleness. These articles may have been written by Calvin (A39-4863). On 27 July 1908 Mary wrote that they were expecting to have a visit from Lord Roberts: "Next week we hope to get a sight of Lord Roberts, Col. Hendrie is to motor him from here to Beamsville, Grimsby, on to Niagara" (6236). Roberts was unable to make the visit and Mary wrote: "What a disappointment that Lord Roberts could not come" (6240).

47 Calvin and Tom regularly had boarding-house problems and Mary worried about their care and meals. This incident appears to have been a "tussle" between Tom and someone who was coming in "after the ball" (A34-4759).

48 Miss Janie James was a missionary in Japan and in China. Her mother, Mrs. George James (Mary) was widowed and lived at 86 Bay Street South with her children (Tyrell 144). They are often mentioned in the letters as: Janie, Willie, Lillie, Nellie, Mary, Connie, and Walter. I am unable to trace their father/husband. They were members of MacNab Church and the WFMS and the children's Mission Band (Latoszek 25 and notes; A38-4835; A42-4977; A50-5199; A63-5512; A79-5868; A80-5898; A97-6446; A101-6636; A102-6676; A138-7136; A113-8787; A109-8867).

49 Likely, Sir John Morison Gibson (1842-1929), lawyer, politician, and businessman. He had been a pallbearer at Isaac McQuesten's funeral. He was prominent in Hamilton development in hydro power, transportation, and steel. He "was a provincial minister in Oliver Mowat's cabinet and Hamilton's foremost Liberal" (Best 5), Attorney General of Ontario (1899-1904), Lieutenant-Governor (1908-14), and was knighted in 1914 for his work with the Red Cross. His third wife Elizabeth Malloch (m.1881) was the daughter of a Brockville judge and likely the sister of Dr. Archibald Edward Malloch (for Malloch, see A25-4582n). The Gibsons were active in philanthropic and community causes: the public library movement, the Hamilton Art School, the Hamilton Health Association and the Sanatorium. They lived at 311 Bay Street South in 1900 and at Ravenscliffe on Aberdeen Avenue in 1912, and were members of Central Presbyterian Church. They had four sons and two daughters. Three sons predeceased Mr. Gibson, leaving Colin Gibson (1891-1974), who also had a distinguished legal, political, and military career (DHB 1:82-3, 54; DHB 3:66-76; DHB 4:98-101; Tyrell 138; A25-4582; A69-5709; A47-MCP1-3a.56; A84-6053; A88-6173).

50 During the construction of the railroad in Canada, many young men took surveying jobs in the West. When Tom's mother refused to "let him go," Tom took a job on a cattle boat and worked his passage over to Europe. He reported to Calvin that he rode to Montreal on the top of a freight train, boarded the "Manchester City," and spent the voyage working, and living, in the hold with the cattle. The meals were very poor. He also asked Calvin not to relate to his mother "the description of the voyage" (4490). Had she heard the details she might have wished that he had gone surveying instead. Tom considered the surveying job again in 1902 but did not go (A25-4582).

51 Mrs. Lyle was Elizabeth (Orr) (1849-1932), wife of Rev. Dr. Samuel Lyle (1841-1919), the minister of the Central Presbyterian Church in Hamilton from 1878 to 1910. The Lyles lived at 136 Bold Street, and had six children and various members are often mentioned in the letters. Mrs. Lyle was president of the WFMS at her church and on the Ontario board, and she and Mary often attended conferences together. She was a member of the IODE and of the Local Council of Women from its inception in 1893. She worked to establish the Hamilton Health Association, "the first purely local antituberculosis association in Ontario," and the Hamilton Sanatorium. The Lyles were leaders in Hamilton's intellectual, cultural, and social development, including the Hamilton Public Library, the Hamilton Art School, environmental reform, slum clearance, and town planning. The Lyles expressed a passion for moral idealism and social reform. Mr. Lyle was a "leading figure in the Presbyterian Church in Canada," and became Moderator of the Synod in 1896, of the General Assembly in 1909, and of the Presbytery in 1914. He was an "articulate spokesman for protestant liberalism in Hamilton" and was "well-read in Scottish philosophy" and "German thought." He favoured Church Union and the modernization of doctrine which was known as higher criticism. Mary McQuesten was opposed to both. She commented on Lyle's sermon on 16 May 1904: "Dr. Lyle has brought a great deal of criticism upon his head by that unfortunate sermon of his Upon Hell. Tom says that Prof McFadyen has all the students at Knox with him they have no use for the other Professors & Prof. Caven will not discuss points … it is said all who can are leaving Knox for Glasgow … I do not know what is to become of the Churches in the hands of men of all kinds of belief. Indeed they may well propose organic union for there is no agreement as to belief among any of the individual denominations now, so they may all mix up as much as they like. But

what is to become of it all, God alone knows. To say that a man is a minister is no longer a guarantee that he us a man to be trusted" (5183; for McFadyen and Caven and higher criticism and Church Union, see A52-5283n).

Lyle's successor, Dr. Wm. H. Sedgewick, also favoured union and "resigned in 1925 when his people voted to remain Presbyterian" (POH 56, 131, 141; 5683). Mary Lyle (daughter) married Alexander Warden, son of Rev. Dr. R. H. Warden, who also favoured modernization and union (A21-4531; A52-5283). John (Jack) Lyle (son) became a prominent Canadian architect and worked with Thomas McQuesten on many of his building projects (A84-6053; Best 54-5; DHB 2:95-99, DHB 3:6, 161-2; Johnston 249; 252; A21-4531; A30-4651; A35-4803; A45-5105; A58-5382; A68-5665; A73-5788; A82-5990; A84-6053; A91-6336).

52 Mr. Glassco was a neighbour suffering from mental illness. The "Glassco affair" is mentioned again in a letter to Calvin from his sister, Mary, 30 April 1901: "Mr. Glassco has been behaving ugly again" and the family was forced to move to the mountain (4462). In 1903 they moved again to the corner of Aberdeen and Queen. Josie O'Brien Glassco, Mrs. Bonnie Glassco, and Reggie and Winnie were members of MacNab Street Church. "Pickle" and "Dot" Glassco were Edna's friends (A37-4815; A38-4835; A43-5012; A87-6135).

In 1900 the Glassco family in Hamilton had four branches with four residences (Tyrell 139). Likely, they were all descended from William Henry Glassco (1819-99) and his six sons and one daughter. He was a prosperous fur trader and furrier. Three sons were in business with him as Glassco and Sons, Wholesale Furs and Hats (DHB 1:84).

53 Dr. McTavish is possibly Rev. Dr. William Sharpe McTavish (1858-1932), a graduate of Knox College in 1884, pastor in Deseronto (1895-1905) and Kingston (1905-11), a field secretary (1911-15), and a pastor in Madoc (1915-22) (BDKC 140; A96-6419).

54 Rev. Dr. Donald Hugh Fletcher (1833-1912) was the minister of the MacNab Street Presbyterian Church from 1872 to 1905 and pastor emeritus to 1912. in 1882 he married Phyllis E. Murray, sister of William Murray, "The Bard of Athol" (for Murray, see A101-6636). Mrs. Fletcher was president of the WFMS at MacNab from 1887 to 1893, at which time Mary assumed the presidency. The Fletchers lived at 116 MacNab Street Street, until 1905 and were then presented a house on Hess Street South. They had two children, Anne (Montague) (A82-5990) and Hugh Murray. Dr. Fletcher became moderator of the Synod of Hamilton and London in 1885 and moderator of the General Assembly in 1903. Dr. Fletcher's brother, Rev. Dr. Colin Fletcher, was also a minister (for Colin, see A28-4635) (BDKC 73-74; POH 78; DHB 2:49-50; Latoszek 25, Buttrum 4-5, Tyrell 137; A47-MCP1-3a.56; A13-MCP1-3b.9; A11-4387; A16-4425; A22-4535; A28-4635; A32-4713; A33-4717; A35-4803; A37-4815; A38-4835; A41-4963; A42-4977; A43-5012; A50-5199; A63-5512; A72-5765; A79-5868; A82-5990; A84-6053; A89-6252; A91-6336; A92-6343; A96-6419; A97-6446; A120-6853; A113-8787).

55 "Grandpapa" was Mary's father, Rev. Thomas Baker. He served in the Royal Navy during the Napoleonic Wars, and on the Great Lakes during the War of 1812 as first lieutenant on the St. Lawrence. He began his Congregational Church ministry in Kingston in 1835. In 1870 he was granted the rank of "Commander in H. M. Fleet" and a retirement pension (3038). His correspondence is in Section 7 of the Calendar (2800 to 4244; Minnes 1).

56 I have found no further information for Rev. Idrisyn Jones.

57 "The Pan-American Exposition was held in 1901 in Buffalo, New York, May 1 to November 2, 1901 on a 342 acre site…. The fair featured the latest technologies, including electricity, and attracted nearly 8 million people…. The Electric Tower was illuminated nightly by thousands of coloured bulbs and floodlights." Thomas Edison had invented the carbon-filament light bulb in 1879. ("Pan-American Exposition, 1901, Buffalo, New York": 1 p. online, Buffalo Free-Net Home Page, 29 November 1998; CBE 298). In the Toronto Evening News, 22 January 1901, Calvin wrote: "The Domin-

ion at the Pan-Am," and reported on the visit of a Canadian delegation led by William Hutchinson of Ottawa to inspect the site of the Exposition grounds. Representatives were from colonization, forestry, mines, agriculture, and archeology. United States President William McKinley was shot at the exposition's "Temple of Music" and died eight days later from a surgical infection. The Exposition has entered American mythology with the fictionalized account by Lauren Belfer: *City of Light* (New York: Dial Press, 1999).

58   This letter gives an indication of the volume of social life that the McQuestens enjoyed (or endured). At times Mary complained that her children did not have enough social life, and at other times she was "simply tired to death of transients" (5392). Because it was summer, many of the visitors were from out of town: Mrs. Davidson from Guelph ("Gracie," see A40-4902); Mrs. MacKay, Blanche, and Maddie from Toronto (A3-4297); Ina and Muriel Hills from Toronto (possibly related to the Hills of Hamilton) (A3-4297 *DHB* 1:103); and the Gilberts from Walkerton (5524). Mattie Davidson (A23-4544); Jessie Brown; the Lockes and Ken [Trigge] (A58-5382; A28-4635); and the Bells (A21-4531) all visited from Hamilton.

59   The gift is likely a wedding gift for Eliza MacFarlane's marriage to James Isaac Buchanan in Pittsburgh, which was her home and his place of business. The wedding took place on 11 July 1901 (1251b). James was a Pittsburgh millionaire and son of the Hon. Isaac Buchanan (see A10-4367).

60   This final paragraph of the letter is obviously *not* the original extension of the above letter dated 13 July 1901. The ending of "goodbye once more" suggests a postscript, possibly to A18-4479, written on 1 May 1901. The references to Calvin's bicycle and Tom's "exams" were both subjects of family letters in late April and early May. On 16 June 1901, Tom had written to Calvin from Aberdeen, Scotland, about his trip across the Atlantic on the cattle boat (4490).

61   I have found no record that Dr. Clark, dentist, was related to Gordon Clark or Sir William Mortimer Clark, but he may have been a cousin. For Clark, see A40-4902.

62   Calvin had moved to the *Montreal Herald* in January 1903 to continue his career in journalism. He worked there until September 1903. While there he wrote a weekly column,"The Tatler," in the tradition of Steele and Addison's "Tatler" of 1709-11 (*OCEL* 804). It featured brief articles on current events and prominent figures, politics, history, religion, and literature (Box13-001 to 059). He also wrote many other articles for the paper but they are unsigned so difficult to recognize.

63   *The Crisis* (1901) was written by Winston Churchill (1871-1947), Missouri historian and novelist (*CBD* 310). A copy is in the Whitehern library.

64   Gordon Clark was the son of Sir William Mortimer Clark, lieutenant-governor of Ontario in 1903. For the Clark family, see A40-4902.

65   Mrs. Sarah Ann Mullin was Mary's good friend and the wife of their family doctor, Dr. John Alexander Mullin (1835-99). He was in attendance at the birth of the McQuesten children and at the death of Isaac (A8-2520n). Dr. Mullin had been introduced to the McQuestens by Mary's father. He assisted in the design and architecture of City Hospital, which opened in 1882, and was on the medical staff and committee (Campbell 180). They were members of St. Paul's Presbyterian Church. They moved from James Street North in 1907 (5832) and lived at 7 Turner Avenue in 1911 (6718). Various family members are often mentioned in the letters. Their children, Heurner, Robin, Willie, and Nellie, studied medicine and Archie went into banking. Heurner married Ethel Lazier in 1907 (*DHB* 1:157; A8-2520n; A21-4531; A23-4544; A25-4582; A31-4686; A32-4713; A84-6053; A91-6336).

66   I have been unable to trace May Cameron or Dr. White, M. D. They were in Indianapolis in 1903 and in touch with Robin Mullin then (A34-4759).

67   For the Lazier family, see A51-5233.

68   May Mewburn's marriage to Dr. McDougal finally took place in 1909 after May's lengthy illness, probably tuberculosis. May and her mother stayed in Calgary from

1904 to 1908 as May was recuperating, and Ruby lived near them there in 1908 when she was ill with tuberculosis (A26-4588; A98-6460; A136-7111).

May, Tom, and John were the children of Sydney Chilton Mewburn (1863-1956) and Mrs. Mary Caroline (Labatt) Mewburn. Sydney was a lawyer (K. C.), politician, businessman, and soldier (major general), and became minister of militia and defence in Borden's coalition Union government in 1917. Their son, John, was killed during World War One at twenty-seven years of age in 1916 (*DHB* 2:112-13). Their son, Tom narrowly escaped drowning in July 1902 (A26-4588). The Mewburns lived at 65 Markland Street and supported the Church of the Ascension (Anglican). Sydney C. Mewburn's biography gives a comprehensive overview of Canada's and Mewburn's involvement in World War One, for which he declined a knighthood. He was "a man of integrity, honour, and a sense of purpose" (*DHB* 3.140-45).

In 1875, Sydney's father, Thomas C. Mewburn, and Hugh Baker and Charles Cory, avid chess players, had organized the West Side Domestic Telegraph Co. and a telegraph line was strung between their houses, approximately seven blocks apart, enabling each player to telegraph his moves (See A78-5854).

69 Jean Vincent was the daughter of Mrs. Jessie S. Vincent and Rev. Edward Vincent of 45 Young Street in Hamilton. They were members of MacNab Church and Mrs. Vincent was secretary of the WFMS in 1896. Penn Yan is in New York State. Mary gave a farewell tea for Mrs. Vincent in October 1902 and regretted the loss of a friend (Latoszek 25; A22-4535; A24-4549).

70 The WFMS conference was held in Toronto, but Mary was unable to attend. Her paper was read and "considered the best" (A25-4582).

71 Kenelm Trigge was a friend from Hamilton but was working in Montreal. He and Calvin lived in the same boarding house in Montreal. Trigge courted Hilda for a time in 1902. For the Trigge family, see A28-4635.

72 Ida Welker and "the Col." were "back" in Montreal from Vancouver (see A24-4549; A21-4531; A24-4549; A26-4588; A39-4863).

73 In 1903 an anti-toxin was being administered for diphtheria; however, it is possible that Dr. Calvin Brooks McQuesten ("Uncle") had arranged early vaccinations for the family. The two deaths from diphtheria created anxiety. Tom's vaccination did finally "take" (see A25-4582). Calvin received a Vaccination Certificate in Montreal dated 16 January 1902 (7940). A news article notes that vaccination parties were in vogue at that time as the "latest social Novelty": the guests are invited and the "physician is the guest of honour, and while he vaccinates the guests one by one, in one room, the others play whist in another. After it is all over, supper is served" (*Evening News*, Toronto, 23 January 1901). Diphtheria immunization in Hamilton schools was administered in 1922 (Campbell 218).

74 B. K. (Bernard Keble) Sandwell (1876-1954) and Calvin had been friends and fellow journalists at the *Evening News* in Toronto in 1901. They also worked together at the *Montreal Herald* in 1902 and 1903. Sandwell was again with the *News* in Toronto in November 1903, and was back at the *Herald* in January 1904, where he was dramatic editor from 1905 to 1911. He was editor of the *Montreal Financial Times* (1911-18) and editor of *Toronto Saturday Night* (1932-51). He taught economics at McGill University (1919-23) and was head of the English department at Queen's University (1923-25). In 1920 he became the first secretary of the Canadian Authors' Association and in 1925 he was elected fellow of the Royal Society of Canada. He was author of *The Privacy Agent, and Other Modest Proposals* (1928), *The Molson Family* (1933), *The Canadian People* (1941), and *The Diversions of Duchesstown, and Other Essays* (1955) (*MDCB* 746). None of Sandwell's published works is in the Whitehern library (Best 104-05, 126; A25-4582; A40-4902; A51-5233; 5798; letters from Sandwell: 7444, 7489, 7553).

In April 1903, Edna notes that she had seen Sandwell "with a young lady, small and quite pretty. I supposed it was Miss Street" (4922). Mary (daughter) notes "he must come up often now. Perhaps it may come to something after all. Miss Street may think it would be wiser to hang on than let him go" (4927). In July 1902, Sandwell visited "but none of the family would hear of" asking him to lunch (4605). In May 1903, Mary comments on an episode in which Cal took a moral stance and left his rooming house because of Sandwell's behaviour with "a woman, such an indecent creature allowing a young man to come into her room in such a way." Mary complimented Cal on being "brave and conscientious … to write to his father … it was a noble thing to do" (4938). In 1907 Ruby reports somewhat humorously an encounter with Sandwell in which he was "still" pursuing a woman and was "no nearer the goal—there is still the other man with the automobile … he has improved—his handshake is less clammy and he looked neater" (5798).

75 Maud Shaw was the daughter of Mrs. G. M. Shaw and sister of Jessie. They lived at 57 Bay Street Street and Maud was planning to visit Ruby at the Ottawa Ladies' College. They were members of MacNab Church and Maud had been treasurer of the WFMS (Latoszek 25; Tyrell 155; WFMS "Minutes" 1890-1900; A24-4549; A66-5630).

76 For the Mullin family, see A20-4521.

77 This item of gossip became somewhat altered in the following letter (A22-4535). William M. Warden married Miss Gooderham and lived at 9 Madison Avenue, Toronto, in 1900 (Tyrell 118). He was one of the sons of Rev. Dr. Robert H. Warden (1841-1905), clergyman, financier, president of the Metropolitan Bank in 1903, college principal, and moderator of the Presbyterian Church (1902). The Wardens lived at 188 St. George Street, Toronto, in 1900 (Tyrell 118). Another son, Alexander Warden, married Mary Elizabeth Lyle, daughter of Rev. Dr. Samuel Lyle of Central Presbyterian Church in Hamilton (A30-4651, *DHB* 2:99). For the Lyle family, see A17-4436.

   Rev. R. H. Warden favoured modernization and higher criticism in the study of scripture, and was an executive of the early Union Committee which led to the formation of the United Church in 1925 and created a split in the Presbyterian Church, (see A52-5283n). (McNeill 65, 67, 107, 146, 252-3; Moir, *Enduring* 199; MDCB 872; A22-4535; A30-4651; A45-5105).

78 I am unable to trace Mrs. Dr. Wallace.

79 Mrs. Emily (Rogers) Bell was the wife of William Bell, attorney and partner in the law firm of Pringle and Bell in Hamilton (*DHB* 3:10; Best 70, 72). The Bells lived near Whitehern, had three children, Charles William, Florrie, and Herbert, and are frequently mentioned in the letters. For Charles Bell and his plays, see A25-4582n. Another branch of the family, Mr. and Mrs. John Bell (nee Park) lived at 52 Hannah Street West and had two children, Madeleine and Hessie (A19-4500; A25-4582; A42-4977; A43-5012; A48-MCP3-5.11; A50-5199; A51-5233; A66-5630; A83-6012; A116-6801; A130-7018; A135-7095).

80 For Ida Welker, see A20-4521.

81 Mary obviously approved of Ken and encouraged the friendship. She frequently asked about him in her letters, but when Ken came to Whitehern to propose to Hilda, Mary rejected him (A28-4635).

82 For more on Mary's will, see A23-4544.

83 Ruby was teaching at the Presbyterian Ladies' College in Ottawa. Mr. Chisholm had been Isaac McQuesten's law partner (see A8-2520).

84 The gossip about the Warden family began in A21-4531. Names may be incorrect, as the script is very faint.

85 Rev. Dr. Daniel Miner Gordon (1845-1925) was born in Nova Scotia and educated at Glasgow University and Berlin University and ordained in 1866. He was professor of systematic theology and apologetics from 1894 to 1902 at Halifax Presbyterian College. He became principal and vice-chancellor of Queen's University (1902-17) after Dr. George Munro Grant resigned (Moir, *Enduring* 189-90). Gordon was author of *Mountain and Prairie* (1880) (MDCB 303-304). Ruby reported that she had heard "two splendid sermons" from Prof Gordon at Queen's (4539). The *Hamilton Evening Times*, 21 November 1902, reported his appointment and noted that he had a son in the

Presbyterian ministry. For his church politics as a "gradualist" on Church Union, see A52-5283; A97-6446. I have found no evidence that he was related to Charles Gordon (see A57-5359).

86 Mrs. Bennett's report about Dr. Barclay suggests that she was possibly related to Jane (Bennett) Sutherland (d. 1916), wife of Canon Sutherland (1854-1921), Anglican clergyman at St. Mark's Church and Christ's Church Cathedral in Hamilton. She was very active in women's organizations in the city.

Rev. Dr. A. Norman Barclay, a prominent Anglican minister in Hamilton, wrote of Canon Sutherland in a church history in 1929 (DHB 2:168-9).

87 For Jean Vincent, see A20-4521.

88 Anna Laidlaw, a musician who "played splendidly" (6395), was likely related to Rev. Dr. Robert James Laidlaw (1839-1895), minister of St. Paul's Presbyterian Church (1878-93). Music was very important at St. Paul's where Rev. Laidlaw was an "initiator and reformer" and installed a new pipe organ in 1880 (Wee Kirks 47). The Laidlaws were associated with St. Paul's organist and choirmaster, Dr. C. L. M. Harris who opened Hamilton's first conservatory of music in his home at Hunter and MacNab Street in 1897. He was director and examiner and made an outstanding contribution to music in Hamilton and Ontario (Campbell 228-29).

89 Rev. Robert Haddow (1860-1949) Princeton, University of Toronto, Knox College, ordained missionary and editor of The Westminster and The Presbyterian (1900 to 1925), and editor of the United Church Record (1926-31) (BDKC 93).

90 This page of the letter is very faint and overwritten. Mr. Graham may be Charles Walter Graham or David Graham, both members of MacNab Street Church, and their wives were members of the WFMS (Latoszek 25). They were likely related to the Sutherlands of 120 Duke Street since Mrs. Sutherland was a Graham (Tyrell 156). For Sutherland, see A16-4425.

91 The McKeands were likely relatives of Mrs. Elizabeth (Fuller) McQuesten, Dr. Calvin McQuesten's third wife. She had tried to pressure her husband to "buy a lot and build a house for them [McKeands] in Hamilton so that she could get them back near her" but he refused (2368). Nellie McKeand came to stay with Mrs. Elizabeth McQuesten when she and Isaac were in conflict over Dr. McQuesten's estate. Mrs. McKeand and Archie and Clarence were living at Wellington Square in Hamilton in April 1873 (2354; A5-4323). It is likely that they returned to the United States when Elizabeth McQuesten retired there after Dr. McQuesten's death in 1885 (235).

92 This is likely Mrs. Robert Grant (see A11-4387). Her letter is not extant.

93 Several letters passed back and forth on the subject of Mary's will and this letter provides some details about the McQuesten's finances. The will was duly signed and daughter Hilda wrote on 26 February 1902 that "mother's mind is at last at rest for her will is signed and witnessed by Mrs. Mullin and Mrs. Irving, one thing off her mind." (4544; 4568; A22-4535).

94 In February 1902 Mary's daughters Mary, Hilda, Ruby, and Edna were 27, 25, 22 and 16 years of age, respectively. At this time there were no prospective suitors.

95 Whitehern and the Bold Street houses required new roofing, which Mary had contracted to have replaced over the previous three years (A8-2520; A22-4535).

96 This is likely Mattie Davidson, a neighbour who lived near Whitehern. She was the caregiver for her mother (Mrs. Davidson), who was confined and "unable to come downstairs" (5640). They may have been related to the Guelph Davidsons (A19-4500; A40-4902) (A60-5464; A105-6738). The elder Mrs. Davidson may have been the widow of Thomas Davidson (d.1861?), builder and owner of the Royal Hotel. The hotel was built at James and Merrick streets on the former site of the foundry owned by Dr. Calvin McQuesten and John Fisher. Dr. Calvin McQuesten held the mortgage on the hotel (DHB 1.58: 198, 305-12).

97 Richard Thomas Lancefield (1854-1911), bookseller, author, librarian, and actor, was the first librarian for the Free Library, the Hamilton Public Library, on Main Street West,

from its inception in 1889 until February 1902, when he disappeared after defrauding the library of $5,300 and destroying the records. He was "gregarious and popular but addiction to gambling led him into trouble." In spite of this he "laid a firm foundation" for the growth of the library system in Hamilton. He had advocated for the political and social emancipation of women (*DHB* 2:88). As recently as 1885 there had been civic resistance to "the formation of a library, when it was feared that domestic disruption would result if women read novels" (*DHB* 1:83). He was an amateur actor who gave recitations at parties and concerts (*DHB* 2:87-89). He wrote *Victoria, Sixty Years a Queen* (1897), which was advertised in the Toronto *Evening News*, 28 January 1901: "By Lancefield, the great librarian ... Only fifty copies left!... $.75." The book has 571 pages and 200 illustrations and is bound in morocco and gilt. The Whitehern library does not contain a copy of this book.

98 Mary may be referring to a mortgage debt owing from the time of Isaac's bankruptcy and death in 1888.

99 Daughter Mary was likely suggesting that her mother pray for similar prospects for her own daughters. Further in the letter Mary expresses her concern that her daughters do not have enough opportunities to meet good prospects.

100 Emily Colquhoun was one of the ten children of Edward Alexander Colquhoun (1844-1904) and Evelyn Esther (Elly) Gourlay. For the Gourlay family, see A83-6012. Emily was a nurse, became "night superintendent in St. John's Hospital" in 1907 (5780), and married Mr. McCarthy (A130-7018). Her father was an accountant, bank manager, politician, and mayor of Hamilton in 1897-98, and won a seat in the Ontario Legislature with the Conservatives. The family lived at Barton Lodge, the Gourlay/Colquhoun estate, a large farm on the Hamilton Mountain brow (*DHB* 1:51, 85). They are often mentioned in the McQuesten letters, especially during their son Gourlay's war service (see A118-9153). (A27-4601; A91-6336; A101-6636; A130-7018; A118-9153).

101 The nature of Leila's illness is unknown.

102 Kenelm Trigge had gone "on the Road" as a traveling salesman.

103 The McQuesten homestead in New Hampshire was Dr. Calvin McQuesten's home before he emigrated to Canada in the 1840s. It was in the family for 136 years. A cousin, John Knox McQuesten, wrote to Calvin from New Hampshire in June 1903 to give his address as 723 South Main Street, Manchester, New Hampshire, "the cradle of the race" (7415). Calvin also received an invitation from Lucy A. Lerned, a relative of Dr. Calvin McQuesten's first wife, Margarette B. Lerned (1809-1841). Lucy was living at Concord, New Hampshire, which was a 7-1/2 mile ride by stage from Manchester (7416). Calvin did visit Boston and the homestead in late June 1903 (4998, 5002).

104 John (Jack) MacKenzie Rioch and Frances "Fanny" Pierson were married on 19 March 1902 and the McQuestens sent a gift. Jack, who had been Calvin's classmate, lived with his mother and sister, Grace, at 118 East Avenue South. Rioch's father died in 1900 (7280). He studied agriculture at Guelph and, in 1902, began to operate a very successful poultry farm in the Adirondacks, New York. Mary stated that she wished she "might get some of the juicy meated fowls he knows how to grow" (4562). They had a son, Stephen Pierson Rioch, on 11 June 1903 and Jack wrote glowingly about his marriage, wife, son, and farm, and was "Ein tickled to death" [sic] (5008). He also complimented Calvin on his writing: "I feel especially interested in 'The Tatler' because of course it gives a fellow an inkling of what is now engaging your attention from time to time and Canadian papers are always interesting" (7343).

105 The Coronation of King Edward VII (1841-1910) was set for 26 June 1902, but was postponed because of his illness (*Globe* 25 June 1902) (see A26-4588). Calvin wrote several articles about the King in his column "The Tatler" at about this time. On 22 February, he wrote of Edward VII's accession to the throne at the "venerable" age of sixty, and the "universal respect" that he had won (Box 13-002). On 12 April, in "The Coronation," Calvin quoted excerpts from Samuel Pepys's diary of 23 April 1661 which

described King Charles II's "ceremonies of the coronacon" [sic] "with the King in his robes, and bearheaded [sic] which was very fine," followed by "the sermon," "the quire" and "the crowne" [sic]. In a second article: "An Old-Time Banquet" Calvin gave Pepys's "exceedingly quaint" description of the Heralds and Knights in armour, and the Lords and Dukes "coming on horseback and staying so all dinner time," and the "Lord of Albermarle going to the kitchin and eatin a bit of the first dish that was to go on the King's table" [sic] (*Montreal Herald*, 22 February, 12 April 1902).

106 In January 1902, Mary reported that Tom's vaccination did not take. The context of that letter suggests that he may have had a vaccination against diphtheria (A20-4521). This letter deals with smallpox and might refer to a second vaccination that Tom may have had in March 1902. Smallpox immunization had occurred as early as 1848 when, in response to an epidemic, a free vaccination program for the poor was instituted at Hamilton City Hall (HPL, *Pamphlet File Weaver*. Harris, Catherine: "The Health of Hamilton 1880-1905").

In Calvin's column "The Tatler," 29 June 1902, he attributed "The Smallpox Epidemic" in Canada and England for the past year to "a set of cranks [who] arose and began to agitate against vaccinations…. They wrote pamphlets and formed societies and waged a vigorous warfare against the only safeguard we have against the most loathsome of all diseases and the most contagious." Also, in "The Scourge of Europe," Calvin gave an historical account of Lady Mary Wortley Montague [1689-1762], who had "traveled in the East, [and] introduced into Europe the practice of inoculation," which was used until "Jenner's great discovery of vaccination" (*Montreal Herald*, 29 June 1902).

107 An example of Tom's annual letter to his mother on the anniversary of his father's death appears here as an epigraph to the "Widow and Matriarch" section in Part One (5440, see also A75-MCP 2-4.37a).

108 I have found no relationship between Dr. Bell, of the Geological Survey, and the Bell family of Hamilton (A21-4531).

109 Dr. Archibald Edward Malloch (1844-1919), son of George Malloch, a Brockville, Ontario, judge. Mrs. J. G. (Margaret) Malloch, possibly his mother, was president of the Hamilton Board of Foreign Missions, 1878-83 (*Wee Kirks* 194). He was physician to Mary's family (the Bakers) in Hamilton in 1880 (4002) and a medical/surgical pioneer in Canada. He worked with Joseph Lister in Glascow who developed the "germ theory" and an antiseptic system of treatment, which Malloch brought to North America and to Hamilton City Hospital in 1871, where he worked with William Osler (Bruce Varcoe, e-mail and *CMAJ* article by James Houston, M.D. Malloch was a trustee for Queen's University, member of St. Paul's Presbyterian Church, and lived at 124 James Street South (*DHB* 1:147-48; *DHB* 3:75). He had three sons and three daughters. Two other Malloch families are listed in Tyrell on page 149: Mrs. Frank S. and Mr. and Mrs. S. E., both residing at 301 Bay Street South (A66-5630; A69-5709; A123-6975).

110 Tom had also considered surveying in 1901 but his mother did not approve. He did not go surveying in the summer of 1902 but joined the militia and "ended up in uniform as a member of the 4th Field Battery, Royal Canadian Artillery" (Best 8; A17-4436; A30-4651).

111 Charles William Bell (1876-1938) was one of the three children of William Bell, attorney, and Emily (Rogers) Bell. In March 1902 he was engaged to Beatrice Emmeline Gates and Mrs. Gates was pressing for the wedding. The date was set for 5 April 1903, however Charles had been delaying for financial reasons. In August 1903, Mary wrote: "Charlie is simply worried to death by his future mother-in-law who is always pressing the marriage and Charlie is in no position to do so" (5059; A48-MCP3-5.11). They were married 21 September 1904.

Charles Bell became a brilliant criminal lawyer, writer, and politician, lived at 17 Homewood Avenue, and attended All Saints Anglican Church. He was also a gifted playwright. "Combining theatre and law came naturally to Charles Bell" and he wrote at least eight successful plays, one of which, *Parlour Bedroom and Bath* (1917) ran on Broadway in 1931 and was produced in Toronto in 1980 as *The Invented Lover*. He also wrote *Who Said Murder?* (1936) a collection of his legal cases. Bell suffered from severe stress, collapsed after an impassioned two-hour address to a jury, was confined to his bed, and died in 1938. "The accused was acquitted" (*DHB* 3:10; Best 70,72).

Mary reported on one of Bell's plays in March 1909: "Nellie Mullin saw Charlie Bell's play last night at the Savoy. It had been greatly written up by manager and talked up by Mrs. Gates, there was a full house and considerable press made, flowers presented to his wife. Nell said it was quite good, and a good many smart bits" (6383b).

112 Likely a humourous reference to Mary's warning to Calvin about marrying the widow landlady (A22-4535).

113 Nellie Mullin was in nursing at Johns Hopkins in Baltimore.

114 The conference was likely held in Toronto, but Mary's injured foot prevented her from attending. She mentioned writing this paper in A20-4521.

115 Rev. William A. Wilson (1851-1940) and his wife Margaret (Caven) Wilson were missionaries in India from 1884 to 1917. Rev. Wilson had been pastor of Knox Church in St. Mary's from 1878 to 84, succeeded by Alexander Grant from 1885 to 1907. Wilson wrote *The Redemption of Malwa: The Central India Canadian Presbyterian Mission* (1903) in which he recognized the role of medical services, orphanages, famine relief, schools, and women in evangelistic work. He recommended that women missionaries be admitted to council to vote on "all matters relating to their own work," and that they be allowed to administer the rite of baptism to the women believers sequestered in the "zenanas" (harems). In a letter to the WFMS, Mrs. Wilson noted that in spite of the violent opposition from the Prince of Indore and other officials, the Christian missions "have opened, and kept open, five schools, where nearly 200 Hindu and Mohammedan children receive daily instruction" (Brouwer 102, 106, 114, 121, 142, 163, 223; Moir, *Enduring* 184). Wilson also wrote *The Popular Preachers of the Ancient Church* (n.d.) and a copy is in the Whitehern library.

116 Mrs. Helen Watson (nee Dewar) lived at 35 Duke Street with her children. Hope Watson was twenty-three years of age, and worked for a wholesale grocery house. He and Tom Mewburn were caught in a storm near Port Carling. The boat capsized and they clung to it for hours but Watson was finally "unable to hold out any longer." Mewburn managed to swim to a rock where he lost consciousness but was rescued (*Globe*, Toronto, 30 June 1902; Tyrell 159). Hope's brother "Strap" was a friend of Tom's (A24-4549; A105-6738; A106-6746; A136-7111).

117 Mary's reference to Tom Mewburn's misguided religious "thoughts" likely refers to the fact that the Mewburns were Anglican, a church of which she was openly critical.

118 The proclamation stated that the coronation was postponed "indefinitely, and great grief prevails throughout the metropolis." "His Majesty III With Perityphlitis [*sic*], a malady resembling appendicitis—An abscess in the right side opened from which pus was evacuated" and surgery was necessary (*Globe*, 25 June 1902). On 30 June the *Globe* stated that the King had made a remarkable recovery, was "completely out of danger," and the bonfires could be lit in celebration. Another article stated that "the King in the sickroom is drawing the hearts of his subjects by his own fortitude ... sorrow has made him a more magnetic personality than he would have been in the trappings of sovereignty.... The allegiance of the masses ... has been strengthened by the pathos of the King's lot stricken down in the supreme moment of coronation glory" (*Globe*, 30 June 1902; A25-4582). The coronation took place on 9 August 1902. Edward VII ruled Britain from 1901 to 1910.

In "The Tatler" 28 June, Calvin gave a brief account of "Some Dreary Coronations," including that of Anne of Denmark, who had to sit through seven hours of hortatory sermons concluding with Dr. Andrew Melville's recitation of "twa hunner lines of Latin verse" [*sic*]. Also, at Charles II's Coronation "at Scone in 1651 [he] was simply preached at and bullied. To hide his indignation and disgust he 'went into the fields to play golf.'" In a second item in his column, "A Literary Baganda," Calvin described the Grand Vizier of Uganda, who had arrived for the Coronation. He was Apolo Kagwa, tall, "well-made," in picturesque costume, had written three books, had electric bells in his house, and rode a bicycle (*Montreal Herald*, 28 June 1902).

119 I have been unable to find the article "Drummond in Britain" in any of the "Tatler" columns or in any other pages of the *Herald* for this period.

120 Mr. Brierley was the managing director of the *Montreal Herald*, and the person to whom Calvin tendered his resignation in September 1903 (7438; A45-5105).

121 A. H. U. Colquhoun was with the *Mail and Empire* in Toronto. He may have been related to the Hamilton Colquhouns who had ten children (A24-4549). Calvin did contact Colquhoun, and on 13 October and 23 December 1902 Colquhoun wrote to him about vacancies in journalism in Toronto (7356; 7374).

122 Calvin and Tom had been plotting a "canoe scheme" and Tom had found a canoe for $11. He asked Calvin to write to his mother about purchasing same: "If you think the scheme is good write to Mamma as soon as possible dwelling upon the advantages and especially the fun you will get out of it" (4592). Apparently, she refused. In July 1904, Tom wrote to Cal that he had purchased a "little bark canoe from Aylmer that you can lift with one hand"; however, he was very nearly "swamped" in it and "had to bale with [his] hat for dear life" (8176).

123 Kenelm Trigge had proposed marriage to Hilda, who was twenty-five years of age. Ken was the son of Captain Trigge and Mrs. Trigge of "Auchmar" in Hamilton, members of the Plymouth Brethren, and his prospects were good (Farmer, *Calendar* 19; Best 16). Their other children, Mary and Arthur, were also friends of the McQuestens. Mary rejected Trigge because he drank alcohol and, as a travelling representative, he was "tempting" others to do so as well. In 1905 a letter from one of Calvin's newspaper friends (incomplete and unsigned) states that Ken "is even less of an abstainer than he was when we dwelt on Sherbrooke. He is still there and still more or less infatuated" (7553). The McQuestens' experience with Isaac's alcoholism, which likely contributed to his death, had created a very strong temperance commitment in the household. Also the temperance referendum was being hotly debated at that time and Mary was actively campaigning for the vote, to be held in December 1902 (A32-4713; A33-4717). The Trigges are often mentioned in connection with the Lockes and were likely related (A19-4500; A20-4521; A21-4531; A24-4549; A29-4647; A30-4651; A31-4686; A36-4810; A40-4902; A51-5233; A58-5382).

124 Rev. Dr. Colin Fletcher (1847-1927), brother of Rev. Dr. Donald Hugh Fletcher (minister at MacNab Church, see A18-4479), was pastor at Thames Road, Kirkton, near Stratford (1879-1916). He married Anna M. Agur in 1879. She was active in the WFMS and attended conferences with Mary (BDKC 73-4; A35-4803; A63-5512; A89-6252; A120-6853).

125 This article appeared in Calvin's column "The Tatler" under the title of "Freak Journalism," in which Calvin referred to a new publication, *The Eagle and the Serpent: A Journal for Free Spirits and for Spirits Struggling to be Free*. He wrote: "A curious publication has recently appeared in England … devoted to the propagation of envy, malice and all uncharitableness. The leading article is entitled 'The Divinity of Hate'…. This periodical appears to be an entirely new departure for journalism. No lunatic asylum should be without it." Mary had abridged the quotation which reads: "People of brains are invited to contribute to this column. We can offer only the small reward of immortality, if immortality is desired, kindly mention it" (*Montreal Herald*, 6 September 1902, Box 13-03).

126 H. W. Nelson had been with Calvin in Chicago at John Dowie's "'Zion' Divine Healing Mission" in July and August 1896 (A13-MCP 1-3b.9, 16). After Calvin left the mission, Nelson wrote to him about his faith and conversion (MCP 1-3b.66).

127 I am unable to find an article about Calvin's meeting with the premier during the Coronation of Edward VII which occurred on 9 August, 1902. The *Montreal Herald* printed a special edition for the Coronation on that date to which Calvin, likely, contributed, but his articles are unsigned. "The Tatler" did not appear on 9 August or 16.

128 At his mother's suggestion (A29-4647) Calvin had contacted Leslie of A. G. Leslie & Company, Iron, Steel & Metal Merchants, Montreal, who invited him and Ken Trigge to tea on 19 October 1902 (7357).

129 Charles Johnson of C. H. Johnson & Sons, Ltd., Wire Merchants, Montreal, replied to Calvin's request for a chat (7358).

130 In Ruby's letter to Calvin, she comments: "[Ken] is really not a fine enough character for Hilda. He hasn't enough strength of will—I'm sure—and his moral senses—if you call them that—are just not keen ... [Hilda] is a real Christian too and would be unhappy to be continually having to live on a lower level" (4657, 26 September 1902).

131 Mary Elizabeth Lyle, daughter of Rev. Dr. Samuel Lyle, married Alexander Warden in September 1902.

132 Nan (Turner) Gilmour was married on 25 May 1902 and her husband died six weeks later. Nan was likely the daughter of James Turner (1826-89) and Caroline Huldah Greene, who had four sons and four daughters. James Turner was a partner in the firm, James Turner & Co., one of the largest wholesale grocery companies in Canada. He was president of the Hamilton Board of Trade, vice-president of the Bank of Hamilton, member of the Senate, and a trustee of MacNab Street Presbyterian Church from its establishment in 1854. The Turner estate was "Highfield" near Aberdeen and Bay streets (*DHB* 1:200-01). Their daughter Carrie's marriage took place in October 1887 (2511).

133 Mrs. Anna (Annie) Ross was the principal of the "Presbyterian Ladies' College" where Ruby was a teacher. She had previously been the first superintendent of the "Ewart Missionary Training Home" in Toronto, a missionary and deaconess training school (1897-1899) (McNeill 150; Brouwer 62). She was very supportive of the WFMS movement, writing letters of encouragement and giving addresses and Bible readings to the groups (Buttrum 5, 7; A72-5765). Anna Ross's daughters, Jean and Eleanor, were teachers at the college also. Her son, David, proposed marriage to Ruby in 1906 (see A65-5622) The Rosses visited frequently and are often mentioned in the letters. For Mrs. Ross and the Wilkie affair, see "Wilkie" note below (A32-4713; A37-4815; A65-5622; A66-5630; A71-5744; A72-5765; A87-6135; A105-6738).

134 Rev. Dr. John Wilkie (1851-1928) had been a missionary in Indore, Gwalior, India, since 1879. He had supported and cultivated women missionaries for their political (and financial) support of his causes. The missions in India became embroiled in a gender struggle and Wilkie was eventually perceived to be the chief cause of the troubles. For a quarter century he had undermined any other authority (male or female) that conflicted with his own. His tactics were manipulative and "transparently self-serving." The rumours abounded as he attempted to rally the WFMS behind him, but his object was to maintain control of the money they raised. He managed to convince Mrs. Ross for a time. Ruby wrote from the Ottawa Ladies' College: "Mrs. Ross is going to show me Mr. Wilkie's statement ... there is going to be a great disclosure but Mr. Wilkie's innocence will be proved. It is one great fakehood about his taking opium" (4643). Mr. Wilkie accused Miss Sinclair of "dancing" and Miss Sinclair and others accused him of taking drugs. Ultimately, documented accusations of his addiction to "pernicious drugs" caused his removal in 1902, after which time the breach between men and women missionaries was healed and separate spheres were created in missionary politics. Wilkie returned to Jhansi in north India to establish an independent mission in 1904, where he worked until his death. He was the founder of Indore College (BDKC 248). When Church Union took place in 1925, the United Church declined to retain Wilkie because he was "reputed to be so difficult" (Brouwer 130-61; McNeill 124-5; Thomson 69; Moir, *Enduring* 230; A49-5172; A50-5199; MCP1-1.28).

135 Miss Jean Sinclair (1866-?) had been a teacher volunteer, then completed the Women's Medical Missionary Society course in Kingston and was sent to Central India in 1888 at the age of twenty-two. She worked with Wilkie in Gwalior and was one of the women embroiled for several years in the gender conflict. She suffered his false accusations and finally denounced him for his betrayal. Mary came to her defence at a conference in May 1904 and Sinclair was vindicated, (see A49-5172). (A50-5199; MCP 1-1.28; Brouwer 99, 103, 185.) (See Wilkie A30-4651n; and Oliver A49-5172).

136 In "The Tatler," Calvin wrote "The Passing of the Sword." He lamented its "discardment" from the "scene of active warfare," as the loss of an "emblem of civilized warfare," and the chivalric and sterling qualities of bravery, skill, courage, and "trueness of eye and hand." Also, in another item about magazines: "British vs. American Periodicals," Calvin debated their relative worth for Canadian readers and noted the elements of "imperial sentiment" in the British, contrasted with the "superior attractiveness" of the American (*Montreal Herald*, 20 September 1902).

137 Col. John McCrae (1872-1918), medical officer and poet, was "very high up in Guelph recruiting" in 1916 (A121-6951). He also served in the South African War. John (Jack) McCrae graduated as an M. D. in 1903 (4988). He was the "author of the war's one deathless poem, 'In Flanders Fields' [and] was the son of a prominent [Presbyterian] elder" (McNeill 268). "He died of pneumonia at the hospital of which he was in charge in 1918.... His birthplace in Guelph is now a historic site" (CE 1258). His poem was preserved by Lt. Col. W. R. Marshall, who sent it to William Hendrie with a handwritten notation: "I thought this v good written by one of our men [sic]" (*DHB* 2:100). Geills McCrae (likely a sister) married Mr. Kilgour, a lawyer in Brandon (see A60-5464).

138 Tom became an expert marksman in the militia in the summer of 1902 (A17-4436; A25-4582; Best 8).

139 A distance of at least eleven city blocks each way.

140 In the "Tatler" article on General William Booth (1829-1912) Calvin reported on Booth's visit to Montreal, where he met and interviewed him. Calvin noted that Booth was the English religious leader and founder of the Salvation Army, and was "the greatest modern apostle of practical Christianity.... At seventy-four years of age, with him as with Moses of old, his eye is not dim, neither is his natural force abated" (*Montreal Herald*, 25 October 1902, Box 13-037). In the "Tatler" article on the Canadian books Calvin gave lengthy reviews of three books: *The Life of Lord Strathcona* by Beckles Willson, *The Fight with France for North America* by A. G. Bradley, and *Maids and Matrons of New France* (1902) by Mary Sifton Pepper, all published by George N. Morank & Co. Ltd (*Montreal Herald*, 18 October 1902, Box 13-036). A copy of the latter is in the Whitehern library.

141 Mrs. McLellan Scott of 88 Bay Street South, two blocks from Whitehern, was a member of the WFMS (Latoszek 25).

142 I have found no record that Calvin wrote a women's column at the *Herald*, although he had done so at the Toronto *Evening News* in 1901 (See 4415n).

143 The "Protest" took the form of a petition headed: "RE THE LIQUOR ACT 1902: We, the undersigned, actively engaged in business in the Province of Ontario are of the opinion that 'The Liquor Act,' which is to be submitted to the people on December 4, 1902 next, is an unwise and impracticable measure, since it permits importation in any quantity from other provinces and countries and would, therefore merely transfer the drinking of intoxicants from licensed and well-regulated places to unlicensed and disreputable resorts and to the homes of the people. We believe that this measure would be detrimental to the best interests, both moral and commercial, of this province, and we therefore urge all voters to mark their ballots 'NO.'"

The petition was then signed by more than fifty names of Hamilton banks, industries, and their presidents or managers, such as The Bank of Hamilton, Hendrie & Co., George Tuckett, Balfour & Co., Dalley, Glassco, Mewburn, Teetzel, "AND MANY

MORE" (*Hamilton Spectator*, 29 November 1902). The "stringent" aspect of the "law" stipulated that a majority vote required that "those in the affirmative must exceed ½ of those who voted in the Provincial general election of 1898 … [e.g.] 212, 723" (*Hamilton Evening Times*, 27 November 1902).

144 The letter did not appear. The *Hamilton Spectator*, 2 December 1903, commented: "The *Spectator* is again deluged today with prohibition and anti-prohibition letters, for which we cannot afford the space." I have found no reference in the *Hamilton Evening Times*, and the *Hamilton Herald* is not available on microfilm for this period.

145 Angus H. MacGillivray (?-1919), Knox College class of 1899, was a pastor in Newmarket, Chatham, and Hamilton, and was a chaplain during the war (BDKC 156).

146 Rev. Dr. Fletcher was sixty-nine years of age. Mary was not pleased with his preaching and was eager to replace him. Fletcher was loath to step down and Mary grew impatient with him (A37-4815;A38-4835;A43-5012;A47-MCP 1-3a.56). The church deficit was a factor and Mary felt that a new and more popular minister would make the church prosper.

147 For Gillies Eadie, see 4605.

148 Ruby's letter to Calvin dated approximately 3 December 1902 also describes the family's poverty at Christmas 1902, and advises that the family should not "spend any money on each other this year." Ruby also notes that she will be minus six weeks pay and "there will be only about $20—however it will help us along" (4263). On 14 January, 1903, Ruby again wrote to Calvin: "It is worrying to think … but I felt that as long as the College went on I'd stick by…. But I can't afford to be out of a job & it is hard to know what to do. But don't let it bother you old fellow. A number of new pupils are coming in Feb…. I didn't let the mither [sic] know to add to other things. I do my best & it isn't my fault that the College had a big debt before I came" (4730). In 1904, Calvin comments to his mother on a family that is "more poverty stricken than our family" (MCP 2-3b.51).

149 Mr. And Mrs. Robert Moncur lived at 222 Bay Street South. Mrs. Robert Moncur was a member of the MacNab WFMS (Latoszek 25; Tyrell 150). "Old Mrs. Moncur" may have been Helen Moncur who "died at her brother's residence on Bay Street" in March 1909 (6383b).

150 Hilda had requested the return of her photo from Kenelm Trigge (see A28-4635).

151 The MacNab WFMS had also discussed the idea of giving a lunch but it was deferred for further discussion (WFMS "Minutes," 2 December 1902). The "Scotch Lunch" at Central was reported in the *Spectator* as A Most Successful Affair at Central Church Schoolroom…. The attendance was exceedingly large…. The young ladies decorated according to their individual tastes and the effect was varied, beautiful and harmonious. The platform was covered with palms…. Duncan Campbell piped, and the guests bought bouquets of heather. The article also described each sale table, named the members of the various committees, and listed the "officers of the Ladies Aid Society" (*Hamilton Spectator*, 4 December 1902).

    The coloured windows at Central Church were installed but destroyed in the fire of June 1906 (see A63-5512.) When the church was rebuilt in 1908, the "features of the new church included beautiful stained glass windows," donated by parishioners (Bailey, *Wee Kirks* 54).

152 The *Hamilton Herald* for this period is not available on microfilm.

153 On the day of the election, 4 December 1902, the *Hamilton Spectator* reported: "WILL ONTARIO BE WET OR DRY? The referendum fight is on all over the province. Liquor men and temperance workers are facing each other and are striving with the people to gain victory…. The dispensers of hard drinks know all the tricks that are worth knowing in connection with the getting out and the manipulating of the vote…. On the other hand the temperance people are without this fine organization. They have not the money…. There was talk of the plugging game being worked along with that of the impersonator."

The women's participation was noted: "One of the pleasant features of the day to the workers was the mid-day remembrance from the W.C.T.U. The ladies are not allowed to vote, but they did the next best thing—they sent hampers to every polling division for the refreshment of the workers of both sides." On 5 December the same paper reported: "The liquor trade has apparently won a victory. That is, through the trickery of Hon. Mr. Ross in imposing an impossible task upon the prohibitionists, [they] have been held in check by a body of men of much less numerical strength. Indeed, the prohibitionists are well entitled to proclaim a victory inasmuch as they polled two votes to the liquor man's one." Rev. T. Albert Moore stated: "All over the Province, the result makes it imperative that we should demand more restrictions on the traffic, with a view to getting rid of the bar-rooms and treating evils."

154 The WFMS made a special effort to convert the "Jews" and other immigrants in Hamilton and elsewhere. Mary was vice-president of the Jewish Mission, which conducted classes for all immigrants (4847). "The women instructed the newcomers in the English language, British social mores and Christianity" (*DHB* 3:6). Mary also tried to find work for the immigrants: "This morning I spent trolling from one end of the city to the other looking for work for a Jew" (5245; A50-5199; A53-MCP 1-1.25).

155 William Alexander (Leander) Logie (Hon. Justice in 1909, colonel/major/brigadier-general) became James Chisholm's law partner after Isaac McQuesten's death in 1888. In 1909 Logie also formed a partnership with Thomas B. McQuesten when Thomas joined his father's old law firm. Logie attended MacNab Street Presbyterian Church. He was also a founding member with James Chisholm and J. R. Moodie (and others) of the 91st Highland Regiment in 1903, later the Argyll and Sutherland Highlanders. He was the first commanding officer and served with them in World War One. He lived at 77 Markland Street with his wife (nee Wylie) and daughter, in 1900 (*DHB* 3.19, 28, 33; Best 26; Tyrell 147; Campbell 204; A117-6805, A119-6828, A122-6967).

156 Dr. White and May Cameron were married in January 1902 in Toronto (A20-4521).

157 Miss Jessie A. Proudfoot was the unmarried daughter of Hon. William Proudfoot (1823-1903), Isaac McQuesten's law (and drinking) partner (Best 2, 5). He was a justice of the High Court of Ontario 1874-90 and was professor of law and vice-chancellor at University of Toronto (*DHB* 1:166; *DHB* 3:5). The Proudfoots were members of MacNab Street Church. Proudfoot had been widowed since 1878 and lived with his daughter Miss Jessie Proudfoot and Miss Sydney Stevenson at 3 Queen's Park Crescent Toronto, in 1900. For William Proudfoot's death in August 1903, see A49-5172 (Tyrell 98; 5074). For Stevenson, see A49-5172.

William Proudfoot's deceased brother, Rev. Dr. John J. A. Proudfoot, had been a theology professor for thirty-five years and was "one of the leading lights at Knox College" (Moir, *Called* 30). Their father, Rev. William Proudfoot (1788-1851) had also been a theology professor from 1844 (the year that Knox was founded) until his death (Moir, *Enduring* 117-18, 84-5; *Called* 23-30). He had come to Canada as a missionary and was a founding member of the Presbyterian Church in Ontario. In the 1830s he had been a circuit rider in the Gore District, preaching the "worde of God" [sic] to the "depraved patrons" of the hostelries (Johnston 89). He also "walked to Goderich and back, gathering groups of worshippers along the way" (*Wee Kirks* 40). He was a "tireless traveller whose voluminous diaries and letters provide an invaluable record, not merely of his own and the presbytery's work, but of the religious and social history of western Upper Canada during the 1830's" (Moir, *Enduring* 84-85; A2-4283; A17-4436; A49-5172; A130-7018; A48-MCP 3-5.11).

158 Since Calvin's articles are unsigned, it is difficult to identify "the scraps" with certainty. However, his column, "The Tatler" of 24 January had five articles: The first, "Ralph and de Blowitz," is a tribute to "two of the greatest journalists" who had recently died. M. de Blowitz, originator of the editorial dispatch, wrote for the *London Times* and "showed a rare instinct for humanity and drama." Julian Ralph wrote about the "war

office and council chamber with the mind of a statesman and a strategist." The second article, "How J. J. Hill Left School," is an anecdote about the railroad king and his schoolmaster, "Rev. Dr. Wetherald, father of Miss Wetherald, the well known Canadian poetess." The third article, "Maori M.P.'s" records the election of four Maoris to political office in New Zealand, who "are now a superior and well-educated class." One MP, Hone Heke, was a descendent of a fighting and fanatical Maori chief who had opposed British colonization and "drove them into the sea." The fourth article, "A Curious Survival," recounts the survival of an ancient custom at Newcastle-on-Tyne in which the mayor presented an ancient coin to each of the judges on circuit. The coins were "a jacobus and a carolus," with which they were to purchase daggers to protect themselves through the border country which was "infested by the Scots." The fifth article, "A Leonine Epidemic," concerns the ranchers of northern Montana who were driven to desperation by the losses of their stock to mountain lions. The lions were trapped in a mountain basin and "then picked off by marksmen." Calvin also included questions from readers about history and literature, and replied in detail and with humour (Box 13-050).

159 Eva Booth was the daughter of Edwin Thomas Booth (1833-93), an American actor who toured with a Shakespearean company in America, Britain, and Germany. He was the son of Junius Brutus Booth, actor and brother of John Wilkes Booth, who assassinated Abraham Lincoln (*CBD* 179).

160 Mrs. Merrill had been renting the houses at 1 and 3 Bold Street from Mary. Mrs. Hill had taken over the rental and the renovations were being done to the boarding houses (see A16-4425).

161 Mary is frequently outspoken in her assessment of preachers (A37-4815; A38-4835; A58-5382; A64-5596).

162 Mrs. Evel was likely Jessie Gay, the wife of James Joseph Evel (1849-1932), founder of the Evel Casket Co. and a director of Mercury Mills. They lived at 51 Stanley Avenue. Evel and his wife worked with Mrs. Lyle and others to found the Hamilton Sanatorium, and the Evel Pavilion is named after him. Evel also helped to found the Hamilton Health Association and was president for twenty-five years (see A17-4436). The Evels were members of Central Presbyterian Church where he was an elder. He was a 33rd degree Mason (*DHB* 3:47-48).

163 Mary Murray Hendrie was the second wife of William Hendrie (1831-1906), prominent Hamilton industrialist, contractor, and horse breeder. He had eight children from his first marriage and three children from the second (five sons and six daughters). He was on the executive of many businesses, including president of the Toronto, Grey and Bruce Railway, Ontario Cotton Co., Hamilton Bridge, and director of Hamilton Gas Co., Canada Life Assurance Co., and the Bank of Hamilton. The Hendries lived at "Holmstead," 57 Bold Street, which was the site of several state occasions and the entertaining of royalty. They were active in the affairs of Central Presbyterian Church, where he was a trustee (*DHB* 1:101; Tyrell 142). Hendrie's eldest son, Sir John Strathearn Hendrie (1857-1923), was the lieutenant-governor of Ontario from 1914 to 1919 (*DHB* 2:63-66; A87-6135). Mary again comments on Mrs. Hendrie in May 1915: "They had a delightful time at the Wentworth Historical Exec. This morning when Mrs. Gov. Hendrie appeared with a letter, which suggested that she should give up presidentship to someone in the city. Mrs. Gates confessed to the letter and there was a great uproar" (6849). See also A47-MCP1-3a.56.

164 For the Donald Fletcher family, see A18-4479. For the Colin Fletcher family, see A28-4635. Calvin had written to Mrs. Colin Fletcher (Anna Agur) on the death of her brother, Mr. Agur (7380, 2 January 1903).

165 Mrs. Irving (nee Fletcher) was visiting her brother, Rev. Dr. Donald Fletcher, at the manse, 116 MacNab Street South (Tyrell 137). Mrs. Irving and her children, Katie and Tom (son or cousin), lived in St. Mary's where Mary visited them in July 1902 (A26-4588). Mrs. Irving had witnessed the signing of Mary's will in February 1902 (4568).

Mrs. Irving had married Dr. Irving (M.D.) in 1880 and he died suddenly in 1901 (A15-4415; A26-4588; A39-4863; A69-5709; A88-6173).

166 This is likely a reference to an article Calvin had written about fox-hunting on snow-shoes: "Snow-Shoers Follow the Hounds" (8108). It is typewritten and dated Montreal, Quebec, 25 February [1903]. It describes the sporting event as a "novel idea" which occurred at Le Montagnard Snow-Shoe Club "last Saturday." He claimed that "it is by no means extraordinary" that good snow-shoers could cover five miles in thirty-seven minutes, and in soft snow conditions could "hold their own in a race with a pack of hounds." Fifty members participated and kept up for a time, but after eight or ten miles of plunging over rail fences and into creeks, the scent was lost. Then the huntsmen started on the run home to the Canadian Hunt Club where they were hosted and "over the bounteous supper congratulated each other upon the discovery of so fascinating a sport and plotted the outwitting of Brer fox." I have been unable to find the published article; it may have appeared elsewhere than in the *Montreal Herald* (A36-4810). Mary commented in her letter of 12 March 1903: "Tom is daring me that the next thing you will do is 'to play the races.' The Sporting spirit will seize you before I know where you are" (4821).

167 Tom was president of the Zetes (Zeta Psi) fraternity (Best 8).

168 Mrs. Francis B. (McCord) Whittemore and her children, Miss Penrose, Harry, and Frank, lived at 133 Bloor Street East, Toronto, in 1900 (Tyrell 120). In 1908 Mrs. Whittemore and some of her family lived near Ruby McQuesten in Calgary and may have been there for the same rest cure which was later diagnosed as tuberculosis (6203). "Reggie" may have been a middle name for Frank. On 19 September 1907, Harry married Miss Florence Haworth (Florrie or Flossie), daughter of Mr. and Mrs. George F. Haworth (nee Yates) of 199 Bloor Street East (Tyrell 61) (5970; A82-5990). Others mentioned in the letters are Henry and Holton (A38-4835; A39-4863; A41-4963; A49-5172; A82-5990; A88-6173; A135-7095).

The fate of the Whittemores' husband and father is unknown; however, he was possibly Dr. J. H. Whittemore, Dr. Calvin Brooks McQuesten's classmate at medical school at Dartmouth College in New Hampshire (CMQPW Sec. 5). Dr. Whittemore and a mutual friend, Dr. George O. Moody, wrote several letters to Dr. Calvin Brooks from Ireland, Germany, Austria, Italy, London, and Boston, where they were studying medicine from 1871-72 and in 1877. They described their travels and studies in the various medical centres in Europe and encouraged Dr. Calvin Brooks to join them, but he did not do so (1256; 1274; 1321; 1327).

169 A Dr. Arnott was consulted for Edna and Ruby. He may have become the family doctor after Dr. Mullin's death in 1899, although Heurner Mullin was attending for a time also (A92-6343). However in the next letter Dr. Clark was summoned for Edna's emotional breakdown (A59-5426).

170 Mrs. A. W. Leitch was a member of the MacNab WFMS for 16 years , secretary for 8 years. Her husband was an elder. They lived at 144 Herkimer Street (Latoszek 25; A38-4835; A40-4902; A47-MCP1-3a.56; A91-6336).

171 David Ross's job involved selling photographs ("Views").

172 Edwin Arthur Henry (1866-1938) was pastor at Brandon, Manitoba, from 1895 to 1902, and at Knox Church in Hamilton from 1902 to 1906 (*BDKC* 101).

173 The Palace Rink, a vaudeville theatre, had been converted from a livery stable and a roller skating rink. It stood at 24-26 Jackson Street West very near Whitehern at 41 Jackson Street West. Daughter Mary also describes the fire: "I do wish you could have seen the Palace Rink 'hop the twig.' I can tell you it was a magnificent sight, no smoke simply red flames" (4855). The Palace Rink and the Star Theatre (on Merrick Street) both provided vaudeville shows every night and Saturday afternoons with singers, dancers and comedy sketches. The *Spectator*, 12 December 1892, reviewed a popular act of male impersonators: "Cort's Cosmopolitan Comedy Co. is the attraction at this popular and cosy place of amusement this week. The company is headed by the great

Hindle, a male impersonator. This lady, or gentleman, is a curiosity in her or his way, she (or he) having been married at one time to Vivian, the celebrated English comique, and since his death, according to the American papers, has been married to a woman" (HPL, Pamphlet File, Weaver). These impersonators likely provided the inspiration for Calvin's pseudonym of "Nina Vivian" for the women's column that he wrote for the *Toronto News* (see A15-4415n).

174 This was likely the family of John Gartshore (?-1906?), of Eglinton Avenue in Toronto (5151), close friends of the McQuestens who visited often and with whom they vacationed together at "Willow Bank," Eglinton, or at Lake Simcoe. They are frequently mentioned in the letters. John was one of the three sons of John Gartshore (1810-73), a pioneer industrial baron in the foundry business in the 1830s and 1840s at the same time that Dr. Calvin McQuesten established his foundry in Hamilton. Gartshore established the Gartshore foundry in Dundas in 1838, and moved to Toronto to establish the Toronto Car Wheel Co. in 1869, which he ran with his son John until his death. Another son, Alexander (1839-1904), remained in the foundry business in Dundas, and then moved to Hamilton in 1870 as Gartshore and Cowrie (later, Canada Pipe Foundry and Gartshore-Thomson Pipe and Foundry (for Thomson, see A15-4415). Alexander married Isobel King Hendrie in 1866. They lived at "Ravelston," 50 Robinson Street, had five children, and attended Central Presbyterian Church. A third son, William Moir, became mayor of London, Ontario (*DHB* 1:80; *DHB* 2:56; Tyrell 138; A37-4815; A40-4902; A42-4977; A43-5012; A63-5512; A67-5654).

175 This letter is in response to Calvin's letter to his mother on the anniversary of his father's death (7 March 1888). That letter is not extant.

176 These are possibly John Alexander Wilson (1872-1935), who graduated from Knox College in 1903, and was ordained in Hamilton in 1904, and Robert James Wilson (1872-1941), who graduated from Knox College in 1903, and was ordained at Westminster in 1903 (*BDKC* 251-52).

177 Samuel Thomas Martin, (1877-1946) graduated from Knox College in 1903, and was ordained in September 1903 (*BDKC* 144).

178 Frederick William Anderson (1871-1954) was at Knox College (1897-99, 1902-03), was ordained in Paris in 1904, went to Winnipeg (1903-04), and was pastor in various churches in Ontario and British Columbia (*BDKC* 4). Anderson did require a rest cure. He wrote to Calvin from Clifton Springs Sanitarium, New York, 12 June 1902, where he was "planning to rusticate and vegetate as much as possible." He had been "working beyond [his] strength" and was "broken down in health" and unable to go to India as a missionary (A37-4815; A40-4902; A97-6446).

179 This was likely James C. Thomson (?-1909), cousin of the "Amisfield" Thomsons (see A15-4415n). He and his wife lived at 201 Bay Street Street in 1900 with their son James A. and daughter Janet (Tyrell 157). James was vice-president and manager of Gartshore-Thomson Pipe Co. and his son James A. was superintendent (*VDCH* 1904; for Gartshore, see A37-4815). Mary noted his death: "James Thomson, Joe's cousin the manager of our church died to-day. He had been sent to Bermuda but left and consulted a New York doctor who told him he was free of tuberculosis & would last long, that is only ten days ago. We all thought so much of his wife & three little children" (22 February 1909, 6359). The *Hamilton Spectator* gives no obituary, simply, "James Thompson of 70 West Avenue South age 46."

180 This was likely Dr. William Barclay (?-1969) from Kirkcudbright, Scotland, who may have been in Hamilton assisting Dr. Samuel Lyle. Years later, in 1926, he accepted the urgent call to the empty pulpit at Central after the abrupt resignation of Dr. Sedgewick and helped to heal the wounds of Church Union. He was chaplain of the Argyll and Sutherland Highlanders during World War II and moderator of the general assembly in 1940. He wrote a history of Central, *A Century of Beginnings* (1941) (*POH* 56; *Wee Kirks* 55; Moir, *Enduring* 242).

181 The letter from Tom is not extant, but an example of Tom's letters to his mother on the anniversary of his father's death forms the epigraph to the section "Mary Baker McQuesten's Widowhood and Matriarchy" in Part One (5440; see also A75-MCP 2-4.37a).

182 In "The Tatler" of 7 March 1903, Calvin wrote "The Social Burden," a criticism of formal entertaining and the demands it makes on both men and women who "are wearing themselves out in the frenzied pursuit of pleasures which do not please and recreations which fail to recreate." In "A Curious Religious Colony" Calvin reported on a bizarre sect in New Mexico in the 1850s begun by Julian Ericson after a break with Joseph Smith and the Mormons. The disciples believed in the transmigration of the souls of the faithful while yet on earth. Believers were promised that they would be changed into the animal or bird of their choice, and each of the frame houses in the colony was built with a cage or den suitable to the needs of the particular animal they expected shortly to become. Ericson and some of his disciples were killed in a battle with the Apaches "and the stronger of the cages, those erected for the would-be tiger men and lion women, were afterward utilized for a brief period as places of confinement for refractory converts" (*Montreal Herald*, 7 March 1903; Box 13-056).

183 Walter "went into the Bank of Hamilton" in April 1903 (4885).

184 Many of the family letters of this period are concerned with the problem of convincing Rev. Dr. Fletcher to retire gracefully. He was seventy years of age and was planning to "hold on for two more years" (4847, 4855). It is likely that Wilson and Anderson both declined, but Dr. Fletcher found an assistant, John David Cunningham, in April 1903.

John David Cunningham (1870-1952) became assistant at McNab Church for 1903-04. He was a graduate student in Edinburgh 1904-06, pastor in Welland 1906-26, and professor at Knox College until retirement in 1944 (*BDKC* 49; A40-4902; A49-5172; A51-5233)

185 There are two books in the Whitehern library on the history of Bedford, New Hampshire, dated 1851 and 1908.

186 "The Bard" was William Murray of Hamilton (see A101-6636).

187 "Annie" is possibly Annie (Agur) Fletcher, Mrs. Irving's sister-in-law and Katie's aunt.

188 Robert Roswell Gamey (1865-1917) was a politician, mining speculator, insurance agent, and Conservative MPP for Manitoulin from 1902 to 1917. "In 1903 he brought against the [Liberal] Ross government charges of bribery and corruption which caused a great sensation, and were partly responsible for the defeat of the government" (*MDCB* 288). The *Montreal Herald* carried the full account of the Royal Commission hearings, which lasted through April and June 1903, and prompted Mary to comment "The Gamey case is beyond me, I cannot afford time to wade through it" (4885). Some of the reporting was likely done by Calvin after his "Tatler" column disappeared with the 28 March issue. The accounts contain verbatim testimony in which Mr. Gamey accused the Hon. J. R. Stratton and other members of the Liberal government of bribery and other forms of corruption to gain his support. It involved large sums of money ($6,000), mysterious parcels delivered anonymously, falsified bank deposits, forgeries, names of members who could be "bought," hidden witnesses and clandestine meetings in the "Piano Factory Episode," "patronage," "mining schemes," "timber concessions," and railroad subsidies. Serious charges were, in turn, laid against Gamey and he was in danger of being "prosecuted for forgery, larceny and mutilation of evidence" (21 April). He disappeared but a reporter discovered him at a "Buffalo Chop House" (22 April). It was finally disclosed that both sides were involved when Frank Sullivan admitted that "Gamey was playing me and I was playing him" (24 April). On 25 April the paper reported that J. P. Whitney came out in support of Gamey and predicted that "the Conservative party had its foot upon the threshold of the Government of the Province." Finally, on 5 June, the Commission "decided that the evidence exonerates Mr. Stratton, the accused, and compromises Mr. Gamey, the accuser." However, Gamey was not expelled and Premier Ross said that he had "no intention of

making him a martyr" (5 June). He was censured (27 June) but held his seat until his death. Nevertheless, the damage was done and Ross's Liberal government fell to Whitney's (and Gamey's) Conservatives at the next election.

Tom, at university at the time, made daily visits to the legislature to witness the workings of government, which he also reported to his mother. The McQuestens were staunch Liberals so when the government fell Mary remarked: "Woe! woe for the Liberals! It is a sad record this morning. And I do dislike Whitney so much. Mrs. Mullin thinks he looks like a Jew, and I think he is like a down East Yankee" (6151, 9 June 1908).

189   Sir Hector Archibald MacDonald, (1853-1903) served with distinction in Egypt, the Sudan, Punjab, and in South Africa, leading to the relief of Kimberly and to the surrender of Boer generals (*WBD* 940).

190   For Lord Roberts and his writings, see A17-4436.

191   Sir Horatio Gilbert Parker (1862-1932), Canadian journalist, author, dramatist, and poet, is best known for his historical novels that introduced French Canadians and the North-West to English literature, such as *Pierre and His People* (1892) and *Carnac* (1922). He settled in England from 1890, became MP for Gravesend (1900-18), organized British propaganda directed at the United States during World War One, and supported British imperialism. He published more than thirty books, notably: *Donovan Pasha* (1902), *The Weavers* (1907), and *The Power and the Glory* (1925). *The Seats of the Mighty* (1896), set in old Quebec, became an international best-seller. Horizon Canada lists him among prominent Canadian authors: "Parker, Connor, Montgomery, Service and Leacock topped the best-seller lists year after year until the 1920s" (*HC* 1614, 210; *MDCB* 647). In Parker's letter to William Thompson from Geneva 10 January 1899 (which came into Calvin's possession, likely at Copp-Clark) Parker wrote: "I think it would be wise to answer in your advertisements (and to inform separate [?] in the newspapers (to the same effect) that 'over 50,000 copies of *The Battle of the Strong* have been sold in England & America in less than three months.' Already over 30,000 copies have been sold in United States alone." Five of Parker's books are in the Whitehern library.

192   John Wilson (Johnny) Bengough, a political cartoonist (1851-1923), was one of the first substantial figures in editorial cartooning. He edited his own magazine, *Grip*, for twenty-one years from 1873, in which he provided a lively portrayal of Canadian politicians. He was a social radical who satirized utopian ideals such as communalism, vegetarianism, and prohibition, and was a "much-loved-but-little-listened-to public scold" in his popular lectures called "chalk-talks." His *Caricature History of Canadian Politics* (2 vols., 1886) is in the Whitehern library. It was reprinted in 1974. Bengough's papers were donated to McMaster University by J. B. Elven, "a relative" and administrator at McMaster from 1903 to 1949 (*DHB* 4:28-29; *HC* 203, 375-76; *MDCB* 58).

193   *The Blue Flower* (1902) by Henry Van Dyke and five other of his works are in the Whitehern library. *The Source* is not.

194   Tom took the job in the lumber camp (see A42-4977).

195   I. P. Buchanan, at Cornell University, was likely a grandson of either Isaac Buchanan or his elder brother Peter (*DHB* 1.31).

196   The missionaries in India became involved in "rescue work" during the famines of 1880-1900 (Brouwer 119-20).

197   In the 21 March "Tatler" article, "Is Britain Indifferent to Canada?" Calvin argued for British postal concessions to encourage British periodical literature in the Colonies and especially in Canada, where the American magazines "by their attractiveness threaten to monopolize the whole field." A second article compared British and American yachts and found them "drawing nearer together in speed ... the element of uncertainty which is the soul of sport is peculiarly large this year." In the "Questions and Answers" section he replied to an inquiry about the "Cost of Horse vs. Motor" and provided an itemized list showing that the annual cost of a gasoline motor vehicle is $2,300.50 and the horse and vehicle is $2,780.00. He also commented on a wide range

of subjects including, "A Hostile Critic on Kipling," "Early decay of teeth," and "Happiness and Friendship" (*Montreal Herald*, 21 March 1903; Box 13-058). Calvin's "Tatler" column disappeared from the *Montreal Herald* after the March 28, 1903 edition, likely because of his increased workload caused by the Street Railway Strike (see A41-4963; Box 13-059). He continued to write for the paper until September 1903 when he tendered his resignation because of a "threatened breakdown." Even though his articles are unsigned, his style and "voice" are sometimes recognizable.

198 Sir William Mortimer Clark (1836-1917), lieutenant-governor of Ontario (1903-08), succeeded the Hon. Sir Oliver Mowat who died on 20 April, after thirty years in office. Clark married Helen "Daisy" Gordon in 1866 and they had two daughters, likely "Jean and Elsie," and one son, Gordon, who died in 1902 (see A20-4521; A24-4549). Clark was born and educated in Scotland and came to Canada and became a writer to the signet in 1859. He was admitted to the bar in Canada (Q.C. 1887), created a knight bachelor in 1907, and was chairman of the board of Knox College from 1880 until his death. He was on the Foreign Missions Committee (FMC) (Brouwer 24; MDCB 158; Tyrell 39; A20-4521; A24-4549; A49-5172). Mrs. Clark was likely related to Mrs. MacKay, who was also a Gordon, and Mary wrote condolences to both at Gordon Clark's death. Mary had dinner with the Clarks at Government House during the WFMS conference in Toronto in 1904 (A49-5172).

199 Mary's grudging acknowledgement of Clark's appointment was echoed by an editorial in the *Montreal Herald*, which may have been written by Calvin: "It can scarcely be looked upon as other than a tribute to the important position which the Scotch Presbyterians hold in the affairs of that province. For while Mr. Clark's high standing in his profession, his dignity of manner, his recognized ability and unimpeachable integrity contribute to make him worthy of the position and equal to any demands that may be made upon him, his elevation cannot but be looked upon as remarkable, in view of the fact that he has never taken any active part in political life."

The editorial concludes with a glowing tribute to Clark's wife: "In view of the preponding part which social duties play in the ordinary routine of a Lieutenant-Governor's life, Mr. Mortimer Clark must be considered unusually fortunate in having a wife with unusual talents for the exercising of hospitality. Mrs. Clark, as all those who enjoy the pleasure of her acquaintance know, combines a stateliness of manner and a kindly cordiality to an extent which is as rare as it is charming. And she may be counted on to perform the duties of a vice-regal hostess in a way that will do credit to herself, her husband and the country" (25 April 1903).

200 A large heart-shaped garden graces the front entrance to Whitehern. Mary had reshaped the original circle into a heart in memory of her husband, Isaac. The heart is in keeping with the Victorian trend to cookie-cutter shapes and is bordered by a walk which converges at the front entrance. Today the heart is a rose garden and contains the yellow hybrid rose developed by White Rose nurseries and dedicated to Thomas B. McQuesten. MacNab Church purchased 200 of these rose bushes and donated seven to Whitehern in memory of the seven McQuesten children. Mary loved the gardens and provides seasonal commentary in the letters (A40-4902; A43-5012; A87-6135). Rev. Calvin McQuesten kept a garden diary from 1918 to 1933 (8296-8421). A study of the garden was done by James C. Haaf in 1987: "Whitehern, A Horticultural Perspective, 1853-85, Dr. Calvin McQuesten's Garden: 'Willowbank'." He notes that there are thirty-five books in the Whitehern library devoted to horticulture. The letters and other writings have assisted in the authentic maintenance of the garden.

201 The book by J. M. Surrie is not in the Whitehern library.

202 Sir Oliver Mowat (1820-1903), lieutenant-governor of Ontario (1872-96), died on 19 April 1903. He was Sir John A. Macdonald's first articled law student and one of the Fathers of Confederation. He was knighted in 1892, and "under Mowat's leadership Ontario came of age economically, politically and socially" (CE 1400).

203 Mary is referring to Ken Trigge's proposal to Hilda, which Hilda rejected at her mother's urging.

204 Montreal suffered general labour unrest from February to May 1903, and Calvin's workload increased. The Street Railway men were demanding a raise to seventeen cents an hour, no more than a ten hour day, promotions from the ranks, and a formal grievance procedure. Electricians were also caught up in the "Strike Fever." After an agreement was settled the company engaged in union-breaking practices and the men went out on strike. the *Montreal Herald*, 23 May, carried the headline: "Montreal is Once More Without a Street Railway Service, and Perhaps Light and Power … less than thirty men reported for work." Threats of violence broke out, the militia was put on guard, and policemen began to accompany some of the cars on their routes. The paper also carried reports of labour unrest in Toronto and in New York, where "American Manufacturers [were] Preparing to Fight Labor Union to Bitter End" and 200,000 men were idle. On 28 May, the paper reported the strike was over and the union had split and reformed.

205 Tom was working at a lumber camp on the Ottawa River (see A42-4977).

206 Tom won the Alexander Mackenzie Scholarship for Political Science in 1903. It brought a small cash prize.

207 Being "starred" represented failure.

208 Rev. Dr. Donald Hugh Fletcher (1833-1912) became moderator of the general assembly of the Presbyterian Church in 1903 (A18-4479; *DHB* 2:49-50).

209 Miss Lerned was related to Dr. Calvin McQuesten's first wife, Margaret Lerned. She lived in Hopkinton, Massachusetts. John Knox McQuesten was living in Bedford, New Hampshire (see A38-4835).

210 James Isaac Buchanan was in business in Pittsburgh.

211 I am unable to identify John Duncan Clarke.

212 Tom was working at the lumber camp on the Ottawa River which he did for the summers of 1903-04. He asked Calvin not to tell his mother about the dangerous work: "I think I will go up the Ottawa this year as a river rat. I will let mama think I am clerking or it will worry her to death" (8160). And again: "I am not letting the Mother know the nature of the work I am doing which is common log-driving. It is pretty hard work for ten hours a day but I will get used to it and the air is fine. The food is enough but very good and that is the most important thing. A person can stand hard work if the food is good. As yet I am not very expert at running on the loose timber but there is not very much danger as the men who are on the whole a fine set of fellows are careful to watch a green hand (8164). The crew too are the wildest looking men. A great many of them are Indians and they are all lousy; Indians and white men both" (8166).

Mary wrote in September 1904: "Tom arrived home … he is literally the colour of mahogany and shows off his muscle with great pride" (5307: A39-4863; Best 9-10).

213 Edna was visiting at the Gartshore's summer home at Roach's Point, Lake Simcoe. Edna and her sister Mary then stayed at Orchard Beach, Lake Simcoe, near the Gartshores, where Mary commented on the social difference between the two vacation spots: "You might call Roach's Point the aristocracy and Orchard Beach the commoners" (5053). Hilda stayed at the Gartshore's in August (5063). Ruby and mother Mary went to Port Carling for their summer vacation in August but found the weather cold and wet (5074). They were near an Indian camp and attended an Indian service (5068). Ruby's letter of 10 August describes the Royal Muskoka Hotel which they visited for an afternoon (5068). While there Mary had to write to Calvin to ask him to send "two dollars or perhaps V" for their "dinners on the way home" (5059, 5 August 1903).

214 For more on Mrs. Hill and the rental houses on Bold Street see A16-4425.

215 In 1903, in honour of his long and distinguished service, Rev. Dr. Donald Fletcher was elected moderator of the General Assembly, and Queen's University conferred on him an honorary D.D. (*DHB* 2:49-50; Johnston 22).

216 On 18 August, Mary wrote to Calvin: "So thankful that Edna's name was in the list of 'passed' in this evening's *Spectator*. In some way it was crowded out of the *Times* and her patience had become exhausted & she was really getting worn out with suspense. You can imagine the wild cheering when Ruby came in with the news that she had passed" (5078).

217 Donald McPhie was chairman of the Board of Managers at the MacNab Street Presbyterian Church from 1893 to 1905 (Johnston 21). Donald McPhie, plumber, had done business with Rev. Thomas Baker between 1876-81 (3996). Stewart Thomson McPhie (1874-1934), architect, was also active in the MacNab Church (A87-6135; *DHB* 3:140; Norman D. McPhie (1878-1977) was treasurer at MacNab Church from 1953 to 65. He was assistant superintendent of the Sunday school, clerk of session for twenty years, became commissioner to the General Assembly in 1950, and was a senior elder until his death.

218 On 2 July 1903 Mary considered purchasing this book: "We have never had George Adam Smith's *Life of Drummond* [1899]. We are thinking of giving him [Tom] something extra as it is his 21st birthday, was not decided. Thought of a pin, but he might lose it, then thought of ebony military brushes. If he goes to Chapter House they would look good on his table, can you suggest anything or which" (5008). This book is in the Whitehern library, as well as Smith's *Wealth of Nations* (1863) and *Essays of A. Smith* (1863).

219 The *Montreal Herald* of 17 August 1903 carried a report of the opening of the "Fifth Congress of Trade Princes of the British Empire" welcomed by Lord Strathcona. Lord Brassey replied, referring to Joseph Chamberlain's proposals for the Empire. Mary wrote on 18 August: "That is a notable Gathering is it not? The British Chamber of Commerce. I was wondering if you were at any of the meetings. I suppose Mr. Brierley himself would be there. Lord Strathcona seems to me to be most remarkable man, (if the papers report him correctly). He seems to be equal to any occasion and his address far superior to Lord Brassey" (5078). Calvin's papers contain a page from the invitation to the banquet: "Plan of Table for Montreal Board of Trade to Delegates to the Fifth Congress of Chambers of Commerce of the Empire, Windsor Hotel, Thursday, August 20, 1903" (8067). The *Montreal Herald* in August 1903 devoted the paper to pictures, biographies, and speeches during the Congress. Lord Strathcona's resolution was adopted by Congress to "strengthen relations" and to "give a substantial advantage" to the trading partners of "the union of the various parts of His Majesty's dominion, based on mutual benefit." There were 500 delegates and a gallery for spectators. An article, possibly by Calvin—"Glimpse of the Traders' Congress"—notes that "the gallery was filled almost entirely with women … the fair visitors," accorded the rival speakers a courteous hearing, and applauded vigorously during a debate on the "fiscal policy of the Empire" (20 August 1903).

220 Sir Wilfrid Laurier (1841-1919) was prime minister from 1896 to 1911 (CBD 866). At the close of the conference Laurier's impassioned speech sought a treaty and a commercial agreement for closer trade relations with the Empire. He paid tribute to all parts of the Empire which enjoyed the "full assurance of the blessings of British equality" and had an "intense desire—to establish closer relations between the Motherland and the colonies." Immediately after the congress, talks began on planning and financing the railway which "would open up to thousands of settlers the great lone land. There were resources there in minerals, timber and agricultural lands … known from the reports of the many explorers" (27 August 1903). Laurier helped to plan the intercontinental railway, the Grand Trunk. On 30 July 1903, the *Montreal Herald* had also reported the full context of Laurier's speech to the Commons (4 pages) on the proposed railroad (G.T.P.) which would continue the line to the Pacific coast and, "in the burning words of the orator," would "bring all parts of our country together in unison to pulsate with one and the same heart."

221 Dr. William P. Caven, physician, lived at 70 Gerrard Street East, Toronto. Mary gave Calvin the doctor's report in her next letter: "Climate had nothing to do with it, but whatever kept your mind easy and happy was the thing for you. He said that newspaper work was the hardest work in the world.... He would take no money for his advice.... I had got a tonic prescription from him." Mary's advice to Calvin was: "In the meantime it seems to me it would be wise for you to come home and thoroughly rest your brains. So as to be ready for any thing & I would like to have you with us for a good visit" (5109). Dr. W. P. Caven was related to Dr. John Caven who knew Isaac "well at college" and examined Ruby in 1908 when Dr. W. P. Caven had "gone back to the old country" (6169). Dr. John Caven and his wife were passengers on the shipwrecked *Republic* in 1909, but were rescued (A91-6336).

Rev. Dr. William Caven (1830-1904) was likely related to William and John Caven. He lived at 76 Spadina Road. He was professor of exegetics and principal at Knox College (1873-1904), convenor of the Committee on Union, and "poured out his soul on behalf of Union." He worked closely with Dr. R. H. Warden and others on Church Union and modernization of the Church, e.g., higher criticism, which Mary did not support (see A52-5283n.) Caven's collected papers are *Christ's Teachings Concerning the Last Things* (1908). This book is not in the Whitehern library (McNeill 37, 79, 251-52; Moir, *Enduring* 182, 189; *MDCB* 142; Tyrell 38; A81-5984; A92-6343; A100-6509).

222 Mary conveyed Dr. Warden's advice to Calvin: "He thought you must consider it well, for to go to the mission field just as a catechist would only be a temporary arrangement and after being engaged so long in the newspaper work it seemed a pity if you could not find something in that line that would not be too much strain. He spoke of the business managerships ... the Westminster was requiring a man to represent them" (5109).

Warden provided a copy of the Mission "Regulations," which listed the salary of a catechist as $5 and board per week for summer and $5.50 for winter (5113).

On 21 September, Rev. Charles W. Gordon also replied to Calvin's inquiry about taking a mission in the West: "I am very sorry to hear of your threatened breakdown, and wish to offer you my earnest sympathy in your trouble. I am not sure whether you would like our work, or whether you would be fitted for it, or whether it would be the thing that would be best for you, but on the whole I feel like recommending you to try it. With this thought in mind I shall give your name to our Committee here, and I think there is reasonable ground to hope that you may be appointed to a mission field in the West. With very kind regards, and wishing you complete recovery and a congenial sphere of labour. Kind regards to your mother" (7439).

223 Calvin wrote a letter of resignation to James S. Brierley, managing director of the *Montreal Herald* on 21 September. Brierley replied: "I trust that your indisposition will be temporary, and that you will soon be in the newspaper harness again, and I hope with the *Herald*. During the two years you have been here, you have shown yourself possessed of very considerable literary ability, of great diligence, and of an earnestness of spirit that quickly won the confidence and respect of all with whom you have been associated" (7438). Calvin accepted a missionary position at Macleod and Standoff, Alberta.

Notes 1904-1908

224 Mary's father, Rev. Thomas Baker, had been the minister of this church.

225 Dr. Fletcher had accepted retirement.

226 Gordon Gibson was likely the son of Sir John Morison Gibson (see A17-4436).

227 William Ewart Gladstone (1809-98), "the great Liberal statesman." He is remembered for his studies in Homer and his political writings, such as *The State in Its Relations with the Church* (1838), *Vaticanism* (1875), and *Gleanings of Past Years* (8 vols., 1879, 1890). John Morley's *Life of William Ewart Gladstone* was published in 1903 (*OCEL* 335). The Whitehern library contains the 1905 edition of the latter in two volumes and *The Vatican Decrees* (1875).

228 This is likely Miss Sydney Stevenson. She and Jessie Proudfoot had lived with Jessie's father until he died in August 1903.

229 This is likely Rev. James MacKay (1879-1940) of Scotland, who attended McGill University (1902-05), Montreal Presbyterian College (1905-06), and Knox College (1906-08), was ordained in Hamilton (1908), and was pastor in Chippawa, Montreal, and London (*BDKC* 132-33).

Tom also criticized MacKay's preaching: "He is a sort of a mess. One of the kind of preachers who uses fine language, deals with vague abstractions, says nothing, but mightily impress most of their hearers and all reporters, simply bull-dogging them by what sounds like a superior education. He is eminently suited to fashionable congregation. Will never set the Thames on fire. One of that sort of minister who begin their prayers with a long intricate simile which they have worked over time to invent and then make a bluff to work it off as if it was spontaneous. That will about hold the Rev. MacKay" (8162, 17 February 1903).

230 Central Church installed an organ in 1875, "the largest in Hamilton," and MacNab installed one in 1877. The introduction of the organ (and of hymns) was heavily debated in the Presbyterian churches from the 1850s to 1900. The objection was later criticized as the "excess of zeal for purity of worship." The organ received several pejoratives such as: "the Kist o' Whustles," [sic], "a prophanation [sic] of a place of worship," ("Memories of MacNab: 1860-1886," William Smith, letter May 2, 1930), and "the instrument of Satan" (John A. Johnston, "The Organ Question" in *Wee Kirks* 205-206). Mary also objected to the installation and use of church bells (see A69-5709). The organ at Central Church was destroyed in the fire of 1906 (see A63-5512). In the new church in 1908 it was replaced by a Casavant organ and was "regarded as one of the most magnificent in Canada" (*Wee Kirks* 56).

231 Possibly, James F. Kerr, son of Alexander Reid Kerr (1835-1900), merchant in dry goods (*DHB* 2:83).

232 Calvin had taken a position as a missionary preacher at Standoff and Slide-out, Alberta (see A50-5199).

233 The occasion was the fiftieth anniversary of MacNab Church which began as a wooden building on the site in 1854. Dr. Calvin McQuesten had donated funds and arranged the financing for the new Free Church (*Wee Kirks* 91; *POH* 77).

234 This is likely Rev. and Mrs. William James Clark (1860-1947), the former a pastor in London, Ontario (1890-1907) (*BDKC*). Mary described him as "a most delightful preacher ... something particularly winning about his way of putting things ... really beautiful" (5157).

235 This is likely Dr. John Pringle, missionary in 1899 to twelve hundred miners in the Klondike, and at Atlin, British Columbia. Moir states: "Pringle made a three-week winter trek to Fort Wrangell, tramping through slush up to his knees, covering only four miles in one six-hour period and eating the netting of his snow shoes to stay alive." He asked the Church to send nurses to the miners and "organized a building bee ... and the result was St. Andrew's Hospital, the first Presbyterian hospital in Canada." He was a very colourful speaker as he travelled about collecting funds for the hospital at Atlin (Moir, *Enduring* 162-63; A50-5199; A92-6343; A97-6446).

236 Mary was attending the WFMS annual meeting in Toronto.

237 Note that these MacKays with whom Mary has been billeted are not related to the Donald MacKays who lived at 5 Queen's Park Crescent, close friends of the McQuestens. These MacKays lived at 84 Madison Avenue, Toronto (5157). However, the Donald MacKays and their two sons also appear in the later part of this letter.

238 For the Wilkie Case, see A30-4651.

239 In January 1904 Mary had reported to Cal on the long-standing gender conflict in the field in India and the rumours that had been circulated by Wilkie against Miss Sinclair: "Four years ago she wrote Mrs. Shortreed that she could keep quiet no longer as to the condition of things there with Dr. Wilkie and her letter was taken no notice of ...

and the ladies received her with the greatest coldness.... Dr. Wilkie had been telling falsehoods about her ... [that she and Dr. Marion Oliver] had gone to a ball at Government House in full dress. So I just asked her and she denied it altogether. It has been a very great injustice, and yet I do not know how to help her" (MCP 1-1.28, 11 January 1904).

Mary's defence of Sinclair at this meeting eventually assisted in her vindication. She was the headmistress of the boarding school at Indore and had a long and successful career in missionary school and evangelistic work "to lift up [her] degraded sisters in heathendom" (Moir, *Enduring* 109; Brouwer 157-58, 54). In 1906 she married Rev. James Sutherland MacKay in the field and they engaged in direct and "district" evangelism in the open bazaars and gatherings. Her husband was a kinsman of Rev. R. P. MacKay, secretary of the Foreign Missions Committee (Brouwer 103). I have found no relationship between these MacKays and the Donald MacKays of Toronto (A3-4297).

240   Dr. Marion Oliver (1855-1913), from Perth County, Ontario, graduated from the Women's Medical College at Kingston (est. 1883) and was one of the first women to go to India as a medical missionary and teacher (1886-1912). She "was a combative participant in Central India's mission politics" involving John Wilkie, and she and Miss Sinclair were involved in the gender wars in the mission field. Initially Wilkie courted their support but later they felt he had betrayed them. Sinclair accused him of being "unscrupulous" in his "policy to crush what he cannot control," and Oliver made the initial accusation that Wilkie was addicted to "pernicious drugs." Rev. John Thomson Taylor and Dr. Margaret Wallace shared these suspicions (Brouwer xiv, 130-61, 196, 208).

241   This is likely Mrs. Andrew Taylor (Margaret Scott) (d.1906), mother of Rev. Dr. John Thomson Taylor (1870-1955) who was born at Galt, Ontario. He and his wife, Harriet E. Copeland, from Collingwood, Ontario, were missionaries at Indore from 1899 to 1945, he as a professor and principal of Indore College, and she as a teacher. He was involved in the Wilkie case and supported Miss Sinclair and Dr. Oliver. He wrote two books on the missionary work: *In the Heart of India: The Work of the Canadian Presbyterian Mission* (1916) and *Our Share in India* (n.d.) These books are not in the Whitehern library (A60-5464) (*BDKC* 232-33; McNeill 119; Brouwer 157-58, 184, 223; A60-5464, A117-6805). (For Copeland, see A60-5464; A116-6801; A117-6805).

242   The "wire-pulling" at the University of Toronto was in aid of Tom's bid for the Rhodes Scholarship (see A50-5199).

243   During the Indian famine of 1900 a Foreign Mission Council resolution had warned against neglecting the evangelical work of the mission for famine relief. The missionaries argued against the resolution and conveyed the urgency and "unspeakable need for giving immediate relief." Taylor noted that by 1916 the famine orphans who remained with the Mission had been converted to Christianity and were becoming mission workers themselves (Brouwer 121-27).

244   Mrs. Mary Shortreed was president of the WFMS senior executive board in Toronto from 1899 to 1911. She had been engaged in a gender struggle at home with the all-male Foreign Missions Committee (FMC), who were determined to set up a Women's Home Missionary Society (WHMS) to minister to the Indians and the immigrants in the Canadian West. She argued that the women missionaries abroad (India, Japan, China) were "doing work that only women could do" since the women were often sequestered. Also the home focus would reduce their abilities and their funds. The FMC wanted access to these funds and accused them of hoarding large sums of money and ignoring the needs of the West. The FMC prevailed and the WHMS was formed in June 1903 as an auxiliary to the FMC. A "spirit of rivalry" and "competition for funds" developed between the two auxiliaries. Those in the West were openly hostile to the work abroad and demanded a united women's missionary society but various efforts at "fence mending" failed. The all-male General Assembly placed restrictions on the WFMS in 1906 and the struggle continued but, eventually in 1910, the WFMS and the

WHMS agreed to "try to work out a basis for union." Mrs. Shortreed complied with the "order," facilitated the change, and promptly resigned in 1911. In 1912 the FMC took a "hard-line" approach and finally, in 1914, they were "forced to unite" to form the WMS. Many of the leaders of the WFMS, including Mary, capitulated and formed the new executive, but felt that they "had been coerced into union" (Brouwer 46-51; A58-5382; A72-5765; A120-6853). Mary continued her resistance in 1915 (see A120-6853).

245   Sir Mortimer and Daisy Clark were related to the Donald MacKays.

246   Mrs. MacKay did not die at this time, but became quite ill and did not recover. She died in March 1907 (5804).

247   Miss Jessie Proudfoot and Miss Sydney Stevenson had moved from Queen's Park Crescent after William Proudfoot's death. On 18 August 1903 Mary wrote to Cal about Proudfoot's death: "On Monday went up to see Jessie Proudfoot, she looks wonderfully well but I see she can hardly speak about her father, at the same time he must have been a constant care and strain upon her. She spoke about your 'lovely letter' and said she fully intended answering them, but not quite immediately" (5078). Proudfoot died suddenly on 4 August 1903 in his eightieth year after a fall and head injury (5053). His death occurred just eight months after the death of his brother, Rev. Dr. John J. A. Proudfoot (A34-4759). Jessie did answer Calvin's letter on 26 August 1903, and described her father's death as "a beautiful ending to a good and noble life" (7432). Miss Sydney Stevenson lived with Miss Jessie Proudfoot and her father until his death in August 1903 (A43-5012; A51-5233; A56-5333; A61-5470; A130-7018: A46-MCP 3-5.7; A48-MCP 3-5.11).

248   Fleming H. Revello Co., a publishing company in Chicago.

249   The Rhodes Scholarship for Tom had been the subject of many family letters for this period in 1904. It would have provided $1500 per year for Tom's education at Oxford. Tom and Mary, and others, did a great deal of politicking, but Principal Maurice Hutton won out with his man, Ernest Riddell Paterson, on the basis of his classical studies, even though President James Loudon favoured Tom (A49-5172; A51-5233; Best 9-10).

Tom wrote to Calvin 24 April: "As to the Rhodes Scholarship, it needs a lot of grafting. Chiefly, I think, owing to the machinations of Hutton … a committee of the senate has been appointed … I have a fighting chance … and I am working all the pull I can … Don't say much to momma about Hutton because she would be calculated to do anything if she got mad with him. It's just a toss-up if I win or not" (8171).

Mary wrote 11 April: "I scarcely dare hope and am so foolishly anxious, though I know perfectly well, that it may not be the best thing for him to have it, and I have put the matter in God's hands day after day but just like a silly mortal cannot leave it there, but carry the burden with me night and day … I am just so unsettled in mind I cannot write" (5122); and on 16 May: "I have really got over worrying about it. The idea of Tom's going away for three years so over-burdens the honour of getting it" (5183).

After Tom lost the bid, Mary wrote on 30 May: "Loudon had tried to console Tom by assuring him that he would be better to go on with his law" (5212). On 6 June she described some of the politics: "Did I tell that 25 out of the 32 Council were for Tom and whilst Loudon was down South, Hutton got the Senate to give it into a committee hands and singly held on and forced it. McGregor Young told somebody, he had talked with Paterson and he was 'an Athletic ninny.' All the same I really think Tom needs just to keep at work, for as he says after having $1500 a year to live on for three yrs. it would have been very hard to come back to a narrow income in a law office" (5225).

The Rhodes Scholarship had been newly instituted in 1904, according to the will of Cecil John Rhodes (1853-1902), prime minister of Cape Colony. He had earned his fortune in diamonds with Kimberley and De Beers (CBD 1234; CE 1867). The *Mon-*

treal Herald of 8 April 1902 commented on the "remarkable and voluminous" will which established colonial, American, and German scholarships to Oxford. Rhodes elaborated in a codicil: "for a good understanding between England, Germany and the United States will secure the peace of the world and educational relations form the strongest tie." The same paper reported the skeptical remarks of Principal Grant of Queen's University: "[Rhodes'] Unpractical and Egotistic Ideas.... Imperialism, in the real sense is not likely to be permanently benefitted by Mr. Rhodes' legacies." For comment from McGill University, see later in letter.

250 Rev. Robert A. King was Wilkie's successor in Indore, India, in 1902. The training classes at Indore Christian College had perpetually experienced staff shortages because of a long-standing "problem of finding affordable, trained staff." King solved the problem by employing qualified women in teaching positions, his wife and other women missionaries (Brouwer 111-12)

251 Rev. Frederick Elliott Howitt (1858-1939), Anglican priest and religious instructor at Hamilton Normal School, lived at 104 George Street with his wife and six children. His son Arthur Hamilton also became an Anglican priest (A51-5233). Although Mary did not generally favour Anglicans, she appears to have respected Howitt. The *Hamilton Spectator* reported on Howitt: He "was a devout man of strong faith ... was widely known throughout Canada and the United States as a missionary and was in great demand as a speaker" at interdenominational conventions. "He lectured on the relationship of world affairs to prophecy in Holy Scripture." During the Street Railway strike in 1906, Howitt preached "a series of interesting discourses" and when "asked to speak on a labor subject," he chose the building of "the Tabernacle from Exodus xxv, 8, 9," the "vast camp" of workers from the orderly twelve tribes, and then related this to the New Testament (*Hamilton Spectator*, 12 November 1906; *DHB* 3:94; A51-5233; A92-6343; A113-8787). For Mary's views on Anglicans in general, see A52-5283; A97-6446.

252 Slide-out was a community near Standoff, Alberta, where Calvin was doing missionary work. He travelled on horseback between the two communities and delivered two Sunday sermons. He was exhausted and depressed.

253 This is Dr. G. G. Kilpatrick (1888-1928), University of Toronto 1905-09, Knox College 1909-12, graduate student at Berlin and Edinburgh, ordained 1914, lecturer Knox 1912, chaplain [World War One], Ottawa 1919-25, to United Church 1925. Kilpatrick preached at MacNab at least three times, and each time Mary gave him a glowing report: "a fine lecture ... he is a noble, beautiful spirited man" (5436). In May 1908, Mary wrote: "It was quite a privilege to hear him, it is so seldom one gets any instruction. In the morning he spoke from 'God is spirit' and in the evening both Paul's prayers in Ephesians 3rd chap 'I bow my knees unto the Father.' It was extremely fine, he said how often we felt our prayers were dry and formal and he counseled us when we seemed unable to pray to take some of the prayers of the Bible and just spread them out before God, applying them to ourselves and noticing that the first need Paul prays for is strength. I wish I could tell you more but my memory is so poor. But do you know, I do think his sermons were appreciated by many, first because he was long. I felt I could not afford to miss it, but I was pretty tired, just because there was so much to be taken in" (6110; A91-6336; A92-6446). For Kilpatrick and the Mormons, see A73-5788.

254 Miss Annie Park lived at 65 Markland Street and was related to the Bell family (see A21-4531; Tyrell 152).

255 Ethel Atkinson was the daughter of Mr. and Mrs. J. T. Atkinson of 90 Hannah Street (Tyrell 128).

256 The Toronto *News* reports: "There is considerable surprise and not a little criticism among the McGill faculty over the action of Toronto appointing a graduate of two years' standing" (21 May 1904).

257 On 16 May 1904, Mary wrote: "Mrs. Bell is worried to death about Herbie, the doctors ... say he must always have bright company must not be left alone. His home

seems to be the worst place for him and to find money to keep him traveling and at the same time provide cheerful company for him is quite a problem. Really one cannot fully realize the blessing of health. I often wonder, if he did not get into the habit of smoking a great deal and destroying his digestion, he was such a wretchedly irritable little fellow that he would smoke to soothe himself, I am thankful neither you nor Tom ever gave way to the destructive habit, but Mrs. Bell quite approved of smoking" (5183). Tom and Calvin did smoke on occasion, but not in their mother's presence.

258 Mary was visiting the MacKays in Toronto, and stayed there for Tom's graduation (A49-5172; A51-5233).

259 W. H. Vander Smissen (1844-?) had been Mary's principal at Newmarket County Grammar School in 1865 (see A150-4220; A151-4221; A152-4222). In April 1904, Mary had solicited Vander Smissen's help in attempting to secure the Rhodes Scholarship for Tom: "Vander is doing his very utmost and others too" (5122). Tom commented to Calvin "Old Vander is working like an Indian for me, he is a pretty kind hearted old chap. I wish his influence was greater" (8171). Edith was likely his daughter. William Henry Vander Smissen, educationist, German parentage, Toronto University B.A., silver medal in classics 1864, M.A. and lecturer 1866, university librarian 1873-91, university senator from 1892, professor of German 1892. "While a student he entered the military service ... and was present with the 'Queen's Own' at the engagement with the Fenians at Ridgeway, June 2, 1866, where he was severely wounded." He was a lieutenant in 1872 and a captain in 1875. He was author of a grammar of the German language and several text books, including the *Shorter Poems of Goethe and Schiller*. He was Lutheran, married Elizabeth Sarah Mason in 1878, and lived at 75 Grosvenor Street, Toronto (Morgan, 1123) (A150-4220; A151-4221; A152-4222).

260 Mary Trigge was the sister of Kenelm Trigge.

261 Sir Ben Greet (1857-1936), Shakespearean actor and director, toured Canada and the United States with "The Elizabethan Stage Society of England." The Whitehern archive contains two programs from the Ben Greet Company. The first is undated except for references to open-air performances on June 4 and 5 of *As You Like It* and *Comedy of Errors*. Ben Greet again played Jacques and Miss Mathison played Rosalind. In *Comedy* Greet played Dromio of Ephesus and Miss Mathison played Adriana (7962). The second program is for *Everyman: The 15th Century Morality Play*, dated the week of 9-14 March 1903, and produced and directed by Ben Greet at The Academy of Music in Montreal. The program contains a synopsis of the play. A final "SPECIAL NOTICE!" provides an insight into the audiences of the day: "This programme is furnished by the Management for your convenience, but not to be used as an annoyance to ladies and gentlemen occupying orchestra chairs. The using of this programme as a missile is a misdemeanour, and will be dealt with accordingly" (8044).

262 It is likely that Mary is referring to Velyien Henderson, see A52-5283.

263 Harold Lister Lazier (1879-1950) lawyer, was a son of Stephen Franklin Lazier, Q.C. (1841-1916) and his wife Alice Maud Mary Lister. They lived at 67 (later 131) Charles St., had two sons and three daughters, attended Centenary Methodist Church and supported Liberal politics. Mrs. Lazier was the daughter of the builder of the Lister Block in Hamilton. Their daughter Ethel was engaged to Dr. Heurner Mullin (son of Dr. John A. Mullin) in 1906 and they were married in 1907 (5636, A20-4521). Another son, Ernest Franklin, became a judge and married Muriel Simpson 17 June 1903 (4988). The Lazier family came to Canada from the Hackensack River Valley in 1791 and trace their descent from Francois Lesueur who came from France to New Netherland in 1657. The Laziers represent five generations of judges and lawyers in Hamilton and Toronto (Tyrell 146; A20-4521, 4988, 5122, A51-5233, 5636, 7040) (Colin G. Lazier to M. Anderson, e-mail, 7 September 2003).

264 This is likely Arthur Hamilton Howitt, who became an Anglican clergyman like his father F. E. Howitt (see A50-5199; *DHB* 3:94).

265 Peter Taylor was likely not related to Sir Thomas Taylor (A58-5382) since Mary's description of his wedding in 1909 to Miss Williams suggests that "her aunts" were "ashamed of Peter's relations" (6466). Miss Williams was likely the daughter of James Miller Williams (1818-90), whose wife and daughter-in-law were members of the WFMS at MacNab (*DHB* 1:211; Latoszek 25). Peter Taylor never reached Brandon. He was born in Hamilton (1883-1940), took his degree in 1904, attended Yale D.S., 1904-05, Knox College, 1902-04, 1905-07, was assistant registrar at University of Toronto, 1907-08, pastor 1909-16, Osgoode Law School, 1916-19, pastor, High Park, Toronto, 1925-27, ordained missionary, Sutton and Mount Pleasant, 1939-40 (*BDKC* 233).

266 Highfield College was founded in Hamilton at Ravenscliffe just west of Bay Street by John Henry Collinson, educator (1861-1941), with assistance from Sir John Hendrie and Sir John Gibson (*DHB*3.37). It was gutted by fire in 1917 and reopened in 1920 as Hillcrest (later Hillfield) at Main and Queen streets. Then it moved to the Dundas Highway and, in 1963, Hillfield and Strathallan colleges opened at the corner of Garth and Fennell streets on Hamilton Mountain as a coeducational school (Campbell 225-26).

267 There were rumours from several sources that Kenelm Trigge was living with a woman, Annie, and that he might have fathered her child. However, it turned out that she was a young widow with a child and that they were married (6256; 7489; 5736).

268 For Herbie's illness, see A50-5199.

269 Mary and Ruby had been visiting the MacKay family in Toronto (see A3-4297).

270 Rev. Dr. Henry Parsons and his wife lived at 235 Jarvis Street, Toronto, with their daughters Jessie and Emma and their son Holly (Tyrell 95).

271 Dr. Parsons and Mary are referring to two related controversial issues that had been developing for several years in the Presbyterian Church: higher criticism and Church Union. Mary (and Parsons) were firmly in the fundamentalist, anti-reform/union camp, and her judgment of various ministers was usually made on that basis. On 16 August 1904, Mary commented on her next meeting with Parsons: "Dr. P. told me that Davidson ... preached there a sermon on Jonah in which he stated how he had come to know it was just a legend ... and the next Sabbath, he said he had been reproved by some 'old fogies' ... but he had received such Enlightenment. Dr. P. is wild & 'no wonder.' To think of men like that going forth with our Bible" (5289). Richard Davidson was one of the "Canadian Presbyterian academics [who] made their mark as leaders in Canadian intellectual life" and "were scholars of international stature" (Moir, *Enduring* 188). In the Presbyterian Church at that time and "closely related to higher criticism ... was the theory of evolution," which became evident in "social Darwinism"—a belief that man was influenced by his environment as well as his will. It placed its emphasis on social reform at home and in the missionary work abroad (Moir, *Enduring* 170-76, 189-90, 199, 204, 211-33; McNeill 203-207, 248-49, 253, 260-61).

The "professors & preachers" that Mary criticizes in connection with the new higher criticism and Church Union are: Lyle (A17-4436), McFadyen (A53-MCP 1-1.25), Caven (A45-5105), Warden (A21-4531), Falconer (A68-5665), Jordan (A74-5794), Richard Davidson (5289), Macdonnell (A58-5382) and McNair (A79-5868). Church Union was proposed as early as 1875, and was debated for many years. In 1904 the leadership of the three churches formed a Committee of Correspondence, including many college principals who were also "hospitable to the new doctrines." The dissenters formed two camps: Principal D. M. Gordon of Queen's and Rev. C. W. Gordon were "gradualists" (Moir, *Enduring* 204; A22-4535; A97-6446), and Prof. Wm. McLaren, principal of Knox College (1905), was one of the "true 'anti-unionists'" (A88-6173n). For more on Union from 1906 to 1925, see A97-6446n and A127-24 April 1923.

272 Mr. and Mrs. Joseph Henderson (nee Ewart) lived at 66 Wellesley Avenue, Toronto, with their children, Miss Constance L., Mr. Velyien E., and Mr. Ernest M. (Tyrell 63; A49-5172, A51-5233, A105-6738, A123-6975). They may have been related to the Gordon Hendersons of Hamilton, see A69-5709.

273 Rev. Dr. John Campbell (1840-1904) was a lecturer at Knox (1870-73), a professor at Montreal Presbyterian College (1873-1904) and its acting principal in 1904. His "wounded" "feelings" likely refers to two incidents in his career: Campbell was one of the first to attempt modernization of doctrine, but at that time was severely criticized for what later became known as higher criticism. Campbell had stood a heresy trial in 1893 for an evolutionary view of life and history, and he was accused of "undermining the literal truth and divine inspiration of the Bible." He was initially found guilty for recognizing "progress in revelation" but, after signing a "typically Canadian compromise statement about Scriptural inspiration" which was acceptable to the Synod, they declared a "victory for the accused." However, ten years later the critical method was being widely adopted by many "professors & preachers" (A52-5283). Also, Campbell had written a two volume work, *The Hittites, their Inscriptions and Their History* (1890), in which "he found the Hittite civilization not only underlying all Oriental cultures, but also traceable in mounds to be seen 'from Alaska to the Gulf of Mexico.'" The work was immediately discredited (McNeill 185, 203, 208-09; Moir, *Enduring* 174, 187, 190, 253). This book is not in Whitehern library.

274 Paul Kane (1810-71), painter, born in Ireland and studied in Canada, the U.S., France, and Italy, travelled by canoe, horseback, and snowshoe to depict the life of the Indians of the North West. "Most of his pictures are now in the Royal Ontario Museum at Toronto or in the Parliament Buildings at Ottawa." Three of his pictures are at Whitehern: *Group of Red Jackets, Dispatch Rider of 1812,* and *General Foch.* Kane published *Wanderings of an Artist among the Indians of North America* (1859) (MDCB 401). This book is not in Whitehern library.

275 The historian and journalist Goldwin Smith (1823-1910) was educated at Eton and Oxford, taught at Cornell, and settled in Canada in 1871. He was called "Annexation" by his opponents because he advocated "union with the US as a prerequisite to moral unification of the Anglo-Saxon race." He favoured the idea "that free trade between nations would lead to interdependence and make war impossible … [a] creed derived from Adam Smith." He contributed to the *Morning Chronicle, Daily News,* and *Saturday Review,* became Regius Professor of Modern History at Oxford, and founded the *Canadian Monthly* and *National Review* with Charles G. D. Roberts (CE 2016). Three of his books are in the Whitehern library: *The English Statesman* (1867), *The Political Destiny of Canada* (1877), and *The United States: An Outline of Political History 1492-1871* (1901).

276 John Ross Robertson, (1841-1918), publisher and philanthropist, founded the *Evening Telegram* (CE 1879).

277 In Mary's letter of 1 August 1904, Gordon MacKay had cashed in an insurance policy for $10,000 and, "in spite of all that Mr. M. could say, went off with it and with his wife, has been spending it as fast as he can" (5275).

278 Mary's criticism of the Anglicans continues in her next letter, dated 16 August: "What a poor set these Anglicans are, and it is deplorable how seldom one meets a true honourable warm loving Xtian. Now this case in Scotland of a handful of free church men (as I understand) holding on to the funds. Isn't that most disgraceful? To think of men calling themselves fellows of Christ, hindering the work of God and making all this terrible disturbance, just to carry their own little point. No spirit of Christ in them but just the spirit of the devil. Supposing they have right on their side how can they put obstacles in the way of carrying on the church's work if they are Xtians at heart? I tell you the devil is getting on finely these days" (5289).

Mary's Anglican criticism likely has its source in an old controversy from the mid- to late 1800s. It involved the Church of England, which considered itself the legal church of the colonies. The Church of Scotland was also setting up its Presbyterian Churches in Canada. When the sale of 2.4 million acres of clergy reserve lands was made to the Canada Company for colonization, one-seventh was to be used for the "Maintenance of a Protestant Clergy," which the Anglicans considered themselves to be. The

Church of Scotland demanded a proportional share but in 1840 received only half the grant that the Anglicans received. Over the years, the dispute over the clergy reserves became "the most fruitful bone of religious contention in Canadian history." A further split occurred within the Canadian Presbyterian Church between those adherents to the mother Church of Scotland and the new church in Canada, which, in turn, had two competing divisions. It is likely that these issues of money and property were coming to the fore again as meetings had begun in 1889 for a Canadian Protestant union. The Anglicans were included in an initial "historic episcopate" but "no follow-up meeting was ever held." Finally, a committee on union was formed in 1904 between Presbyterians, Methodists, and Congregationalists, which resulted in the creation of the United Church in 1925 (See A52-5283n above on Union, and A53-MCP 1-1.25 below; Moir, *Enduring* 49, 69, 75-76, 84-94, 101-107, 138, 182).

279 Calvin had decided to go back to the University of Toronto for his pass B.A. On 13 September, Mary suggested that he go to Knox College, the Presbyterian College at Toronto: "I have not heard from you why you do not go to Knox, it would be so much cheaper, I think … you will have to consult economy because I am afraid everything will be high this year and I want you to have as good food as you can and a comfortable warm room" (5313). Calvin went to Knox College.

280 "Mounts" are photo mounts (see 5303). Calvin had been preparing an article and pictures for the *News*, upon which Mary comments on 22 August: "It was really too bad of the 'News' to treat your article in such a way. I never saw it at all, July 30th was the first Saturday I was in Toronto there I was watching for your pictures expecting the article to be with it. It was very annoying" (5297).

281 In Mary's letter to Calvin of 22 August, she wrote: "Imagine our feelings when the reply came on Friday that it was a mistake & my daughter had won *The Governor-General's Scholarship in Classics*. I was out that morning & when I came in sight of the door all the family was out waving, gesticulating, I didn't know what was up. Our heads were nearly turned. Just to think of little Edna…. Edna thinks now that after this year's rest, she will try Queen's next year, if she only goes a year. In fact she is full of projects. She is going to try for pupils to coach and thus make a little towards paying her music lessons" (5297).

On 29 August Mary wrote "There is a women's residence under the care of a Mrs. Goodwin a niece of Sir Oliver Mowat, which makes Queen's an ideal college for girls. Of course Edna does not intend to go *this* year" (5303). Edna's mental health continued to be fragile, she had another breakdown in September 1904, and was never able to go to Queen's (see A59-5426).

282 In Japan's war with Russia in 1904-05 Japan gained several victories and then "defeated the Russian fleet at Tsushima in 1905" (*CBD* 1465-66). On 13 September 1905 Mary wrote: "It is sad poor old Tojo's battle ship lost, the Japs are having a hard time lately with the Scots &c" (5406). The *Hamilton Spectator*, 12 September 1905, reported: "Fire Did What the Russians Failed To Do: Admiral Tojo's flagship, the *Mikasa*, was destroyed by fire and the explosion of her magazine at an early hour…. The cause of the fire is under investigation." On 13 September, "peace was declared between Russia and Japan and the Chinese in Manchuria were very happy since for 18 months the war had been fought on their land while they were obliged to 'play the game of neutrality to each side.'"

283 For Mary's work with the Jewish Mission, see A33-4717.

284 This is partly explained in the note on Anglicans in the previous letter. It refers to a dispute that occurred within the divisions of the Presbyterian Church in Canada, the Free Kirk and the Old Kirk. In 1843: "Dr. Thomas Chalmers led 202 other commissioners out of the General Assembly of the Church of Scotland to found the Free Church…. The basic issue … was the relation of church and state rather than any doctrinal grievance. The specific controversy concerned that old grievance … to restore the Reformation practice of congregations [lay patrons] 'calling' ministers …

[However, the secessionists still] held that the state was obliged to support the church" Chalmers and the "seceeders" [sic], over one-third of the ministers, resigned in 1843 to found "not a voluntary Church, but a voluntarily endowed and supported Church." The dispute over division of money and properties, the clergy reserves, the funding of universities, and other power struggles followed, including slavery issues between Canadian Free Church and American Presbyterians who "replied bluntly that slavery was no concern of the Canadians." The negotiations toward union revived the old grievances and controversies in a "Backwash of Disruption" (Moir, *Enduring* 101-103, 127, 82, 98, 189; A52-5283n).

285 Rev. Dr. John Edgar McFadyen, professor at Knox College from 1898, was one of the foremost proponents of the higher criticism in theology and biblical scholarship. He had studied in Germany, married a German woman, graduated as the best theological student in Scotland, published nine books in as many years, and was a "scholar of international stature" (Moir, *Enduring* 188). Five of his books are in the Whitehern library: *In the Hour of Silence* (1902), *Introduction to the Old Testament* (1906), *Ten Studies in the Psalms* (1907), *The Prayers of the Bible* (n.d.), and *A Guide to the Understanding of the Old Testament* (1927). The new critical method became a storm centre and caused a conservative backlash, which Mary and Mrs. Ross are reflecting. Mary reported: "Tom says that Prof. McFadyen has all the students at Knox with him" (5183); and she cautioned Calvin at Knox College to "keep him [Tom] straight for his Knox College friends are all carried away by McFadyen" (5289). She also notes a meeting in which McFayden was criticized and Dr. Lyle "took up 15 minutes eulogizing him" (5157); for Lyle, see A17-4436; McNeill 185, 203; Moir, *Enduring* 174-75, 188-89, 235; A52-5283; A74-5794; A98-6460).

286 Tom had taken a job before returning to school. Mary wrote: "Tom has most providentially come in for a good thing.... On Sunday ... Mr. Chisholm told us he had had a messsage from Mr. Gibson, that they were wanting a man on military survey at $75 month ... in Niagara District, so Tom telephoned Mr. Ballentine, if he could let him off for a month ... he thought he could catch up in lectures at Osgoode, as $75 seemed too much to miss" (5313).

287 Tom was writing exams.

288 William Alexander Fraser (1859-1933), engineer, began his writing career with stories published in the *Detroit Free Press*. Most of his writing life was spent in Georgetown and Toronto. He wrote popular fiction, such as *The Lone Furrow* (1907) and *Bulldog Carney* (1919). "He wrote with a strong air of moral didacticism" (*OCCL* 433).

Fraser's article covers three columns and provides commentary on many magazines and authors' works in Canada, America, and England. He finds American and Canadian literature morally superior to English: "there is next to no market for degrading literature, unless, unfortunately, it has had a previous great success in England." He applauds Canadian literature because "In the first place Canadians are a clean-living, God-fearing people; they have little inclination to filth either in their literature or in their lives" (*The News*, Toronto, 15 May 1905).

Of Mary August Ward (Mrs. Humphrey Ward) (1851-1920), Fraser found her work "exotic" and hoped that editors "would eliminate useless depravity or refuse" it altogether. He also criticized Ward, Charlotte Bronte, and Marie Corelli because they "take great cognizance of the legs of Churchmen." The *OCEL* notes that Ward was a social activist and embodied in her most famous novel, *Robert Elsmere* (1888), her view that Christianity could be revitalized by emphasizing its social mission and discarding its miraculous element (*OCEL* 871).

Sir Anthony Hope Hawkins (1863-1933) was the author of *The Prisoner of Zenda* (1894), *Rupert of Henzau* (1898), *The Dolly Dialogues* (1894), and other novels and plays (*OCEL* 373). *Trilby*, a novel by George Louis Palmella Busson DuMaurier (1894), is about "an amiable artist's model in Paris, with whom various young English art-students fall in love" (*OCEL* 832). These books are not in the Whitehern library.

289 The *Macassa*, *Modjesca*, and the *Turbinia* were steamships that carried passengers between Hamilton and Toronto across Lake Ontario (Campbell 247). It was a very convenient method of travel. Mary used the ships for visits to friends and to her dentist in Toronto (A68-5665). "On the Macassa we can get 10 trips for a dollar or 25 cents return. The Turbinia 50 cents" (5313). Meals could be purchased in the dining room on board. Tom reports that the Royal Hotel in Hamilton took the overflow from a medical convention in Toronto, and that the convenient travel by steamship made this possible (8193).

290 Calvin took a position as minister at Staney Brae, Muskoka. Mary was very pleased that he had finally completed his exams and was "situated" with a regular stipend. On 6 July 1905, she wrote: "My heart is full of gratitude to God for all his wonderful goodness to us. When I look back at times when we could not look ahead at all, it all seems wonderful. It seems to me that patience is what I need more than anything else" (5347).

291 I have found no further record of Kerr. In the summer of 1905, Tom made frequent business trips—Toronto, Newmarket, and Ottawa—likely for the law firm of Royce and Henderson to which he was articled until graduation. It was during this time that he acquired the Beach Strip properties for the railroad and the hydro companies (Best 13; A58-5382). Tom also spent time at home this summer doing repairs and gardening. In September he was "so tired of the city and so glad to get off to his dear lumber camp" before going back to school (5410).

292 Rev. Dr. Hugh Beverly Alexander Ketchen (1872-1961) Knox College 1901-04, ordained Hamilton, MacNab Church on May 5, 1905-46, D.D. Knox, 1928, moderator, 1943. He married Maude McAlpine McMahen of London in 1905, and they had one son and two daughters. "He was considered an outstanding expository preacher, strong on poetic quotation and choice of language." He wrote two books: *Sons of Martha* (1938), which is in the Whitehern library, and *The Harper of the Hills*. More than four thousand sermons came from his pen and reprints regularly appeared in *The Presbyterian Record*. He had a "sparkling wit" and was in great demand as a speaker on Charles Dickens and Robert Burns (*DHB* 3:103). Mary had been very critical of many of the aspiring ministers who were tested as replacements for Dr. Fletcher, but she strongly endorsed Ketchen. He delivered her eulogy (see A144-Eulogy; BDKC 115; A58-5382; A67-5654; A68-5665; A71-5744; A76-5800; A85-6063; A91-6336; A98-6460; A118-9153; A124-9180).

293 Rev. Dr. Charles William Gordon (Ralph Connor) (1860-1937) was born at Indian Lands, Glengarry, Ontario, son of Rev. Daniel Gordon and Mary R. (Robertson) Gordon. In 1899 he married Helen Skinner King, daughter of Rev. John M. King, and they had one son and six daughters. B.A. University of Toronto 1883, Knox College 1884-87, professor, ordained missionary to miners in Alberta, and lumbermen in North West Territories, pastor, Winnipeg 1894-1937, chaplain E.E.F. 1914-18, moderator 1921, F.R.S.C, D.D. Knox College 1906, Glasgow 1919, Edinburgh, L.L.D. Queen's. Gordon was an articulate speaker on the "Social Gospel" and wrote books and many articles for the Presbyterian Church. The *Toronto News* of 15 May 1905 reports a speech/sermon by Ralph Connor with the triple headlines: "Attacks Evils of Society," "He Is Sick at Heart," and "Revelations Which Have Come to Him Have Filled Him with Sorrow and Shame." Gordon was on the "delaying" or "gradualist" side of the Union debate: "the proposal for union meant three things: first, halt; second, confer; third, report" (*Hamilton Spectator*, 9 June 1923; see A52-5283; A127-24 April 1924).

Gordon, under the pseudonym of Ralph Connor, wrote at least twenty-eight works of fiction. His first three books sold five million copies: *Black Rock* (1898), *The Man from Glengarry* (1901), and *Glengarry School Days* (1902). The latter became a minor classic in the United States and Britain. He wrote *Postscript to Adventure: The Autobiography of Ralph Connor* (1938). Several of his works are in the Whitehern library:

The Life of James Robertson: Missionary Superintendent of Western Canada (1908), *Beyond the Marshes* (1900), *Christian Hope* (n.d.) and *The Dawn of Galilee* (n.d). His fiction combines the "didacticism of moral and social reform with adventure, frontier stories and lively characters." His mother was the inspiration for the "saintly Mrs. Murray" and was "the informing spirit behind many other idealized women" in his books. In 1889, he credited "women's missionary societies as the most important agents in the missionary movement in the preceding half-century" and commended their "almost perfect organization" (Brouwer 31). His work has attracted critical interest in cultural studies in "efforts to define English Canada's identity," and in studies of "religion, imperialism, women, labour and Canada's native peoples." Several biographies have been written about him and his works (*OCCL* 474-76; Moir, *Enduring* 188, 193-99; *BDKC* 86; *MDCB* 303; McNeill 184, 195-96, 240). I have found no evidence that Charles Gordon was related to Dr. David Miner Gordon of Queen's (A22-4535), or to the "old Mr. Gordon" in the letters (A93-6347). While in Winnipeg in 1903, Gordon invited Calvin to do missionary work in the West, which Calvin did, see A45-5105n. (Best 18; A57-5359; A45-5105n; A60-5464; A61-5470; A79-5868; A94-6363; A97-6446).

The Gordons, Clarks, and MacKays were interrelated: Mrs. Mortimer Clark (nee Gordon) and Mrs. Donald MacKay (nee Gordon) were related and Mary wrote condolences to both at the time of Gordon Clark's death (A20-4521; for MacKay, see A3-4297, A79-5868n; for Clark, see A40-4902; Tyrell 39). Charles Gordon's mother, Mary R. (Robertson) Gordon, gave an address to the MacNab WFMS in 1885 (Buttrum 3) and wrote articles for the *Knox College Monthly* (1885 and 1889).

294   Possibly, Adam Jamieson, ordained 1896 but the record shows no pastorate or missionary postings (*BDKC* 107).

295   The Locke family members—Helen, Charlie, and Mary—are often mentioned in the letters. They were related to the Trigge family. See A28-4635 (A19-4500; A42-4977; A88-6173).

296   Sir Thomas Wardlaw Taylor (1833-1917) and Lady Margaret (Vallance) Taylor (daughter of Hugh Vallance, merchant, of Dundas and Hamilton). The Taylors lived in Hamilton from 1902 to 1917, during which time he was an elder of St. Paul's Presbyterian Church, Hamilton: "For seven generations a member of his family was an elder in the Church" (*POH* 139). Sir Thomas Wardlaw Taylor had been the Chief Justice of Manitoba and presided at the trial of Louis Riel who was hanged for treason in 1885. In 1897 he was created a knight bachelor by Queen Victoria (*MDCB* 821; *POH* 139). Taylor's son, Thomas Wardlaw Taylor (1865-1952) distinguished himself as a barrister, lecturer, minister, missionary, and professor at Montreal College (*BDKC* 233; *POH* 139). Their daughter Margaret Wardlaw Taylor married J. J. C. (Joe) Thomson in 1905. Another Taylor daughter married Dr. Gilbert Gordon, son of "old Mr. Gordon" (see A93-6347). Sir Thomas Wardlaw Taylor (judge) should not be confused with Judge Thomas Taylor (1778-1837) of Hamilton, writer of the first volume of law reports issued in Upper Canada (*DHB* 1:192; Campbell 57; A33-4717; A84-6053; A93-6347; A117-6805).

297   For Thomson family and Laura Hostetter, see A15-4415.

298   John P. Baker, son of Mary's half-brother, James Alfred Baker, lived at Komoka, Ontario, near London (*CMQPW* 88a-b).

299   In August and September Edna's mental health had been failing and on 7 August Mary sent her to stay with her cousin John Baker. Mary was very concerned about her "excitable" condition and "fearful state of nervousness" and "really was terrified that her brain had given way" (5398). Edna stayed with Baker until 6 September, became disturbed, and left very suddenly. On 13 September Mary wrote to Calvin: "On Saturday evening Edna came home in the most terrible nervous condition, never ceases talking she was commencing with this before she left home, but according to her John drinks and comes home every Saturday in particular raging, insults Lorrie, argues con-

tinually till Edna had hysterics; then she declares she was too ill to come home, so Winnie kept her for a few days at Hattie's to try and get her better. Irritable beyond description we are at our wits end to please her.... Before we could get Edna quieted for the night, she had a violent fit of the hysterics, such as I had never seen before, which kept us up till nearly 2 o'clock.... Altogether such a time! I shall not soon forget it. Yesterday E. seemed a little more like herself but this morning she is very irritable. But Dr. Arnott assures me she will be alright in time.... It takes all of us to attend to Edna" (5406).

On 19 September Mary wrote: "We have been having a very anxious and trying time with Edna. But I think she is considerably better on the whole. But she is simply crazy on the subject of going to school. The failing in physics has never been out of her mind and the craze to go to Queen's so that she could really say she was there. Sometimes I have been afraid her mind had become unhinged. But I trust God in his mercy will save her from that. Everything is so exaggerated in her mind" (5418).

For the balance of September and early October Mary advised Tom and Calvin not to come home since "Edna needed to be kept as quiet as possible" (MCP 2-4:51). On 10 October, Mary reported a complete breakdown, see (A59-5426).

300 Logie Macdonnel was Rev. Dr. Samuel Lyle's assistant at Central Presbyterian Church in Hamilton. He may have been related to Daniel James Macdonnel (1840-?), minister of St. Andrew's Church, Toronto, in 1875. Daniel had caused a disruption in the Church with his almost heretical views on "the changing theology of the age," and on shortening the Confession "in view of a coming union of the Churches" which was being debated as early as 1893, and which finally occurred in 1925. Mary's faith was fundamentalist and she was strongly opposed to union (see A127-24 April 1923). (For higher criticism and union see A52-5283. (McNeill 204-07, 248-49; Moir, *Enduring* 172-74, 181, 187, 188.)

301 Tom had brought Dr. Hutchison to Whitehern to visit in July (see A57-5359).

302 The family often objected to the noise of the T.H.& B. railroad trains on the track near Whitehern.

303 Edna's mental health had been deteriorating since the summer. She was taken to Montreal by the nurse, Miss Hutton, and on 19 October Hilda wrote to Calvin about the need for secrecy: "In Tom's letter I warned him that if people become too inquisitive about Edna to say that the nurse came from Montreal and that Edna went back with her as the doctor advised change of scenery and invigorating air, we do not mention her name unless people ask about her particularly" (5430). An enclosure in the above letter, dated 20 October, from Mary states: "We had word from the Doctor to-day, 'Miss McQuesten has been quieter to-day (Wednesday) and has taken her nourishment fairly well.' To me, this is very encouraging, as she had taken nothing for days and we were powerless to make her. Have been writing Ida Welker, whom I have taken into my confidence, to send her some flowers on her birthday next Monday. Have not yet heard if we may write her.... [P.S.] Pray earnestly" (5434).

Ida Welker lived in Montreal. (Calvin had visited the Welkers there, see A20-4521.) At this writing, I have found no letters between 19 October 1905 and 6 March 1906, so it is not known how long Edna stayed in Montreal. Edna was with Ruby in Ottawa in April 1906, but it not known for how long. She started home on 4 June (5445; 5448; 5477; 5495). Mary was away in the West for five weeks and returned 16 June 1906. Edna recovered for a time but remained fragile and suffered several more episodes until she was finally institutionalized at Homewood in Guelph in October 1920. She had several shock treatments and a partial lobotomy, and died there in November 1935. Her healthy periods and deterioration are described in many of the family letters (A59-5426; A53-MCP1-1.25; A58-5382; MCP2-4.51; A62-5487; 5367; 5371; 5377; 5398; 5406; 5418; MCP2-4.51; 5422; 5430; 5434; 5445; 5448; 5477; A62-5487; 5495; 5502; A63-5512; 5691; A69-5709; 5876; A124-9180; A126-8734; 7040; 7044; A138-7136; 5297).

304 Mary was greatly concerned about the cost of medical care for Edna. In a letter to Tom of October 1906, she notes that Dr. Clark charged $25 for consultation in the home, the doctor at a Mimico asylum was charging $100, and that Mrs. B[?] was paying $50 a week for her daughter's care at Guelph (MCP 2-3b.47).

305 There are three copies of the *Works of Horace* in the Whitehern library, dated 1859 and 1860.

306 Mary traveled to Winnipeg to attend a Missionary Society Conference and to inspect some of the Mission schools in Western Canada. She traveled with twenty-eight people, all prominent missionary society members, many of whom are mentioned in the letters during the trip from 10 May to 15 June 1906 (5453; 5502). She was billeted with various well-respected missionaries and political officials. I will annotate only those who are significant to the larger body of letters.

307 I have been unable to locate a copy of this speech.

308 Dr. and Mrs. Gilbart were missionaries at Rolling River, about sixteen miles from Winnipeg. Mrs. Gilbart's death is noted in letter of 15 January 1907 (A72-5765; A61-5470).

309 Daniel H. MacMillan was lieutenant-governor of Manitoba (1900-11) (CE 1296).

310 Geills (McCrae) Kilgour married Mr. Kilgour and went to live in Brandon where he had a law office (5388, 7738). His parents, Mr. and Mrs. Robert Kilgour (nee Govan) lived at 144 Bloor Street East, Toronto, in 1900, and had a summer home at Roach's Point on Lake Simcoe (Tyrell 71). Mary's daughters, Mary and Hilda, vacationed near them at Orchard beach and visited often for play and prayer-meetings. Mary commented: "The Kilgours are such nice people, so religious and yet—jolly … [They] have an elegant house beautifully situated with a smooth lawn stretching to the river and a number of large acacia trees scattered around. In fact everything is as perfect as it can be. It seems so fortunate that they should be such good people, for of course what the Kilgours do is the thing. There is very little communication between the Roaches Point people and the Orchard Beach ones. You might call the Roaches Point the aristocracy and the Orchard Beach the commoners" (5053, A60-5464).

311 This is possibly Mrs. Alex McLagan of 360 Main Street East (Tyrell 148). She also attended the WFMS conference in Vancouver in June 1912 (A111-6780).

312 Hon. Colin H. Campbell (later Sir) was attorney-general of Manitoba in 1905 (*Manitoba: A History,* 1957, 292) (A60-5464).

313 Edna had been in Montreal recovering from a mental breakdown since October 1905.

314 Augustus Albert Laing (1872-1942) and his wife Marion S. Noble were missionaries at Fort Qu'Appelle, Saskatchewan from 1905 to 1910. His father was John Laing (1828-1902), pastor in Toronto, Ottawa, and Dundas (BDKC 118-19).

315 This is likely Elizabeth (McDougall), the wife of John Shepherd Davidson (1863-1950); they were missionaries in Manitoba and Saskatchewan for thirty-seven years, from 1903 to 1940 (BDKC 53).

316 I have found no further record of Mr. Heron.

317 During the Boer War (1899-1902), "the 3rd contingent, Strathcona's Horse, was funded entirely by Lord Strathcona, Canada's wealthy high commissioner to the UK" (CE 2048, 2015).

318 Mrs. Jaffary was the wife of John Ashton Jaffary (1859-1930), minister and missionary at Macleod, Alberta, from 1897 to 1904. He then moved to Edmonton as librarian of the provincial library there (BDKC 107; A49-5172; A63-5512).

319 Mary was billeted with Mrs. Bryce at 372 Assinaboine Avenue, Winnipeg, at the beginning and end of her trip.

320 On 15 June 1906 Mary described the balance of her trip: "Here I am at last and glad to be at home after five weeks of wandering. Well, owing to a mud slide at Medicine Hat, my train on the Saturday was cancelled so I did not get to the Lake of the Woods at all, but went over to St. Boniface and wandered about the old cemetery. Then Monday morning we took the train to Fort William, we had a beautiful view of the Kee-

watin Lakes and the Kaurauistiqua River and reached Fort William at 9 p.m. We had to have three beds placed in parlour of C.P.R. Hotel, but were quite comfortable. Then Tuesday morning took the Steamer Manitoba, a most beautiful steamer and the lakes were smooth as glass and the steamer works with scarcely a tremor, so it is really a fine trip down through the Sault. Mr. Duncan, our minister there, was on board, and gave me all the information about Clergy's works and the locks. We were two days and two nights on board, reaching Owen Sound on the Thursday morning (yesterday). We arrived at Toronto 1 p.m." (5502).

321 Miss Middleton and Miss Robinson were Ruby's fellow teachers at Ottawa Ladies' College (5508).

322 Mary notes Edna's progress in letter of 15 June 1906: "Edna looks fat and cheerful, but is still quiet and not inclined to do anything, but will be all right in time" (5502). Mary often expresses concern for the mental health of both Calvin and Edna, and sometimes her own. She is ever on guard for signs of the family's inclination toward "nervous prostration." In her letter to Calvin 4 July 1906 she fears that he "is not up to work of any kind" (5524) and declares "You are very like myself in temperament" (A103-9058).

323 These McKays were neighbours of the McQuestens, and Miss Christina McKay and her sister, Mrs. John Lauder (Elizabeth), were members of the WFMS at MacNab Church (Latoszek 25).

324 Central Presbyterian Church was built in 1858 at Jackson and MacNab Streets. In 1908 it was rebuilt at Caroline Street and Charlton (formerly Hannah) Avenue, where it stands today. The architect was John MacIntosh Lyle (see A84-6053, A17-4436).

325 Bessie Richardson may have been related to Rev. Dr. James Richardson (1791-1875) "Bishop M. E. Church," a friend of Mary's father (4172). Hilda wrote in August from the Richardsons (Bessie, Uncle Bob, Edwin) at Walkerton to describe canoeing on the Saugeen River and fishing for speckled trout. She stayed four weeks (5602).

326 David Ross was the son of Anna Ross, principal of the "Presbyterian Ladies' College," where Ruby was a teacher. Mary's objection to the marriage and the need to delay may have been motivated by the fact that Ruby's salary was needed for Tom's tuition at university (A71-5744). Tom would not be graduating for another year (June 1907) and his future was not yet secure. On 4 September 1906, Mary wrote of Ruby's teaching: "I do hope this will be the last year for Ottawa" (5636). David wrote to Tom on 9 October 1906 from the West about his engineering job with the railroad, and he mentioned his "week in Muskoka.... Your mother let me take her out in the canoe once— and once only—for, the very next day I upset myself close to shore and so ruined my reputation" (MCP 2-3b.48). David and Ruby's relationship continued secretly for two years and terminated while Ruby was being treated for tuberculosis in Calgary in 1908 (5908).

327 Mary's father was born in Portsea, England (now a suburb of Portsmouth), in 1795/6 (Minnes 1).

328 On 12 July 1907 Mary gave Mrs. Ross's report of their first year in the West: "Mrs. Ross writes of her Western home in glowing colours, but I understand why, she enlarges on the beauty of David's as well as her own. In the meantime they and their belongings are crowded into D's small house, theirs will not be built till next year. Poor David has to build it, it will be of logs plastered over. Of course I can understand Mrs. R.'s satisfaction in having a spot she can call her own and being with David, but when the winter comes it will not be so delightful. Eleanor had received letter from Jean telling of her trials, she had bought some hens and put 12 doz. eggs (Plymouth Rock) under them but they ate and broke the eggs and two chickens were the result" (5908).

329 Mrs. Jennie (Ault) Robertson—widow of Charles Robertson (1851-92), educator and principal of Hamilton Collegiate Institute—was a member of the MacNab WFMS, lived at 115 George Street, and had two sons (DHB 2:130; Latoszek 25; A74-5794).

330 Mr. and Mrs. Charles S. Proctor (nee Campbell) lived at 223 Bay Street (Tyrell 152). She was a member of the MacNab WFMS. In her letter of 4 June 1909, Mary notes that Mrs. Proctor received a legal settlement resulting from a medical judgment that Mr. Proctor's death had been caused by a "very peculiar disease" that had also weakened his mind (6436).

331 Donald MacGillivray was with William McClure, M.D. in Honan, North China, during the Boxer rebellion of 1900. In the bloody attack by nationalist Chinese militants on the "foreign devils," 231 people, mostly missionaries, died. They were forced to flee hundreds of miles overland or by water and many more were wounded. After the rebellion was quelled by European, American, and Japanese forces, the "mission work developed even more rapidly than before" (McNeill 122-23; Moir, *Enduring* 152).

332 This act and reflection and note of regret came at a time when Mary had already refused marriage proposals from suitors for Hilda (A28-4635) and Ruby (A65-5622).

333 Miss Jane Buchanan, daughter of the Hon. Isaac Buchanan and a member of MacNab Church (A10-4367).

334 Harold Thomson was related to Mrs. Robert Thomson and her son Joseph J. Thomson, possibly a cousin. He joined the Rhodesian Mounted Police in 1903 (A37-4815) and shot himself in 1906 (A68-5665), which may have been suicide. In Mary's letter of 8 October 1906, she provides the latest gossip about his colourful career: "By the way Mrs. Mullin says that Mr. Wilton thinks Harold Thomson might have shot himself accidently, as he was out shooting in the Rockies he went out there because he had deserted from the American Army, which he joined for the second time after coming from S. Africa. You remember he deserted from the N.W. Mounted Police and the Thomsons had to buy him off. It seemed too bad altogether the way he used his life" (5675).

   Others mentioned in the letter appear to have been brothers of the deceased. His mother was not the Mrs. Robert Thomson of Hamilton since the letter discloses that his mother and aunt were dead in 1906 (A37-4815).

335 For Dr. Lyle and his stand on church politics, see A17-4436; A52-5283.

336 Sir Robert A. Falconer (1867-1943) was a clergyman, educator, and scholar, and was educated at London, Edinburgh, and Germany. He was principal of Knox College and became president of the University of Toronto in 1907, which he completely reorganized and integrated. He was very active in church politics and favoured higher criticism and Church Union. He was on the committee for church union which began in earnest in December 1904 (CE 744). For Falconer's politics, see A52-5283.

337 Mary had written to Calvin on 30 October 1906: "So I want you to tell me all about it and not to feel badly or worried about it, for we will manage it somehow and make it up again. I have the idea that in connection with the Bible Study classes, you ordered books largely and the students did not pay you. Well you did it with the best intention and we all make mistakes.... You see you were just in such an excited state at that time, that I can quite understand you may not have kept a correct account of anything. So in that case we had better just pay the bill and say nothing more. Do not fret about it, I am not, for it was not your fault, your health gave out and it is just like paying a doctor's bill. Were any of the books returned? Could they be returned? Is there any one of the students I could write to see about them?" (5701).

   In July 1907, Mary wrote: "I was very glad to know the bill was paid at Methodist Book room no wonder it was a large one when they charged for what you had not got" (5912).

338 Mrs. Gordon Henderson (nee Muriel Sanford) was a member of the WFMS in Hamilton (A135-7095). "Idylwild" was located near the mountain brow. It became a nursing home (*DHB* 1:177). She may have been related to the Joseph Hendersons of Toronto (see A52-5283).

339 I have been unable to identify Miss Evans.

340 Mrs. Robert Thomson and Mrs. and Mrs. Joseph Thomson lived at "Amisfield" (see A15-4415).

341 Miss Honeycomb was a seamstress. She often stayed with the family for several days while sewing and sometimes brought another seamstress and another sewing machine. In 1906 Ruby paid for a new sewing machine: On 8 November 1906 Mary wrote to Tom: "We have had to buy a new sewing machine but what Ruby sends will nearly pay for it" (MCP 1-3a.20; A110-8848; A113-8787; 6683; 6820; 8836; Box 12-179).

342 Auchmar was the family home of the Buchanans. The tea was likely for the wife of James Isaac Buchanan, son of Isaac Buchanan and a Pittsburgh millionaire (A10-4367; A19-4500).

343 I have found no record for Mr. Dulcos, but Moir notes that "by 1904 French Evangelization had been placed under Home Mission Board control" (Moir, *Enduring* 154). The Point-aux-Trembles School was taken over by the Presbyterian Church in 1880 and was influential until about 1900, largely through the efforts of Charles Chiniquy, formerly a prominent Quebec Catholic priest. He "detached himself from Romanism, and with many of his people entered the American Presbyterian Church." In 1876 he was transferred to Montreal. "He was greatly in demand as a speaker.... His fearless exposure of the evils he had witnessed in Romanism, his extraordinary eloquence and ready pen, made him a notable force in the life of Quebec, and for a time it appeared that a mass movement into Protestantism was to sweep the French population." Chiniquy died in January 1899 and "in 1902 the number of French-Canadian converts in all evangelical churches in Quebec was estimated at between 30,000 and 40,000." Since then there has been "less antagonism" and McNeill in 1925 speculates that "recent notable advances in education among Roman Catholics" may have been due to the influence of Presbyterian schools (McNeill 99-100).

344 The *Hamilton Spectator*, 12 November 1906, reported on "THE NEW CHIMES": "Dedicatory Sermons Preached.... For a week past workmen have been busy installing the chime of eleven bells recently purchased for St. Paul's Presbyterian Church, and on Saturday night the first concert was rung on them for the public. The bells were given to the church by those who were or had been members of the church except one donated by Hon. Senator Gibson ... and on the occasion of Saturday night's concert the streets were lined by hundreds who enjoyed their sweet tones and were not slow to express their appreciation of the music pealed forth."

The chimes played ten hymns preceding the Sunday morning service. The *DHB* notes that the chimes were designed "to reproduce that at St. Giles, Edinburgh" (*DHB* 2:85). For Mary's disapproval of the chimes, see A70-MCP 2-4:34.

345 Florence Mary Gibson married John Morrison Eastwood (1864-1927). Eastwood was proprietor of John Eastwood and Co., Liberal, alderman 1903-06, a director of the Yacht Club and Incline Railway and of several large industries. Eastwood was a trustee of Central Presbyterian Church. Florence Mary Gibson was the daughter of Senator William Gibson, banker, politician (1849-1914). She was one of five children from his first marriage to Jane Hill Davidson, died 4 Feb. 1902. Senator William Gibson's obituary in the *Hamilton Spectator* 4 May 1914 states that he was survived by five daughters: Mrs. John Jennings, Mrs. C. W. Darling, Mrs. D. M. Finnie, Mrs. J. M. Eastwood and Miss Evelyn H.

We have been unable to establish a relationship between Senator William Gibson and Sir John Morison Gibson (1842-1929) 4436, *DHB* 3:66).

346 Mary wrote to both *The Hamilton Spectator* and the *Hamilton Evening Times*: The *Times* caption reads: "A WOMAN'S OPINION: Prominent Lady Writes in Support of the Men." Mary wrote: "To the Editor of the *Times*: Sir,—This morning it is reported that unless the citizens support the employees in this street railway trouble and refuse to ride in the cars—until their demands are granted—the men will be worsted in the struggle. We who are outsiders cannot be thoroughly acquainted with the working of the street car system, or presume to say just where the fault lies, which has driven the employees to desperation; but we feel quite sure that all our citizens believe that whatever the difficulty may be the men should not suffer.

When we think of all these faithful men endure in all sorts of weather, at all seasons, and at all hours of the day and night, whilst we enjoy the comfort, it makes one's blood boil, to think of them having to fight in this way for their daily bread. No wonder there is no love between employers and employed, when nothing is given graciously, because it is well deserved.

We who are housekeepers, know full well the tremendous increase in cost of living and no matter what the disagreement at headquarters, it is a very great sin to take the services of these men and not sufficiently pay them. To many this walking seems an impossibility, but let every one of us resolve to get up a little sooner and we shall be surprised how far we can walk, and enjoy it too. If we really sympathize with these men and their families let us be willing to deny ourselves and support them. Thanking you very much for your valuable space, Yours sincerely—Mary B. McQuesten. 'Whitehern' Saturday."

The strike grew violent before it ended. On 24 and 26 November, the *Spectator* headlines reported "Wild Mob Was in Complete Control, Police Were Powerless" and "Mob and Military Clash: Disgraceful Saturday Night Scenes on the Main Streets of Hamilton Bring Blush and Shame to Citizens," and on 30 November, "All Ordered Back to Work: After long discussion they were crowned with success."

347 On 13 and 26 November 1906, Mary again expressed her disapproval of the bells: "On Saturday morning began the chimes and yesterday they rang away, but really I cannot say I admire them very much. It is too much noise and they are certainly not worth the money" (5728). "You have had your trials with calves and we have had ones with chimes. They started to ring the quarters also, but people in the vicinity protested against them at night, but they started the hours. The whole thing has been a frightful waste of money. As the cities are now, all noise unnecessary should be avoided" (5740). And on 3 December 1909, Mary planned to protest: "St Paul's actually got another bell. But it really looks very pretty and quaint, a little Cupola on the S.S. [Sunday school]. I am waiting to get hold of the first St. Paul's man to rate them for their noisiness" (6557).

348 The Hamilton Street Railway strike had been settled and the employees—"the old men"—did not lose their jobs. (See A70-MCP 2-4.34.)

349 Tom had one more year to complete at Osgoode Hall. He graduated in law June 1907 (A79-5868).

350 This cookbook is in the Whitehern library and was obviously a favourite as it is much used. In a previous letter, Mary had given Calvin a list of books suitable for Christmas presents: "You might just send to the Westminster Co. for one of Ralph Connor's books or Marian Keith's 'Duncan Polite' or 'The Silver Maple'; the first is the best, $1.25. 'The Prospector' is fine, I think, if they have not read it" (5736). Marian Keith's *The Black Bearded Barbarian: The Life of George Leslie MacKay of Formosa* (1912) is in the Whitehern library.

351 Mrs. Needham succeeded Mrs. Anna Ross as the principal of the "Presbyterian Ladies College" in Ottawa. Eleanor Ross had pneumonia (A70-MCP 2-4:34). Eleanor did not go West with David, his mother, Anna, and his sister, Jean (see A65-5622).

352 The "Homework" is the Women's Home Missionary Society (WHMS). It was formed in 1903 to minister to the men in the gold fields of British Columbia and Alaska. Mary held executive positions in both auxiliaries and was exhausted. However, on 5 February she gave another address to WFMS auxiliary : "The subject for our Mission study this year is 'The Islands of the Pacific' and as the London Miss. Society was the first to send Missionaries to the South Seas and as I had heard that it had published a report of its work from the beginning at the time of its Centennial, I determined to write for it hoping the cost would not be much. So on January 8th I wrote to Rev. Wardlaw Thompson, the Secretary whom I met at Ecumenical Conference. So on Friday I received a <u>very</u> nice note from the Ass. Sec. and on Saturday the book, a <u>very</u> nice one <u>bound in</u> <u>cloth</u> and <u>illustrated</u> for <u>one shilling</u> and six pence

for postage. I was just delighted. There was the full account with portraits of Capt. Wilson who commanded the Mission ship, having been converted under Rev. John Griffin at Portsea Chapel (Grandpa's Church) and Dr. Bogue who was principal of the Missionary Seminary Grandpa attended and full of names most familiar to one in childhood" (5784).

I have been unable to locate Mary's finished paper or the book. In March 1907 Mary had another of her "blind turns" (5804) and she remained exhausted throughout the year. In May she was in Brantford at an annual meeting of the Presbytery WFMS (5844). At the annual meeting of the MacNab WFMS in December 1907 she resigned "her office as president on account of ill health," but a plan was adopted that the society retain Mrs. McQuesten as president and that ten of the members be asked to preside at the monthly meetings (WFMS "Minutes," December 1907; *DHB* 3:6). For a note on the conflict between the FMC and the WFMS and the WHMS, see A49-5172n.

353 Mary visited the Gilbarts while touring the Western missions during May 1906.

354 The Railroad had made an offer to expropriate the house (see A74-5794).

355 John ("Jack") McIntosh Lyle was the son of Rev. Dr. Samuel Lyle of Central Presbyterian Church in Hamilton. He was a noted architect in Ontario (*DHB* 2:99; A84-6053).

356 Prof. Kilpatrick and Hon. Frank Oliver (see below) had a running debate in the *Globe* about the Mormons. Oliver claimed that Kilpatrick had "made reference to the unwisdom [*sic*] of Government allowing the Mormons to settle in Alberta"and that "the Mormon invasion was a sin to be laid at the Government's door." Oliver countered and described the Mormons as a "benefit to the West" since they had brought "arid lands under cultivation ... increased the value of some twenty or thirty million acres" and were "industrious, peaceful and law-abiding" (*Globe*, 15 February 1907). Kilpatrick replied that Oliver's "attack" was merely of the "vote-catching order and was meant for consumption in Alberta and not in Ottawa." Kilpatrick objected to the "block system" of settlement and noted that the Mormons were now a "political body" with the intention of throwing their vote "where the most good could be accomplished for the Church." Kilpatrick had two other objections: (1) "[Mormons] maintain as a religious belief ... Polygamy ... which is held to be immoral ... a crime under Canadian law." (2) Other more diverse settlement could have been accomplished in the West. He concluded: "We want Canada to be a great country ... whose people shall be homogeneous.... The Mormon invasion was therefore, in my judgment, no necessity of State, and has brought with it moral and political dangers which it would have been possible to have avoided" (*Globe*, 16 February 1907). Mary had also commented on the Mormons on 20 April 1904: " As to the Mormons one could never believe Joseph Smith anything but a vile old beast, and no pure minded man could ever follow him" (5151).

357 Hon. Frank Oliver (1853-1933), newspaper publisher, founded the *Edmonton Bulletin* in 1880. He was elected to the North-West territories in 1888 and 1894, to the House of Commons (1896-1917), and was minister of the Interior and of Indian Affairs (1905-1911). Mary's reference to Oliver's "origins" likely refers to the fact that he "took his mother's maiden name." Oliver continued the policies of Sir Clifford Sifton (1861-1921), who "established a vigorous organization to seek out ... most controversially ... east-central Europe" settlers to the Canadian West, and he "defended the 'stalwart peasants in sheep-skin coats' who were turning some of the most difficult areas of the West into productive farms" (*CE* 1564, 2000; A73-5788; A134-7085).

358 Dr. and Mrs.Thomas Husband lived at 33 Jackson Street West in 1900 (Tyrell 143). Whitehern is at 41 Jackson Street West.

359 The previous T.H.& B. Railroad expropriation was mentioned (A15-4415) when a portion of "Whitehern" property was taken by the railroad (1901).

360 For discussion of the Rhodes Scholarship, see A50-5199.

361 For Dr. McFadyen and his church politics, see A53-MCP 1-1.25; A52-5283.

362 Dr. William George Jordan, theology professor at Queen's, was a prolific writer in the Old Testament field. His *Prophetic Ideas and Ideals* (1902) is an interpretation of the Prophets. He also wrote children's Bible stories (McNeill 185-95, 203). Mary is less critical of Jordan in 1908 (see A89-6252). For his connection with McFadyen and church politics, see A52-5283n.

363 Mary may be referring to the "published report" of the work of the London Missionary Society (see A72-5765). I have been unable to locate this work.

364 "This day" is the anniversary of Isaac Baldwin McQuesten's death.

365 The Hamilton Club (an exclusive men's club) had suffered severe damage in the tornado of June 1906. Mary describes some of the damage: "Found there had been a tornado in Hamilton, which took down entirely our poor cherry tree, took the centre out of one of the maples next it…still we escaped wonderfully. Hundreds of chimneys were blown down….There was great destruction at Dundurn and elsewhere; elsewhere numbers were killed…. We hear the Ham. [Hamilton] Club is considering our place. Its roof was blown off" (5691).

　　On 13 March 1907, Mary wrote: "As to our house I think it is almost certain to go on. I was at Dr. Osborne's yesterday…and he said there was nothing else to do, but go on for they all knew already that the cost of building would be great, and when they give us an indemnity of $200, it looks pretty certain. At any rate we will have a cottage for the summer…. When Mr. Mason and the steward and cooks were over on Monday, he decided they would not take attic (which seems too good to be true) but every inch of cellar space. I was horrified to hear the bar was to be in back cellar, had not quite realized that feature, but it seemed as if I had gone too far to draw back, and wondered if I were doing wrong and yet it is just the same as an hotel" (5804).

　　The Hamilton Club considered purchasing Whitehern, but rented it instead, from April 1907 to January 1908. Letters for this period describe preparations for moving, storing furniture, and renting a cottage in Oakville for Mary and daughters. Several letters describe the condition of Whitehern when the Club moved out, and the extensive cleaning and redecorating required to restore it (A77-5820; A83-6012).

366 This is likely Sir Wilfred Thomason Grenfell (1865-1940), English physician and medical missionary to Newfoundland and Labrador. He founded hospitals, hospital ships, orphanages, and other social services (*CBD* 626). He was a forceful speaker, prolific writer, publicist, and fund raiser. He often used artistic licence in accounts of life on the northern coasts. His main financial support came from the U.S. and his papers are in the Yale medical history library (*CE* 938).

367 Miss Oates was the landlady.

368 In a letter to Calvin, Mary added a note for Tom: "Tell Tom to get raw eggs too" (5812, 7 April 1907).

369 Mary is referring to the rental income from the Hamilton Club, and the prospect of rental income from the Bold Street houses when repairs are made (see A76-5800).

370 For Rev. Dr. John McNair, see A79-5868.

371 Hugh Cossart Baker Jr. (1846-1931) was not related to Mary Baker McQuesten. He was a prominent businessman in Hamilton, a banker and stock broker, and was instrumental in forming the Hamilton Street Railway. He "conceived the idea of using a telegraph line between his house and the houses of two fellow chess players … enabling each player to telegraph his moves to his opponents" (7 blocks apart). In 1875 they organized the West Side Domestic Telegraph Co. These were replaced with telephone lines in 1877 and he leased the second telephone in Canada in 1878 (the first went to Prime Minister Alexander Mackenzie in 1877). He became the manager of The Bell Telephone Co. in Hamilton. His father had opened the first life insurance company in Upper Canada in 1847 (A84-6053; *DHB* 1:12-14; HPL *Burkholder* 139-40; for more on telegraph, see A91-6336; A20-4521 *Mewburn*).

372 This is the first mention of *any* "extravagant" purchase for Mary. The income from the Hamilton Club's rental of Whitehern likely made the purchase possible.

373 Tom wrote to Calvin in June 1907 (8198) that there had been some confusion about Calvin's courses at Knox College. Tom visited Calvin's professors several times and tried to sort out the problems in Calvin's program of studies and his exams. After four visits, the professor "finally intimated that you [Calvin] might confer with him and if you wrote on Astronomy that would be sufficient" and "there should be no difficulty about your obtaining an M.A. next Spring." However, Calvin did not receive an M.A. in the spring of 1908, but in June 1908 he received news of his B.A.(see A84-6053). Calvin continued his studies and wrote his final exams in April 1910, but still did not receive an M.A. (8198, 15 June 1907; A81-5984; A84-6053; A102-6676).

374 Principal Maurice Hutton at University of Toronto, see A51-5233. Hutton was largely responsible for the Rhodes Scholarship being awarded to Paterson and not to Tom (A50-5199).

375 Sir William Ralph Meredith (1840-1923), chief justice of Ontario (1894-1923), practised law in London and in Toronto. He was elected to the legislative assembly in 1872, and became leader of the Conservative opposition in 1878. He was knighted in 1896 and elected chancellor of the University of Toronto in 1900, a position he held until his death.

376 Grey was likely a fellow student. For Miss Elliott, see below.

377 Miss Mary Taylor is often referred to as "little Mary Taylor." She was a special friend of the McQuesten daughters and they visited frequently. She lived in Toronto at 44 Isabella Street in 1908 (A84-6053). In 1909 Mary wrote: "We have little Mary Taylor with us, she came back from England last month and is just as chatty and pleasant as ever ... [She] is engaged to an Englishman, now in Winnipeg. She visited his house when in England and they are very well off people, but her poor chap has, I'm afraid nothing yet to marry on and no definite prospects and poor little Mary so hates I think, to have to go back to taking some position" (6501). She continues to be mentioned in the letters by her maiden name so she likely did not marry the Englishman. The final mention is in 1916 (A121-6951; A124-9180). I have found no evidence that she was related to Sir Thomas Taylor (at A58-5382), or to Rev. John Thomson Taylor (at A49-5172), or to Rev. Peter Taylor (at A51-5233).

378 Mrs. MacKay died in March 1907 (5804). This letter helps to establish that she was a Gordon.

379 Tom had been engaged to article with Royce and Henderson (Robert) of Toronto at $75 per month. He assisted in the purchase of properties on the Burlington Beach strip to provide a right of way for railway and hydroelectric development between Niagara and Toronto (Best 13). Mary commented "he is getting quite a man of affairs, having the buying of the Beach properties for the Railway people, he has already paid out $25,000" (5636). The firm was pleased with his work and even paid him while he took his exams (A75-MCP 2-4.37). I have found no evidence that Robert "Bob" Henderson was related to either the Gordon Hendersons of Hamilton (A69-5709) or the Joseph Hendersons of Toronto (A52-5283).

380 In July 1907, Tom's prospects with Masten, Starr, and Spence, Toronto, became a little more definite: When Robert Henderson returned from his honeymoon business trip to England, Tom would "go in" with Masten at $1,000 per year. Mary commented: "I feel very thankful as it seems to be an excellent opening, and they are not always obtainable" (5912). For Tom's work with Masten at Elk Lake, see A82-5990.

381 Mrs. James suffered from "nervous prostration." It is described by Mary in letter of 15 June 1907: "Mrs. James completely upset Edna, and got her into such a state that I was worried to death. When Mrs. J. came she had a turn of her nervous prostration and talked without ceasing, and while I was away in Toronto at convocation, she never left the girls for a moment, as she was better she was able to come downstairs and follow them at their work so they were nearly worn out. E. never slept at all one whole night" (5876).

382 Rev. Dr. John McNair (1862-1954) University of Toronto, Knox College, University
of Gottingen, Edinburgh, lecturer Knox College (1890-92), ordained Guelph (1893),
pastor Waterloo (1893-99), Oakville (1899-1909), Petrolia (1909-14), retired (1914-
20), lecturer, London Normal School. This colourful gossip about an altercation
between minister and layman "after the sermon" perhaps accounts for the small size
of the congregation attending the Oakville Presbyterian Church (A78-5854). It is
possible that the dispute is a reflection of the storm centre within the church at that
time over higher criticism and Church Union. McNair's background at Gottingen, Germany, suggests that he might have been on the "experimental religion" side of the
debate (see A52-5283; Moir, *Enduring* 174-75).

383 Miss Elliott (escorted by Grey) was the woman to whom Tom was rumoured to be
engaged. Mary objected to the relationship and Miss Elliott attempted to win Mary's
favour by arranging to have Mary's miniature painted by a Miss Ramsay; however,
Mary found fault at each stage of the painting and retouching (A83-6012). The
romance continued in secret for a time and Miss Elliott wrote letters to Tom at Whitehern "in a masculine hand" from October 1906 to April 1907, but the relationship
ended and Tom never married. Mary makes very few comments about this relationship
in her letters (MCP 3-5.69,74,75,76,77; A81-5984; A83-6012; Best 17-18).

384 Annie Fletcher was the daughter of Rev. Dr. Donald Fletcher (see A18-4479). She
became engaged to Price Montague in May 1907 (5850), with the marriage to be in
September 1907 (A82-5990).

385 This is likely Charles Gordon, (pseudonym, Ralph Connor) who would have been
forty-seven years of age at this time (see A57-5359).

386 Likely, Rev. James Alexander Macdonald (1862-1923) University of Toronto, B.A.,
Knox College, University of Edinburgh, managing editor *Knox College Monthly* (1889-
91), pastor St. Thomas (1891-96), first editor of *The Westminster* (1896-1902), founder
and editor of *The Presbyterian*, principal Presbyterian Ladies' College (1896-1901),
managing editor the *Toronto Globe* (1902-16), L.L.D Glasgow (1909), Birmingham
(1911) (*BDKC* 128). He gave a series of impassioned speeches on evangelism and radical social reform during the Social Gospel conferences in 1908 and at the National
Missionary Congress in 1909. MacDonald was critical of the church's failure to Christianize civilization. He and others were angry that the "churches did not extend the
right-hand of fellowship to new Canadians…. There is nothing more un-Christian,
more utterly pagan, than the flaunting ostentation and pride and idleness of the members of the House of Have." He also lectured on settlement work such as Toynbee
Hall in England and others in New York and Chicago (*CBD* 1471, 4785), and he
helped to pioneer the settlement movement in Canada by the Presbyterian Church and
its "energetic Committee on Moral and Social Reform," also inspired by Charles Gordon, (see A97-6446, A92-6343). "In 1911 the Board opened St. Christopher's House
in Toronto as its first settlement" and the movement soon spread to Montreal, Winnipeg, and Vancouver (Moir, *Enduring* 184-85,187,195; McNeill 19; Gordon 162-63).
Ruby, in Ottawa, commented on a similar lecture given by a "young" and "unabashed"
"L. M. King" in 1903 (4785). This was likely, William Lyon Mackenzie King (1874-
1950), social activist and Presbyterian, who became deputy minister of Labour in 1900
and prime minister in 1921. King wrote *Industry and Humanity* (1918) (CE 1136), a copy
of which is in the Whitehern library.

387 Knox & Co was owned by John Knox (1824-1915), merchant, executive, and one of
the founders of the Cataract Power Co. He lived at 54 Hunter Street West in 1900
(Tyrell 145) and was a member of St. Paul's Presbyterian Church and chairman of its
Board of Managers for twenty-two years. St. Paul's owes its chimes to him (see A69-
5709). His dry goods business was at 18-22 King Street East, Hamilton, in 1905. In 1908
the firm was planning a move to Toronto; however, after delays caused by a workers'
strike, the business was sold to Gordon, MacKay, and Co. of Toronto (*DHB* 1.85; A84-
6053). For the MacKay family who owned the business in Toronto, see A3-4297.

388 Robert Buchanan was likely related to the Isaac Buchanan family (see A10-4367).

389 Rev. Malcolm McGregor (1852-1908) was special writer and editor of *The Presbyterian* (1900-08).

390 Likely Dr. W. P. Caven (see A45-5105).

391 For Annie Fletcher's wedding, see A82-5990.

392 Likely a mention of Miss Elliott, but no mention of her relationship with Tom (see A79-5868; A83-6012).

393 The "Bard of Athol" was William Murray (1834-1923), uncle of the bride. The Murrays lived at "Athol Banks" at Queen and Herkimer streets. He and his brother Charlie were the sons of Peter Murray, poet and businessman in wholesale and retail dry goods. William was a partner in the family business. Critics of the day acclaimed him for his "fine literary taste" and he was elected senior bard of the Caledonian Society in 1889. Many of his poems appeared in magazines and newspapers, often anonymously. Some were political, as in "Passing the Hat," an attack on Sir John A. Macdonald. He is listed in *Scottish Poets in America* (1889). He wrote poetry on biblical themes and historical events; he wrote several poems for the McQuesten family on special occasions, as well as acrostic poetry and two poems for William Blair Bruce. The Murrays were members of MacNab Street Church and his sister Phyllis married Dr. Hugh Fletcher, the minister of the church (for Fletcher, see A18-4479n; *DHB* 2:49, 119-20; A82-5990; A101-6636).

394 Dr. and Mrs. Montague lived at 5 West Avenue in 1900 (Tyrell 150;). In May 1907, Annie Fletcher's engagement to Price Montague was announced. Mary was "sorry" that Rev. Dr. Fletcher's name was to be associated with Dr. and Mrs. Montague, "quite impossible," but she did not state her reasons (5850): "Nevertheless it would make me very uncomfortable to be connected with Dr. M." She also noted that Dr. Montague was "worth about a million. Price is to manage his father's affairs in W. [Winnipeg]" (5960). Mary stated her regret that Annie was very young "It really gives one quite a shock to realize that the time has come for Edna's friends to be married.... It seems to me Annie need not be in such a hurry. But I know her mother always seemed to be in quite a hurry to have her married" (5942). On 7 September 1907, Mrs. Fletcher wrote and thanked the McQuestens for their "most useful and handsome" gift, and described the generosity of the Montagues: "Dr. Montague sent home a cheque for $1000 to furnish their home, and Mr. Montague besides many other nice things is giving her a beautiful fur coat which she was being fitted for in Toronto today. They are really exceedingly good to her" (5976; A96-6419).

395 Tom remained with Royce and Henderson until the fall of 1907, and then began work with Masten, Starr, and Spence, Toronto, at $1,000 per year (5912). He made several trips north on law business and, from January to June 1909, took charge of their new law office at Elk Lake which served the mining boom. His letters home describe frontier life. He started in Mr. Chisholm's office in Hamilton in June 1909 (see A98-6460). (A75-MCP 2-4.37; A79-5868; A84-6053; A90-6318; A91-6336; A92-6343; A95-6391).

396 The Hamilton Club had rented Whitehern from April 1907 to January 1908. Mary was indignant at the poor condition of the home when the club moved out. On 30 January, she again wrote: "I was quite upset to find the sideboard would have to be taken away and need about 5 weeks before being finished has to be scraped.... Then the ledges of the bookcases had to be scraped too, so very badly stained by the wine glasses of those wretches.... A gas leak was discovered in Grandpa's closet, a large leak.... The only part of the house which is bad now is the sitting room and it is the most wretched place. If it were not for the pictures it would be uninhabitable; but I try to think of the people in the shades and be thankful and have patience" (6020; A76-5800).

397 Aleck Gourlay was likely a grandson of Colonel William Gourlay. I have been unable to determine why he was "unfortunate." Colonel William Gourlay (1794-1867), soldier and gentleman farmer, married Emily Esther Elizabeth Whyte, daughter of Isabella Hyde Whyte, in 1850. She was reputed to be a daughter of the Duke of Kent, about

whom "clung an aura of romance and mystery which in Victorian days set whispers circulating behind fluttering fans" (Campbell 145). They had two sons and one daughter and lived at Barton Lodge, an estate on the mountain brow. Evelyn Esther Gourlay married Edward Alexander Colquhoun in 1881, had ten children, and also lived at Barton Lodge (*DHB* 1:51, 85; A87-6135; A92-6343).

398 Miss Ramsay was the artist commissioned by Miss Elliott, Tom's lady friend, to do Mary's miniature (see A79-5868). Mary found fault with each of her features on the miniature, but gave a grudging acceptance of it in January 1908: "Well, I think the miniature is now in a fair way to be good. Miss R. was here to-day and having friends to stay with, will come back in the morning and that will do I think. I am afraid, have been a difficult subject" (6020). Then in February 1908, Mary found fault with the face and the eyes: "I was afraid you would not be satisfied with the miniature. At one time thought it was fair except lower part of face, too heavy altogether and then at the last I found she had worked at the eyes and spoiled that. I would not care, if she had been practising for her own benefit, but I am more than sorry to have you disappointed. I should have stood firm by my former experience of artists and not allowed you to be drawn in. How long will Miss R.[Ramsay] stay? You had better let Miss Elliott know, you are not yet pleased with it. With much love, dearie" (6035).

Again in February 1908, Mary found fault with the nose: "find out if Miss Ramsay is coming up here again to see Mrs. Gartshore, if so she might as well come here. It occurred to me yesterday that my nose is too broad" (6039). The miniature is in the collection at Whitehern Museum.

399 For Tom and his work with Masten, Starr, and Spence, see A82-5990.

400 Mary had not been feeling well for the past year; she complained of having "blind turns" in March 1907 (5804, A72-5765; A87-6135; A103-9058).

401 For more about Calvin's "M.A.," see A79-5868.

402 John ("Jack") McIntosh Lyle, noted Ontario architect, was the architect for the new Central Church after Central burned down in 1906 (*DHB* 2:98-99). He was the son of Dr. Samuel Lyle, minister of Central Church. He attended the Hamilton School of Art, the Yale School of Arts, and L'École des Beaux-Arts, Paris, and he worked in New York for twelve years and lectured at the University of Toronto. Jack was the architect for the Royal Alexandra Theatre (1906), the Union Station in Toronto (1913-27), Memorial Arch, RMC, Kingston (1923), the original Toronto Stock Exchange, more than fifty bank branches, the High Level Bridge in Hamilton (now the Thomas B. McQuesten Bridge), and many other buildings. Lyle developed a distinctively Canadian style which parallels the Group of Seven. He integrated Canadian floral and faunal motifs into his building designs, and his designs influenced contemporary Canadian coinage (*CE* 1253; *Hamilton Spectator* 16 September 2000). He was a leader in the "City Beautiful" movement, based on a renaissance ideal, and he worked closely with Thomas McQuesten, Noulan Cauchon, and other artists and visionaries, in their urban planning projects (A125-MCP 1-3b.15).

403 Thomas Lees (1841-1936) jeweller, watchmaker, and optician, was trustee and member of the board of managers of Central Presbyterian Church (*DHB* 1:125).

404 St. James Church was first known as the Locke Street congregation. It was a small church at the southwest corner of Locke and Herkimer Streets and their building fund had grown to $2,700 in 1906. They did build a new church that opened in 1909 (*POH* 124; dates differ slightly in *Wee Kirks* 186).

405 Central Presbyterian Church had been completely destroyed by fire on 25 June 1906 (see A63-5512). It was rebuilt at at the corner of Charlton and Caroline streets, and formally opened on 14 June 1908.

406 Dr. Heurner Mullin and his brother Archie.

407 7 March was the twentieth anniversary of Isaac's death.

408 The "comfort and luxury" is relative to their former circumstances. Two months later, in a letter of 16 May, Mary is still short of money (A86-MCP 3-5.4), and on 22 May 1908, she is still carrying debts (A87-6135).

409 Likely Calvin was coming home and then going out to Glenhurst, Saskatchewan, as a missionary preacher. The "bale" of supplies had been sent ahead.

410 Rev. James Black was a retired Presbyterian minister. Mrs. James Black and Mrs. P. H. Black were members of the WFMS at MacNab Church. They lived at 112 Herkimer Street. A daughter, Jean, was married to Rev. William McKeracher, minister at Gravenhurst (see A100-6509). (Latoszek 25; Tyrell 129; A120-6853).

411 For more on Ruby's illness, see A87-6135.

412 See A17-4436 for a news account about the women of Hamilton raising the money for a statue of Queen Victoria for Gore Park.

413 The house required extensive repair and redecorating after the Hamilton Club moved out in January 1908 (A76-5800). Aleck Gourlay was helping with renovations.

414 This is the first report that Ruby's illness may have been very serious. It was variously diagnosed as grippe, cough, or bronchitis. Tom showed some concern but was hopeful when he wrote to Calvin on 25 July 1907: "The family are pretty well with the exception of Ruby who looked very badly when she came home but slowly improving and I think she will be all right again in a month or so" (8200). In June 1908 a Dr. McDunnough examined her throat and Mary was falsely reassured at his report: "Dr. McD. said it was just a muscular affection of the throat brought on by teaching, using her voice when she was tired. Dr. Caven says Dr. McD. is one of the very rare men who knows the throat so it was worth a great deal to go and hear from them that there was not a thing the matter, no bronchitis at all, but just run down a little and she needed a good change. So you can just imagine how happy we all are to-night. I had got nervous about her lungs, but both doctors said there was not a single symptom.... Dr. D. knew exactly what it was" (6169).

    In July 1908 Ruby was sent to Alberta for a rest cure where she was treated for "the con" [consumption] for nine months, then sent to a tuberculosis sanatorium in Muskoka in April 1909 and, finally, the family took a cottage on Hamilton mountain where she died on 9 April 1911 (A86-MCP3-5.4; A88-6173; A100-6509; A102-6676; A103-9058; A113-8787n; 8200).

415 Mary had been complaining of tiredness, "nervous heart," and "heart palpitations" for several months (A84-6053).

416 Mary is referring to the romantic relationship between Ruby and David Ross, son of Annie Ross, principal of Presbyterian Ladies' College at Ottawa where Ruby was teaching. See A65-5622 for David's proposal and Mary's objections. In September 1908, while Ruby was convalescing in Calgary, she wrote to Calvin in response to a suggestion that she visit the Rosses: "I couldn't do it ... without Mama's knowledge—she would certainly hear. And I wouldn't mention the name to her again. It would spoil any good she may have rec'd and I'm afraid from the last letter she is really very poorly again" (6281). In October 1908, from Calgary, Ruby informed Calvin: "I suppose I may as well tell you, if it will make you happier, that it's all over between David and myself. It was his decision & everything is now over and done for. So you can burn this letter and we will not mention the subject again" (6302).

417 Dr. and Mrs. Thomas H. Husband (nee Emma Magill) lived at 33 Jackson Street West. In June 1904 the YWCA garden party was held in the Husbands's garden, and Mary noted: "we were obliged to go. So we actually saw the inside of the house, although Hilda is not satisfied because she did not see the upstairs" (5245)

418 This is likely the wife of one of William Hendrie's five sons. I am unable to locate her father's name (her maiden name). William Hendrie had died in June 1906 (5516). For Hendrie family, see A35-4803. It is also possible that Mary had written in sympathy at (or near) the second anniversary of William Hendrie's death.

419 Likely Sir John Morison Gibson (see A17-4436).

420 For Irving family, see A35-4803. Mr. Irving was likely a relative of Dr. Irving, who died in 1901. Dr. Irving was Mrs. (Fletcher) Irving's husband (7296).

421 Rev. Colin Fletcher had abdominal surgery for "peritonitis" in May 1908 (6125) and was not expected to be well enough to preach again for at least six months (6223).

422 This is likely Prof. William McLaren, principal of Knox College from 1905. In 1875 he was convenor of the Foreign Missions Committee (FMC) and instrumental in establishing the first Woman's Foreign Missionary Society (WFMS). His wife, Marjorie, was the first president and they were closely involved in the first training centre for women overseas missionaries. In 1906 "the venerable" McLaren spoke against a union with the Western auxiliaries to form the WHMS, which Mary also resisted because it would effectively deplete funds and personnel for the women in the overseas effort, but they were defeated (see A49-5172). McLaren was also involved in attempting to resolve the gender conflict and the Wilkie case, see A30-4651 (Brouwer 21, 24, 26, 36, 48, 133, 135). In the higher criticism and Church Union debate he was firmly on the side of the fundamentalists and the "anti-unionists" (as was Mary). See "professors & preachers" at A52-5283n (Moir, *Enduring* 176, 199, 204; A88-6173). It is not known if he was related to Rev. W. W. McLaren (1873-1915), missionary pastor and principal of Birtle Indian Boarding School when Mary visited the West in 1906 (see A124-9180n).

423 Robert ("Bobby") Kerr (1882-1963) was "a blond Irish-Canadian ... track great, whose remarkable career as a runner climaxed hundreds of victories and new records ... with a 1908 Olympic championship in the 220 yards." Some of his records stood for 20 years. He worked at International Harvester and was a fireman in Hamilton (Campbell 185, CE 1133).

424 For Dr. Jordan, see A74-5794 where Mary is critical of Jordan's and McFadyen's preaching. Here she appears more accepting of it, from Tom's report. For the "professors & preachers" of higher criticism see A52-5283n.

425 Tom started in Chisholm's office on 19 June 1909 (see A98-6460, 6458). Tom was somewhat reluctant to settle down in Hamilton. He wrote to Cal: "If I did have the idea of going into politics I would have to consider where to settle down. It would be almost hopeless for a liberal to try to get elected in Toronto. I think I would stand a far better chance in Hamilton, but then I could not afford to be a stranger there" (8176).

Notes 1909-1934

426 The *Republic* steamship was shipwrecked in collision with an Italian vessel, the *Florida*, 23 January 1909. It sank 39 hours later in 40 fathoms (240 ft) 15 miles off Nantucket, while being towed in for repair. During the 39 hours, the 1,500 passengers were transferred twice. The heroic wireless operator Jack Binns remained at his station "summoning aid by wireless, using it for the first time at sea for this purpose" and "subsequently every soul aboard the *Republic* was saved ... and Sealby [Captain] was the last to leave the ship." The cargo was lost: $3,000,000 in American Gold Eagles destined for the Imperial Russian Government of the Czar, as well as all luggage and personal possessions. The *Republic*, similar to the *Titanic*, was considered unsinkable. "This golden cache still rests in its watery tomb ... waiting" (*Official RMS Republic Web site*, 8 December 1999. AltaVista Sites). Another shipwreck rescue by telegraphy occurs in a letter of 5 February 1910: "Isn't that wireless telegraphy a wonderful thing? The rescue of the Kentucky another instance" (6630). For Mary's report of the *Titanic's* sinking, see A110-8848.

427 Marconi's first experiments with wireless telegraphy occurred in 1895 and 1899. However, it was "conceived in N. America by Samuel Morse in 1837 and in Europe by the English partnership of William Cooke and Charles Wheatstore.... In Canada, the first telegraph company, the Toronto, Hamilton and Niagara Electro-Magnetic Telegraph Co. was formed in 1846." By 1881 it had been taken over by Western Union Co. of the United States which, for a brief time "controlled virtually all telegraphy in

Canada, after which it was taken over by the railroads" (*CE* 2123; *CBD* 969; see also Hugh Cossart Baker A78-5854; *DHB* 1:13; and Burkholder 139-40).

Marconi's wireless system created a revolution in communications technology. The *News*, Toronto, 21 May 1904, ran an ad offering an investment opportunity in the new wireless telegraphy:

MARCONI WIRELESS EARNINGS MR. MARCONI SPEAKS. Mr. Marconi stated that he was very anxious to get the daily wireless news service to steamships started "not only because it will be very profitable to the company, but because it will be very profitable to the publishers of the ship's daily newspapers, as well, through the publication of advertisements".... "But see the advantage we have over wire systems" said he "to send a news dispatch of 1,000 words to fifty differ-ent newspapers by wire requires the transmission of 50,000 words. We can serve fifty ships or more with 1,000 words each by sending only 1,000 words. Each of the ships will receive the message simultaneously. At the same time no vessel, not carrying our system, can receive a single word of the dispatch." ... A net annual profit to the system of $730,000.... Mr. Marconi is busy with big plans which promise great results for the future ... If you want to be one of those to profit by the extraordinary opportunity offered by the Marconi investment ... at $5.00 each you must have your application in our hands on or before June 20th ... Marconi expects to put this girdling of the earth into operation about the mid-dle of August.... The magnetic device will take forty words a minute ... long-distance tests will be made by British war vessels in different parts of the world. NOW ACT! Marconi Wireless Telegraph Company of America.

428 Mr. and Mrs. J. W. Woods, Miss E. B. Woods, Miss I. L. George, and Dr. and Mrs. John Caven, were on the passenger list of the *Republic*. Mr. and Mrs. James W. Woods lived at 91 Breadalbane Street, summer residence 170 Centre Island; they had two daughters named Effie and Mary, and Mrs. Woods's maiden name was Douglas. They were all from Toronto, and all were first-class passengers travelling to the Mediterranean. Mary stated that Dr. John Caven had "known your father well at college" and he had examined Ruby in 1908 (A45-5105; 6169). It is not known if Mr. Woods is the same person who suffered a fall in February 1909 and was not expected to recover (A93-6347).

429 Daughter of Mr. and Mrs. MacKay (A3-4297). Mrs. Mackay had died in March 1907 (5804) and Mr. MacKay had died in February 1909 (6359).

430 Rev. R. P. MacKay (1847-1929) was secretary of the Foreign Mission Committee (FMC) from 1892 to 1916. He travelled a great deal inspecting the various missions in the East, in China, Korea, and India. In 1911 he became Moderator of the General Assembly. He was from East Zorra, Ontario, and was educated at University of Toronto and Knox College. His son-in-law, Rev. Andrew Thomson, wrote his biography: *The Life and Letters of Rev. R. P. MacKay, D.D.* (1932) (Thomson 97, 108; McNeill 66, 144, 192; *BDKC* 133). In the gender struggles between the Committee and the WFMS, MacKay "was particularly anxious to resist any accretions of power by the WFMS." This usually involved decision making about the distribution of monies collected, which the women had mandated for women missionaries and for work with women and children, but which the committee wished to appropriate for the larger political body. This money is likely the "account" that Mary would like to "bring back" (Brouwer 38-39). MacKay also favoured Church Union, which Mary rejected. Mary comments: "Every where we went in the West we heard of the badly planned tour of R. P. Mackay and the little good done when he did arrive and all spoke of the difference between him and Miss Craig ... and what sort of results can you expect from such visitations ... it is waste of time. Well, I will waste no more on the subject" (5964). I have found no relationship with the D. MacKays, Mary's friends in Toronto (A3-4297).

431 Mrs. Janet McGillvray was editor of *Foreign Missionary Tidings* (Brouwer 51). Her husband, Donald, was "chiefly engaged in the extensive translation and other publication work for the society" (McNeill 123).

432 Possibly, Donald Calvin Hossack (1862-1937) ordained minister and barrister in Toronto (*BDKC* 104).

433 Prof. Kennedy was a teacher at Knox College (see A98-6460).

434 For Rev. Samuel Harper Gray (1873-1916) see A106-6746n; A118-9153.

435 James Burnside Paulin (1879-1969) University of Toronto (1904), Knox College (1902-03), Glasgow (1907-08), ordained and pastor at St. Giles Church, Hamilton (1908-16), Toronto (1918-30), teacher, Aurora (1930-32), St. John's Newfoundland, (1932-34), Toronto, Rosedale (1934-50), D.D. Knox College (1930).

436 Dr. John Pringle had been a missionary to the Klondike (see A49-5172).

437 Rolland was likely the son of Albert H. Hills, a Hamilton architect (A3-4297).

438 Mr. and Mrs. William Symington lived at 134 Duke Street. She was a member of the WFMS at MacNab Church and was treasurer of the Presbyterial (Latoszek 25; A109-8867).

439 Dr. and Mrs. John Caven had been passengers on the shipwrecked *Republic* (see A91-6336).

440 *The Letters of Queen Victoria* (3 volumes, 1908) are in the Whitehern library. Mary's comment about this collection of letters helps to establish that she appreciated the importance of letters in a historical/cultural context. She also notes her great regard for Queen Victoria.

441 "Old Mr. Gordon" was the father of Dr. Gilbert Gordon, who "died of consumption of the bowels" (4847). He left his wife Mary (Taylor) Gordon with three children and a farm in Waterdown, with "no servant and things looked poor"(5675, 5683). She lived for a time with "old Mr. Gordon" and then with her mother, Lady Taylor, in 1909, at which time Mr. Gordon went into a sanatorium "where he has a fine room and finds the electrical treatment very beneficial" (6436). I have found no evidence that "old Mr. Gordon" is related to Rev. Charles Gordon (A57-5359) or to Dr. David Miner Gordon (A22-4535). For Thomson relationship, see A15-4415.

442 I am unable to identify Mr. Woods. It is not known if he is the same Mr. Woods who survived the shipwreck of the *Republic* in A91-6336.

443 Ethel Caroline Kinrade was murdered on 25 February 1909. Her sister Florence claimed that she and Ethel answered the door to a man who asked for food and then demanded money. When Florence went to get the money, Ethel was shot to death. When Florence returned, she quickly handed him the money and fled out the back door. In spite of a good description, the man was never found. Another theory "holds that Florence may have been collaborating with him or may herself have committed the crime. However none of these allegations was ever proven. The murder remains unsolved." The Kinrades lived at 105 Herkimer Street and Mr. Kinrade had warned the girls not to turn away any vagrants who requested food, because the family should "share the comforts" with which it had been "blessed." However, Mrs. Kinrade was frightened by the "suspicious characters" "hanging about" their home and at the time of the murder "was at the police station demanding protection for the family" (*DHB* 2:85). On 1 May 1909 Mary commented: "Our papers are full of the lawyers' contentions over the Kinrade affair. Do not know the use of Stanton prolonging affair by keeping Florence out of witness box, but perhaps he knows. People give family a terribly bad character, thoroughly <u>bad</u>, except the mother" (6409).

444 Daughter of Mr. and Mrs. MacKay of Toronto (see A3-4297).

445 For Hostetter and Thomson connection, see A15-4415.

446 Maggie (MacKay) White and her sister Leila (MacKay) Senkler (A3-4297). Their father had died earlier in February 1909 (6359). The reference is to the disposition of the estate (see also A99-6483). Mr. Hammond was likely a bank official or a business associate.

447 I have been unable to establish the nature of Calvin's illness; however, it may have been another nervous collapse, which often occurred under stress, such as during exams, or overwork.

448 On 8 April Mary wrote: "In the meantime a new site for Public Library is required. Carnegie having offered $25,000. There is scarcely any likelihood of us being taken on account of the Railway" (6387). The Hamilton Public Library was built near Whitehern, at Main and MacNab Streets It was funded by Andrew Carnegie and opened 5 May 1913. The first library in Hamilton was the Mercantile Library in 1854, then the Mechanic's Institute with the first reading room. In 1883 a lending library was established by the Lancefield brothers and R. T. Lancefield became the first librarian for the new public library (see A24-4549). There was strong opposition at first to the Free Libraries Act of 1885 because some men thought that "libraries were just for the purpose of letting women read novels, while their children were being cared for at the kindergartens," and the term "dime novel" was "about the last word in the demoralization of the youth system" (Burkholder 86). Mary and her family were very much in favour of the public library as were many other prominent Presbyterians and Hamiltonians.

449 Tom had been at Elk Lake since January 1909 practising law for Masten, Starr and Spence during the silver boom at Cobalt, Ontario (see A82-5990). In Mary's letter of 24 April 1909, she tells of Tom's long walk at Elk Lake: "He had just returned (on the 20th) from Gowganda having walked there and back 66 miles. A pretty rough trip and lots of lice, it is a beastly hole. Wasn't that a terrible experience. Do not know how he did it" (6398).

450 The *Globe* of 20 April 1909 carried an article about the revolution in Turkey: "Report that the Sultan has Fled on a Warship: Young Turks threaten to hang him in front of his palace. Macedonian army of nearly 30,000 men closing in on Constantinople. The officerless soldiery here are in a blue funk and say they won't fight.... They are determined this time to hang the sultan in front of his own palace. There is to be no mistaken clemency now.... The crowned assassin will assassinate no longer. The sultan's complicity in Tuesday's mutiny has been overwhelmingly proved. The reactionary Mohammedan society which caused the mutiny was led by the chief of the palace eunuchs, and included ... his son, his chamberlain and many of the Old Regime spies, all living in the palace. The Mutinous troops in St. Sophia Square ... were well provided with gold pieces ... these facts are conclusive. There is no fear of Christian massacre here as the Christians are well armed....The worst feature of it, if not the starting point, was the fanaticism of the Moslems and their bloodthirsty treatment of the Christians ... one of the most injurious despotisms known to history.... Turkey may now be left unmolested to show what her people can do in the way of self-government."

A young Canadian seaman, "Ransford D' Bucknam," was part of the Court of Sultan Abdul Hamid. "Bucknam Pasha" was vice-admiral of the empire, in command of the Imperial navy and of all naval construction. "Twice already he has saved the life of the Sultan, and present indications are that he will not have long to wait for a third opportunity" (the *Globe*, 21 April 1909). On 15 May, the *Globe* included an advertisement for subscriptions (donations) "For the Adana Christians": for the relief of Christian "refugees in Asia Minor devastated by fanatical Turks." They claimed to be in "constant telegraphic touch with the missionaries at all the points where the Armenians were slaughtered ... victims of Moslem fanaticism."

451 Rev. Dr. John A. Carmichael was the missionary in charge of the synod of Manitoba (1902-11) (*BDKC* 36). When Calvin first wrote inquiring about the Western field, Carmichael stated: "I could give you a field where you would have long journeys every week and abundance of time in the open air. Our work requires men of high purpose and average preaching ability." Carmichael travelled a great deal and wrote to Calvin on 10 May 1909 describing his very heavy schedule and noting that Friday, 21 May was the only day he would be free. Presumably the ordination took place on the previous Sunday (7441, 7797, 7769).

452 Calvin was ordained at Glenhurst, Saskatchewan, where he was a missionary preacher and homesteader.

453 For Tom's work at Elk Lake, see A82-5990.

454 Herbert Henry Asquith (1852-1928), British Liberal, became prime minister of Britain in April 1908 (*CBD* 71).

455 For the Coronation Oath, see A97-6446.

456 Rev. Norman MacEachern (1882-1945), University of Toronto (1903-07), Glasgow (1907-08), Knox College (1908-09), Montreal Presbyterian College (1909-10), M.A. University of Toronto (1909), ordained Toronto (1910), pastor Brampton (1910-16), overseas chaplain (1916-19), Smith's Falls (1919-21), Toronto (1921-26), Winnipeg (1926-31), D.D. Montreal (1937), editor Presbyterian publications (1931-45) (*BDKC* 130).

457 I have found no record of Mr. Cooper.

458 The *Globe* 15 May 1909, reported that Mr. Asquith, prime minister of Britain "Favors the Amendment of Coronation Oath" to remove the "Catholic Disabilities." The bill passed its second reading with "Asquith's cordial support" and he said that the declaration was an "unnecessary safeguard of the Protestant succession, dated from probably the worst period in our history." The Roman Catholics named as "Objectionable Clauses" those who denied that "in the sacrament of the Lord's Supper there is any transubstantiation of the elements of bread and wine into the body and blood of Christ ... whatsoever, and that the invocation or adoration of the Virgin Mary or any other Saint and the sacrifice of Mass are superstitious and idolatrous." The Orangemen of Canada protested and drew up resolutions and mailed them in large numbers to the British Protestant Alliance in London and demanded "the retention of the oath as at present." In 1901 the same issue had been raised and Rev. J. L. Gordon, of Toronto, defended it and said that "Catholics should amend their own oaths." The Cardinal in London declared that the language used in the declaration was "stupid, silly, cruel, painful, shameful, and most wicked." Mr. Gordon replied that the oath was "one of the strongest bulwarks of the British Constitution and the backbone of Protestantism" (*Evening News*, 1 April 1901).

459 I have found no record of Principal Forrest of Halifax. He may have been related to George Forrest who came from Scotland and the United States to become pastor of St. Gabriel Street Church in Montreal in 1802.

460 Dr. William Patrick was principal of Manitoba College in 1899 until his death in 1911. He favoured Church Union and made a "devastating attack on John MacKay" for his delaying tactics and concern for property settlements. See note for John MacKay below (A97-6446n) (McNeill 82; Moir, *Enduring* 197, 199, 200, 203).

461 For a discussion of Church Union from 1875 to 1905, see A52-5283. The publication of "The Basis of Union" occurred in 1908. In 1909 the sides began to form and by 1910 the movement became intensely political and debates raged in the Colleges and at the Assemblies, which "divided the church sharply." In 1913 "The General Committee of the Organization for the Preservation and Continuance of the Presbyterian Church in Canada" was formed in protest, the debates raged for years, and the fear of schism was strong (Moir, *Enduring* 199, 207). The world war intervened and a "truce" was "scrupulously observed" until the early 1920s when it was found that many churches had formed "union churches" of "double affiliation," especially in the West, where congregations were small and widely separated. After the war, returning servicemen, pressure of immigration, and the need for missions at home and abroad fostered a united emphasis on "social activism," "moral reform," and education. In 1925 union finally took place by a two-thirds majority and the United Church was formed. The remaining one-third, the same number as in 1911, voted to perpetuate "a distinctive Presbyterian denomination in Canada." The "leading exponents" of higher criticism and "Union" departed into the United Church; however "the tradition of biblical criticism that McFadyen and others had represented went into eclipse with Union, and "with them too had gone the Social Gospellers." Moir laments that "each parted without charity for the other" (Moir, *Enduring* 176, 189-90, 199, 203-204 206, 211-12, 235; McNeill 245-61). "Significantly, no woman was ever included" in the various

committees, and in 1913 "The Women's League" was formed as an anti-union group. By 1923 Mary was "violently opposed" to union and organized a group of women to hold a session of their own at the conference, see A127-24 April 1923.

462 I have found no record of Dr. Duval.

463 Dr. John MacKay was principal of Westminster Hall, a new seminary in Vancouver. He was opposed to union, was concerned about property settlements in the advent of union, and he demanded agreement of the people "with reasonable unanimity." He was a "gradualist" and recommended "delay and co-operation" (Moir, *Enduring* 203).

464 Rev. Dr. Robert Campbell, minister of St. Gabriel Street Church, Montreal, had been clerk of the Presbyterian Assembly since 1892 and had written and worked for "reconciliation" and "forbearance." He was on the General Committee ... for the Preservation ... of the Presbyterian Church in Canada" in 1913, and "published a book-length attack on organic union." He also challenged the Assembly on union in 1916 on the grounds of irregularities in the voting. Campbell wrote an exhaustive *History of the Scotch Presbyterian Church, St. Gabriel St., Montreal* (1887) (McNeill 191, 252; Moir, *Enduring* 137, 207). This book is not in the Whitehern library.

465 This is possibly an older relative of Rev. Dr. William H. Sedgewick of Central Church (A124-9180), in which case they would have been on opposite sides of the Union debate, but it was not unusual for families to be split on the issue.

466 Rev. Dr. George Pidgeon and C. W. Gordon (Ralph Connor) collaborated with J. G. Shearer of Hamilton in his work on social reform following his political success with the "The Lord's Day Act." They formed the Department of Moral and Social Reform (1906). They did an "exhaustive survey of temperance, gambling, Sabbath observance, 'social evil' [prostitution], industrial relations, and pornography ... and of the pressing work remaining to be done in these fields, as well as an account of the interdenominational federated Moral and Social Reform Council of Canada" a political body of which Shearer was secretary. Together they did a "two-year study of urban living—'The Problem of the Twentieth Century'" (Moir, *Enduring* 179, 184, 193-96, 209, 217, 223)

467 Gordon influenced the theme of the 1908 National Missionary Congress: "Will Canada Evangelize her share of the world?" and the 1909 Congress was a culmination of that work. Nearly 5,000 people attended as Gordon spoke on "The Place of the Church in the Making of the Nation" and had specific, radical recommendations to make. He was "angered that the churches did not extend the right-hand of fellowship to new Canadians." One concrete form of such evangelical outreach was the social and settlement work pioneered by the Presbyterian group in Toronto, Montreal, Winnipeg, and Vancouver, all inspired by Toynbee Hall in England (See A80-5898n; Moir, *Enduring* 179, 184, 194, 196; Gordon 162-63).

468 Rev. Donald Campbell MacGregor (1875-1946), educated at University of Toronto, Glasgow, and Knox College, and pastor at Orillia (1909-11), was assistant secretary Department of Social Service and Evangelism of the Presbyterian Church in Canada (*BDKC* 130).

469 Murdoch A. McKinnon, from the West, was also a social activist. In his speech of 1913, "The New Patriotism," he "warned that the existing social system based on apathy, materialism, injustice and religious indifference must give way to a 'social order where the good of each is based upon the good of all'" (Moir, *Enduring* 195).

470 Principal Gordon of Queen's also advocated social activism and "In 1909 practical field experience in 'Christian or Social Work' became a requirement for all students of the college." He was also a moderate, a "gradualist," on the question of union (see A97-6446n) (Moir, *Enduring* 190, 204).

471 For Mr. Byers, I have found no record.

472 Rev. James Little (1875-1935) born at Hamilton, son of Rev. James Little, was the assistant at Central Church (1904-05), pastor Brampton (1905-10), Westminster, Toronto (1917-35), United Church (1925) (*BDKC* 123-24).

473 Tom began working as a partner in the law office of James Chisholm for $1,000 per year (A98-6460). Chisholm had been his father's junior law partner. Mary had been urging Tom home to get him involved in politics, which he also desired, although he was somewhat reluctant to return to Hamilton (A90-6318; 8176). In Mary's letter to Calvin 19 June 1909 she commented: "Tom came home last night and started to the office this morning, think it will be quite a change to settle to regular work; has had a lazy time of it up north" (6458).

474 For James Chisholm, see A8-2520. His sister was likely the Alice Chisholm mentioned in 5876, 15 June 1907.

475 I have found no record for Rev. Jos. Nite Cory of British Columbia.

476 Prof. Kennedy was a teacher at Knox College (A91-6336). Tom reported to Calvin that Kennedy was going "across" to take a postgraduate course, likely to Scotland. He also stated to Calvin: "[Kennedy] was quite in your line was he not. Well after you have had a year or two preaching probably we could manage to send you across for a post-graduate course" (8212).

477 I have found no record for Prof. Seyas.

478 Ruby had been with May in Calgary when both were convalescing. Ruby had tuberculosis and May likely the same. May recovered but Ruby did not and died in April 1911 (see A87-6135).

479 Likely, Laura Hostetter and Mrs. Thomson (see A15-4415).

480 Hamilton's East End Incline Railway ran from the base of the mountain at Wentworth Street to the top of the mountain. It consisted of "two cable cars owned and operated by George Webb. The cars had a passenger cabin and an area large enough to accommodate horse-drawn wagons, motor vehicles and theatre-goers during the season." Summers Mountain Theatre overlooked Hamilton at the top of Wentworth Street. The incline was favoured by tourists for viewing the city (*DHB* 3:201; Bailey, *Around and about Hamilton* 117). It was converted to electricity in 1914. Unfortunately, the line suffered losses and was closed on 15 August 1936 (HPL Web site).

481 Maggie (MacKay) White, one of the MacKay children from Toronto, had disclosed to Mary some of the details of the disposition of Mr. MacKay's will (died February 1909, 6359). Leila was married to Dr. Senkler. Small, the cook, and Mary were likely servants of the MacKays at 5 Queen's Park Crescent in Toronto. Drummond did marry a Miss Smith (6540).

482 I have found no record of Mrs. Williams Helms or of the "Event."

483 Likely Dr. W. P. Caven.

484 Gordon Gates's death had been reported in Mary's letter to Calvin of 21 August 1909: "he died of consumption, ill a long time, his sister will be very lonely without him" (6501). He and his sister were likely related to the Gates family mentioned in the note for the Bell family at A25-4582.

485 Dr. Parfitt was in charge of the sanatorium at Gravenhurst where Ruby was being treated for tuberculosis (A113-8787; A87-6135; A103-9058).

486 Jean (Black) McKeracher was likely the daughter of Rev. James Black, a retired Presbyterian minister. Her husband, Rev. William McKeracher, was a minister at Gravenhurst. He invited Calvin to take his services for him on 17 September during his holidays so that Calvin could visit with Ruby (6540).

487 Calvin did visit Ruby at Gravenhurst (6574).

488 The *British Weekly: Journal of Social and Christian Progress* for 20 January 1910 displays a front page editorial during the election campaign, entitled "Points for Progressives." It is a direct attack on the Tory "Protectionists" and their tariffs, as opposed to the Liberals (Progressives) and their "Free Trade." The editorial foresees the danger of war with Germany under the Protectionists, and declares: "We may say with joy that Protectionism, if not dead, is at least in a dead faint." On 27 January 1910 the paper reports a victory for the Progressives: "Back again after the most terrific electoral battle

fought within living memory." On 3 February, the paper notes a "victory by a round majority of 124" and attacks the "pretensions of the House of Lords" who "have striven for" the "absolute destruction of representative government in this country." The Free Trade Liberals under Prime Minister. Asquith gained the support of industry and unions and won by promising employment and social benefits (Owen 185-88).

489 For Murray family, see A82-5990.

490 Gordon Hamilton Southam (1886-1916), athlete, publisher, and soldier, worked for his father's printing company and became assistant manager of the *Hamilton Spectator*. He was killed in World War One.

491 Crawfords' Confectionery Store, see A10-4367.

492 On 26 April 1910, Mary wrote to Calvin about his exams: "Amidst all my cares, I feel I am not half thankful enough for your health. It really is such a great blessing and such a comfort to send you off in perfect health, and after all the disappointments it is a most wonderful achievement to have finally passed all your examinations and be finally launched, for which we have great reason to thank God. One cannot forget the time, when we both decided that nevermore must you attempt examinations. It is truly wonderful, the goodness of God!" (9033).

493 Mai Mathewson was from Goderich (6732). Nell was, likely, Nellie James, who attended Mai's wedding on 22 August 1911 (6758).

494 Rev. Dr. David George McQueen (1854-1930), ordained missionary (Edmonton 1887-1930), was also Protestant school inspector for Alberta (1887-94), chaplain at Alberta penitentiary (1906-30), D.D. (1905), L.L.D. (1912), and moderator in 1915 and 1925 (*BDKC* 172).

495 Rev. Frederick Smeaton Dowling (1879-1949) Knox College 1906-09, ordained and assistant First Church Edmonton 1910, Toronto, New Brunswick, and Nova Scotia 1911-25, United Church 1925 (*BDKC*).

496 Ruby left the cottage at Muskoka (A102-6676) in October 1910 when the family took a cottage on the Hamilton mountain near Chisholm's house on the brow, and Hilda became her caregiver there. They named it "Cosy Cottage." Hilda wrote to Calvin on a very windy day, 14 December 1910: "I hope we won't be swepted [sic] over the mountain, but we are very cosy inside" (9050; 8709; 8722). The family visited regularly and Ruby died on 9 April 1911. The only letter in the Whitehern *Calendar* reporting Ruby's death is a letter of condolence from a friend: "I heard from mother this evening—and of your loss. I knew it must come soon and yet I cannot realize it. I did not know how much I loved her till that day and what a comfort it must be to know how happy she was being at Home again and seeing you all so often—she spoke of it to me and said—'And dear old Tom comes up every day—if it is only for a few minutes' ... Helen J. R. Locke" (6680). A commemorative journal is in the archive and Whitehern.

497 Mary is referring to Edna's mental illness (A58-5382; A59-5426).

498 Mary is likely referring to Ruby's death (A87-6135; A103-9058n).

499 I have found no record of a Dr. Thornton as moderator. The reference is likely to the discussion of the changes in the Coronation Oath in Mary's letter of 11 June 1909 (see A97-6446).

500 Mr. Sillars is again mentioned in A106-6746.

501 The *Hamilton Spectator*, 28 July 1911, describes the "Aviation Meet" as a contest between three "birdmen" and their respective flying machines: "Hamilton had its first taste of flying in the air when McCurdy, Willard and Martin, three well-known aviators made their initial flights.... Seven flights were made, four by Willard, two by McCurdy, and one by Martin, the efforts of Willard to please the crowd proving the most enjoyable, as he made prolonged flights directly over the field throwing in a few dips and turns as extra measure.... Willard is the man to look to for sensations.... McCurdy flew a new machine a little bit of a bi-plane."

On 29 July the heading read: "Aviator Had a Close Call: Martin's engine failed to work and he came down, descended in the Marsh but escaped injury ... McCurdy had his little baby Wright in good working order ... the little machine showing all kinds of speed.... Willard was undoubtedly the most popular one of the three birdmen ... supplied lots of thrills." The object of the meet was to establish new records in altitude and speed, and at one point McCurdy flew to a height of "over two thousand feet." Mary saw the meet on the following Monday and Willard and Martin (the Englishman) did not fly.

502   John Alexander Douglas McCurdy (1886-1961), aviation pioneer, made more than 200 short flights before flying the *Silver Dart* off the ice at Baddeck, Nova Scotia, in February 1909, the first controlled flight by a British subject in the British Empire. He designed the *Silver Dart* and it was built by the Aerial Experiment Association formed by Alexander Graham Bell. He also made the first ocean flight from Florida to Cuba while sending and receiving the first messages while aloft (*National Aviation Museum*. December 28, 1999, online <www.aviation.nmstc.ca>).

503   Mary had written to Calvin that Hilda had "a terrible nose ... a similar one after last Christmas work.... Doctor declared it had been poisoned, probably her veil, and gave her some remedies ... the swelling is all down, but it is literally the colour of a beet all over the tip of the nose and the poor girl cannot be seen" (6564, 11 December 1909). Again in August 1911 Hilda took treatments for her nose at the Hiscott Institute in Toronto: "It has been three weeks now and I feel it is on the mend" (6762).

504   The reference to a visit with "the family" suggests that the Joseph Hendersons of Toronto (A52-5283) may have been related to the Gordon Hendersons of Hamilton (A69-5709).

505   It is not known which McKay she married.

506   Tom's salary was increased to $1,200 per year. Tom wrote to Calvin, 17 August 1911: "I am getting a larger office, which I suppose will be a gratification to Mrs. McQ. She sniffed every time she came into the present office" (8239).

507   The *Hamilton Spectator*, 8 August 1911, reviewed the show at the Temple Theatre in the "Music and Drama" column and described the Coronation pictures of George V in 1910 as a grand tour round the world by ... this marvelous invention.... How perfect this color motion photography is by Kinemacolor.... It was possible to see the coronation procession as it actually took place with the rich colors of the ... military, the gaudy decorations in the streets, and the multitudinous shades of the thousands of horses. These were not tinted pictures, but the actual reproduction of the scene as it was. Foods and wines were depicted. Then came a trip of Lake Garda in Italy.... Then a film dealing with ships that were reviewed by the King.... Then the growth of flowers ... a performance which had a distinct attractiveness from a scientific as well as a purely pictorial point of view as the blossoms were shown from their growth from a bud to full bloom.

       Mary did not normally approve of going to the theatre and her children were not allowed to attend, but presumably the Coronation pictures were considered acceptable theatre fare. Also live theatre was permitted and Mary describes the Shakespearean plays they attended in June 1904 (A51-5233). See A122-6967 for Mary's comment on "theatricals."

508   Rev. Dr. Samuel Harper Gray (1873-1916) B.A. Queen's University 1894, M.A. 1895, Knox College 1895-98, ordained Calgary 1898, missionary Banff and Canmore 1898-99, Knox Church, Dundas 1899-1911, Toronto 1911-16 (BDKC 91; A91-6336; A118-9153). He was the son of Rev. Patrick Gray and Jane (Harper). He died at the age of 43. He was married to Laura Laing who graduated from University of Toronto with a B.A. 1896.

509   For Mrs. J. Emily Steele, see A11-4387. In 1911 she was elected president of the national WFMS, at which time she moved to Toronto (Brouwer 41).

510   Several letters at this time describe plans and purchases to furnish Calvin's manse at Bracebridge. In her letter of 8 April 1912 Mary opens with: "I went down this morning

to see about that brown carpet at Watkins. They had got another in like you saw and also some Brussel squares like you saw. I was so undecided that I telephoned Tom and we finally decided on the Brussel, it is a lovely brown, but the floor will need to be painted about 1 ft wide all round, the carpet is a rich golden brown. Then Tom saw a Moravian rug large enough for "living room" that is 9 x 12 for [$110.00?] and he was quite determined to have it. The centre is a beautiful [crimson?], so you must try and have the new paper a very colourless affair, for the rug is very bright, with [?] effect. Is the paint yellow?" (8872).

511 Duncan Chisholm, handyman (A133-7074; A139-MCP 2-3b.40). He may have been related to James Chisholm, Tom's law partner (A8-2520).

512 Ruby and Calvin were kindred spirits and they often wrote long "stavers" to one another.

513 The Thomsons' summer home was in Burlington.

514 Miss Honeycomb was a seamstress (see A69-5709).

515 Thompson's Art Store was located at 64 King Street East. It was the oldest retail art business in Canada, est. 1860. It started at 47 James Street North and drew "customers from all over the Dominion" (HPL, Special Collections). Mary is likely referring to an art show or sale, in which case some of Ruby's and Edna's paintings may have been sold. Many of their paintings are on display at Whitehern, as well as a collection of engravings. Ruby was a good artist and won acclaim at a Hamilton Art School exhibit: "In sepia work the best thing shown for years is a castor plant leaf by Ruby McQuesten" (News clipping n.d., Box 08). This work, or one similar, is on display at Whitehern.

516 The *Titanic* sank on 15 April 1912. She was considered unsinkable, but on her maiden voyage, at high speed, she struck an iceberg in the North Atlantic near midnight and sank in less than three hours. There were insufficient lifeboats for all aboard so only 705 passengers were saved, and more than 1,500 people perished in the icy water. The confidence in the ship was so strong that the first news reports indicated that the passengers were safe and that the wonder of the wireless had averted the disaster: "Wireless Played Noble Part in Saving of Lives: The Drama Enacted on the Atlantic To-day Would Have Been Turned Into a Tragedy But For Marconi's Invention"; "Other Liners Rushed After Getting the Flash to the Aid of the Crippled Titanic—Passengers Safely Transferred." The next day, the headlines read "OCEAN'S WORST TRAGEDY": Appalling Shipwreck Has Stunned Humanity ... Titanic's victims now estimated at not less than 1200"; "News was Terrible Shock After the False Reports Sent Out from Various Sources Yesterday"; "Titanic Disaster Thrilled Hamilton" (the *Hamilton Spectator*, 15 and 16 April 1912). For a comparison with the averted disaster on the *Republic*, a similar ship, see A91-6336.

517 I have found no record for D. C. McGee. Possibly, Mary heard a reading of a speech made by Thomas D'Arcy McGee (1825-1868) a "zealous reformer," politician, journalist, poet, historian, and "Probably the most eloquent Father of Confederation." He was occupied with the welfare of Irish immigrants, the settlement of the West, a transcontinental railway, and the development of a distinctly Canadian literature. McGee was assassinated "likely by a Fenian extremist" (CE 1265). The newspapers of the early twentieth century carry many reports of social reform lectures, meetings, and activists who "Attack Social Evil Vigorously" (the *Hamilton Spectator* headline, 16 April 1912).

518 Mary and her daughter Mary and a contingent of women from the WFMS had attended missionary meetings in Vancouver, and were vacationing as well.

519 Grace Weir Hastings of Vancouver met them "at the elevator" of Glencoe Lodge in Vancouver (6769).

520 These Hendersons may be the Gordon Hendersons from Hamilton (A69-5709) or the Joseph Hendersons from Toronto (A52-5283), or both.

521 Mrs. McLagan was also on the WFMS trip to Winnipeg in May 1906 (see A61-5470).

522 In February 1912 Dr. Calvin Brooks McQuesten (Mary's brother-in-law) died and left Mary $36,000. The inheritance likely accounts for the financial contrast between this

relatively expensive vacation and Mary's vacation of the previous year in which she was relieved to find room and board for "only $5.00 a week" (A107-6752, August 1911; see also A43-5012n).

523 Mary visited Calvin at Bracebridge after her trip to the West Coast. She arrived in early August and stayed until late September. Edna, Hilda, and Mary visited at times as well.

524 The spelling of this name may be incorrect. When Calvin received his "call" from Bracebridge, it was signed by a Mr. Naismith (Box 03-116). I have found no record of Mr. Nasmith's reply to Mary or of what was done to relieve Calvin; however, Calvin remained at Bracebridge until December 1914, although his condition was precarious at times (A115-8756).

525 Monck was a small community on the Monck Road which runs between Lake Couchiching (near Gravenhurst) and the hamlet of York River (now Bancroft, Ontario). It was named after Charles Stanley Monck (1819-94) governor-general of British North America (1861-67), and the first governor-general of Canada, 1867-68 (CE 1374). The Monck Road was constructed in 1864-65 at the time of the American Civil War "for the dual purpose of opening up a wilderness area to settlement and providing an alternative less vulnerable military route between the Upper Great Lakes and the Ottawa valley" (Mrs. Walker, curator, Bancroft Museum, from a brass plaque at Bancroft, Ontario).

526 Janie James and Mr. F. E. Howitt were both missionaries, but with different denominations. He was an Anglican priest and an interdenominational lecturer (see A50-5199).

527 Miss Honeycomb was a seamstress (see A69-5709).

528 Rev. Dr. Fletcher died 25 December 1912. Mrs. Fletcher lived into her hundredth year.

529 Dr. Parfitt was in charge of the sanatorium at Gravenhurst where Ruby had gone for treatment of tuberculosis . In 1916 Mary blamed the doctors for Ruby's death: "Ruby in that horrid Ottawa had a succession of colds and grip and the doctors evidently did not look after [her]" (A100-6509; A87-6135; A103-9058).

530 Rev. J. H. Jowett wrote *The Preacher His Life and Work: Yale Lectures* (n.d). The book is in the Whitehern library, as well as seven other of his religious works dated from 1898 to 1922. He may have been related to Dr. Benjamin Jowett (1817-93), a professor of Greek at Oxford who wrote on Plato and Aristotle, and also on the interpretation of scripture in a way that was "notable for the freedom and freshness of its treatment, the orthodoxy of which was criticized" (OCEL 438).

531 It is not known what the problem was with Mary's face.

532 Tom was elected alderman, a "position he maintained for seven years" (Barnsley 22). Tom and his family worked very hard to get the voters out, especially the women who had been "enfranchised for municipal elections" (Best 26). Women could vote even earlier for certain by-laws: on 23 August 1892 the *Hamilton Spectator* reported "everyone who owns property may vote on the T. H. & B. by-law." This did not include single women since they could not own property. The provincial franchise was not received until 1917, the federal in 1918 (Bashevkin 6); however, some restrictions still applied until 1923. The *Hamilton Spectator*, 22 February 1923, notes: "Extending the right to vote to women comes into force this year."

533 John Allan (1856-1922), builder and politician, was elected mayor of Hamilton in 1913 and had been an alderman since 1908. "His administration was noted for its business-like methods, and he was popular with all classes [and] was elected Liberal MLA for Hamilton West in 1914." He was a Presbyterian, a member of the Commercial Club and the Scottish Rite, and assisted in the formation of the National Bricklayers' Union.(DHB 2:1). He worked well with Tom on many issues including the struggle with the T.H.&B. Railway to depress their lines in the West End near Whitehern.

534 This is a reference to Tom, who had worked very hard for the Liberals in the election.

535　This is likely Newton Galbreaith (1848-1925), a philanthropist, who came from United Empire Loyalist stock. He worked in his father's general store and retail grocery on King Street East and earned his wealth in real estate speculation. His mother established Hamilton's first art class, later part of the Wesleyan Ladies' College, and he created Hamilton's largest and most valuable private art collection. He was an early proponent of an art gallery for Hamilton, and "wanted beautification of the city." He was a Liberal, a Freemason, and a member of Central Presbyterian Church. His art collection was donated to "the proposed future gallery" and a room was named for him (*DHB* 3:65-66).

536　John C. Milne (1838-1922) businessman, senator, member of the Board of Directors for the Library, owner of the Pure Milk Co., director of Steel Co. of Canada, and in charge of the Wentworth Street Incline Railway and many other business interests. He was a Freemason and a member of Knox Presbyterian Church (5297; A91-6336; *DHB* 1:154; Henley 28).

537　Thomas Skinner Morris, merchant and alderman (1892-95, 1909-10, and 1912). He was instrumental in establishing the five-mile stretch of land that became Mountain Face Park, which had been denuded by quarries, brick manufacturers, and railroads. He worked closely with Tom on several city beautification projects (Best 44). He was on the board of control from 1913 to 1917 and acting mayor in 1916. He ran for mayor twice and was defeated. He was a Liberal, member of the Scottish Rite, a firm believer in social reform and assisted in the establishment of Methodist Sunday schools and churches (*DHB* 3:153).

William Henry Cooper, contractor, was elected alderman in 1909 and to the Board of Control in 1910, ran for mayor in 1917 and lost. He was president of the YMCA for twenty-five years, worked for the Big Brothers' Association, the General Hospital and the library, was a Methodist, a Mason, and a United Church supporter. He was a man of "unashamed religious convictions" and "believed that education must go hand in hand with Christian faith." To that end he worked to bring the Baptist McMaster University to Hamilton in 1930, and was citizen of the year for 1942 (*DHB* 4:52-53).

Charles W. Gardner, clothier and Conservative, was elected to city council (1907-09), to the Board of Control (1910-13), and ran for mayor in 1915 but was defeated. He was a member of the Scottish Rite (*DHB* 3:66).

Charles G. Bird, labour organizer and salesman, was elected alderman in 1912 and to the Board of Control in 1913-14. He was a Roman Catholic (*DHB* 4:32).

538　A reference to the temperance part of the election.

539　On 30 March 1914, Mary suggested to Calvin that he take an ocean voyage to the old country: "You come home fast as you can and talk it over" (8752). It is doubtful if he took the voyage and, since there are no letters, he appears to have been at home. He was home "playing bowls as usual" in the summer of 1914 (A117-6805), and on 10 December he was back at Bracebridge for a brief time (8785). In December 1914 he accepted a "call" as co-presbyter in Buckingham, Quebec (8748; A118-9153).

540　David Lloyd George, 1st Earl of Dwyfor (1863-1945), Welsh Liberal statesman, Chancellor of the Exchequer from 1908 to 1915. "He had been regarded as a pacifist," but the "threat of invasion of Belgium by Germany dispelled all pacifist tendencies" (*CBD* 906). In 1915 he became minister of munitions and in 1916 war secretary, and succeeded Asquith as coalition prime minister, a post he held until 1922. He was a brilliant orator and the speech that Mary heard was likely one of his anti-war speeches at a time when he was concerned for the "financial crisis which the War-storm had produced" (Owen 264-65). On 5 August 1914 Britain declared war.

541　Sir Winston Leonard Spencer Churchill (1874-1965) became Lord of the Admiralty in 1911 "and organized the navy for the war he foresaw." In 1917 he became Lloyd George's minister of munitions and he and Lloyd George worked closely together throughout the war of 1914-18 (*CBD* 310). He became prime minister in May 1940 and led Britain through World War Two.

542 World War One was declared by Britain on 5 August 1914. In Mary's letter of 5 August to Tom, she wrote: "The war trouble is so terrible, it makes me quite ill, and we are powerless to do any thing. One cannot see why these things are permitted. It doesn't seem possible that Mr. Chisholm should have to go. It is to be hoped something will have happened to stop it, before they reach the front. I am thankful you did not belong to the regiment. I would not live through it" (6809). For more information on Mary's opposition to Tom's desire to enlist, see A123-6975n.

543 Mary's daughter Mary was on a European tour and narrowly missed the trouble in Europe.

544 William Alexander (Leander) Logie was a law partner with James Chisholm and Thomas McQuesten in 1909. He was a captain in the 13th Regiment and enlisted for service in World War One. This letter suggests that he may have been killed; however, the letter of 30 April 1915 (6836) reveals that he had been wounded (A119-6828).

545 See A115-8756, 17 March 1914. In December 1914 Calvin took a position as co-presbyter at Buckingham, Quebec, which he held until August 1916 when he came home exhausted and discouraged.

546 Edward Blake (1833-1912), lawyer and politician, became leader of the Ontario Liberal Party in 1868 and second premier of Ontario in 1871. "He established the Liberal dynasty that ruled Ontario from 1871 to 1905." "In 1892 he entered the British House of Commons as an Irish nationalist." He "retired to Canada in 1906, and served as senator and chancellor of University of Toronto (from 1873)." He was described as "intensely ambitious" and "absurdly sensitive to criticism." "[He] often behaved like a spoiled child" and "possessed a manner as devoid of warmth as is a flake of December snow"; however, he did leave his mark by recruiting both "Oliver Mowat … and Wilfrid Laurier, two of Canada's most effective and electorally successful politicians" (CE 240).

547 For Rev. Samuel Harper Gray, see A91-6336; A106-6746n.

548 Stephen Leacock was touring to raise funds for the Belgian Relief Fund: "that little nation, which was almost wiped from the European map … by the violation of its neutrality by Germany." The *Hamilton Spectator*, 26 March, reported the coming event: "Great Rush Seems Probable for the Evening with Canada's Humorist" at the Temple Theater, Tuesday, 30 March, at 8:15 p.m. On 31 March, the paper reported the performance: "Canada's Mark Twain … Stephen Leacock is a master of satire and he stood out last evening a living embodiment and perfect interpreter of the humor which he has originated … and one who could get a strangle-hold on Old Man Gloom." After the introduction he "immediately got in touch with the risibilities of his audience." He read from his own works, did a "spoof" on a romance novel "in his best vein." He also performed a "problem play in three acts … the first two acts were 'hum-dingers,' the problem being that the plot was so twisted that only the professor could bring it to a conclusion." The closing was "the reading of an alleged copy of the London Times bearing the date of 1916, wherein … the entire house of commons leaves arm in arm, the objective point being a moving picture palace where the film is entitled, The March of the Allies into Berlin. It was real satire, the kind Hamiltonians have been denied for many a day."

549 Gourlay Colquhoun joined the Canadian Permanent Force in April 1909. At that time, Mary stated: "Think it is rather a good thing as he is rather wasted in the bank" (6395). On 26 February 1915 Mary had relayed a report to Cal: "There is a report through a letter from Mrs. Watson's son to her that Gourlay Colquhoun is to have the Victoria Cross for conspicuous bravery in rescuing a comrade. It is not yet confirmed, and I am sure it will be difficult to confer all that are deserving in this terrible war" (9111). The above letter gives the 26 March report, and on 31 March 1915, Mary gave a further report about war events and Gourlay's capture: "From their house on Bloor Street they saw the great parade of 9000 men, but people could not cheer, every one feels too badly to see them go. Kate Colquhoun phoned us yesterday, that they had a cable from Gourlay's wife, that he had been found in a Red Cross Hospital in Germany.

Nothing more and they asked us not to tell this to any one for some reason.... The paper has just come in and says Mrs. Colquhoun has received message from Adjutant Gen., confirming report that Gourlay is a prisoner at Meintz [sic]. Hope he will not be ill-treated" (6813; A24-4549).

The *Hamilton Spectator*, 31 March 1915, reported that "Lieut. W. Gourlay Colquhoun, the brave Hamilton officer who distinguished himself with the Princess Patricia's Canadian Light Infantry in France, first reported missing, and whose body it was later claimed, has been found in a German trench, is safe in the citadel of Metz, a prisoner of war.... Mrs. Colquhoun never gave up that her son might be alive."

550 Lloyd George made a widely publicized speech at Bangor on 28 February 1915 in which he declared: "Drink is doing more damage in this war than all the German submarines put together. Reports of what was represented as being almost a tidal wave of drunkenness had been pouring in for months past from all over the country. Amongst shipyard workers, now getting really good wages for the first time, it appeared especially serious." A temperance crusade was launched and the nationalization of drink was proposed, but it received opposition from both the beer barons and the teetotalers. The first did not want to lose their profits to the State and the second would not "countenance that the State should sully its soul by dealing in the evil trade." This "unacknowledged coalition" brought the matter to a end (Owen 284-86).

551 The Duke of Connaught (1850-1942), third son of Queen Victoria and soldier, was governor-general of Canada (1911-16) (*CBD* 337).

552 The "enclosed" is a notice from the Upper Canada Tract Society stating that "Smith 'Geog of Holy Land'" [sic] is "out of stock at present, will send soon as stock arrives." A copy of George Adam Smith's *The Historical Geography of the Holy Land* (1910) is in the Whitehern library, as well as four other of his works on Isaiah and Jerusalem.

553 Rev. Dr. Daniel R. Drummond (1868-1931) was inducted at St. Paul's in Hamilton in 1905. He had won several scholarships at Queen's, did postgraduate work in Edinburgh, became a trustee at Queen's University, was chaplain (major) of the Argyll and Sutherland Highlanders during World War One, and he encouraged military service. He sat on the board of foreign missions and the general assembly. He was a moderate on Church Union and wrote a pamphlet, "Is There No Way Out," to promote the position of a federation of churches instead of an organic union. This would have allowed each church to retain their own "denominational traditions." He "resigned as chairman of the general board" in 1925 because "he was unable to reconcile the division which left 30 percent of Presbyterians outside the union." He was stricken with meningitis in 1925 and never fully recovered (*DHB* 3:43-4; Moir, *Enduring* 204, 219; *Wee Kirks* 48; A138-7136). For "Church Union" see A52-5283, A97-6446n.

554 22 April 1915, Mary wrote: "The war news seems terrible just now, it hangs over one, and we feel as if we didn't know what would happen next. It seems so fearful to think of the awful slaughter, thousands of men handed over to death. Such fine fellows too! It makes one ill to think of it, and no one can stop it, we are just helpless" (6820).

555 In Mary's letter of 30 July 1914 (A117-6805) it appeared that Logie might have been killed; however, this letter clarifies matters somewhat. Mary's daughter Mary describes the injury in her letter to Calvin: "Col. Logie had been thrown from a mortar, had had his head badly cut, a shoulder dislocated and other injuries" (6836).

556 Calvin had planned to deliver a talk/sermon on Dr. Geddie. Mary wrote on 22 April, "Am glad you are going to preach on John Geddie, it is such a good thing for a minister to improve these occasions, the people know very little about the lives of missionaries and I always find them most inspiring and I think you can make such an interesting address out of them" (6820). John and Charlotte Geddie were the first Presbyterian overseas missionaries. They went to the New Hebrides and encountered "the savage and cannibalistic natives.... Natives were converted one by one ... a chapel was built

and a congregation of one hundred organized within a decade." Natives were taught to abandon polygamy and infanticide and learned crafts and skills. Geddie was their doctor and Charlotte taught sanitation. Other missionaries (George W. Gordon and his wife) were sent to Erromanga Island nearby, but they were murdered in 1861 by the natives who blamed them for the measles epidemic. Gordon's brother and wife went to the same island and suffered the same fate in 1872. The Geddies wrote "descriptive letters" that were widely reprinted and they did speaking tours. When he died in 1872 a memorial tablet was erected and inscribed: "When he landed, in 1848, there were no Christians here, and when he left, in 1872, there were no heathen" (Moir, *Enduring* 147-48; Brouwer 6, 82).

557   The "Home" party is the WHMS. See A49-5172 and note for Shortreed for the history of the struggle between the FMC, the WFMS, and the WHMS, which finally led to the formation of the WMS in 1914, by "coercion." Mary's remark discloses that the resistance continued after the merger as Mary and many others continued to favour expenditures on the foreign work (A49-5172, A72-5765, A121-6951, A124-9180).

558   Sir George-Etienne Cartier (1814-73) lawyer, railway promoter, politician, prime minister of the Province of Canada, descendent of Jacques Cartier, Father of Confederation, reconciled the majority of French Canada to Confederation (CE 367-68).

559   Miss Margaret (Dr. Maggie) McKellar (1861-?) medical missionary. Brouwer notes that Miss McKellar was an example of the young single women who were often attracted to missionary work by a desire for travel. As a young milliner in southwestern Ontario, she first tried giving money for the "world's evangelization," but found that "it did not work." Then, in 1883, she went back to school to get an education as a doctor so that she could participate directly in the field, and was sent to India. She was often very outspoken and during the gender wars and the Wilkie problems, she "wryly observed, 'I am not half so much surprised at the state of the heathen as I am at the state of the missionaries.'" Her work was exemplary, and Dr. R. P. MacKay payed her this tribute: "When I landed in India I started with the strongest prejudice against lady doctors and I confess that this prejudice still obtains so far as home is concerned. As concerns India, however, Dr. McKellar and Dr. Oliver ... have entirely converted me.... Both these ladies have earned my highest respect and liking for their arduous and conscientious work and their breadth of mind" (Brouwer 71, 88, 144, 179).

560   Miss Josephine Smith was Calvin's new housekeeper. On 2 February 1916, Mary wrote: "Hurrah! Miss Smith is coming, but am sorry she cannot get started til Tuesday am sending fare to her, am writing her to write you, if anything should occur to prevent her coming Tuesday. I offered her $16.00, did not like to say less, but she has some of her own. I am giving her $10.00 to take down, but that is my treat, it is such a relief to my mind, it is quite worth it (6944; A122-6967; A123-6975).

561   Rev. A. B. Winchester was head of the mission in British Columbia. It was not very successful in converting the Chinese immigrants. The mission gave free English courses beginning in 1892. "Unfortunately the desire for salvation fell off rapidly once the Chinese immigrants learned enough English to ensure them good jobs, and in any case only about one percent of all Chinese Canadians were attracted to this mission" (Moir, *Enduring* 167).

562   This is possibly the Rev. Donald George McPhail (?-1918). He became a war chaplain and died at sea.

563   This letter indicates that the finances between WMS and the WFMS were still being kept separate.

564   Miss Annie I. Robinson was Calvin's former housekeeper. She left because her sister died (7836).

565   Miss Smith was Calvin's housekeeper (see A121-6951). Ethel MacLaren was likely a friend that Edna had made when she visited Calvin at the manse in 1915 (9175).

566 Likely, Thomas Lees, church trustee (see A84-6053).

567 Calvin may have been considering applying for a position as minister in a Hamilton church.

568 See A106-6746 for note on Mary's views on the theatre.

569 Mayor Chester S. Walters was in the forefront of the local recruiting drive, as well as Mewburn (A20-4521) and Chisholm, Tom's law partner (A8-2520) (*DHB* 4:178). Walters was deputy minister of highways (Tom was minister) when he attended Mary's funeral in 1934 (*Hamilton Spectator,* 10 December 1934). In 1948, in Tom's obituary, Walters wrote: "Thomas Baker McQuesten was one of Canada's great men. He was the soul of honour. As was said of Christopher Wren, 'if you would seek his monument, look about you'.... He was my dearest friend" (Best 189). Rev. Ketchen had made a similar statement to Tom in a letter of 12 July 1947 (Box 08-202).

570 Mary's "violent opposition" to the war is coloured by the fact that Tom wanted to enlist, just as his friend and law partner, Chisholm, had done. This caused a family crisis since Mary did not favour the war and feared losing her favourite son and his income. During this long crisis, Calvin wrote brief prayers for the family in his diary: "April 10, 11, 1916, that Tom may go ... that mother may tell him so ... April 8, 1918, that all may know His peace in anxiety about possibility of Tom being called to the colours." In spite of many arguments, Mary managed to keep Tom at home (*DHB* 4:178; Best 26; see also A117-6805).

571 Ethel McLaren was likely related to W. W. McLaren. Mary and her family met the McLaren girls at a "five-o'clock tea" at Whitehern in June 1906. At this time Mary noted that "they were new friends, their father a clergyman"(5516). Rev. William McLaren was a principal of Knox College in charge of student missionaries. In 1906 he was in charge of the Birtle Missionary School when Mary visited there. Mary wrote to Calvin from Winnipeg that McLaren "was on the Knox Coll. Com. that sent you first to Alberta. He won the Traveling Scholarship but came here six months ago a nervous wreck" (5474). And again: "some get on in the West, but a great many have a hard time. Would not live there for anything. Mr. W. W. McLaren told me his liver was affected and his nerves had gone to pieces" (5502, 15 June 1906). McLaren was a "true anti-unionist" (Moir, *Enduring,* 176, 199, 204; 6173, 6574, 7287). Mary reports in August 1907 that McLaren died after a long illness and "it was a mercy for Mrs. McL. was worn out, as he had to be very often moved" (5936).

572 "Dr. Grinch" was likely Dr. R. P. MacKay, secretary of the FMC, who was involved with the negotiations between the WFMS and the WHMS to create the WMS and had been in contention with the women's groups over control of funds collected by the WFMS (see A91-6336; A49-5172n).

573 This is the last extant letter in which Mary mentions the women's missionary auxiliary work. It is likely that she grew somewhat disillusioned after the political problems with "Dr. Grinch" and the FMC in general (A91-6336; A49-5172n; 8725). This letter suggests that the missionary work in Canada was no longer as vitally needed as it had been. The communities and the government social agencies had taken over much of the medical, educational, and welfare aspects of the work (*Wee Kirks* 195). Mary's letters after 1916 indicate that she transferred some of her missionary zeal to the Social Gospel reform agenda and to Tom's "City Beautiful" movement, and was the inspiration behind his vast and successful enterprises in building parks, highways, and bridges, and in bringing McMaster University to Hamilton. Her vision for Tom became apparent soon after his graduation: "[I] hope that here I may get him interested in some good work besides his business" (A90-6318).

574 Miss H. Elsie J. Buchanan's avoidance of "meetings" suggests that she also was disillusioned with the missionary effort, and had now turned her efforts to private charitable enterprises. She was a charter member, with Mary, of the Women's Auxiliary at the McNab Church in 1876 and had also spent many years on the executive.

575 Mary's first viewing of moving pictures was the Coronation pictures in 1911 (A106-6746). She also described "a photoplay 'Cabiria' said to be the most wonderful spectacular display ever shown" (20 November 1915, 9096).

576 Rev. William Henry Sedgewick (1876-1945), Presbyterian clergyman. Educated at Halifax, Glasgow, doctorate at Knox College, ordained 1901 at Nova Scotia, postgraduate studies, Scotland, Church in P.E.I. (1904-06). He was "virtually whisked away by Dr. Samuel Lyle of Central Presbyterian Church.... He was a happy combination of young life, scholarly tastes, personal gifts and a very engaging personality." He shared the ministry with Dr. Lyle and assumed full charge in 1910. He was a leader in the Church Union Movement and when the Central congregation voted to remain Presbyterian, he resigned. He was on the Board of Home Missions and Social Services, chairman of the Home Missions Committee and was a member of the Scottish Rite (A124-9180; 5683; DHB 4:223-24; POH 56). He may have been related to "Old Dr. Sedgewick" (see A97-6446).

577 Possibly Derwyn Trevor Owen, Anglican primate and rector of Christ's Church Cathedral. In 1934 he became Archbishop of Toronto and fifth primate of Canada. He was a member of the Scottish Rite and was one of the fathers of the ecumenical movement in Canada. This meeting appears to be an interdenominational service for the Bible Society (DHB 3:163).

578 Noulan Cauchon (?-1948) of Ottawa, a noted railway engineer and pioneer of town planning, collaborated with Tom on many of his public works and "City Beautiful" projects in Hamilton and throughout Ontario. Theirs was a renaissance movement influenced by Cauchon's experience in classical design and reconstruction in Greece. Tom was appointed to the Hamilton Town Planning Commission in January 1916, to the Board of Parks Management in 1922, and to the provincial Highways portfolio in 1934, and he and Cauchon worked closely together to build many Hamilton Parks: the Rock Garden (RBG), Desjardins Canal, Cootes Paradise, High Level Bridge (now named for McQuesten), McMaster University and park grounds, Scott Park, Gage Park, and many more. Within ten years Hamilton "had the largest acreage of developed parkland in any Canadian city." The provincial projects include: The Niagara Parks system and School for Apprentice Gardeners, the Queen Elizabeth Highway, the Rainbow Bridge, the restoration of the forts, and many more. They worked with the team of Dunington-Grubb garden designers, sculptors Frances Loring and Florence Wyle, and architect John Lyle (Best 51-68, 113-18; Barnsley 26; A84-6053). This group subscribed to the social reform philosophy that healthy surroundings have a moral effect on the population, and they envisioned and implemented it with a missionary zeal. Cauchon presented A Book of Bridges (1915) to Tom with the inscription: "To my friend T. B. McQuesten 'Enthusiast' Hoping that the spans of Hamilton may rank with the noblest of these, September 1918." This book is in the Whitehern library. Cauchon often stayed at Whitehern when he was in Hamilton. Cauchon was Tom's visionary, and his mother's passion for beauty was his inspiration, see (A134-7085).

579 Mr. Donald MacKay died in 1909, so this Mr. MacKay is likely one of Maggie's brothers.

580 Tom worked for Royce and Henderson in 1906-07. Robert "Bob" Henderson was married on 20 July 1907 (A79-5868; 5912).

581 Likely, Dr. Arnott, see A37-4815.

582 Edna suffered another mental breakdown and was hospitalized with "irrational and hysterical behaviour" at Homewood Sanatorium at Guelph on 23 October 1920. The family visited her and sometimes took her out: On 21 July 1928 Mary wrote to Calvin: "We had a delightful afternoon yesterday at Guelph Tom drove us up in our fine car leaving here about 1:45 and reaching Guelph before three.... At [?] Lake to which Edna wished to go, it was really too cold, but revived Tom greatly after excessive heat of previous days. Edna said we could have tea there so we drove about, down thro' Hespeler, till time for six o'clock "supper." It was excellent, thin sliced tongue, scalloped

potatoes, a tomato with salad dressing, celery, lovely tea biscuits and to top off, a little ice-cream with a chocolate sauce and small cakes, bread & butter, tea or coffee with good cream, properly made tea & coffee. We all enjoyed it immensely and really it was very pleasant to have no strange driver. E seems to have no desire to come to H.[Hamilton]" (7044; A59-5426n).

Edna remained at Homewood until her death on 10 November 1935 of "Haemorrhage, duodenal ulcer" (Minnes 3).

583   Calvin had written to Knox College requesting the use of the library while working on his "war book" and for accommodation as a postgraduate. He describes himself as "crippled" with "emotional problems" and he details the family's history of health and financial problems. He was granted a room, and the manuscript bears the title: *The King of Fighting Men*. It is about Christ as soldier and saviour. It was never published (MCP 2-3b.35, 6909, Box 04-028). Calvin also wrote a second book which was also not published: *The Healing Ministry of Jesus in His Day and Ours* (Box 14-078).

584   Rev. Dr. W. G. Brown was from the West. Like Dr. Drummond on Church Union he "hoped that a federation of churches might create the desired unity" and tried to "discontinue negotiations.... Dreading the very real prospect of disruption, he argued for more discussion." He also "represented the traditional middle of the road conservative" and advocated more emphasis on "welfare programs" and "social action" (Moir, *Enduring* 204, 207, 235, 238).

585   Rev. John McClung (1844-1924), at Knox College in 1870-73, and ordained in 1874, was a retired Ontario minister. He served at Ancaster and Alberton (1888-89), where in 1925 the congregations voted overwhelmingly against union. He also served at many other Ontario churches for periods of three to eight years. He retired to Hamilton in 1915 (BDKC 149). I have been unable to establish a relationship with Nellie McClung or her husband, Robert Wesley McClung (CE 1256).

586   Mary was seventy-five years of age at this time. Mary and Tom both made impassioned speeches at meetings, with the result that the Hamilton vote was negative on Union and it was the only Presbytery in Canada which unanimously opposed union. Tom determined to take the fight to Parliament but despite his pleas the Church Union Bill was passed; however, he did win some concessions which preserved the Presbyterian Church in Ontario, settled property disputes, and ceded Knox College to the anti-unionists (Best 33-34). In 1925, when the United Church was formed, many congregations were fractured by the vote; however MacNab lost only seventy members, including six elders, and the Hamilton Presbytery remained.

The debate caused some dissension in the McQuesten family. Calvin was in favour of union and in complete opposition to the stance taken by other members of the family. Following a shouting match with his brother, Tom, at a congregational meeting on the subject," Calvin was chastised by some members of the congregation. He was reconciled to the family and "in later years graced MacNab Sunday by Sunday with his presence, his gifts and his prayers." Calvin became a United Church minister and was chaplain of the Hamilton Sanatorium from 1920 to 1950 (Johnson, *Strong Wind Blowing* 28; Moir, *Enduring* 170-96 and 197-223; McNeill 203-207, 248-89, 253, 260-61; see also A52-5283; A97-6446).

587   Mary, Tom, and Hilda were touring England with the Canadian Bar Association delegation to a convention with English lawyers. The *Daily Mail* of 22 July 1924 carried pictures and reports of the English and Canadian lawyers as they welcomed the American Bar Association at Westminster Hall on 21 July 1924. They visited the historic sites and were introduced to royalty and Britain's leaders (Barnsley).

588   "Sorosis" is the brand name of a boot that was usually front-laced with a pointed toe and hourglass heel (Jonathan Walford, fashion historian, Font Hill). The name may be related to "sorosis," a women's club or society, and may suggest a particular fashion or style of the day (*WNCD* 808). In 1930 Mary refers to using a lorgnette glass (see

A134-7085). The Whitehern archive contains a lorgnette glass and several pairs of boots from that era.

589   The Covenanters are members of the Solemn League and Covenant, an agreement made in 1643 between English Parliament and the Scottish Covenanters during the English Civil War, by which the Scots would provide military aid in return for the establishment of a Presbyterian system in England, Scotland, and Ireland. Although the Scottish support proved crucial in the Parliamentary victory, the principal Presbyterian leaders were expelled from Parliament in 1647 and the covenant was never honoured. (*OED* 330, 1378)

590   Calvin was vacationing in Gaspe, Quebec. He loved the wilderness and had become an avid naturalist, birdwatcher, and member of the Audubon Society. For a number of years he was president of the Hamilton Bird Protection Society, Inc. (Protection Society Program, 1931-32, Box 08).

591   This is likely Mrs. Charles Bull, wife of Tom's associate, friend, and "Hamilton Club crony" (Best 136). Mr. Welby was a member of Tom's "old law firm" and a pallbearer at Tom's funeral in 1948 (Best 131, 189).

592   The make and model of the car is not known. It was likely not a Ford because on 10 July 1928, Mary noted: "fearfully hot, could not have stood it in a Ford car" (7033). Hilda, Tom, and Mary became drivers, with Tom and Hilda doing most of the driving. Daughter Mary was nervous and did little driving (7033). On 7 July, Tom drove the family to Grimsby (7030). On 21 July Mary wrote: "We had a delightful afternoon yesterday at Guelph. Tom drove us up in our fine car leaving here about 1:45 and reaching Guelph before three.... M & H. have about mastered the car; which is a relief for at one time M. was so nervous for fear of injuring such an expensive car, that she almost gave up" (7044). On 14 August, Mary wrote " Mary [Daughter] ventured out by herself in car this morning so we hope soon to have full use, but girls have not nerve enough yet to go so far as Guelph, and Tom cannot always get away, as he is off on other things often, but we hope to get up on Friday" (7064). At this time they were visiting Edna at Homewood in Guelph.

593   Possibly Woods of "Woods' Fair" (A93-6347).

594   Calvin had taken the position of chaplain at the Hamilton Mountain Sanatorium sometime in 1920. It was a semi-volunteer position which he held for thirty years (Minnes 3).

595   Calvin did not go to Barbados. On 14 July, Mary wrote to Calvin: "Sorry to hear you are disappointed about the sailing trip, but you may have escaped hardships of which you were not aware.... Now you will just enjoy your comfortable quarters and canoe at Gaspe" (7040).

596   James Chisholm had given Mary a gift of money on the occasion of his seventieth birthday. I have found no record of the amount of the gift. On 24 December 1928, Chisholm wrote: "Will you kindly accept the enclosed cheque as a slight acknowledgment of my feeling of gratitude for Mr. McQuesten's kindly interest and kindly assistance in the long ago, developing as time went on into a close association that has lasted a lifetime. It will give me pleasure to have you make use of it in any way that will minister to your pleasure or comfort. I was fortunate in being trained in an office that conducted its business on high principles and the same high principles were in evidence in the conduct of the home. I therefore, look back with grateful remembrance to associations that have been so stimulating and helpful and pray that you may be spared for many years yet to your children and friends. Sincerely yours, Jas. Chisholm." See note to Chisholm in "Excerpts from Mary's will" (A143).

597   Ferdinand, Vicomte de Lesseps (1805-94), French diplomat and canal promoter, cousin of the Empress Eugenie. He campaigned for the construction of the Suez Canal, which was completed in 1869. He was also involved in the scheme to build a sea-level Panama Canal, but work was abandoned in 1888: "management was charged with breach of trust, and five directors were condemned—Lesseps, now a broken old man,

to five years' imprisonment for embezzlement, but the sentence was reversed." He wrote *Histoire du canal de Suez* (1875-79) and *Souvenirs de quarante ans* (1887) (*CBD* 887). These books are not in the Whitehern library.

598 James Chisholm had an appendectomy at seventy-two years of age (see A135-7095; A136-7111). He died in 1944 at eighty-six years of age (*DHB* 3:33).

599 In her letter of 18 June 1928, Mary wrote: "[P.S.] Very large individual contributions coming in for McMaster; nearly the $500,000" (7010; see also Whidden A135-7095). Tom and his family and colleagues were instrumental in bringing McMaster to Hamilton from Toronto. Tom as head of the Parks Board and C. V. Langs as chairman offered McMaster fifty acres of property and committed to develop a park setting free of charge for the campus, and "a citizens committee pledged to raise $500,000." Tom saw the acquisition of McMaster for Hamilton as the greatest coup of his career: "We've never landed such a fish as this.... Our whole development has been on mechanics lines. And the result has been, the owners don't live here ... and Hamilton has become too much a factory town. This is the first break toward a broader culture and higher educational development. It was sorely needed. Did I ever think what a great work "university" is?—It has never been let down, never become stale or commonplace, always dignified and lofty" (Best 58).

600 At this time Tom had many parks and building projects under development (see Cauchon; A125-MCP 1-3b.15). He frequently took his mother on inspection trips. In 1909 they made a trip by train to Fonthill Nurseries and Mary describes "the botanical wonders they saw" (6521). On 3 July 1930 Mary wrote: "We are having beautiful weather and on Tuesday morning Tom took me to Gage Park and as it was rainy and a holiday at noon he drove over the grass. The ramblers over the bed and roses in the bed in front of greenhouse are beyond description; and long rows of scarlet geraniums etc." (7080); on 15 May 1931: "Rock Garden brilliant" (7124); on 19 May 1931: "Had been down to Gage Park the day before (Sunday). The honesty is a sight to behold in that bed against the fence. The whole place beautiful" (7128; also A138-7136). Also, Mary's letters give seasonal descriptions of the Whitehern gardens. In Mary's obituary, Tom gave his mother full credit for his dedication to beauty: "Mr. McQuesten himself has told of the large part his mother has played in molding his tastes, his standards and his plan of life. Not the least of her contributions to him was to give him a love for beauty that was large enough to spread out and influence the appearance of a great city.... Large areas of Hamilton are, in the last analysis, a reflection of her love of beauty" (the *Hamilton Herald* 7 December 1934).

601 Hon. Charles Dunning (1885-1958) businessman, Liberal politician, premier of Saskatchewan 1922-26, then minister of railways and canals, and then minister of Finance under Mackenzie King, 1926-30 and 1935-39 (*CE* 636). On 3 July 1930 Mary wrote: "Last night we heard Dunning from St. Thomas, his own constituency, heard him very clearly, so I was tempted to listen till nearly eleven when my head rang. I think the broadcasting worth the money. I doubt if ever the people knew before how much the Government had done. I am sure I had not the faintest idea and he gave such a presentation of conditions all over the world including the US. You probably heard it all from Cobourg" (7080). The *Hamilton Spectator*, 9 July 1930, reported that in Dunning's previous address he had presented the budget and had upheld Mackenzie King's move toward greater Empire trade. This involved $250,000,000 "worth of trade [that] would be taken away from the United States and given to the Empire." See also A136-7111.

602 For the Hon. Frank Oliver, see A73-5788. On 5 July 1930, The *Hamilton Spectator* reported on Oliver's "Strong Criticism of Pool Methods Made in Winnipeg.... The Pool as a business organization has achieved bankruptcy. The prices paid to farmer members for their wheat is lower than at any time since formation of the joint pool in 1924."

603 Mary purchased a lorgnette when she was in England in 1924 (see A128-8719).

604 The first woman Senator was Cairine Wilson (née Mackay) (1885-1962), nominated in 1930 by the King government, shortly after the "Persons" judgment conferred full political rights upon women as "persons" in Canada. She had been very active in Liberal politics, and her father also held a Senate seat. "She had raised a large family [eight children], was active in church and charity work and believed firmly in traditional moral and family values" (Bashevkin 19-20). "She was active in the organization of Women's Liberal clubs and youth groups in the 1920's.... She was president of the League of Nations Society in Canada (1936-42), and Canada's first woman delegate to the UN in 1949. As chairman of the Canadian National Committee on Refugees 1938-40, she was outspoken against Anti-Semitism in Canada" (CE 2310).

605 This is likely Laura Hostetter, who may have been a patient at Homewood.

606 It is impossible to be certain about the identity of these patients and their visiting families at Homewood in Guelph, a sanatorium for treatment of mental illness and alcoholism. The reference to "booze" suggests that some of the patients were being treated for alcoholism.

607 The Whittemores were likely vacationing in Oakville.

608 James Chisholm was recovering from an appendectomy (see A134-7085).

609 I have found no record for Harry O'Brien, but the papers for this date refer to the debate about the preference for trade with the Empire rather than with the United States. This caused some dissension in party politics, and caused some to break ranks. The vote was to take place on 28 July. In a headline "Former Tory Speaks Out and Ascends Liberal Platform as Exponent of Empire Trade" the *Globe* reported that J. H. Burnham "made no apologies" for "speaking on behalf of Liberal policies." He appealed to the women and "stressed the intelligent viewpoint being taken by the women electors who, he said, would make or break a candidate's political chances. He appealed particularly to the Conservative women tonight" (*Globe*, 9 July 1930). Women received the franchise in Canada in 1918 (Bashevkin 6).

610 Howard P. Whidden was chancellor of McMaster in 1927 and retired in 1941. He collaborated with Thomas McQuesten and others to bring McMaster to Hamilton. Whidden gratefully acknowledged the university's indebtedness to Thomas and the Parks Board for their generosity in offering what he called "exceedingly reasonable terms." He also stated that Tom was "one of the great big factors which has made the whole thing possible" (Johnston 7, 14, 161, 176, 200; A134-7085n). An early news account exults at the prospect: "The new university starts with a plenitude of groves of Academe.... right on the brink of a sylvan paradise. Its scholars will at their back door have cool ravines and marsh meadows in which to meditate the theological and other muses.... And they will have red-winged blackbirds and whistling swans and canorous Canada Geese to keep them company. Hamilton is proving itself a generous host to higher learning.... A broad tree-lined avenue ... a sunken garden ... lily ponds and grottoes containing fountains and flower beds suggesting the work of La Notre, the famous architect of Louis Quatorze" (*Hamilton Spectator*, 5 October 1929).

Unfortunately, the Sunken Garden was razed to make way for the Medical Building. In 1934, after Tom's appointment to cabinet, The *Hamilton Spectator* reported at great length on Tom's contributions to Hamilton: "Far-Seeing Plans Bring University.... Crusades for City Improvement.... Venerable Mother Shares His Triumph" (30 June 1934). In 1941 Whidden again wrote to Tom: "Do not forget that from the beginning I have been under indebtedness to you for constant support and inspiration in connection with the bringing of McMaster to Hamilton and the making possible of its beautiful surroundings and setting" (Box 08-138a, 21 March 1941). Whidden was a pallbearer at Tom's funeral in 1948, as was G. B. Gilmour, chancellor in 1948.

611 The Mewburns lived at 65 Markland Street. Nearby Chilton Place may have been named after Sydney Chilton Mewburn's son, John Chilton Mewburn, who died in World War One (1916).

612 Mackenzie King and Dunning were defeated by the Conservatives under R. B. Bennett in 1930 (CE 1136).

613 The "Rock Garden" is the Royal Botanical Garden in Hamilton, which Tom and his associates developed in an old quarry as part of their "City Beautiful" movement, and which has become one of the most beautiful features of Hamilton.

614 Mary, Tom, and Hilda had made a trip to England in 1924 (see A129-8716, A128-8719). Her letters at this time are punctuated by her memories of same.

615 The *Globe's* "new lady correspondent" was Judith R. Robinson. She wrote an account from London of the "Debate at Westminster." It is highly descriptive and moves from awe to disillusionment: "The policeman on duty at St. Stephen's entrance wore even such a helmet as those whose outline has grown dear to the hearts of Toronto Communists.... Awe mounted in a child of the Dominion Overseas who tiptoed past the Great Hall of William Rufus, clomb—a lovely word, clomb—clomb the broad steps, passed the carven doors.... [entered] the frescoed antechamber under the cold marble gaze of pedestalled [*sic*] parliamentarians.... One after another, honorable members were led to believe, made each other fully aware, did not disguise the fact, had every hope that.... Er-er-er-circumstances over which we have no control [and in the end] the ties of Empire were knotted tight" (29 April 1931).

616 For Mary's trip to England, see A129-8716; A128-8719.

617 Duncan Chisholm was Mary's handyman (see A108-8817). He may have been related to James Chisholm (see A8-2520).

618 Calvin did the "grand tour" beginning in May 1931 and returned in August (Calvin's diary). Extant letters are from 8 May to 18 June (7115 to 7144 and A139-MCP2-3b.40). Calvin's final letter to his mother before her death is dated 2 September 1934 from Gaspe. He wrote: "Have never enjoyed a holiday more, but shall be so glad to see you again, dear little thing" (7154).

619 Saint Dunstan, Anglo-Saxon prelate and Archbishop of Canterbury from 959.

620 It is likely that the card enclosed a monetary gift.

621 For Laura Hostetter and Thomson family, see A15-4415.

622 The *Hamilton Spectator*, 30 June 1934, notes Tom's devotion to his mother on the occasion of Tom's appointment to Cabinet, less than four months before her death. He had stated that his mother was his "best chum": "Mr. McQuesten has a "chum." Sometimes long miles from home and fighting his earliest battles of life he could only be with her in his thoughts.... A venerable lady who sits in the beautiful garden at the rear of the historic old McQuesten mansion ... followed the campaign battles of her son with intense interest.... Happiest Moments Spent With Mother ... He found time an hour a day to take his mother for a motor ride. Time also to spend an hour or so sitting with her reading to her and answering the questions of a still keen mind about public affairs.... Today Mrs. McQuesten is sharing her son's honour and he is enjoying the success in life that attends respect of parenthood."

623 Mary Baker McQuesten died at Whitehern on Friday, 7 December 1934, at the age of eighty-five. The newspapers in both Hamilton and Toronto carried many obituaries: "Mother of Hon. T. B. McQuesten Dies at Great Age—Will Be Deeply Mourned.... Mrs. Isaac Baldwin McQuesten, A prominent figure for many years in the W.M.S. of the Presbyterian Church, whose death occurred last evening.... Her Passing will be the occasion of the deepest regret in many walks of life where her beneficent influence was felt" (Minnes 3). "Mrs. McQuesten was a woman of beautiful character, high culture, and wide interests" (M49 Misc. Clippings, Whitehern archives).

624 "According to her will, Mrs. Mary Baker McQuesten's estate was just under $54,000." "All of her living children (Mary, Calvin, Hilda, Tom & Edna) received 1/5th residue of the estate or $10,746.70. In addition, Tom received $100 and pictures (pictures he once gave her). In addition, all the girls (Mary, Hilda & Edna) received 1/3rd share of jewelry & clothing (value of $33.33, $33.33 $33.34)" (Minnes 7, 3). For letters about Mary's concerns during an early preparation of her will in 1902, see A23-4544.

625 I am unable to locate this "impressive deliverance." A news clipping in the archives at MacNab Street Presbyterian Church states simply: "A silk gown was presented to Rev. Mr. Ketchen on behalf of the Ladies Aid Society. Mrs. McQuesten made the presentation.... Preceding this, there had been several speakers" (n.d. 1905).

626 Mrs. Jellyby is a character in Charles Dicken's *Bleak House* who "sacrifices her family to her selfish addiction" to the cause of an African charity (*OED* 95).

Bibliography

❧

Primary Sources

The letters selected for this book may be found among the extensive correspondence in the Whitehern Museum Archives and on microfilm in the Ontario Archives, Toronto, Ontario.

The newspapers used in this book may be found in: the *Montreal Herald* (1902-1903), on Microfilm at the National Archives, Ottawa, Ontario. Citations from the *Hamilton Spectator*, the *Globe*, Toronto, and the Toronto *Evening News*, are on microfilm at the Mills Library, Reference and Special Collections, McMaster University, Hamilton, Ontario. The *Hamilton Times* citations are on microfilm at the Hamilton Public Library, Special Collections.

Works Cited or Consulted

Allen, Richard. "The Social Gospel in Canada and the Reform Tradition in Canada, 1890-1928." *The Canadian Historical Review* 49 (1968): 381-91.

Anderson, Mary J. "The Life Writings of Mary Baker McQuesten (1849-1934): Victorian Matriarch of Whitehern." PhD dissertation, McMaster University, 2000.

Arnold, Matthew. "Sweetness and Light." *A Cultural Studies Reader: History, Theory, Practice*. Ed. Jessica Munns and Gita Rajan. London: Longman, 1995, pp. 21-32.

Ashcroft, Bill, Gareth Griffiths, and Helen Tiffin. *The Empire Writes Back: Theory and Practice in Post-Colonial Literatures*. London: Routledge, 1989.

Bailey, Melville Thomas, ed. *Dictionary of Hamilton Biography*. 4 vols. Hamilton: W.L. Griffin, 1981-99.

———. *Presbytery of Hamilton: 1836-1967 (POH)*. Hamilton: Presbyterian Church Committee, 1967.

———. *Wee Kirks and Stately Steeples*. Burlington: Eagle Press, 1990.

———. *Around and About Hamilton: 1785-1985*. Hamilton: The Head-of-the-Lake Historical Society, 1986.

———. *Biographical Dictionary of Knox College: 1845-1945*. Presbyterian Church of Canada, unpublished.

Ballstadt, Carl., ed. *Roughing It in the Bush or Life in Canada*. Ottawa: Carleton University Press, 1988.

———. "'The Embryo Blossom': Susanna Moodie's Letters to Her Husband in Relation to Roughing It in the Bush." In McMullen, ed., *Re(dis)covering Our Foremothers: Nineteenth-Century Canadian Women Writers*, 137-45.

319

Ballstadt, Carl, Elizabeth Hopkins, and Michael A. Peterman, eds. *Susanna Moodie: Letters of a Lifetime*. Toronto: University of Toronto Press, 1985.

——. *Letters of Love and Duty: The Correspondence of Susanna and John Moodie*. Toronto: University of Toronto Press, 1993.

——. *I Bless You in My Heart: Selected Correspondence of Catharine Parr Traill*. Toronto: University of Toronto Press, 1996.

Barnsley, Roland. *Thomas B. McQuesten*. The Canadians. Markham: Fitzhenry & Whiteside, 1987.

Benson, Eugene, and William Toye, eds. *Oxford Companion to Canadian Literature* (*OCCL*). Toronto: Oxford University Press, 1997.

Best, John C. *Thomas Baker McQuesten: Public Works, Politics, and Imagination*. Hamilton: Corinth Press, 1991.

Blom, Margaret Howard and Thomas E. Blom, eds. *Canada Home: Juliana Horatia Ewing's Fredericton Letters 1867-1869*. Vancouver: University of British Columbia Press, 1983.

Bridge, Kathryn. *Henry & Self: The Private Life of Sarah Crease, 1826-1922*. Victoria, BC: Sono Nis Press, 1996.

Brouwer, Ruth Compton. *New Women for God: Canadian Presbyterian Women and India Missions, 1876-1914*. Toronto: University of Toronto Press, 1990.

Bruss, Elizabeth. *Autobiographical Acts: The Changing Situation of a Literary Genre*. Baltimore: Johns Hopkins University Press, 1976.

Buss, Helen M. *Memoirs from Away: A New Found Land Girlhood*. Waterloo: Wilfrid Laurier University Press, 1998.

Campbell, Marjorie Freeman. *A Mountain and a City: The Story of Hamilton*. Toronto: McClelland and Stewart, 1966.

Canary, Robert, and Henry Kozicki. *The Writing of History: Literary Form and Historical Understanding*. Madison: University of Wisconsin Press, 1978.

Coleman, Linda S. *Women's Life Writing: Finding Voice/Building Community*. Bowling Green: Ohio State University Popular Press, 1997.

——. "Public Self, Private Self: Women's Life Writing in England, 1570-1720." PhD dissertation, University of Wisconsin, 1987.

Conrad, Margaret, Toni Laidlaw, and Donna Smyth, eds. *No Place Like Home: Diaries and Letters of Nova Scotia Women 1771-1938*. Halifax: Formac, 1989.

Cook, Elizabeth Heckendorn. *Epistolary Bodies: Gender and Genre in the Eighteenth-Century Republic of Letters*. Stanford: Stanford University Press, 1996.

Cook, Ramsay, and Wendy Mitchinson, eds. *The Proper Sphere: Women's Place in Canadian Society*. Toronto: Oxford University Press, 1976.

Crerar, Queenie. *Diary* (1887 & 91-92), unpublished. Hamilton Public Library, Special Collections.

Crystal, David, ed. *Cambridge Biographical Encyclopedia* (*CBE*). Cambridge: Press Syndicate of the University of Cambridge,1998.

Daiches, David. *The Paradox of Scottish Culture*. Oxford: Oxford University Press, 1964.

Day, Robert Adams. *Told in Letters: Epistolary Fiction Before Richardson*. Ann Arbor: University of Michigan Press, 1966.

Easthope, Antony, and Kate McGowan, eds. *A Critical and Cultural Theory Reader*. Toronto: University of Toronto Press. 1992.

Farmer, Mary Harrington. "The McQuestens and Their Letters." The Bailey Memorial Lecture, 15 October 1976. *Wentworth Bygones: (From the Papers and Records of The Head-of-the-Lake Historical Society)*, 12. 1977.

———. *Calendar of the McQuesten Papers at Whitehern, January, 1973* (CMQPW). Hamilton: Whitehern Museum, unpublished.

Gay, Peter, ed. *The Enlightenment: A Comprehensive Anthology*. New York: Simon and Schuster, 1973 (CMQPW).

Goldenson, Robert M. *Encyclopedia of Human Behavior*, 2 vols. (*EHB*). New York: Doubleday, 1970.

Gordon, Charles W. *Postscript to Adventure: The Autobiography of Ralph Connor*. New York: Farrar & Rhinehart, 1938.

Gregg, William. *History of the Presbyterian Church in the Dominion of Canada*. Toronto: Presbyterian Publishing, 1885.

Hall, Roger, William Westfall, and Laurel Sefton MacDowell, eds. *Patterns of the Past: Interpreting Ontario's History*. Toronto: Dundurn Press, 1988.

Halsband, Robert. *Dr. Johnson and "The Great Epistolick Art."* Ann Arbor: University Microfilms International, 1980.

———. "Editing the Letters of Letter-Writers." In R. Gothesman and Scott Bennett, eds., *Art and Error: Modern Textual Editing*. Bloomington: Indiana University Press, 1970.

Harmon, William, and C. Hugh Holman. *A Handbook to Literature*. 7th ed. Upper Saddle River, NJ: Simon & Schuster, 1996.

Harvey, Paul, Sir, ed. *Oxford Companion to English Literature* (*OCEL*). Oxford: Clarendon Press, 1967.

Henley, Brian. *The Grand Old Buildings of Hamilton*. Hamilton: The *Spectator*, 1994.

Hinz, Evelyn, ed. and Introduction. *Data and Acta: Aspects of Life-Writing*. Mosaic. Special Issue 20.4 (Fall 1987): v-xii.

———. "Mimesis: the Dramatic Lineage of Auto/Biography." In Kadar, ed., *Essays in Life Writing*.

Hoffman, Frances, and Ryan Taylor. *Much to Be Done: Private Life in Ontario from Victorian Diaries*. Toronto: Natural Heritage/Natural History, 1996.

Houston, James Kirk, M.D. "An Appreciation of A. E. Malloch, MB, MD, (1844-1919): A Forgotton Surgical Pioneer." *Canadian Medical Association Journal* 160 (1999): 849-53

Hutcheon, Linda. *The Canadian Postmodern: A Study of Contemporary English-Canadian Fiction*. Toronto: Oxford University Press, 1988.

Jameson, Anna Brownell. *Winter Studies and Summer Rambles in Canada*. Toronto: McClelland and Stewart, 1990.

Jones, Peter, ed. *The "Science of Man" in the Scottish Enlightenment*. Edinburgh: Edinburgh University Press, 1989.

Johnson, Charles M. *The Head of the Lake: A History of Wentworth County*. Hamilton: Wentworth County Council, 1967.

———. *McMaster University: 2/The Early Years in Hamilton 1930-1957*. Toronto: University of Toronto Press, 1981.

Johnston, John A. *Strong Wind Blowing: MacNab in Celebration*. Hamilton: MacNab St. Presbyterian Church, 1979.

Kadar, Marlene, ed. *Essays on Life Writing*. Toronto: University of Toronto Press, 1992.

———. "Behind Every Great Man: Frida Kahlo's Letters to Ella Wolfe." *Mosaic* 20.4 (Fall 1987): 143-53.

———. Afterword. In Staebler, ed., *Haven't Any News: Ruby's Letters from the '50s.* Waterloo: Wilfrid Laurier University Press, 1995.

Katz, Michael B. *The People of Hamilton, Canada West: Family and Class in a Mid-Nineteenth-Century City.* Cambridge, MA: Harvard University Press, 1975.

Kauffman, Linda. *Special Delivery: Epistolary Modes in Modern Fiction.* Chicago: University of Chicago Press, 1992.

Latoszek, Ania. "The Women's Foreign Missionary Society Auxiliary of MacNab Street Church (1887-1907): A Preparation for Change." Unpublished, 1993.

Lessing, Doris. *The Golden Notebook.* London: Michael Joseph, 1962.

MacGillivray, Royce. *The Mind of Ontario.* Belleville: Mika, 1985.

MacNab, Sophia. *The Diary of Sophia MacNab.* Ed. Charles Ambrose Carter and Thomas Melville Bailey. Hamilton: W. L. Griffin, 1968.

Magnusson, Magnus, ed. *Chambers Biographical Dictionary* (CBD). Edinburgh: W & R Chambers, 1993.

Marsh, James H., ed. *The Canadian Encyclopedia* (CE). Edmonton: Hurtig, 1988.

McBeth, R. G. *Our Task in Canada.* Toronto: Presbyterian Home Mission Board, 1912.

McGahan, Elizabeth W., ed. *Whispers from the Past: Selections from the Writings of New Brunswick Women.* Fredericton: Goose Lane, 1986.

McMullen, Lorraine, ed. *Re(Dis)covering Our Foremothers: Nineteenth-Century Canadian Women Writers.* Ottawa: University of Ottawa Press, 1990.

McNeil, Bill. *Voices of a War Remembered: An Oral History of Canadians in World War Two.* Toronto: Doubleday, 1991.

McNeill, John Thomas. *The Presbyterian Church in Canada 1875-1925.* Toronto: General Board Presbyterian Church, 1925.

McQuiston, Leona Bean. *The McQiston McCuiston and McQuesten Families 1620-1937.* Louisville, KY: Standard Press, 1937.

Minnes, Georgina. *The McQuesten Family of Hamilton.* Hamilton: Whitehern Museum, unpublished, 1999.

Moir, John S. *Enduring Witness: A History of the Presbyterian Church in Canada.* Hamilton: Eagle Press, 1987.

———, ed. *Called to Witness: Profiles of Canadian Presbyterians: A Supplement to Enduring Witness.* Vol 3. Hamilton: Presbyterian Church of Canada, 1991.

Moodie, Susanna. *Roughing It in the Bush.* Ed. Carl Ballstadt. Ottawa: Carleton University Press, 1988.

Morgan, Henry J. *Canadian Men and Women of the Time.* Toronto: William Briggs, 1912.

Morton, W. L. *Manitoba: A History.* Toronto: University of Toronto Press, 1957.

Munns, Jessica, and Gita Rajan, eds. *A Cultural Studies Reader: History, Theory, Practice.* London: Longman, 1995.

Pearsall, Judy, and Bill Trumble, eds. *Oxford English Reference Dictionary* (OED). Oxford: Oxford University Press, 1996.

Perry, Ruth. *Women, Letters and the Novel.* New York: AMS Press, 1980.

Peterson, Linda H. *Traditions of Victorian Women's Autobiography: The Poetics and Politics of Life Writing.* Charlottesville: University Press of Virginia, 1999.

Prince, Leslie A. *Over the Ivy Wall.* Hamilton: McMaster University Alumni Assoc., 1975.

Raab, Elisabeth. Life Writing: *And Peace Never Came*. Waterloo: Wilfrid Laurier University Press, 1997.

Redekop, Magdalene. "Alice Munro and the Scottish Nostalgic Grotesque." *Essays on Canadian Writing* 66 (Winter 1998): 21-43.

Richardson, Samuel. *Pamela, or Virtue Rewarded*. Ed. Peter Sabor. Harmondsworth, Middlesex: Penguin Books, 1985.

———. *Clarissa, or History of a Young Lady*. Boston: Houghton Mifflin, 1962.

———. *Letters Written to and for Particular Friends on the Most Important Occasions*. London: 1741.

Rubio, Mary, and Elizabeth Waterston. *Writing a Life: L. M. Montgomery*. Toronto: ECW Press, 1994.

———. *The Selected Journals of L. M. Montgomery*. 4 vols. Toronto: Oxford University Press, 1985.

Rusk, Lauren. "Three-Way Mirrors: The Life Writing of Otherness." PhD dissertation, Stanford University, 1995.

Staebler, Edna, ed. *Haven't Any News: Ruby's Letters from the '50s*. Waterloo: Wilfrid Laurier University Press, 1995.

Taylor, Claire Drainie. *The Surprise of My Life: An Autobiography*. Waterloo: Wilfrid Laurier University Press, 1998.

Traill, Catharine Parr Strickland. *The Backwoods of Canada: Being Letters from the Wife of an Emigrant Officer, Illustrative of the Domestic Economy of British America*. Toronto: McClelland & Stewart, 1929.

Trombley, Stephen. *The Lynchburg Story*. PBS television documentary, 16 November 1999.

Tyrell, William. *Toronto, Hamilton and London Society Blue Book*. Toronto: Tyrell, 1900.

Van Norman, Catherine Bell. *Catherine Bell Van Norman Her Diary 1850*, with a preface by Ethel V. Gudgeon. Burlington Historical Society. Hamilton: W. L. Griffin, 1981.

Van Peer, Willie. "Two Laws of Literary History: Growth and Predictability in Canon Formation." *Mosaic* 30.2 (June 1997): 113-32.

Verduyn, Christl, ed. *Marian Engel's Notebooks*. Waterloo: Wilfrid Laurier University Press, 1999.

Vernon Directories. *Vernon's Directory of the City of Hamilton* (VDCH). Hamilton: Vernon's Publishing, 1896 to 1970.

Wallace, W. Stewart. *Macmillan Dictionary of Canadian Biography* (MDCB). Toronto: Macmillan, 1978.

Weaver, John C. *Hamilton: An Illustrated History*. Toronto: John Lorimer, 1982.

———. *Shaping the Canadian City: Essays on Urban Politics and Policies 1890-1970*. Kingston: Institute of Public Administration of Canada, 1977.

Webster-Merriam. *Webster's New Collegiate Dictionary* (WNCD). Toronto: Thomas Allen, Limited, 1960.

White, Hayden. "The Historical Text as Literary Artifact." In Canary and Kozicki, eds. *The Writing of History*.

———. "Narrativization of Real Events." *Critical Inquiry* 7.4 (Summer 1981): 793-98.

Whiteley, Marilyn Fardig, ed. *The Life and Letters of Annie Leake Tuttle: Working for the Best*. Waterloo: Wilfrid Laurier University Press, 1999.

Winslow, Donald J. *Life-Writing: A Glossary of Terms in Biography, Autobiography, and Related Forms*. Honolulu: University of Hawaii, 1980.

York, Lorraine M. "'The Things That Are Seen in the Flashes': Timothy Findley's *Inside Memory* as Photographic Life Writing." *Modern Fiction Studies* 40.3 (Fall 1994): 643-55.

Index

઒

Italicized page numbers refer to the photographs. Bolded numbers refer to a larger biographical or descriptive note. Please search the Web site (www.whitehern.ca) for possible further information.

Aboriginals, 24, 30, 32
Addison and Steele, 12, 251n.62
Adirondacks, 255n104, 150
Alaska gold fields, 24, 288n.352
Alberta, 142; penitentiary, 303n.494
alcoholism, 7, 96-98, 133
Allan, John, 205, 306n.533
America, 191, 302n.488
American, 56, 267
Anderson, Annie, 103, 104, 109
Anderson, James, J., 63
Anderson, Rev. Frederick W., 109, 111, 112, 114, 185
Anglican, 56, 57, 275n.251,133, 278n.278
appendicitis, 109, 111
Argyll and Sutherland (91st Highlanders), 243n.16, 262n.155, 265n.180, 309n.553
Arnott, Dr., 264n.169, 282n.299, 171, 174, 179, 220; Arnott, Mrs., 264n.169
Ashbury Park, NJ, 77, 244n.7
Asquith, Herbert, 183, 300n.454-58, 302n.488, 207, 307n.540
Association Hall, 105, 154
Atkinson, Mr. and Mrs. J. T., 275n.255; Ethel, 129
Atlin, BC, 272n.235; Hospital, 128
Auchmar, 153, 217
autobiography, 55, 60
automobile, 267n.197, 133, 141, 218, 312n.582, 222
aviation meet, 195, 303n501, 304n.502

Baker, Hugh, C., 161, 290n.371; See also telegraph, 251n.68
Baker, Rev. Thomas, xix, 3; Royal Navy, 3; *Antelope* and HMS St. *Lawrence*, 3;

Napoleonic Wars, 3; War of 1812, 3; emigration to Canada 3; Congregational Church minister, 3, 121, 271n.224; Lieutenant and Commander, pension, 3; Calvinist 4; character 4, 5, 10, 11, 65, 66, 77; death, 78, 242n.14, 79; grandpapa, 86, 289; first wife, Sarah Hampson, 3; James Alfred, 10, 11; Maria (Mudge), 10, 11; John, 138, 282n.299, 193; Lorrie, 138; Winnie, 138; Hattie, 283; second wife, Mary-Jane McIlwaine, xix, 3, 4, 9, 64, 77; Mary Jane, xix, 3. See also McQuesten, Mary Baker
Ballstadt, Carl, 62
Baltimore, MD, 114, 123, 136
Bank of Hamilton, 160, 170
Barbadoes, trip, 223, 314n.595
Barclay, Dr. A. Norman, 90, 254n.86
Barclay, Dr. William, 111, 265n.180
Bard of Athol. See William Murray
Beardmore, Mr., 96, 97, 98
Beatty, Dr. Elizabeth, 27, 38
Bedford, NH, 266n.185, 269n.209
Bell, Alexander Graham, 304n.502. See also aviation meet
Bell, William, 89, 106, 129, 148, **256n.111**; Mrs. Emily (Rogers), 94, 116, 123, 128, 148, 171, 226; Florrie, 86, 89, 106-07, 129, 168; Charles W., **256n.111**, 106-07, 123; Beatrice, E. (Gates), 256n111, 123; Herbie, 89, 123, 107, 119, 123, 129, 275n.257, 132, 134, 148, 168; See also tuberculosis
bells, MacNab Church, 154
bells, St. Paul's Presbyterian Church, 272n.230, 153, 287n.344, 154, 288n.347.
Bengough, John W., 113, **267n.192**